# So Long! Walt Whitman's Poetry of Death

# So Long!
# Walt Whitman's Poetry of Death

HAROLD ASPIZ

THE UNIVERSITY OF ALABAMA PRESS
*Tuscaloosa and London*

Typeface: ACaslon

∞
The paper on which this book is printed meets the minimum requirements of
American National Standard for Information Science–Permanence of Paper for
Printed Library Materials, ANSI Z39.48 1984.

Library of Congress Cataloging-in-Publication Data

Aspiz, Harold
  So long! Walt Whitman's poetry of death / Harold Aspiz.
     p.  cm.
Includes bibliographical references and index.
  ISBN 0-8173-1377-X (cloth : alk. paper)
   1. Whitman, Walt, 1819–1892—Criticism and interpretation. 2. Death in literature.
3. Whitman, Walt, 1819–1892. Leaves of grass. 4. Whitman, Walt, 1819–1892—Prose.
I. Title.
  PS3242.D35 A87 2004
  811'.3—dc21

                                                                    2004010210

British Library Cataloguing-in-Publication Data available

"In the future of these States must arise poets immenser far, and make great poems of death."—*Democratic Vistas*

# Contents

# Preface

The theme of death pervades the text and the subtext of *Leaves of Grass*. Although some of his contemporaries hailed Whitman as America's inspired poet of death and many of his death-saturated poems have earned critical acclaim and popular affection, this is the first book-length study to examine his treatment of death by considering the entire range of his poetry and the way his attitudes toward death define his career as an intellectual, a poet, and a person. This is also the first full-scale study to relate his developing views of death and his literary treatment of death to his social and intellectual milieu and to the wide-ranging contemporary debate about the meaning of death. We can fully appreciate Whitman's poetry of the material world or his poetry of the soul only when we comprehend how vitally these themes are entwined in his emotional and philosophical engagement with death. Neither an orthodox believer, a skeptic, or a philosopher, Whitman generally interprets death in terms of his experience and his intuitions, so his death-oriented poems tend to be personal and poignant. Although he treats death imaginatively and with a certain latitude, he will not view it as a total cessation of personal identity; rather, he interprets it as a momentous forward leap in the cycle of human advancement. Nor does he forget that his splendid body (about which he boasts in prose and verse) carries the seed of death; an unflagging awareness of death colors his treatment of all phases of life. Death is a vital component of his gospel of universal brotherhood and sisterhood, of his luminous vision of the progressive unfolding of the human race (particularly its American component), and of his profound spirituality. And it is a vital element in the yearning for love that permeates the poems.

Although he was acquainted with many of the scientific and religious movements of the age, Whitman could not accept the prevailing secular

and scientific theories concerning death or those advocated by estab-
lished religion. He viewed death as an eternal and benign mystery that he
was destined to interpret for himself and to translate for his readers. At
times his poems approach death gladly, as if to embrace it; at times they
treat it quizzically, revealing an uncertainty about his own assumptions.
*Leaves of Grass* depicts not only the poet-persona's observations of the
dying and the deaths of a great range of persons and his moving medita-
tions on death, but it also discloses those moments when the persona
contemplates, or even "experiences," his own death.

In order to explain how death is treated in the broad range of Whit-
man's poetry, this study has been organized in a loosely chronological
sequence that extends from his sentimental apprentice writings to the
sophisticated verses of his later years. The introduction examines the
background of his development as a poet and thinker and shows how his
poetry of death is related to his literary and intellectual milieu. Chapters 1
and 2 examine death and dying in the first edition of *Leaves of Grass*
(1855), particularly in the magisterial "Song of Myself," which contains
some of the most affecting death scenes in all of poetry. They show the
development of the Whitman persona, his musings about death, his con-
frontations with death, and his inspired role as an interpreter of death.
Other poems in the 1855 edition—notably "To Think of Time" and "The
Sleepers"—are examined in chapter 2.

In preparing the successive editions of *Leaves of Grass* after 1855, Whit-
man generally included the poems that had been published in the pre-
ceding edition and supplemented them with his new poems. In order to
create a chronological record, chapters 3 through 6 cover those poems
that were newly added to each edition. Chapter 3 deals with the poems
that first appeared in the second edition of *Leaves of Grass* (1856), with
special attention to the poet-persona's role as a folk prophet who confides
his gospel of democracy and immortality to his fellow citizens. High-
lighting this edition are "Crossing Brooklyn Ferry," Whitman's haunting
visualization of his postmortem self, and "This Compost," in which the
persona confronts his own death with alternating moods of terror and
acceptance. Chapter 4 considers the new poems of the third edition of
*Leaves of Grass* (1860). It explores the persona's mating urge in the "Chil-
dren of Adam" poems as an expression of species immortality; the inter-
play of homoerotic love and the preoccupation with death in the "Cala-
mus" poems; the myth of the poet's childhood initiation into the mystery

of death in "Out of the Cradle Endlessly Rocking"; his despairing confrontation with mortality in "As I Ebb'd with the Ocean of Life"; and the sensuous ritual of his dying and transfiguration in "So Long!" Chapter 5 reviews the *Drum-Taps* poems (1865–1866), which are predicated, as Whitman explained, on the centrality of death. We witness the invention of the healer-persona who moves among the wounded and dying in Washington's military hospitals and his empathetic reactions to agony and death. The chapter also includes an extensive analysis of the magnificent Lincoln elegy "When Lilacs Last in the Dooryard Bloom'd." And chapter 6 spans the quarter century of Whitman's post–Civil War poetry, a rich and varied body of poems that features a renewed emphasis on religious spirituality and an eager anticipation of his approaching death. Such poems as "Prayer of Columbus," "Passage to India," and an array of charming lyrics welcome his own dying and speculate about the unknown afterlife that may await him.

In my longtime acquaintance with Whitman I have found him always companionable and always ready to reveal new insights, new linguistic surprises, and new perplexities. My undertaking has been assisted by many colleagues at California State University, Long Beach, and by its ever-helpful library staff. My special thanks to Jerome Loving, Arnold T. Schwab, and Sue Breckenridge.

I dedicate this book affectionately to my wife, Sylvia, and to my son, Ira (both of whom have provided inspiration and invaluable assistance), and to Rosie and Aaron.

So Long! Walt Whitman's Poetry of Death

# Introduction
## "Great Poems of Death"

I

Walt Whitman is a great poet of the joys of life, but he is equally a great poet of death. Few poets have been so immersed in the mystery of death or lived so close to death as he did. Fewer still have treated death with such an eloquent voice or created such an awesome persona. Death is a major component in the richness and variety of *Leaves of Grass,* providing a window into the poet's thoughts and an insight into his achievements. Whitman's poetry illustrates the universal truth that death is not only the most overwhelming and the least understood event of our existence but also the most intriguing. He realized from the outset of his poetic career that if his poetry were to reflect the essence and scope of our life experiences—and those of his own life—it must speak of death openly, imaginatively, and unswayed by clichés or established doctrines. He became a sensitive student of death and dying, familiar with disease, anguish, violence, and the displays of both fear and courage among the many dying persons he observed. Throughout *Leaves of Grass* he proclaimed his faith that death was not a plunge into the terminal *nada* and was convinced that we can live our lives fully only if we are prepared to welcome death as a transition in a continued, but still mysterious, process of spiritual evolution. Underlying this conviction was his belief that death promised some sort of future continuity for everyone—and particularly for himself. And as the poems reveal, this belief did not come easily but was part of a trying personal and ideological struggle. Moreover, he felt that a profound respect for death was fundamental to his aesthetic and to all great art. His expressions of faith in an afterlife—for himself, for his book, and for humanity—though sometimes clouded by uncertainty, resound like an iron chord in *Leaves of Grass*. In fact, he was proud of his achievement as a poet of death. Comparing his own pronouncements on death to those of the religious thinkers of the day, he declared boldly, "I say better things about death than orthodoxy with all its boasts is saying." And he agreed with the comment by his devoted amanuensis Horace Traubel that "if 'Leaves of Grass' is remarkable for anything, it is its celebration of death." "That's what we think," he responded, "but they don't, or won't, see it."[1]

Although Whitman's treatment of death has not been a primary concern of Whitman scholars in recent years, many of his contemporaries recognized his preeminence as a poet of death. Ethnologist Daniel G. Brinton displayed a sharp insight into the role that death plays in Whitman's poetry:

> Saturated as they are with the zest of life, marvelously sensitive as they are to every passing thrill of pleasure, to every glad sound or sight, they are essential peans [*sic*] of Death. Whatever is, is of worth as part of the I, and only of worth as that I is immortal, is the defiant conqueror of Death and Time. This was no matter of tradition or education with Walt. It was the inevitable product of his genius, the logical result of his conception of man and the universe. Both, to him, were futile and worthless without the continuance of the mortal life hereafter. This alone, to his mind, offered a rational cause for existence. Unless the individual survives the mutation of matter, the universe is purposeless. . . . To Walt it was the positive conclusion to the severest ratiocination. It is only with this thought constantly in mind that we can read the poems intelligently or sympathize with his acute love of life.[2]

Assessing Whitman's literary achievement, physician and sexologist Havelock Ellis ranked Whitman as "one of the greatest English artists," one who "aspires to reveal the loveliness of death" and "speaks not only from the standpoint of the most intense and vivid delight in the actual world, but [one who] possesses a practical familiarity with disease and death which has perhaps never fallen to the lot of a great writer." And in an effusive oration at Whitman's gravesite, orator and skeptic Robert Ingersoll evaluated the importance of death in the poet's art:

I thank him for the great and splendid words he has said in favor of liberty, in favor of man and woman, in favor of motherhood, in favor of fathers, in favor of children, and I thank him for the brave words he has said about death.

He has lived, he has died, and death is less terrible than it was before. Thousands and millions will walk down into "the dark valley of the shadow" holding Walt Whitman by the hand. Long after we are dead the brave words he has spoken will sound like trumpets to the dying.[3]

A few years later D. H. Lawrence put his unique spin on Whitman's achievement as a poet, asserting hyperbolically that Whitman "would not have been the great poet he is if he had not taken the last steps and looked over into death. . . . Whitman was a very great poet, of the end of life. A very great postmortem poet, of the transition of the soul as it loses its integrity." Lawrence conjectured that, like Moses glimpsing the Promised Land, Whitman imagined that he had caught a glimpse of the Land Beyond. Irish poet Padraic Colum asked, "Did Whitman feel an unwonted power upon him when he sang of death?" and answered: "It would seem as if he did." And in a rather Hegelian vein, the Cuban poet Jose Martí called the "harmonious relation between life and death a basic link in Whitman's dialectic chain."[4]

Granted, Whitman's work is vast in its scope and exquisite in its probings into human nature and into the world around him and is best appreciated as a whole. Nevertheless, to approach Whitman's total achievement through his treatment of death affords invaluable insights into the man and his work. He looked at death (as he looked at everything) from every possible angle; hence *Leaves of Grass* explores the many meanings and resonances of death. He viewed death as a tragic loss, as a phase of species immortality, and as a momentous prelude to an afterlife. His pronouncements on death may even strike the reader as tentative, contradictory, or provocative, for the poems play games with the reader, including some that involve death. But he carefully avoids being trapped into foolish consistency. He is rarely doctrinaire; he never develops an overarching or consistent theory of death. And, as his poems attest, he is aware of his limited ability to grasp cosmic truths as he struggles to maintain a humane and ameliorative faith, thus the shifting strategies in the treatment of death that appear in *Leaves of Grass*. Confronted on all sides by contradictory evidence and conflicting ideologies, he chooses to keep his own counsel, convinced that his insights into death are as valid as any argument or body of evidence. "Having pried through the strata, analyzed to a hair, counseled with doctors and calculated close," he declares in "Song of Myself," "I find no sweeter fat than sticks to my own bones." He remained steadfast in his belief that death serves a useful purpose in the course of human development and that an individual death is to be accepted calmly and hopefully. Having demanded "great poems of death" from America's future poets, he set the noblest of examples.

*Leaves of Grass,* where the word *death,* together with its compounds and variants, appears well over two hundred times, employs many strategies to express Whitman's engagement with death. Death is represented by many images, including passageways, roads, gates, embouchures, twilight, autumn, leafless trees, and frequent versions of spirit launchings and voyages across uncharted seas. Typical of the latter images is this 1871 lyric:

> Gliding o'er all, through all,
> Through Nature, Time, and Space,
> As a ship on the waters advancing,
> The voyage of the Soul—not life alone,
> Death, many deaths, I'll sing.[5]

As he tries to persuade his countrymen and countrywomen that death is not an inglorious closure to life and that immortality is a reasonable expectation, the Whitman persona assumes many guises. He witnesses (and imagines) many kinds of death experience, contemplates his own death, and even fantasizes about his own death and transfiguration. Thus as the Whitman persona stands in a graveyard in "Song of Myself," section 6, he appears ingenuous and mystified by death, humbly confessing that "I wish I could translate the hints about the dead young men and women" but nonetheless concluding that "They are alive and well somewhere." He sings the praise of all the dead; he presents himself as a prophet of an immortality that embraces even the most humble and rejected mortals and as a translator of the auguries of universal immortality that he finds everywhere. His words, he feels, are as inspired as those of any man or god. He pictures the Whitman persona as a Christlike intervener with death—one who confronts death as a force equal to himself, whether it appears as a mother, a lover, or an adversary. In his limitless empathy, the persona "becomes" one of the dead, descending into the Gehenna of dead souls and rising to the Heaven of pure spirit. For all that, he remains human and keenly aware of his own limitation and fallibility.

In evaluating Whitman as a poet of death, we cannot separate the personal and the ideological: For to him (and to the Whitman persona) the personal is ideological and the ideological is always personal. Whatever rings true to his (or the persona's) observations, his senses and his instincts, is deemed valid and universally applicable because he is certain that his capacity for inspiration exists at the highest level. Whitman speaks of immortality "not as an intellection, but as a pervading instinct" related to "the inner light of the Quakers, the pure conscience, rising over all the rest like pinnacles to some elaborated building." This is the faculty that he celebrates (in the preface to the first edition of *Leaves of Grass*) when he declares, "from the eyesight proceeds another eyesight, and from the hearing proceeds another hearing." Somehow, he feels that death's secret is ultimately discoverable by those endowed with extraordinary sensitivity—a capacity he attributes to the genuine poet—and that his instincts and insights are attuned to the universal soul, what he calls "pure consciousness." Therefore they serve as sources of the highest truth. In poem after poem he seems to be convinced that death is part of a beneficial cosmic plan or "moral law" that governs every phase of existence.[6] But his assurance is often affected by the cruelties and contradictions of the material world, by the rising tides of science and skepticism, and by his own fallibility as a seer and as a speaker. After all, there is precious little evidence to indicate any existence beyond the grave; the return of Lazarus from the grave must be taken on faith. And distrusting any form of logical argument concerning death, he offered none himself. His faith in immortality was strengthened by the (seemingly tautological) belief that he shared with Emerson, William James, and others, that there is an afterlife because there exists an almost universal belief that it is so. Whitman saw his poetic function as that of a "translator" who conveys to humanity that which he feels or "knows" to be a higher truth. Thus, in calling *Leaves of Grass* "a language experiment" (the phrase is generally understood to refer to Whitman's innovative freeing of poetry from traditional stanzaic forms and his perfecting a vernacular style of poetry), might he not have been testing whether any poet who is able to perceive or intuit the highest truths can invent a language that will convey these visions or truths to the reader? Perceiving tokens of divine truth in the emblem-filled world in which he lives, the persona declares ("Song of Myself," section 20), "All are written to me, and I must get what the writing means."

What the poet knows about the meaning of death—what he *feels* has been revealed to him—is likely to be something intangible or even un-translatable; and his task, therefore, is to discover or invent an "idiom" that will make this revelation translatable and comprehensible even to those whose language skills are far weaker than his own. Whitman is keenly aware of the difficulty of conveying his vision of death, both to the individual reader and to the masses. Thus, near the end of "Song of Myself"—a poem in which the Whitman persona melds his vision of death with his vision of a rich and ample life—the persona voices his frustration in having apparently perceived the truth about the unbroken cycle of life and death but having failed to find the language that would make the reader "see" what has ostensibly been communicated to him or her. "Perhaps I might tell more," he cries falteringly. "Outlines! I plead for my brothers and sisters." But these "outlines," he is obliged to admit, are only the rudimentary linguistic approximations of the inspired messages he wishes to convey. So he cries out, almost in desperation,

> Do you see O my brothers and sisters?
> It is not chaos or death—it is form, union, plan—it is eternal
> life—it is Happiness.

In a note that is related to "Song of the Answerer" (a composite poem, many of whose lines are related to the prose preface of the 1855 edition of *Leaves of Grass*) Whitman attempts to explain his critical role as poet and "translator" of cosmic truths:

> Every soul has its own individual language, often unspoken, or lamely, feebly, haltingly spoken; but for a true fit for that man, and perfectly adapted to his use.—The truths I tell to you or any other, may not be plain to you, because I do not translate them fully from my idiom into yours.—If I could do so, and do it very well, they would be as apparent to you as they are to me; for they are truths.—No two have exactly the same language, and the great translator and joiner of the whole is the poet. He has the

divine grammar of all tongues, and says indifferently and alike
How are you friend? to the President in the midst of his cabi-
net, and good day my brother to Sambo, among the hoes of the
sugar field, and both understand him and know that his speech
is right."[7]

Basic to an understanding of Whitman's interpretation of death is his
dualism of outlook regarding, on the one hand, the mortal body and the
palpable world around him and, on the other hand, the spiritual force
within him and surrounding him that he equates with his soul and with
the world soul. This is no simple matter, for it hinges on his (not always
clear or consistent) concepts of the relation between the body and the
soul. Thus the persona exalts his physical grandeur throughout "Song of
Myself" and in this self-advertising boast from "Excelsior" (1856): "for
who possesses a perfect and enamour'd body? for I do not believe any one
possesses a more perfect or enamour'd body than mine." But this celebra-
tion of the body (especially in the poems of the 1850s) generally treats the
physical self as the material embodiment of the spiritual essence.

Such dualism, of course, has classic roots, particularly in Christianity,
which often defines the body as finite and expendable (or in Whitman's
startling term "excrementious")—something to be voided at death in or-
der to release the soul for its continued and presumably higher level of
existence. Whitman's formative exposure to Christianity was by way of
Hicksite Quakerism, which may have helped him to emphasize the cen-
trality of his own beliefs and develop a distrust of doctrinal formulas. As
he wrote in the late 1850s, "the true religious genius of our race now seems
to say, Beware of Churches! Beware of priests! above all things the flights
and divine extasies of the soul cannot submit to the exact statements of
any church, or any creed." In his disaffection with organized religion,
Whitman even toyed with the idea of "writ[ing] a new burial service."[8] A
decade later the poet, who pictured his spirit striving to reach the god-
head and perhaps eventually becoming a god himself, conjectured that
with "modern knowledge" and an enlightened outlook the five-thousand-
year-old belief in the existence of a god may soon disappear.[9] The 1855 and
the 1856 editions of *Leaves of Grass* show the democratic Whitman per-
sona straining to persuade the common folk that they, too, may eventually
aspire to become splendid specimens and learn to trust their inner light
in matters of life and death. But as he grew older and his body weakened,

he concentrated less on the physical self and increasingly on his own impending death and the capacity of his own soul to test the implications of life and death. "Compared to the vast oceanic vol[ume] of the spiritual facts," he questioned in 1857, "what is all our material knowledge before the immensity of that which is to come, the spiritual, the unknown, the immensity of being and facts around us of which we cannot possibly take any cognizance[?]"[10] This dualism, which grants primacy to the soul by de-emphasizing the material world, was buttressed by various influences, including popular religious movements, the Romantic philosophy of Kant and Emerson and Hegel, and Eastern religions. But because the poet so delighted in the human body and the senses and was so profoundly rooted in his physical world, he sometimes appears uneasy with this sort of dualism. Some fragmentary notes possibly predating the appearance of *Leaves of Grass* show his struggle to distinguish between body and soul:

Divine is the body—it is all—it is the soul also
How can there be immortality, except through mortality?
How can the ultimate realities of things be visible?
How can the real body ever die and [?][11]

The note ends inconclusively. Another early fragment shows the poet wrestling with the distinction between body and soul, invoking a spiritualist terminology. The physical body, it says, is not the "real" body but only the "visible" body, adding that "there is the real body too, not visible."

These early speculations do not clarify whether Whitman assumed the invisible "real body" to be coterminal and coextensive with the physical body or whether he thought it to be somehow discrete from the physical organism. Nor is it clear whether he believed that following death, when the worldly body no longer functions, another "real body" will house the soul and they will coexist in some unitary but joined relationship. In the poems of the first three editions that celebrate both the bodies and the souls of men and women, young and old, the tension between the persona's corporeal and spiritual selves constitutes a major source of the poems' excitement. "Song of Myself" pictures the persona as the inspired receptor of the spiritual emanations that surround him and inspire his powers of utterance. But the poet cannot easily define the essential self—

whether it is some manifestation of the body, body and soul together, or the soul alone—that will enjoy a continued existence beyond the grave: "I know I shall not pass like a child's carlacue cut with a burnt stick at night," the persona exclaims confidently. But the poems of the first three editions (1855, 1856, 1860), which celebrate the body's exuberance and name it as the seat of the soul, struggle to distinguish between body and soul as unified, separable, or separate entities. They often construe the body's "satisfactions" as auguries or indicators of the still greater satisfactions that will accrue in the afterlife. Yet "To Think of Time"—Whitman's first full-scale meditation on death—while striving to confirm his belief that all indications point to a satisfactory afterlife, reveals a profoundly troubled mind struggling with his not necessarily congruent thoughts on life, death, body, soul, and the afterlife.

In the late 1850s Whitman came to a decision of sorts concerning his poetic treatment of body and soul. "Starting from Paumanok," the rambling introductory poem of the 1860 edition (but essentially written in the middle to late 1850s), while seemingly affirming both the spiritual world and the material world and their convergence in the human body, makes this bold but misleading promise:

> I will make poems of materials, for I think they are to be the
>     most spiritual poems,
> And I will make the poems of my body and of immortality,
> For I think I shall then supply myself with the poems of my soul
>     and of immortality.

But the poet would make no more poems about his body until many years later when, as an ailing paralytic, he compared himself to the dying Columbus and to a redwood tree in the process of being felled and, in the years preceding his death when he was already something of a celebrity, when he wrote "rivulets" of little verses to inform the public of the status of his failing health. Even in so germinal a poem as "Crossing Brooklyn Ferry" (1856), where the dead persona hovers above the East River in some sort of spiritual habiliment, his cast-off physical body is only a memory. And although *Drum-Taps*, Whitman's collection of wartime poems, and his wartime diaries show him to be an incomparable observer of bodily ailments and dying, they rarely allude to an afterlife. Perhaps

Whitman's daily witness to the bleak reality of death and dying inhibited him from conjecturing about the satisfactions of the afterlife.

Even during the war years Whitman was abandoning his stance as the poet of both body and soul to become almost exclusively the poet of the soul. The watershed year for this change was 1867, two years after the war's end, when England's *Broadway Magazine* published a group of five lyrics depicting the soul's eager embarkation on its spiritual journey into the infinite—poems with titles like "Whispers of Heavenly Death" and "Darest Thou Now, O Soul"—that set the tone for the soul-oriented poems of the poet's last quarter-century. Four years later when he published the imposing "Passage to India" and a number of similarly themed poems in a small collection, he had clearly staked out his position as the preeminent poet of the soul and of the soul-journey. "*Preface 1872*—As a Strong Bird on Pinions Free" hints that Whitman was also positioning himself as the poet of the "New Theology" whose poems illustrate that "mortality" is "but an exercise . . . with reference to results beyond." Nevertheless, the later poems do not always differentiate between the mind and the soul. Although it is generally assumed that the mind and the emotions have a physiological basis, a number of the later poems, including "Passage to India," picture the persona's postmortem entity as dual—the "soul" accompanied by the "self" (which retains the faculties of the sentient mind)—twin interlinked companions and lovers journeying to the paradise of their heart's desiring. Aware that his views remain paradoxical, the poet attempts to explain his position:

> Body and mind are one; an inexplicable paradox, yet no truth truer. The human soul stands in the centre, and all the universes minister to it, and serve it and revolve around it. They are one side of the whole, and it is the other side. It escapes utterly from all limits, dogmatic standards and measurements and adjusts itself to the ideas of God, of space, and to eternity, and sails them at will as oceans, and fills them as beds of oceans.
>
> The varieties, contradictions, and paradoxes of the world and of life, and even good and evil, so baffling to the superficial observer, and so often leading to despair, sullenness or infidelity, become a series of infinite radiations and waves of the one sea-like universe of divine action and progress, never stopping, never hasting.[12]

Whitman also backs away from his early contention that these cosmic truths may be accessed by the broad masses—the "superficial observer," proposing instead that they are revealed only through the superior insights of poet and sage.

Whitman's self-esteem as a poet of the soul is clearly stated in an unpublished letter of 1874. Speaking of himself through a fictitious third person, he says, "Out of [Whitman's] apparent materialism, an unerring spirituality always & certainly emerges. A distinguished scientist in Washington told me not long since, that, in its tally & spirit, Whitman's was the only poetry he could mention that is thoroughly consistent with modern science & philosophy, & that does not infringe upon them in a single line."[13] His intent to focus now on the soul is articulated in "*Preface 1876*—Leaves of Grass and Two Rivulets," in which he proposes "a further Volume" that features "the unseen Soul" as the earlier editions had featured "the Body and Existence"—a volume "which would be based on those convictions of perpetuity and conservation, which, enveloping all precedents, make the unseen Soul govern absolutely at last" and show the soul as it enters "the sphere of the resistless gravitation of Spiritual Law." Using a photographic metaphor, he proposed to "shift the slides [from his previous volumes] and exhibit the problem and paradox of the same ardent and fully appointed Personality entering the sphere of the resistless gravitation of Spiritual Law, and with cheerful face estimating Death, not at all as the cessation, but as somehow what I feel it must be, the entrance upon by far the greatest part of existence, and something that Life is at least as much for, as it is for itself." "[T]he last enclosing sublimation of Race or Poem" he declares, "is, What it thinks of death . . . in my opinion it is no less than this idea of immortality, above all other ideas, that is to enter into, and vivify, and give crowning religious stamp, to democracy in the New World." Death had become for him "the crowning fact of physical existence" and the primary focus of its American poet:

> I am not sure but the last enclosing sublimation of Race or
> Poem is, What it thinks of Death. . . . . .[*sic*] After the rest has
> been comprehended and said, even the grandest—After those
> contributions to mightiest Nationality, or to sweetest Song, or
> to the best Personalism, male or female, have been glean'd from
> the rich and varied themes of tangible life, and have been fully
> accepted and sung, and the pervading fact of physical existence,

with the duty it devolves, is rounded and apparently completed, it still remains to be really completed by suffusing through the whole and several, *that other pervading invisible fact* (is it not the largest part?) of life here, combining the rest, and furnishing for Person or State, the only permanent and unitary meaning to all, even the meanest life, consistently with the dignity of the Universe, in Time.[14] (emphasis added)

The "Spiritual Law" Whitman invokes in *"Preface 1876"* (and as "the law" in numerous poems) posits the existence of an unbroken continuum encompassing the material and the invisible worlds and further assumes that this unifying spirit pervades "the moral universe" and operates within the soul of each man and woman to create a nobler existence. And it is the poet, says Whitman, who is charged with illustrating how this "Law" operates in life and in death. One who perceives "the endless process of Creative thought" and sees beyond life's apparent contradictions understands that the universe has "one consistent and eternal purpose. . . . As life is the whole law and incessant effort of the visible universe, and death only the other or invisible side of the same, so the *utile,* so truth, so health, are the continuous-immutable laws of the moral universe, and vice and disease, with all their perturbations, are but transient, even if ever so prevalent, expressions."[15] Whitman felt certain that a cosmic master plan governs all phases of existence as a moral imperative that can be ascertained, or at least sensed by the poet. The influence of Eastern thought strengthened what became a downgrading of the material world—poetically, at least—in favor of some sort of pure spirituality. An extreme version of this view occurs in the twenty-one quatrain stanzas of the poem "Eidòlons" (1876), which denies the primacy of physical reality in favor of the "eidolon," or soul image, which pervades everything and inspires everything. The visible, tangible world is labeled the "ostent evanescent"—the world of fleeting appearances. The "eidolon" world is the immaterial force that inspires noble deeds and noble souls. The "prophet and the bard" (recognizable identities of the poet) propose to interpret "God and eidòlons." Not "the mountains and oceans" or "this world" or the visible "universes" are the ultimate reality, he tells them, but these "eidolons" that pervade the soul and inspire its self-discovery and its quests for godliness. The poem rejects outright the idealization of the physical body that had characterized the earlier editions of *Leaves of Grass* in favor of a mystic body—an *eidolon* body—that transcends mortality and has affinities with the souls of the living and the dead:

> Thy body permanent,
> The body lurking there within thy body,
> The only purport of the form thou art, *the real I myself*,
> An image, an eidólon. [emphasis added]

## 2

Whitman's foreground provides some clues to his mature writings about death. He seems to have been always sensitive where death is concerned. He frequently recalled his intense emotional reaction when, as a Brooklyn schoolboy, he heard the explosion of the steamboat *Fulton*, which jarred the city, and his fascination with the "strange and solemn military funeral for the officers and sailors killed by the explosion at the Navy Yard . . . the impressive service and the dead march of the band, (moving me to tears) and the led horses and officers' trappings in the procession, and the black-draped flags, and the sailors and the salutes over the grave, in the ancient cemetery." (He also remembered another explosion in Rockaway, Long Island, some years later.) As an impressionable ten-year-old he served as an errand boy to a Brooklyn physician who had participated in Admiral Decatur's North African campaign in 1804 and who related tales of battle carnage—tales that apparently lingered in the memory of the poet, whose gory imagery of "an old-time sea-fight" in "Song of Myself" is unexcelled in its sensuous evocation of violent death. And he recalled his fascination with graves and burial sites during his boyhood rambles through Brooklyn and its rural surroundings—a fascination that remained throughout his life as these modest rustic cemeteries gave way to large, anonymous cemeteries accessible to rich and poor city dwellers.[16] According to William Roscoe Thayer, those who knew Whitman "in early and middle life" found him to be a "preternaturally emotional" man who gave free rein to his feelings. Whether through intellectual curiosity or an inborn empathy with suffering, Whitman seems always to have been susceptible to the allure of suffering and death. His family friend Helen Price recalled a conversation about death in which

Whitman participated: "For a few moments his face wore an expression that she had never seen before—he seemed rapt, absorbed . . . he appeared like a man in a trance."[17]

In an era characterized by a shorter life expectancy and a high incidence of child mortality, journalist Whitman inveighed against Brooklyn's life-threatening health conditions—the foul dwellings of the poor, crude health practices, deplorable sanitation, contaminated water, and what he called "swill milk." These circumstances were periodically worsened by devastating epidemics of cholera and other lethal diseases; during some of these trying times young Walter appears to have visited the afflicted and dying poor, many of them immigrants. He was also drawn to the city firemen and the drivers of the horse-drawn omnibuses on New York's Broadway, among whom the incidence of injury and death was very high—drawn perhaps by their rugged individuality, by their sexual masculinity, and by a sort of "motherly" compassion that a number of his acquaintances attributed to him.[18] These same motivations later spurred his visits to the wounded soldiers in New York hospitals at the outbreak of the Civil War and his heroic labors among the hundreds of injured and dying soldiers of Washington's camps and hospitals. To some degree, however, this compassionate conduct was linked to his attraction to suffering and violent death, evidence of which appears in passages of luminous poetry that are often associated with episodes of heroism or of vicarious suffering.

Joseph Jay Rubin observes that although young Whitman lived amid a "vibrant" Long Island milieu, "he chose at first to sing of stricken youth rather than of farm kitchens, headlands, morning glories, swimming, and bluefish trolling" that would appear in some of his mature poems.[19] The undistinguished tales and verses that young Whitman wrote mirror the sentimentality and moralizing that characterized the popular press, but they also provide clues to his brooding over death and to his abiding fascination with death. Thus the protagonist in "Tomb Blossoms," a tale Walt may have composed while still in his teens, strikes the pose of a romantic young "man of feeling" who yearns for a gentle death and who praises the grave as a palliative for human suffering. In this sentimental tale about a poor, aged widow whom the protagonist watches as she decorates two adjacent graves because she does not know which of them contains the remains of her late husband, the narrator utters this paean to the grave:

The grave—the grave. What foolish man calls it a dreadful place? It is a kind friend, whose arms shall compass us round about, and while we lay our heads upon its bosom, no care, temptation, nor corroding passion shall have the power to disturb us. Then the weary spirit shall no more be weary, the aching head and aching heart will be strangers to pain, and the soul that has fretted and sorrowed away its little life on earth will sorrow not any more.

In sentiments resembling the outpourings of the consolation literature written by clergymen and their wives, the reader is advised, when troubled by vexation and sorrow, to consider the comfort that death will bring. The suggestion that death can solve human woes was a commonplace in this sort of writing, so it is difficult to judge the seriousness of Whitman's words or to know what state of mind produced them. The author, who affected a number of literary poses, may have been affecting the fashionable pose of a world-weary young man who is preoccupied with death. However, the tale does hint at the young Whitman's moments of self-doubt. His praise of death (coupled with the implied denial that he is terrified by it) gives way to a death wish that sometimes surfaces in his mature poems:

There have of late frequently come to me times when I do not dread the grave—when I could lie down, and pass my immortal part through the valley and shadow, as composedly as I quaff water after a tiresome walk. For what is there of terror in taking our rest? What is there here below to draw us with such fondness? Life is the running of a race—most weary race, sometimes. Shall we fear the goal, merely because it is shrouded in a cloud?[20]

The postmortal "goal" alludes to the preceding rhetorical question and foreshadows the theme, richly developed in *Leaves of Grass*, that life and immortality are integral parts of the same evolutionary cycle.

The sentimental verse "The Love That Is Hereafter" (1840) foreshadows those 1860 poems in which the persona expresses the hope that his failure to meet and attract mortal soul mates may be remedied in the next life:

For vainly through this world below
We seek affection. Nought but wo
Is without earthly journey wove,
And so the heart must look above
    Or die in dull despair.

"Fame's Vanity" has echoes of Gray's "Elegy Written in a Country Churchyard" and the sentimental poems of young Bryant. "Time to Come" (1843), with its echoes of "Monk" Lewis's "the-worms-crawl-in-the-worms-crawl-out" style of poetry is an uninspired declaration that following death the soul will divest itself of the physical body. But in questioning, "where will be *my mind's* abiding place" following his death (emphasis added), the young poet raises an issue that will continue to trouble him, as it has troubled most immortalists, namely, Following death, what *is* the relation between the human mind and the presumably imperishable soul? Young Whitman seems untroubled that the mind is generally assumed to be a function of the brain and the nervous system—and therefore the mind's functions cease when the body dies. Yet the mature poems that depict the afterlife of the Whitman persona—such as "Crossing Brooklyn Ferry"—generally show him retaining the highest degree of mental acuity and sensitivity. Lightly passing over such vexing matters, however, "Fame's Vanity" concludes by reassuring its readers of their immortality, in which state, it hints, their "*re-purified*" souls may be housed in astral bodies and clad in "*robes of beauty*."[21] "A Sketch" (1842), recently attributed to Whitman, also presents a scenario that appears in a number of later poems. Standing at the seashore and looking into the heavens for relief from his "darkened thoughts," the youthful persona discovers that nature has sent him a sign to bolster his faith in life everlasting. He beholds a star and declares that "the rich radiance of its beams, / Tells me of light beyond the tomb."[22] But perhaps the most intriguing image—one that haunted the poet for half a century—occurs in a first-person version of the poem "My Departure," written when the poet was twenty years old. In this version of *Waldeinsamkeit*, or forest solitude, so dear to the Romantics, the fledgling poet prays that when his time comes he may experience a solitary and peaceful release from life in a setting of pristine nature. He expresses a wish to go alone into the woods, where all is pure and serene, to lie down in an opening among the trees where there is a view of a bay, and there at sunset to "leave this fleeting world"—to "step down to the Unknown World alone" while he is "looking on water, sun, and hill, / As on their Maker's face." The imagery of departing this life in nature's bosom, solitary and content, so appealed to Whitman that it reappears in "Death's Valley," one of his last poems.[23]

"Revenge and Requital," one of the sentimental tales that young Whitman composed, casts an eerie light on the man who would later become a legendary hospital volunteer. The tale dramatizes Whitman's fascination with New York's "humane institutions" and foretells the devoted volunteer who will be drawn to the sick and dying in the hospitals of New York and Washington. During one of the cholera epidemics that struck the city, we are told, many residents fled; but others, whom the tale calls "God's angels," stayed behind to succor the afflicted. One such "angel" anticipates the image of the selfless "wound-dresser" of *Drum-Taps* and the later Whitman's own devotion to the hospitalized soldiers who, according to his own testimony, he rescued from abandoning their will to live.

> There were the men and women ["God's angels"], heedless of
> their own small comfort, who went out amid the diseased, the
> destitute, and the dying, like merciful spirits—wiping the drops
> from hot brows, and soothing the agony of cramped limbs—
> speaking words of consolation to many a despairing creature, who
> else would have been vanquished by his soul's weakness alone—
> and treading softly but quickly from bedside to bedside—with
> those little offices which are so grateful to the sick, but which
> can so seldom be obtained from strangers. . . . .*One* among them
> seemed even more devoted than the rest. Wherever the worst
> cases of contagion were to be found, he also was to be found. In
> noisome alleys and foul rear-buildings, in damp cellars and hot
> garrets, thither he came with food, medicine, gentle words, and
> gentle smiles. By the head of the dying, the sight of his pale calm
> face and his eyes moist with tears of sympathy, often divested
> death of its severest terrors. . . . And when he wandered through
> the most wretched streets and alleys of the city [at night] his
> well trained ear caught those familiar sounds, those wailings of
> anguish and fear, how unerringly would he direct his feet to the
> spot whence they proceeded. There, like an unearthly help, vouch-

safed from above, he would at once take the measures experience had proved most efficacious, not seldom finding his reward the next day in the recovered safety of his patient.[24]

If the tale is autobiographical we can conclude that early experiences honed the skills with which he comforted the sick and the dying and learned to speak the words of assurance they most wanted to hear. Most dying individuals, as Elisabeth Kübler-Ross discovered during years of observation, are concerned with issues of life, not the fact of their own dying. "They wanted honesty, closure, and peace," she says. "How a patient died depended on how he lived"—a sentiment with which the poet concurred. A successful counselor to the dying, she concludes (and Whitman was one of the best), must be concerned with "the practical and philosophical realms, the psychological and the spiritual."[25] From the beginning Whitman seems to have recognized his ability to comfort the ailing immigrants, and later the hospitalized horse-car drivers and injured firemen and soldiers, by speaking with them in the simple manner that characterized his—and their—humble origins and by entering into their mode of thinking. The hero of this "fact-romance," who would not allow a dying man to be "vanquished by his soul's weakness alone" and whose consoling "tears of sympathy . . . often divested death of its severest terrors," is a rough model of the persona of the healer-poet in *Leaves of Grass.*

And death was no stranger to him. Harold Bloom remarks that death was part of the Whitman family history, "and its enigma is assimilated into the mystery of origins, where it is granted its true priority."[26] Although many of the Whitmans were relatively long-lived, an infant sister died at six months of age when Walt was only six years old; his father died at sixty-six, during the birth year of *Leaves of Grass;* his brother Andrew died, aged thirty-six, of tuberculosis (from which Walt also suffered); his beloved mother and his sister-in-law Martha Whitman both died in 1873, the year he was stricken by paralytic hemiplegia; and both infant children of his brother George, with whom he was then living in Camden, died soon after their births.[27] And many of the soldiers with whom he developed emotional bonds—he sat beside some of them as they expired— died during his years of service in the Washington military hospitals. Devastated by the death of his cherished mother, the middle-aged poet kept an all-night vigil beside her coffin and was still sitting there the next day, thumping with his cane on the floor and seemingly oblivious to the funeral service being conducted in the adjoining room.[28]

Whitman's role as America's poet of death was shaped in part by his intellectual milieu. Christian tradition had long stressed the importance of preparing for death, often warning of terrors beyond the grave for those whose faith had lapsed or failed. On the other hand, religious moderates tended to picture death in a hopeful light. The century's advances in geology, anthropology, and various life sciences, which Whitman credited with buttressing his arguments in favor of immortality by demonstrating the antiquity of existence, the evolution of life toward higher forms, and the ever-expanding dimension of the universe, undercut the argument (favored by Emerson, William James, *and* Whitman) that one's fervent belief in immortality (the belief of millions throughout the world) may be the best proof of its reality. And although he did not accept the trappings of spiritualism, remarking on several occasions—once after he attended a séance—that it was a fraud, spiritualists found many of his views compatible with their own; and by way of reciprocation, perhaps, he sprinkled hints in some of his poems that he, too, might be something of a spiritualist. Like Whitman, the spiritualists were interested in the reforms of the day. Typically, the radical spiritualist, free speech advocate, labor reformer, and "free love" enthusiast Ezra Heywood—who taunted the nation's moral censor Anthony Comstock by reprinting some of Whitman's "offensive" poems—maintained that death is no more than a transient illusion, "born of limited mortality, and transcended by Life and Immortality, revealed in convincing evidence of immaterial Intelligence"—that is, the spirit world. Heywood's radical view of death motivated him to become a founder of the New England Anti-Death League, which denied the reality of death. And although Whitman's poems occasionally indulge in flights of fancy (some of them erotic) about the persona's excursions into the afterlife, he declined to speculate about the nature or the specifics of the postmortem scene.[29]

Whitman was apparently well acquainted with the literature of death. His claim (in the preface to the first edition of *Leaves of Grass*) that he had gone "thoroughly" through the Old and New Testaments and that he had read a range of classical writers, including Homer (several translations!), Shakespeare, Milton, and Blake may be hyperbolic. Yet his brother George recalled that young Walt frequented libraries, and Walt himself claimed that he had read the Bible, Homer, Shakespeare, Aeschylus, Epictetus, Horace, Virgil, Ossian, Hafiz, and Walter Scott in his youth.[30] Among the still-popular poetic meditations on death that he may have read—some of them written by Christian ministers—were Thomas Parnell's "Night Piece on Death" (1722), Edward Young's "Night Thoughts" (1742), Robert Blair's "The Grave" (1743), and Gray's "Elegy" (1751). In fact, the literature of mourning and consolation had a mass readership in his formative years. Prior to the Civil War, when child mortality was high, popular periodicals were filled with mawkish tales and poems—characterized by their confident promise of immortality—about the deaths of children. During Whitman's formative years, Lydia Sigourney's seemingly endless flow of sentimental stanzas charting the progress of children from death to burial and an instant elevation to angelhood achieved great popularity. And, as Ann Douglas observes, contemporary writers like Dickens, Harriet Beecher Stowe, and Elizabeth Stuart Phelps published works that assumed "a pseudoscientific spirit of assurance" regarding the existence of Heaven.[31] Mortuary art also reached a peak of popularity in this period. Not only did cemeteries, like the famed Auburn Cemetery in Cambridge, develop a high level of landscape and statuary art, but hundreds of painters—including some whom Whitman knew—painted mortuary subjects, including the portraits of recently dead adults and children.[32] But childhood deaths are conspicuously absent from *Leaves of Grass*. The only dead children pictured there are victims of sea disasters—"the silent old-faced infants" in "Song of Myself," section 33, and the dead cabin boy in section 36; however, Whitman assures us in "Faith Poem" (1856, later titled "Assurances") that "the deaths of little children are provided for" in the cosmic scheme of things.

Moreover, the writings of the major American literary figures of the first half of Whitman's century—Irving, Poe, Bryant, Emerson, and Melville—were steeped in death. And, unknown to the author of "Crossing Brooklyn Ferry" and of other poems that dramatize his posthumous persona, his younger contemporary Emily Dickinson, concerned with the fate of *her* soul, speculated in dozens of poems about her life on both sides of the grave.[33] Although Whitman and Dickinson built on the tradition of their death-oriented antecedents, their poetic confrontations with death are presented as intense poetic dramas that are, at the same time, both personal and cosmic. Of American poets Whitman was most impressed by William Cullen Bryant as a writer of poems "pulsing the first interior verse-throbs of a mighty world—bard of the river and wood, ever conveying a taste of open air ... always lurkingly fond of threnodies—beginning and ending his long career with chants of death, with here and there through all, poems, or passages of poems, touching the highest universal truths." Indeed, echoes of "Thanatopsis," young Bryant's celebrated hymn to death, resound in Whitman's work, and faint strains echoing Bryant's "unfaltering trust" in a benign future existence linger in some of his mature poems.[34] However, Whitman goes far beyond Bryant's patient acceptance of death. He and his persona struggle hard to find the meaning of death and to affirm the possibility of an afterlife. They wrestle with death; taunt it; plead with it; pursue it as a lover; travel to the realms of death both celestial and hellish; exalt it in various ways; plead to be its spokesman and its translator.

As Whitman began planning his book of poems in the early 1850s, convinced that great art must show a proper regard for death, he realized that death was fundamental to his aesthetic. A talk that he made at the Brooklyn Art Union in March 1851 shows him gestating the "language experiment" that four years later would give birth to *Leaves of Grass*. He proposes the appropriateness of death as a subject for the highest artistic endeavor. Decrying the frequent association of death with terror and proposing that death be rendered in a context of beauty and hope, the talk shows the poet developing the theory by which he will subsequently be guided. Despite its conventional elements and a fleeting hint that death may turn out to be only the eternal *nada* (a recurrent note throughout the poems), the talk signals the emergence of a poet who will picture death as an event to be approached with serenity, awe, and trust. He rejects the frightening traditional imagery of death in favor of a softer Grecian—possibly homoerotic—imagery that anticipates his own poetic practice:

> Nay, may not death itself, through the prevalence of a more artistic feeling among the people, be shorn of many of its frightful and ghastly features? In the temple of the Greeks, Death and his brother Sleep, were depicted as beautiful youths reposing in the arms of Night. At other times Death was represented as a graceful form, with calm and drooping eyes, his feet crossed and his arms leaning on an inverted torch. Such were the soothing and solemnly placed influences which true art, identical with a perception of the beauty that there is in all the ordinances as well as the works of Nature, cast over the last fearful thrill of those olden

days. Was it not better so? Or is it better to have before us the idea of dissolution, typified by the spectral horror upon the pale horse, by a grinning skeleton or a mouldering skull?[35]

The strategies Whitman employed in *Leaves of Grass* reflect, directly or indirectly, his attitudes toward death. *Leaves of Grass* is replete with references to death; the word *death* and its variants appear there well over two hundred times. The poems depict deaths he witnessed, death-scenes he invented, scenes of the persona's own fantasized death, and moments when the poet seems to be resigned and eagerly anticipating death. The Whitman persona in "Song of Myself" assumes many guises. In the graveyard setting of section 6 he appears ingenuous and mystified by death, humbly admitting, "I wish I could translate the hints about the dead young men and women," but nevertheless proclaiming his certainty that "they are alive and well somewhere"—a recurring theme in the poems. He praises all the dead, however humble or rejected during their mortal lives. He portrays himself as a prophet of death and a translator of the signs and auguries of an immortal future that are planted throughout his world; he equates his own words and insights with those of any man or god. He is a Christlike intervener with death. In his limitless empathy, he "becomes" one of the dead, even descending into and emerging from the murky realm of death. He confronts and challenges Death as an equal. And in a spectacular finale, he melts effortlessly into the realm of Death, where he loses neither his identity nor his capacity to benefit humanity nor to retain a mystic contact with generations of the living. "Great Are the Myths" (the concluding poem in the 1855 edition) ends—like every successive volume of poems that Whitman published—on a note of praise for death. "To Think of Time" (1855)—Whitman's first full-dress meditation on death—apparently reflects a bitter crisis of confidence in a meaningful death and a fear of annihilation that are resolved by a kind of mystic revelation when he surveys the splendid world around him, one of several such moments in *Leaves of Grass*.

The sublimated fear that death might extinguish his conscious identity crops up throughout *Leaves of Grass*. Some poems show how fiercely Whitman resisted the thought that his consciousness could end with his final breath; he considered such an ending to be a cosmic fraud, incompatible with his trust in an orderly and purposeful world. And there is more than a grain of truth in Arthur E. Briggs's observation that Whitman's treatment of death is often rooted in his loneliness and his moments of despair—transient feelings that are offset by his conviction that his poetry must not only be "an apostrophe to the fullness of life in the compact, concrete, and visible, but in comradeship with the unseen, roving, general soul of man."[36] He developed a sort of secular mysticism that viewed death, confidently but vaguely, as the passing into another evolutionary stage with one's conscious identity somehow preserved. His acceptance of death as part of the cycle of existence, as many critics have noted, was a vital factor in his zest for life and in his belief that mortal life is to be relished as a glorious adventure. The suppressed terror of death, which is the subtext of many of his poems, subsided in the post–Civil War years as he reached the relative calm of old age and became a prophet of what Keats calls "easeful death." His greatest literary invention, the Whitman persona, always relishes life but knows that he lives on the edge of death and trusts that death will prove to be a meaningful advance in the cycle of existence. The presumably imperishable persona is seemingly autonatal, reborn each day into a sort of divinity and inspired anew to venture forth on the limitless mythic road that leads to self-realization and perfection—a process glowingly depicted in such poems as "Out of the Cradle Endlessly Rocking," and "Song of the Open Road." As he traverses the everyday world, he discovers it teeming with vibrant life and lined with emblems of divinity and immortality which he aspires to read and to translate for mankind. And everywhere along this endless road looms the ghostly image of death, whether as a nebulous specter, a motherly comforter, or as the gatekeeper of the god with whom the persona aspires to form a comradely relationship, to identify, or eventually to merge. Even after the horrors of the Civil War and the corruption of postwar American society had shaken his faith in America's capacity to achieve a real democracy, Whitman remained steadfast in his belief that the cycles of death and the ameliorative workings of time would ultimately provide a vehicle for personal development and national salvation. As his streetcar-conductor comrade Peter Doyle affirmed, Walt always expressed a firm faith in an afterlife.[37] In his later years, some of his admirers accepted the idea that Whitman had somehow absorbed the meaning of death through a sort of spiritual osmosis and had become death's greatest prophet.

In the 1856 edition—a virtual manual of "democratic faith"—the persona often appears as a friendly guru and would-be companion of the common folk, persuading them that their lives and their deaths can be meaningful and satisfying and that he sees auguries of universal immortality throughout the visible world. The crown jewel of the edition, "Crossing Brooklyn Ferry," is the only extended depiction of the persona as an all-seeing, all-empathizing postmortal being, dwelling in a mythical hereafter, endowed with heightened powers of sympathy that bind him to the living and afforded a superior view of the orderly workings of the universal law. (Other poems, notably "So Long!" [1860] and "Passage to India" [1871], depict varied but wishful versions of the persona's happy existence in a postmortal state.) Indicative, however, of Whitman's vacillations concerning death and immortality, the original version of "Crossing Brooklyn Ferry" reveals the persona undergoing a crisis of faith in which he questions his own certainty that there may exist a meaningful life beyond death. And another 1856 poem, "This Compost," depicts a traumatic crisis of faith that is seemingly resolved by an epiphanic vision of universal goodness and continuity and followed by a strong affirmation of immortality. The 1860 edition of *Leaves of Grass* is replete with such affirmations of immortality, even though two of its masterpieces—"Out of the Cradle Endlessly Rocking" and "As I Ebb'd with the Ocean of Life"—also reflect deep crises of faith in which the persona questions his ability to perceive an orderly universe and to interpret life and death. However, in both poems, the episodes of personal crisis are momentarily resolved by mystic signals from the heart of nature—a pattern found in several poems. But they leave unresolved the question: To what extent are these crises literary strategies to reflect the triumph of faith over doubt, and to what extent do they reflect Whitman's genuine crises of belief?

*Drum-Taps,* the elegant poetic record of Whitman's witnessing of so many deaths on the battlefields and in the hospitals and his empathetic involvement with the dying soldiers, chiefly focuses on the grim reality of death and dying as the central realities of the war. Whitman stresses the fact that the soldiers whom he witnessed died calmly, even serenely, perhaps to illustrate that dying is essentially devoid of terror. Few of the poems describe his agonized reactions to these fatalities, and relatively few declare that the dead soldiers are immortal, or they only suggest it vaguely and by indirection. And although many of the postwar poems celebrate the impending journey to a mystic beyond, some resonate with the subdued cries of pain. Thus even "Passage to India" and "Prayer of Columbus," which voice the persona's eager readiness for death, incorporate prayers for his release from physical suffering. And referring to his own "grave illness," Whitman labeled the 1876 edition of the *Leaves*, and its "mostly sombre" poems, as "almost Death's book," one that introduced "diviner songs" based on a "more splendid Theology" that emphasized the bodiless soul.[38] Thereafter, as his twilight days drew nearer, he wrote many haunting lyrics welcoming his death and his voyage thither and voicing his composure and his expectation of a life beyond.

## 3

Whitman firmly embraced some form of future life. "Have you any doubt of mortality?" he asked himself in an early notebook, and answered, "I say there can be no more doubt of immortality than of mortality."[39] And although he appears convinced that he will continue as a distinct entity in some future state, he cannot define what that state may be like or what the relation may be between his mortal, material self and any future manifestation of himself. Thus he remarks in his informal autobiography *Specimen Days*, "the most profound theme that can occupy the mind of man . . . is doubtless involved in the query, What is the fusing explanation and tie—what the relation between the (radical, democratic) Me, the human identity of understanding, emotions, spirit, &c., on the one side, of and with the (conservative) Not Me, the whole of the material objective universe and laws, with what is behind them in time and space, on the other side?" He relates the material and spiritual worlds by defining them as the "necessary sides and unfoldings . . . in the endless process of Creative thought," which ultimately are parts of an essential unity governed by "one consistent and eternal purpose." Given the right powers of perception or inspiration, he assumes, one could possibly understand the essential unity between the material and the spiritual. And although he does not say it in so many words, he appears to equate "Creative thought" with "the Mind of God." As he draws closer to philosophical idealism with the passage of years, he subsumes life and death under a continuous and purposive law governing "the visible universe" and the "invisible side of the same."[40]

Like many of his contemporaries, Whitman reasoned that his fierce desire for an afterlife and the corresponding desire that he believed to exist among peoples throughout the world were the best indicators of a possible immortality. Nevertheless, he remained deliberately vague about the nature of the existence that may follow one's death. He was not tempted to describe or define the nature of a future world; to have been more specific would place him in the same ideological trap as those immortalists of the Gilded Age whose graphic images of a comfortable anthropocentric heaven bordered on the ludicrous.[41] His staunch belief in immortality was certainly related to his keen awareness that mortal existence could be unsatisfying to the "formless, feverish" children of Adam and Eve with "never-happy hearts"[42] who deserve something better than the travail that seems to be their allotted portion. It may be true, as Marxist philosopher Howard Selsam asserts, that the oppressed masses have conjured up "a heaven, another and better world for which the present is but a trial and a preparation" as an imagined compensation for their earthly poverty and distress, trusting that "if this life is bad, men made it worse that the future life might be better."[43] Nineteenth-century America was a fertile ground for new creeds, many of them intent on redefining death as an ultimate palliative for the harsh realities of mortal travail. Although critics have detected Buddhist, Quaker, Spiritualist, Hegelian, Transcendentalist, and Darwinian influences in Whitman's writings, it is safe to say that his views of death and immortality have a liberal Protestant base. However, he distrusted all religious orthodoxies because they imposed rigid formulas upon the individual and thwarted his or her abilities to seek inspiration and truth; but like some religious reformers he, too, aspired to usher in a "new" democratic religion of his own devising, in which an open acceptance of death would be a purposeful goal.[44] As Arthur E. Briggs observes, "this new religion of Whitman's was not atheism, agnosticism, or skepticism" but rather one that promoted the "encouragement and assurance" that "'nothing is ever lost'" and that "'we are 'all surely going somewhere.'"[45] When Robert Ingersoll challenged Whitman's views because they lacked "definiteness," the poet defended his ideological vagueness as a rejection of those who attempted to reduce the mystery of life and death to some formula, stressing, as he often did, that his own profound feelings and intuitions were as valid an approach to the ultimate truth as anyone else's dogma or formula.[46]

Immortality has always been a troublesome concept. Socrates conjectured that death may be a removal to another place where one can join one's deceased friends in a fairly congenial setting—an idea that Whitman toys with in the "Calamus" poem, "These I Singing in Spring."[47] Plato was more cautious. "But surely," he said, "it requires a great deal of argument and many proofs to show that when a man is dead his soul yet exists, and has any force or intelligence."[48] Some ancients dreaded the very thought of a perpetual existence in what they conceived to be an interminable Hades. To the ancient Jews, Greeks, and Romans, and to the Hindus the prospect of an afterlife or resurrection was often terrifying.[49] The Book of Ecclesiastes comments dourly that "in the days to come shall all be forgotten. . . . For the living know that they shall die: but the dead know not any thing, neither have they any more a reward, for the memory of them is forgotten." And the Psalmist declares that "the dead praise not the Lord, neither any that go down in silence." But influenced by their Greek and Near Eastern neighbors, the Hebrews made life after death a key tenet in their belief system; and in the eighth century B.C., when they faced massive threats, Isaiah advanced the doctrine of personal and national resurrection. Two centuries later, Ezekiel prophesied the resurrection of the Hebrew dead, both the individuals and the nation.[50] And although some early Christians cloaked the idea of immortality in a pall of terror, Platonic Christianity became a major source of the belief that mortal life could indeed be transcended, maintaining that because death represents a beneficial change from earthly existence, grief over the loss of a mortal life should be curbed. In the New Testament (where Heaven is mentioned some 140 times) the promise of immortality forms the heart of Paul's message. He tells the Corinthians that "if the dead rise not, then is not Christ raised: And if Christ be not raised, your faith is vain." And he interprets Christ's resurrection as the emblem of universal resurrection. Yet, Paul's words (like those of Whitman) challenge the reader to pin down an unambiguous explanation of physical or personal immortality.[51]

Like both Emerson and Elias Hicks, the radical Quaker whose person and beliefs Whitman esteemed, the poet rejected established theological creeds. Hicks praised Christ chiefly as an inspirer of the human spirit. Whitman quoted with admiration Hicks's dictum that God had breathed life into "the immortal and invisible soul . . . and it became alive to God." And in view of Whitman's frequent reference to the "law" that prevails throughout the universe and is generally manifested in the human spirit as feeling or intuition, it is illuminating to note Hicks's contention that "the cross of Christ . . . is the perfect law of God, written on the tablet of the heart, and in the heart of every rational creature," a law that humans cannot "erase or obliterate." Anticipating both Whitman and Emerson,

Hicks remarked that "Christianity brought a new wisdom. But learning," he added cautiously, "depends on the learner."[52] Emerson's essay "Immortality" also interprets immortality as an extension of the life of the mind and the power of the imagination—a yearning for perfection in a context of an eternal existence. Assuming, like Whitman, that we live in a divinely ordered universe, Emerson said, "I think all sound minds rest on a certain preliminary conviction, namely, that if it be best the conscious personal life shall continue, it will continue; if not best, then it will not: and we, if we saw the whole, should of course see that it was better so." Emerson's essay echoes many of the concepts that permeate *Leaves of Grass,* among them that humanity yearns for "stability" and takes "delight in permanence" and in a sense of "immense time." Like Whitman, he posits an orderly universe where "nature never moves by jumps, but always in steady and supported advances." Also like Whitman, for whom "a vast similitude interlocks" the visible and invisible worlds, Emerson perceives many signs of immortality in the visible world, declaring that "all I have seen teaches me to trust the Creator for all I have not seen." And, like Whitman, he feels that the strongest indications of immortality are the individual's *feeling* that it exists and the supposedly universal yearning for its existence. "Belief in the future is a reward kept only for those who use it," he maintains; and, like Kant, he interprets the belief in eternity and immortality as part of the universal "moral sentiment" that links man to God. "It is curious," Emerson says, "to find the selfsame feeling, that it is not immortality but eternity—not duration, but a state of abandonment to the Highest, and so the sharing of His perfection— appearing in the farthest east and west." For both Emerson and Whitman, this mystic inner enlightenment and conviction are indicators of eternity and immortality.[53]

Eastern religious beliefs concerning the continuity of the species-life and of the individual lives also impinged on Whitman's views on death, particularly in his later years. Like his own thought, the stream of Buddhist thought about these matters is far from unitary. In fact, his conception of immortality both as some sort of personal survival and an inexhaustible reservoir of the life-essence is prefigured in Buddhist thought. According to Bruce R. Reichenbach,

> Buddhist literature follows the Vedic tradition of avowing a belief in life after death; what is not so clear is the sense in which this belief, as a form of immortality, is to be understood. For example,

on the one hand, immortality is likened to the vital energy, which, flowing from time immemorial, is passed from one organism to the next—from the first tree to its seed, on to another tree. On the other hand, all kinds of evidences from parapsychology are introduced to justify the belief that the person survives as a discarnate, insubstantial spirit and returns to human existence. Between these two views there lies an enormous difference: whereas the first substitutes a nonindividual continuing vitality for any persistence of the person, the second presupposes such persistence.[54]

Likewise, the nineteenth century's fascination with (and its revulsion from) scientific theories of evolution also shaped Whitman's conception of death. David Kuebrich observes, "modern science and democratic thought enabled the poet to arrive at a new, and in his mind more exalted understanding not only of this world but also of the afterlife," so that "he conceived of the afterlife as a process in which the soul attained to successively higher levels of illumination and participation in the divine consciousness . . . [a] belief in humanity's infinite potential for spiritual development."[55] Whitman also interpreted evolution as evidence of the inexorable advancement of the race and of his own exalted destiny; he might have applauded Darwin's assertion that "as natural selection works solely by and for the good of each being, all corporeal and mental endowments will tend to progress toward perfection." But he credited science with making only limited advances toward the highest truths. The "facts" of science "are not my dwelling," he declares in "Song of Myself"; "I enter by them to an area of my dwelling." The scientific evolution of Huxley and Darwin, he remarked late in life, is only a "working hypothesis"; but "when it comes to explaining absolute beginnings and ends," it doesn't clear up "the mystery any better than the philosophies that have preceded it." He admired the evolutionary hypothesis, he said, essentially because that sort of thinking "always keeps the way beyond open—always gives life, thought, affection, the whole man, a chance to try over again after a mistake—after a wrong guess." ("The way beyond" can refer, ambiguously, either to the terrestrial or the post-terrestrial future.)[56]

*Leaves of Grass* explores the many resonances of death because Whitman chose to look at death (as he looked at everything) from every possible angle, and so depicted death as a tragic loss, a personal drama, an aspect of species immortality, or as a point of departure on his quest to attain godliness. Because of the poet's empathy and compassion, his insight into the human condition, and his struggle to maintain an ameliorative and humane faith, readers may find his treatment of death to be inspiring or provocative. Yet they may remain puzzled by the subtle verbal games that the poems play with them. Even his strongest utterances are tempered by an awareness of his human fallibility; hence his many shifting strategies to present a rounded view of death. Confronted on all sides by conflicting evidence and contradictory ideologies, he preferred to keep his own counsel, perceiving his world as a palimpsest of divine messages that he yearns to decipher for himself and his fellows. "All are written to me, and I must get what the writing means," he declares, finding confirmation everywhere for his faith that death serves a beneficial purpose in the course of human development and that the individual death is to be accepted calmly and with a measure of hope—beliefs he illustrated in a rich variety of ways.

Horace Traubel, who perpetuated the image of a prophetic and saintly Walt Whitman, recorded the poet's words during the last four years of his life, including many of his observations regarding mortality. The poet's views on death remained generally consistent over the years. Although he did not object to being thought mistaken in his views, says Traubel, he disliked having his ideas challenged. Conceding that neither he nor anyone else could defend the belief in immortality on purely logical or scientific grounds, Whitman seemed to say that his belief was essentially based on the depth of his own feelings. Reiterating earlier claims that his pronouncements about death may have been mystically inspired, he told Traubel that "the most of what I have said about death came to me once long ago in a vision." The truth about death and immortality, he contended, is not arguable: the true poet simply "sees" (or at least glimpses) it. "Nowhere I look on this side of what is called death, do I see extinguishment, effacement of the Individual." When asked by a skeptic whether immortality could be proved, he reportedly answered: "Proved—in reality proved: yes. Proved as you understand proved: no. There are certain sorts of truths that may yield their own sorts of evidence. Immortality is not speculative—it does not come in response to investigation—it also does not give up its secrets to the chemist: immortality is revelation: it flashes itself upon your conscience out of God knows what." Whitman's vision of the afterlife, according to Traubel, included "no heaven or hell, no saved or damned, no ecstasy or horror—just men and women." Stressing that he views death as a sort of ultimate democracy, Whitman declared that "death allows for no accidents, no withdrawals:

death offers no options: the same gates are open to all." Throughout *Leaves of Grass* those "gates" serve as passageways that lead somewhere beyond our mortal existence and beyond our mortal understanding.[57]

Expressing a grudging admiration for scientists and all the other "ists and isms and haters" for attempting to make sense of their world, Whitman insisted (as he had in "Song of Myself") that scientific and secular knowledge alone is insufficient to reveal the ultimate truths of life and death. Only "tyros," he insisted, could be "certain either way." He valued science largely because he felt that its evidence substantiated his "own feeling, conviction" of the possibility of immortality.[58] Emphasizing his rejection of all orthodoxies, he remarked that "the tendency of belief" in this period is "not to be so damned certain we are certain . . . not so sure—any of us," and he added that "the not-too-damned-sure spirit is the glory of our age." As for the scientists' insistence on hard evidence concerning immortality, Whitman said, "I know nothing that better satisfies my own feeling, conviction" than an open-minded attitude toward the unknown. John Burroughs disputed the poet's acceptance of immortality as impossible to verify, arguing that "one cannot conceive of the thing until after it is proven! Life, and consciousness without the body, without the limitations of time and space! It is unthinkable, and therefore incredible." And he further mused: "I am convinced there are no terms by which we can express the truth of these things. Creation is infinite, and we cannot prescribe its ends or its bounds without a contradiction. It is too large for the mind to grasp. What is life for? Well, what, then, is immortality for?" Nevertheless, Burroughs accepted *Leaves of Grass* as an "inspired utterance." In turn, Whitman called Burroughs something of a "heretic" who, like other scientists and rationalists, "is not so sure he is sure and as long as this is the case, he will not say he is sure."[59] Whitman's rationale was not very distant from Emerson's view (or from that of many *fin de siècle* intellectuals) that "the blazing evidence of immortality is our dissatisfaction with any other solution." Emerson, whose roots were deeply theological, cautioned that a disbelief in immortality could result in pessimism and despair; without such a faith, he warned, "the affections die away—die of their own conscious feebleness and uselessness. A moral paralysis creeps over us."[60] The aging Whitman said, "I am more firmly than ever fixed in my belief that all things tend to be good, that no bad is forever bad, that the universe has its own ends to subserve and will subserve them well. Beyond that, when it comes to launching into mathematics—tying philosophy to the multiplication table—I am satisfied: if they can explain, let them explain: if they can explain they can do more than I can do." He conceded that his convictions "are not reasons—not reasons: they are impressions, visions. What the world calls logic is beyond me: I only go about my business taking on impressions— though sometimes I imagine that what we see is superior to what we reason about—what establishes itself in the age, the heart, is finally the only logic—can boast of the only real verification." To the very end Whitman retained his almost desperate faith in the ultimate perseverance of the good. "[W]ithout immortality," he said, oblivious to the ironic ambiguity of his words, "all would be sham and sport of the most tragic nature."[61]

*Democratic Vistas* (1871) asserts that nature has provided ample evidence for a belief in immortality in "the eternal beats, eternal systole and diastole of life in things—wherefore I feel and know that death is not the ending, as was thought, but rather the real beginning—and that nothing ever is or can be lost, nor ever die, nor soul, nor matter." And it predicts a succession of literary artists who will inspire "a real beginning" for the American people and for humanity with a spirit of renewal that involves a proper reverence for death:

> Faith, very old, now scared away by science, must be restored, brought back by the same power that caused her departure, restored with new sway, deeper, wider, higher than ever. Surely, this universal ennui, this coward fear, this shuddering at death, these low, degrading views, are not always to rule the spirit pervading future society, as it has in the past, and does in the present. . . . It must be done positively by some great, coming literatus, especially poet, who, while remaining fully poet, will absorb whatever science indicates, with spiritualism, and out of them, and out of his own genius, will compose great poems of death. . . . In the future of These States must arise poets immenser far, and make great poems of death. The poems of life are great, but there must be the poems of the purports of life, not only of itself, but beyond itself.[62]

One is not hard pressed to identify the model and the avatar of the "coming" literatus—America's premier bard of death.

# I

# "Triumphal Drums for the Dead"

## "Song of Myself," 1855

I

Like Dante, who was "midway upon the journey of our life" when he entered the darkened woods,[1] Whitman launched his poetic excursion in midcareer. When *Leaves of Grass* appeared in 1855 he was thirty-six years old, halfway through his allotted life span. A young man's fancy may turn lightly to thoughts of love, but middle-age fancy becomes tempered by thoughts of death. Carl Jung's dictum that a philosophical acceptance of death invigorates the second half of one's existence certainly applies to the fashioning of Whitman's literary career. "From the middle of life onward," says Jung, "only he remains vitally alive who is ready to *die with life*. For in the second hour of life's midday the parabola is reversed; death is born. The second half of life does not signify ascent, unfolding, increase, exuberance, but death, since the end is its goal.... Waxing and waning make one curve."[2] Jung probably did not have Whitman in mind when he made this statement, but the "curve"—the awesome parabola inscribed by Whitman's imagination as he strove to encompass life, death, and eternity—is a defining metaphor both for *Leaves of Grass* and for its poet, who undertook to suck life to its dregs and, simultaneously, to welcome and embrace death, sometimes with complaisance, sometimes with cheer, and often with a shiver of uncertainty. He accepted the Hegelian principle that "death is an essential factor of life ... the *negation* of life as being essentially contained in life itself, so that life is always thought of in its relation to its necessary result, death, which is always contained in its germ."[3] Like many of his contemporaries, he wanted to believe that dying meant neither the end of one's existence nor the loss of one's conscious identity. He reveled in the feeling that some sort of personal continuity beyond mortality was inevitable, even though he could not cite any decisive evidence. But he believed that the sum of human knowledge (which he conceived as a harmonious blending of personal experience, "hard" science, certain pseudosciences, and broadly based religious ideas) tended to buttress his belief in immortality. Above all, he trusted his own perceptions and his intensely felt instincts as the best proofs concerning the nature of life and death. Small wonder then that broad range of experience encompassed by "Song of Myself" and its dynamic persona always includes death.

The innovative structure of "Song of Myself" has opened the poem to a broad range of interpretations.[4] Whitman probably sensed the shape the poem would ultimately take, yet he seems to have fitted various disparate sections (sections 6 and 34–36, for example) into its loose fabric.[5] Most readers know the poem from its final arrangement in the "Deathbed" edition of *Leaves of Grass,* where it is divided into fifty-two numbered sections, perhaps to make it more accessible to readers who needed to absorb one section at a time. However, in the first edition of *Leaves of Grass* the poem is divided into unnumbered "stanzas" of a single sentence, varying in length from one to sixty-nine lines (in present section 15). These sentence-stanzas form the poem's essential building blocks. To emphasize their importance, the 1860 edition numbered them sequentially, like verses in a Bible. Within the poem's loose structure, words, images, motifs, and ideas appear and reappear in nuanced variations. Although only section 6 and sections 49 through 52 (as numbered in the final edition) are devoted exclusively to the theme of death, interspersed throughout the poem are dozens of passages on dying, death, the possibility of an afterlife, and the place of the persona in the timeless cosmos. As "Song of Myself" develops from beginning to end it becomes increasingly focused on mortality. And in one of the most memorable farewells in all of literature, it concludes with an imagined enactment of the persona's own death and his disintegration into earth, water, air, and spirit. This ritual death is only the most impressive of several such farewells in *Leaves of Grass,* all of whose successive editions, as well as the smaller collections of poems that Whitman issued during his lifetime, end on a note of death—sometimes the imagined death of the Whitman persona himself.

From the poem's outset the persona celebrates his existence as a democratic visionary whose hopeful gospel is intended to encourage the American masses to acknowledge the divinity latent in each of them.

I celebrate myself,
And what I assume you shall assume,
For every atom belonging to me as good belongs to you.

I loafe and invite my soul,
I lean and loafe at my ease . . . . observing a spear of summer
      grass.[6]

By loafing (and thus relaxing his physical and mental tensions) and by
inviting his soul to a spiritual communion, the persona attains the calm
that mystics claimed to be the precondition for entering into a visionary
state and uttering inspired words. He rejects the "perfumes" that signify
artificial doctrines in favor of the rarefied air of the inspirational afflatus,
and he delights in the good health that makes him feel so vital a part of
the divine scheme. But by inviting his soul to merge with whatever part
of himself is *not* his soul, the persona introduces the concept of philo-
sophic (and personal) dualism that permeates much of *Leaves of Grass.*
"Clear and sweet is my soul," he declares, "and clear and sweet is all that
is not my soul," thus suggesting that the visible and the tangible serve as
analogues of the invisible and the unknown:

Lack one lacks both . . . . and the unseen is proved by the seen,
Till that becomes unseen and receives proof in its turn.

The coexistence and interaction of the "unseen" and indestructible spirit-
self with the physical/material-self is basic to Whitman's interpreta-
tion of personal immortality, particularly in the first three editions of
*Leaves of Grass.* "To elaborate is no avail," he asserts, unwilling to have his
intuitions subjected to logical dissection or tests of religious correctness.
Hence his assertion (in section 3) that "learned and unlearned *feel* that it
is so."

The persona illustrates the accessibility of spiritual illumination to
himself and to his fellows in section 5 by reconstructing the scene of
his purported mystic awakening—an epiphany similar to one that Whit-
man himself had reportedly undergone not long before he composed the
poem. His devoted physician and friend Richard Maurice Bucke claimed
(apparently drawing on Whitman's own statement) that in June 1853 or
June 1854 the poet had experienced a revelation "that gave him the mental

power, the moral elevation and the personal joyousness" that wrought "the change . . . in his mind and heart" and that marked "the birth within him of a new faculty."[7] In the poem's dramatic reconstruction of this mystic experience, the persona's godlike soul, depicted in the passage as a sexually seductive and "loving bedfellow,"[8] spends the night with the persona and, before departing, leaves him baskets filled with the bread of life—assurances of his self-worth and an awareness that little can be gained by "ciphering" out the mysteries of life and death by logical or mechanical means. The harmonious union between his body and his indwelling spiritual essence is dramatized as a rapturous, but rather nebulous, sexual coupling during which the conscious self appeals suggestively to his spiritual seducer to "loose the stop from your throat" and to inspire him with "the hum of your valved voice" by plunging "your tongue to my barestript heart." Above all, he appears to be asking his spirit-lover to be granted the power of language that will enable him to become America's master poet. (Throughout the poems, in fact, the power of utterance is equated with the afflatus and the life-force itself.) The mystic moment ends with the persona's conviction that he has experienced "the peace and knowledge that pass all argument of the earth," convinced that he is immortal, and that a godlike element pervades him as it pervades every part of creation. Whatever biographical or religious implications this celebrated passage may have, it certainly conveys the impression that a divine presence has conferred its imprimatur upon this poetic work, thus sanctioning Whitman to become an inspired interpreter of life and death.

Like all of the persona's mystic experiences, this one is solitary. Possibly looking back at this mystic incident of "interior consciousness" Whitman wrote in *Democratic Vistas:* "[O]nly in the perfect uncontamination and solitariness of individuality may the spirituality of religion positively come forth. Only here, communion with the mysteries, the eternal problems, whence? whither? Alone, and identity, and the mood—and the soul emerges, and all the statements, churches, sermons melt away like vapors. Alone, and silent thought and awe, and aspiration—and then the interior consciousness, like a hitherto unseen inspiration, in magic ink, beams out its wondrous lines to the senses."[9] Having momentarily shut out that part of his dual selfhood that is rooted in the everyday world of joys and frustrations, his spiritual "self" rejects the "linguists"—the purveyors of uninspired, and therefore false, language—and "the contenders"—the advocates of the unpersuasive religious teleologies and of the secular doctrines that flourished at midcentury. Like the blind John Milton who was willing to "stand and wait" for divine guidance, the persona declares: "I have no mockings and arguments . . . I witness and wait." The true poet's access to uncorrupted speech comes only with the influx of inspiration.

The persona first attempts to explain the meaning of death in the celebrated sixth section of *Leaves of Grass,* whose distinctively naive and wistful tone may indicate that it was written as an independent piece and then fitted into the poem's larger structure. Section 6 begins with the persona's somber-playful response to a child's simple question, "What is the grass?" The grass, of course, is the poem's (and the volume's) core symbol, its leitmotif, seemingly inexhaustible in its ramifications and embodying the mysteries of nurture, decay, death, and renewal. The grass that grows by absorbing the life-giving energy of the sun becomes a metaphor of "the ceaseless springing forth of life from death."[10] Like Tennyson's "flower in the crannied wall," it is a microcosm that embodies and encodes the entire mystery of existence. The awesome challenge to explain the mystery of life and death is expressed in words of startling ingenuousness:

A child said, What is the grass? fetching it to me with full hands,
How could I answer the child . . . . I do not know what it is any
    more than he.

However, the persona's disarming admission that he cannot translate this master symbol into words that will satisfy the child—or satisfy himself— is a rhetorical device that serves to introduce a series of tentative answers meant to show how deeply Whitman has probed into this mystery.

In response to the child's challenge to explain the meaning of the grass, the poet resorts to analogy and metaphor—a rhetorical strategy that he follows throughout the poems in attempting to interpret the meaning of death. The grass is itself a master metaphor, of course, and as is the case with metaphors, it is defined by employing other metaphors. Although the grass appears in the Psalms as a symbol of mankind's helpless susceptibility to mortality and dissolution,[11] the persona, employing a pathetic fallacy, offers the playful (and subjective) conjecture that the grass that blankets the earth may be the objectification of his own self—"the flag of my disposition, out of hopeful green stuff woven,"

Or I guess it is the handkerchief of the Lord,
A scented gift and remembrancer designedly dropped,
Bearing the owner's name someway in the corners, that we may
    see and remark, and say Whose?

The above conceit pictures God playing a game of drop the handkerchief with the favored persona in order to illustrate the principle that God's world is carpeted with decipherable emblems of universal benevolence. To those who can read their meaning, the handkerchief, the letters, and the grass are universal signifiers of the wonders of nature. Speculating in a related metaphor that the grass may be "a uniform hieroglyphic," the persona foresees the time when nature's emblems will be readable by all human beings. In the art of ancient peoples, eighteenth-century scholar Andrew Michael Ramsay declared, "the source of this primitive hieroglyphical language seems to have been the persuasion of the great truth that the visible world is representative of the invisible, that the properties, forms, and motions of the one were copies, images, and shadows of the attributes, qualities, and laws of the other."[12] Subsequently, the persona seems to have gained a mastery of the ancient skill of "reading" the objective world, for in section 48 of "Song of Myself" he appears confident that he can interpret nature's encoded messages. No longer feeling obliged to say "I guess," he declares boldly, "I find letters from God dropped in the street, and every one signed by God's name."

But these hopeful images become darkened in the final twenty-one lines of section 6. One becomes aware that the persona's meditations may be taking place in a graveyard, where it is only natural to associate the grass with the thoughts about those who lie beneath it. He longs to translate the arcane language of the grass that covers the graves of young and old. He sees the grass as "the uncut hair of graves," growing from the breasts of young men whom he might have loved—tender mates, perhaps, or mute inglorious Whitmans. (In "Scented Herbage of My Breast," 1860, the persona pictures himself as deceased, the grass sprouting from *his* breast, and uttering emblematic "leaves" of poetry to readers yet unborn.) In another emotional conceit he pictures the grass issuing from the corpses of the elderly and from children "taken soon out of their mothers' laps, / And here you are the mothers' laps," he cries. Such sentiments were not unusual in an era marked by a high incidence of childhood mortality, when legions of minor poets and portrait painters memorialized the deaths of children. And death is personified in *Leaves of Grass* not only as a merciful mother who receives the dying and cradles them in her soothing embrace but as a mother from whose womb offerings emerge into a new, postmortem, life. In a related image, the persona beholds the grass as "so many uttering tongues" issuing from "under the faint red roofs of mouths" of the interred, seemingly trying to reveal to him what no mortal has yet understood—the secret of the grave. Yearning to read the emblems inherent in every aspect of existence, he hopes to translate the still unintelligible secrets that the metonymic tongues of graveyard grasses seem to be trying to tell him. Thwarted by his inability to read their mystic language, he laments,

> I wish I could translate the hints about the dead young men
>     and women,
> And the hints about old men and mothers, and the offspring
>     taken soon out of their laps.

And as though he were soliciting the reader's sympathy for his temporary failure to explain death, he asks rather plaintively, "What do you think has become of the young and old men? / And what do you think has become of the women and children?" At midcentury, when millions of Americans reportedly believed in spiritualism and other doctrines that affirmed the possibility of life after death, he is safe in assuming that his auditors will share his faith in an afterlife. Although most of section 6 is notable for its gentle and understated tone, its concluding lines, which proclaim the immortality of those who lie beneath the grass, are unusual in their assertiveness:

> They are all alive and well somewhere,
> The smallest sprout shows there is really no death,
> And if ever there was it led forward life, and does not wait at the
>     end to arrest it,
> And ceased the moment life appeared.
>
> All goes onward and outward . . . . and nothing collapses,
> And to die is different from what any one supposed, and luckier

That "sprout" of grass is an effective metaphor for nature's perpetual renewal and for human progress both within and beyond the bounds of mortality. Nevertheless, the assurance that the dead "are alive and well somewhere" is not altogether convincing. For as Ivan Marki remarks, in his analysis of the first edition of *Leaves of Grass,* these "nebulous" lines, these "shouted pronouncements," indicate an evident strain in which "a lapidary stridency replaces the early lines' easy breathing" and show the poet trying "to make up for the conviction which is not there and his effort to extricate himself from the terror of death."[13] In fact, the lines are uncomfortably close to what has been called "the pseudoscientific spirit of assurance which the writers of consolation literature brought to the subject of heaven."[14] Among liberal religionists, says Corliss Lamont, the image of heaven tended to blur into little more than a sentiment; this attitude follows "the example of the eighteenth-century German philosopher Immanuel Kant, who concentrated on proving immortality as a postulate of the moral law and wasted scarcely a word in *describing* it." Certainly, Whitman shows the strain of announcing his faith in a future life whose nature he cannot explain. The vague proclamations that "they [the dead] are alive and well somewhere" and that "to die is different from what any one supposed, and luckier," identify neither the "they" who are dead nor the "somewhere" in which they may exist. Nor do they clarify the sort of good luck the dead will enjoy. But beneath their strenuous rhetoric, the lines affirm a stubborn faith, reiterated throughout *Leaves of Grass,* that death is an essential element of the universal continuum in which the soul may be said to progress. By making an accommodation with death, observes Robert K. Martin, the persona "realizes that he has escaped the trap of mortality."[15] For Whitman "the trap of mortality" most likely implied the fear that there may be no possible existence beyond the grave. Whitman's assertion of certainty concerning his own immortality was for him a source of comfort, a stay against the terrors of the unknown that sometimes darkened his thoughts about dying. But although the fear was usually kept in check and barely noticeable, the trap seemed to be forever there, yawning in the background.

The little lecture on death is resumed in the opening lines of the present section 7, which repeats the claim that it is "lucky to die, and I know it." How does he know it? Seemingly through surges of the divine afflatus that inspire him with a sense of his own infinitude. Having affirmed his faith in a benign cosmic order, the persona then prepares to launch himself on a vast imaginary journey, during which he will test his extraordinary visionary and sympathetic powers and will enter into the consciousness of hundreds of his contemporaries from all walks of life (sections 8 through 15). As though he were airborne and impervious to the workings of time and causality, he views the world below him. And like a mesmerist or a visionary, he appears able to penetrate the realms of life and death. "I pass death with the dying, and birth with the new-washed babe," he boasts. And further illustrating Whitman's "psychic disposition which inclined him to mystical experiences—excursions from what seemed to be the margins of himself,"[16] the persona asserts that his true dimensions are not circumscribed by the six-foot span "contained between my hat and boots." For such reckoning would not encompass his immeasurable spiritual divinity, which will survive his physical demise and become integrated into his immortal self. (Whitman could not imagine separating some of his mortal attributes from the identity he hoped to retain when he was no longer mortal.)

In these sections of "Song of Myself" the persona prophesies a spiritual democracy whose advent depends, in no small part, on the workings of death. "I am the mate and companion of people, all just as immortal and fathomless as myself," he asserts. "They do not know how immortal, but I know." His proclamation that the mass of humanity are eligible for immortality casts him in the role of an egalitarian, but his assumption that he possesses insights into their immortality of which they are still incapable positions him above the masses. In the course of the persona's panoramic mental journey across America, he claims to see "through the broadcloth and gingham whether or no" and to penetrate the minds and hearts of his fellows in all walks and conditions of life. He appears to receive a "resonance" from every person he sees, as though his mind were a mental sonar that responded to every vibration emanating from man and woman. He observes and "identifies with" infants, young lovers, farmers, craftsmen, boaters, trappers, slaves, a sex-starved woman whose yearnings for intimacy become his own, and a suicide who "sprawls on the bloody floor of the bedroom," but who, in a draft version of this passage, has hanged himself.[17] In section 14 he identifies with horses, moose, and, significantly, with wild geese:

The wild gander leads his flock through the cool night,
Ya-honk! he says, and sounds it down to me like an invitation,

The pert may suppose it meaningless, but I listen closer,
I find its purpose and place up there toward the November sky.

In Romantic poetry the bird call serves as the voice of inspiration from a higher power. After all, it is a "spotted hawk" that, at the end of "Song of Myself" appears to summon the persona to quit his earthly existence for whatever unknown fate may await him. By stating that "I believe in those winged purposes," the persona implies that the bird's call and its flight are subject to the same universal laws that govern his own being. The flight of the "wild gander," in particular, parallels the persona's spiritual journey in this section of the poem. Indeed, many religions have equated the gander's flight with the trance-flight of the shaman or mystic. During their trance-state, the mythologist Joseph Campbell explains, Hindu yogis are known as "wild ganders" or "supreme wild ganders," and he observes that

> in the image of traditional Hinduism, the wild gander is symbolic of *brahman-atman*, the ultimate transcendent yet immanent ground of all being, with which the yogi succeeds in identifying his consciousness, thus passing from the sphere of waking consciousness, where A is not A, passing even beyond dream, where all things shine of their own light, to the nonconditioned, nondual state "between two thoughts, where the subject-object polarity is completely transcended and the distinction between life and death dissolved."[18]

In order to zoom his poetic lens over the broadest range of life and to translate what the persona has seen and felt into poetic language, Whitman developed a unique version of the poetic catalogue. Just as Newtonian science had undertaken to classify and label all the phenomena of the known universe, so—as though he were the poetic heir of Linnaeus—Whitman developed a unique poetic catalogue that could record every aspect of human experience in tightly packed lines, evocative clauses, or brief cinematic vignettes. Packed into the sixty-five lines of section 15 of "Song of Myself"—in one continuous sentence—is a remarkably inclusive sequence of verbal snapshots of more than four dozen persons or groups of persons, all of whom have been so completely "absorbed" into the persona's heightened consciousness that the viewer and the object almost become one. The extensive panorama ends with the persona's declaration that "these one and all tend inward to me, and I tend outward to them, / And such as it is to be of these more or less I am." And section 16, which follows, reaffirms his belief that his thoughts harmonize with those of men and women in all eras, of "every hue and trade and rank, of every caste and religion." Yet amid all this diversity he still insists on his essential uniqueness and his appointed place in the overall scheme of things: "I am not stuck up and am in my place," he declares. His words, like the life-giving grass and "the common air that bathes the globe" with its "breath of songs and behaviour," are said to incorporate "the riddle and the untying of the riddle." He feels certain that what he calls "a living principle"—the universal spiritual "law" that cannot be codified or analyzed—is nevertheless most accessible to those, such as himself, who are attuned to nature and to their own true instincts. He believes that these unitary "laws of promotion and transformation" (as he calls the "living principle" in "To Think of Time") govern humanity's perpetual progression through all phases of existence during one's mortal life and beyond. In interpreting this principle of continuity as an "irrevocable" law of nature, his "science friend" Anne Gilchrist explained that "everything [is] the result and outcome of what went before; no gaps, no jumps; always a connecting principle which carries forward the great scheme of things as a related whole, which subtly links past and present, like and unlike. Nothing breaks with its past."[19] Whitman excluded no one, no matter how humble or corrupt, from the operation of the law, which embraced "the endless races of working people and farmers and seamen" and the losers and unsung heroes as well as the seemingly fortunate. Existence is not "a sham, a sell," he insisted. And indicating that his poetry encompassed the entire range of existence, he declared, "I am the poet of commonsense and of the demonstrable and of immortality." Comparing his heady pronouncements to the triumphal sound of a marching band of a thousand players, he announces:

> I play not a march for victors only . . . . I play great marches for
>     conquered and slain persons . . . .
> I sound triumphal drums for the dead . . . . I fling through my
>     embouchures the loudest and gayest music to them. [section 18]

Changing the figure of speech, he characterizes his inspired words as "the meal equally set . . . the meat and drink of natural hunger" from which no one is excluded. Thus, his words become the Bread of Life, and he becomes the godlike lover who yearns to instill his message of personal infinitude and immortality into everyone.

The persona insists upon his own infinitude, rejecting religious dogma and portraying himself as though he were one of Emerson's Representative Men whose life demonstrates the eligibility of every human to a meaningful mortal existence and to the immortality that may follow. Having, like an archeologist, "pried through the strata and analyzed to a hair," he feels sure of his own centrality in the universe. Reflecting Whitman's interest in Egyptology during the 1850s, the lines that follow picture the persona as a sort of Champollion, intent on translating the richly emblematic world as though it were a Rosetta Stone.[20]

To me the converging objects of the universe perpetually flow,
All are written to me, and I must get what the writing means.

I know I am deathless,
I know that this orbit of mine cannot be swept by a carpenter's
    compass,
I know I shall not pass like a child's carlicue cut with a burnt
    stick at night.

These lines confidently assert that his essential selfhood is inextinguishable and immeasurable by any known geometry. Spiritually imperishable, he maintains that he will not "pass" into the dark night of death and nothingness. (The word *pass* is used here and elsewhere just as the term was used by spiritualists and mystics, to suggest the transcendence from mortal life to a higher state of being.) As the self-appointed interpreter of both the "demonstrable" world and the realm of "immortality," the persona appears eager to demonstrate that he can suffer no cessation and that he will remain a primal force to be reckoned with. Small wonder, then, that this ostensibly limitless being can fancy himself as a god who is capable of mating—copulating as an equal and lover—with the "voluptuous coolbreathed earth" and with the "amorous" sea, which (as the poem implies) are yearning to receive *him*. The "bright juice" of his spermatic discharge which "suffuse[s]" the very heavens is an audacious metaphor for his virile and transcendent selfhood and for his inspired utterance in *Leaves of Grass*.[21]

2

By the mid–nineteenth century the meaning of time had changed. As American society became industrialized, time was measured in ever more finite units in the manufacturing and scientific processes, thus acquiring new connotations in the popular mind. Meanwhile, the traditional concept of time was vastly expanded by the discoveries of astronomers, geologists, archaeologists, and anthropologists. The labors of Lyell, Chambers, and Darwin radically broadened the concept of time, whose unlimited capacity for expansion is a cornerstone of Whitman's faith.[22] Both these tendencies are evident in *Leaves of Grass,* where time is assumed to be dichotomous, spanning both the chronometricals and the horologicals, as Melville called the finite and infinite measures of time. So the persona's references to time generally assume the continuum of limited, worldly, time and cosmic, or boundless and ever-expanding, time.

> A word of the faith that never balks,
> One time as good as another time . . . . here or henceforward it is
>     all the same to me . . . .
> A word of reality . . . . materialism first and last imbuing.

An 1853 letter to the *New York Times* that has been attributed to Whitman declares, "It is difficult to comprehend how the least cultivated mind can be made acquainted with the beautiful harmonies that pervade every department of nature without being excited to the highest degree of wonder and admiration."[23] And although the persona of "Song of Myself" concedes that science has reinforced his "faith that never balks," a faith that is grounded (at least in part) on worldly evidence, he maintains that the discoveries of science are still too narrow to unlock the mysteries of existence. Unlike our contemporary scientists who take their cues from Einstein's principle of relativity and from Heisenberg's uncertainty principle, many scientists in Whitman's day—like Whitman himself—were attuned to what might be called a "certainty principle."

Although Whitman was averse to rigid formulas, he was not alone in seeking a synthesis that included the material and spiritual worlds or in assuming the existence of an overarching "law" that could apply equally to both realms. The spiritualist Andrew Jackson Davis, who, like Whitman, resided in Brooklyn in 1854, called his own synthesis of science and spirit "Harmonial Philosophy," and credited the material progress of the nineteenth century to its steady rapprochement with the spiritual world; conversely, he predicted that a growing emphasis on the world of the spirit would be efficacious in promoting material progress. Similarly, the physiologist Joseph Buchanan claimed to have discovered a steady gradation reaching from the material world to the spiritual world. And other unorthodox thinkers speculated that with the mastery of "psychology" (the nascent "science of mind") spiritual phenomena would soon become subject to scientific study.[24] Obviously, Whitman was not alone in seeking to forge a unified field theory of science and spirit. His English admirer Edward Carpenter agreed with him that science is merely "a stage *that has to be passed through* on the way to a higher order of perception."[25] Edward Livingston Youmans, the preeminent popularizer of science in the three decades beginning in the mid-1850s, and a possible acquaintance of Whitman's, claimed that Mosaic Law was being replaced by the law of evolution, and that the universe was guided by "Omniscience" and "divine laws." And an 1879 article significantly entitled "Cosmic Emotion," intended to illustrate the idea that our mortal experience is only part of "something higher," pronounced Whitman "more in harmony with advanced science than any other living poet."[26]

The preface to the 1855 edition of *Leaves of Grass* asserts that "the sailor and traveler, the anatomist, chemist, astronomer, geologist, phrenologist, spiritualist, mathematician, historian and lexicographer are not poets, but they are the lawgivers of poets and their construction underlies the structure of every perfect poem"—an implication that poets and scientists pursue the same truths. This statement is somewhat modified in section 23 of "Song of Myself," which acknowledges that although the labors of scientists have shed light on the meaning of existence, their findings do not come as close in unlocking universal truths as do the intuitions of the true poet. After voicing an ambiguous "Hurrah for positive science!" and "exact demonstration!" the poet repeats his roll call of scientists and semiscientists—including a lexicographer, an Egyptologist, and "one who works with the scalpel," with some of whom he appears to have been personally acquainted.[27] In a half-ironic tone he acknowledges that although their "facts are useful and real . . . . they are not my dwelling . . . . I enter by them to an area in my dwelling." In a related notebook entry Whitman made this comment about "pure and positive truths": "I guess that after all reasoning and analogy and their most palpable demonstrations of any *thing*, we have the real satisfaction only when the soul tells and tests by its own arch-chemic power—superior to the learnedest proofs, as one glance of the living sight, [*sic*] is more than quarto volumes of description and maps." Concerning "professors, lawyers, authors teachers and whate not," he added: "Of them we expect to be learned and nothing more."[28]

Concluding the first segment of "Song of Myself," sections 24 and 25 present the persona as a living miracle, a personification of the "law" that pervades the universe, his personal grandeur demonstrating the possibilities latent in every human being. "Through me the afflatus surging and surging," he boasts in striking electrical imagery; "through me the current and index." The "current," or electrical life force, flows through him as it does through every man or woman; but by calling himself the "index," he defines himself as the inspired poet through whom the divine afflatus courses so that his words can teach his fellows how to understand their lives. He is able to utter "the password primeval" because, like the hero of Emerson's essay "The Poet," he feels the unmediated pulse of nature surging through him and enabling him to speak truths that are impervious to time. (Whitman would later boast that the universal spirit that created *Leaves of Grass* and the spirit that formed the Rocky Mountains are one and the same.)[29] Although "dumb," oppressed, and despairing humanity still must learn to recognize the inspirational forces that pervade creation, the persona positions himself as the spokesman of nature's "law" and believes himself to be capable of demonstrating how seemingly ordinary phenomena are actually miracles in a world that is filled with miracles: The wonders of the universe may be studied in their microcosmic manifestations, he says. As "the plenum of proof" of his argument, he proposes that his readers—many of them familiar with the pseudoscience of physiognomy—examine the photograph of his face that appears opposite the title page of the 1855 edition, thus implying that his face may be read as a dial plate (or "index") of his own being and as a microcosm or an emblem, of his universe. And he further illustrates the relation between macrocosm and microcosm in a delightful pun by declaring that "a morning-glory at my window satisfies me more than the metaphysics of books," thus suggesting that the ever-renewed glorious morning of the world manifests itself in this humble flower as in all things. The morning glory, which was commonly used as a symbol in mortuary portraiture, is also an appropriate symbol for Whitman's American drama of life and death. The morning glory, says one authority,

> was not a European symbol. But their growth cycle suggests a particularly dramatic birth-to-death progression. First the green vine sends out heart-shaped leaves and long clinging tendrils. Slowly the petals of the bud grow, remaining tightly wrapped up as buds around a spindle. Then, suddenly, the translucent petals open to the morning sun, wilt as the sun's rays become more intense, and drop from the vine. Because their stems are short, and because they bloom for a single half-day, the blossoms are generally not picked.[30]

Asserting that his "voice goes after what my eyes cannot reach" among the wonders of the visible and invisible worlds, the person now proclaims that "speech is the twin of my vision," thus stressing his role as a visionary who probes nature and the farthest reaches of the "invisible world," and is able to articulate their secrets. Nevertheless, since these matters can only be learned at first hand, he challenges "whoever hears me" to set out on his or her own road to self-realization. Having, in the poem's first major phase (sections 1 through 25) experienced a series of epiphanies, having "absorbed" the secrets and the essences of hundreds of lives, and having become vocal and prophetic, the persona now attains a spiritual calm and is content to wait for another influx of the divine afflatus.

### 3

Sections 26 through 30 of "Song of Myself" show the persona absorbing his world through his exquisite senses of hearing and touch, what Roger Asselineau calls his "hyperesthesia."[31] His stimulated senses induce reveries of sexuality and death. The first absorptive exercise of his senses (section 26) occurs when he decides to do "nothing but listen" and to test the limits of what Lawrence Kramer labels his "auditory imagination." The act of listening exhilarates his senses and excites him sexually, eventually producing a sort of postcoital depression and nightmarish death fantasies in a "step-by-step dissociation of the poet's identity."[32] It is important to recognize, however, that these fantasies are self-induced—

Whitman compares them to taking an opiate—by the persona who wishes to test how close the senses can bring him to the brink of death and self-destruction and a consequent sense of illumination and transcendence.

Sounds reminiscent of death constantly intrude upon his senses—the judge pronouncing death sentences; ominous fire alarms; the "low-march" of a funeral procession. But it is the sound of music (to which Whitman was passionately devoted) that produces the most intense reactions. The music of instruments, chorus, and opera produce "sweet pangs through my belly and breast," says the poem's persona. In a related note Whitman expresses the wish to taste a sort of surrogate death and then to be returned again to life—to be "convulsed" by orchestra and chorus filling him with passions, "unknown ardors and terrible extasies . . . lulling me drowsily with honeyed morphine opium—writhing about me the coils of collapsing death . . . tight'ning the fakes of death about my throat, and awakening me again to know by that comparison, the most positive wonder in the world, and that's what we call life." He is enthralled by the voice of the brilliant tenor, an apparent reference to Allesandro Bettini, "the orbic flex of whose mouth is pouring and filling me full." (That last phrase may imply fellatio.) But the emotions underlying the tenor's portrait run deeper than the poem suggests, illustrating once again Whitman's association of sexual passion with death. A notebook entry praising Bettini's singing declares that the tenor's voice had filled him with thoughts "of the spirit of life, and hope and peace" as well as thoughts "of the red fire of passion, the cavernous vacancy of despair, and the black pall of the grave." The "trained soprano," in the 1855 poem, "convulses me like the climax of my love-grip," the sublimity of her voice possibly bringing him to sexual release. (The celebrated contralto Marietta Alboni "roused whirlwinds of feeling within me.")[33] And orchestral music excites a range of emotions encompassing sublimity, terror and death:

> The orchestra whirls me wider than Uranus flies,
> It wrenches unnamable ardors from my breast,
> It throbs me to gulps of farthest down horror,
> It sails me . . . . I dab with wet feet . . . . they are licked by
>     indolent waves,
> I am exposed . . . . cut by bitter and poisoned hail,

Steeped amid honeyed morphine . . . . my windpipe is squeezed
in fakes of death,
Let up again to feel the puzzle of puzzles,
And that we call Being.

In this reverie, the allure of beauty converges with the persona's fantasies
of possible rape and of death by strangulation, for those "fakes of death"
are, literally, ropelike coils wound around his throat that can strangle him
and silence the voice that he equates with his selfhood and his immor-
tality. Lulled by the "honeyed morphine" of orchestral sound, he seems
almost to have swallowed the music (fellatio again?) in "gulps of farthest-
down horror." Subsequently awakening from this music-induced night-
mare vision of death and sensing the calm that generally follows his in-
tense emotional arousals, his spirit becomes liberated and he is again
able to contemplate "the puzzle of puzzles, / And that we call Being."
The word *Being* (in Jonathan Edwards's usage, for example) can refer to
the ineffable name of God. The persona's adventures in listening thus
appear to have carried him from the sounds of everyday life to a sexual-
emotional arousal, thence to a sense of experiencing death by strangula-
tion, and, finally, to the state of calm during which he once again becomes
able to contemplate his place in the divine order. The experience of in-
tense beauty, as Keats knew, can induce an apprehension of death. Such
an experience, says Rainer Maria Rilke, is all the more terrible because
beauty can dangle us over the chasm of death: "Beauty is only / the first
touch of terror, we can still bear / and it awes us so much / because it so
cooly / disdains to destroy us."[34]

In sections 27–29 the persona tests the limits of his tactile imagination.
These sections of "Song of Myself" are essentially the reworking of ex-
plicit draft materials in which Whitman explores the limits of pain and
pleasure, and the degree of physical and emotional intimacy that he may
be able to derive from homosexual (and possibly of masturbatory) activity.
Thus he notes that "there is something in the touch of an [*sic*] candid
clean person—what it is I do not know . . . but it fills me with wonderful
and exquisite sensation."[35] Like a hallucinogen or an emotional trauma,
the exploration of touch activates his libido, his imagination, and his
dream power, but it ultimately induces a loss of self-control. The tamer
version developed in "Song of Myself" differs radically from the draft
original, portions of which are completely suppressed in the completed

poem. *Leaves of Grass* could not include overt references to the presumably sordid sexual activities that were decried by clerics and reformers as unnatural acts of self-pollution. The persona's exploration of his tactile senses roughly parallels the cycle of his auditory experiences in section 26. He passes through a sequence of intense sexual arousals, intimations of beauty, feelings of guilt, depression, hysteria, and near-death, and eventually attains the calm that enables him to behold visions and to prophesy. When he exclaims during an apparent sexual spasm that "my breath is tight in its throat," his intense sexual feeling is once again accompanied by the threatened loss of speech, the inability to inhale the inspirational breath-afflatus, and intimations of death by strangulation. Like other passages in the poems, this episode of sexual arousal, climax and an ensuing calm is followed by visions of beauty and by a resumption of the persona's powers of inspired utterance.[36] His seminal release (section 29) appears to clear his brain and to germinate "prolific sprouts"—visions of golden landscapes and endless generations of loving human beings, and it reinstates him as a godlike visionary who appears certain of his place in an evolving universe (sections 30, 31). This sequence once again illustrates Whitman's principle that everything from "a leaf of grass" to "the journey-work of the stars"—including phallic experiences—can open a window on the wonders of the universe. In this connection it is noteworthy that classical Greek statuary often employed representations of the phallus and the seed to illustrate the (presumed) masculine source of eternal life.[37]

In the next dozen sections of "Song of Myself" the persona seemingly overcomes the limitations of time, space, and causality to become fully visionary and "absorb" his world through his senses, his imagination, and his intuition. As though he were re-experiencing the successive cycles of geological and animal evolution, from the primal magma to the human present, he exclaims (in section 32), "I follow, I ascend," thus implying that—whether as species prototype or as poet—he is the end product, so far, of an ongoing process. Evolutionary forces have operated through the millennia to produce a "Walt Whitman" who is gifted with a racial memory that enables him to replicate the evolutionary steps through which his "embryo" has progressed. Thus he preserves, as Donald Pease phrases it, "an impression of man's former presence . . . on its way into the human form."[38] And the persona substantiates his claim to a sort of geological immortality by professing to discover traces, or "tokens," of his former selves among the (supposedly lesser) animal orders through which he and humanity have evolved. In language reminiscent of his finding God's emblematic handkerchief in section 6, he says,

I wonder where they got those tokens [of myself],
Did I pass that way huge times ago and negligently drop them?

This imagery of species evolution may owe something to Constantin Volney's *Ruins, or Meditations on the Revolution of Empires,* which depicts the human soul as the culmination of a "physical metempsychosis, or the successive movement of the elements, of bodies which perish not, but, having composed one body, pass, when that is dissolved, into other mediums, and form other combinations. The soul is but the vital principle, which results from the properties of matter, and from the action of the elements in those bodies, when they create a spontaneous movement."[39]

Sections 33 to 37 demonstrate the persona's capacity to process the crowding and contradictory impressions, both objective and subjective, that impinge on his consciousness.[40] The deeper he probes into the human condition, the more he beholds the universality of agony and death. His absorptive powers are most impressively displayed in section 33—the greatest sustained poetic catalogue in our language. Although most of the section seems to be based on the poet's keen observation, some death-drenched episodes of heroism in section 33 as well as all of sections 34 through 36, are based on semihistorical secondary sources, some verging on pulp fiction.[41] As the persona identifies more closely with agonies and with the attractive-repulsive allure of death, he grows increasingly despondent, ultimately undergoing his most profound emotional crisis, but a crisis from which he will again emerge calm, refreshed, and prophetic.

The opening line of section 33 reads: "Swift wind! Space! [later clarified as "Time and Space!"] My Soul! Now I know it is true what I guessed at," that is, his assumption of the infinitude of space and time in which he exists and in which he will continue to exist.[42] A belief in immortality, as Frederick J. Hoffman explains, "serves to regulate the pace of human time," because it enables one to view each moment as both finite and infinite, "and one may say that each physical phenomenon touched by eternity gains a symbolic quality from the exposure to it." A sense of immortality, he declares, confers on each moment or object "a compensatory grace of objective value" and "an eternity in depth."[43] In this sense, the persona "enters into" every person, object, or occurrence that he beholds during his progress through the realm of life and death both through his powers of human perception and through his powers of cosmic perception."[44] Everything he beholds when he is "afoot with my vision" is compacted into the massive catalogue of section 33, which is structured as a single virtuoso sentence, its clusters of adverbial clauses and balanced participial phrases displaying countless snapshots of his observations, and coming to a close with a finite subject and verb in the sentence's eightieth line. The catalogue exhibits the inspired persona "speeding through space, speeding through heaven and the stars," speeding from place to place, from era to era, from person to person, and absorbing ("becoming") many identities whose essence he integrates into his own transcendent and multifaceted self. Insistently intruding into this panoramic overview of (mostly American) life, however, are the painful images of death—"the life-car . . . drawn on a slip-noose"; "the half-burned brig [which] is riding on unknown currents, / Where shells grow on her slimy deck, and the dead are corrupting below"; the "burial-coaches enter[ing] a cemetery"; and, in lines mirroring Whitman's fascination with the hospitalized and the dying, the sympathetic (and possibly autobiographical) figure of an attendant standing

> By the cot in the hospital reaching lemonade to a feverish patient,
> By the coffined corpse where all is still, examining with a candle.

Envisioning himself negating time and "speeding" through the boundless universe, oblivious to "material and immaterial" limits, he is able to picture himself "walking the hills of Judea" alongside Christ—an association repeated several times in the poems. And once again he expresses his absorption of vibrations from his fellow humans and from the divine afflatus in terms of orality, describing himself as "a fluid and swallowing soul."

Following the massive catalogue, section 33 develops a montage of multiline vignettes in which death becomes increasingly palpable. One vignette pictures the persona as a soldier entering "some vast battlefield in which we are soon to be engaged" and beholding "some vast and ruined city" that, like Petra, is a silent monument to death. Another vignette conjures up a vision of the past—a mother is burnt as a witch while her horrified children look on. And in an odd montage of violence, sexual excitement, and the terror of death, the persona "becomes," in rapid succession, an aggressive lover enacting a rape fantasy, a drowned bridegroom (death by water seems to have haunted the poet), and the grieving bride herself:

> I turn the bridegroom out of bed and stay with the bride myself,
> And tighten her all night to my thighs and lips. . . .
> My voice is the wife's voice, the screech by the rail of the stairs,
> They fetch my man's body up dripping and drowned.

So closely does he identify with the grieving woman that when she beholds the body of her drowned mate her agonized "screech" seems to issue from *his* throat. Throughout section 33 the persona identifies with those who endure anguish and death: "All these I feel or am," he proclaims. In another vignette he "becomes" the "hounded slave," whipped insensate and murdered by the slave master's "buckshot and bullets." As these passages demonstrate, Whitman is not only the poet of life and death, but he is the poet of agonies. "Agonies are one of my changes of garments," the persona testifies, as though to indicate that he is the very personification of agony. "I myself become the person," he asserts. His declaration is all the more poignant when one considers that *agony* can be defined as the final painful struggle that precedes death. A ten-line passage converts a *New York Tribune* report of the tragedy that befell the steamship *San Francisco* in 1854, with a loss of 150 lives, into graphic poetry. Although the episode serves as a tribute to the ship's chief officer, who succeeded in saving the ship and the lives of many passengers and whose heroism Whitman recorded in one of his notebooks, the poet transforms the vessel into a Coleridgean death ship, "Death chasing it up and down the storm." He paints a horrifying scene of the gaunt and dying women and children.[45] Witness the "oral" imagery of the vignette's concluding couplet, in which death is once again associated with tasting and swallowing. The persona ingests death and agony as though they were delicacies and he were a living Christ savoring the woes of the world:

> All this I swallow and it tastes good . . . . I like it well and it
>     becomes mine,
> I am the man . . . I suffered . . . I was there.

Another scenario pictures a "mashed fireman" with a crushed "breast-bone" who lies beneath the rubble of a collapsed building. (Whitman's attraction to the daring and masculine firemen is recorded in various autobiographical notations, and firemen are mentioned in several poems.) In this remarkable vignette the persona himself "becomes" the agonized fireman, sharing his pain and his half-conscious thoughts as he lies prone and helpless and appears to be watching his fellow firefighters struggling to extricate him and "tenderly lift me forth." The dying fireman's imagined thoughts are touchingly ambiguous:

> I lie in the night air in my redshirt . . . . the pervading hush is for
>     my sake,
> Painless after all I lie, exhausted but not so unhappy,
> White and beautiful are the faces around me . . . . the heads are
>     bared of their fire-caps,
> The kneeling crowd fades with the light of the torches.

These may be the thoughts of the half-conscious fireman anesthetized by pain or those of the persona who has "absorbed" his conscious and half-conscious thoughts. But viewed from another perspective, the injured fireman who is apparently at peace with himself as he looks into the transfigured faces that encircle him like an aureole suggests that Whitman may be depicting an out-of-body experience of the fireman who may be dying or may already be dead.[46] In the same way Whitman depicts the disembodied specter of a dead person looking at his own corpse in "To Think of Time." As the persona delves deeper into the mysteries of life and death, he "becomes" the clock of eternity; and his words become a dial plate for all to read his vision of resurrection:

> Distant and dead resuscitate,
> They show as the dial or move as the hands of me . . . . I am
>     the clock itself.

He who (in section 7) claims the power to "pass death with the dying and birth with the new-washed babe" now peers into the farthest reaches of eternity. And he concludes that the fireman's life, like all lives, is not extinguishable by his fatal accident, because his essence will somehow survive mortality. As David Kuebrich reminds us, "in limning the violent deaths of firemen, soldiers, swimmers, etc., Whitman may have intended to illustrate the principle that the human soul must prove superior to circumstance."[47]

In the final death-saturated sketch of section 33 the persona assumes the guise of a battle-hardened veteran whose memory is haunted by the horrors of an unnamed battle as he recalls "the ambulanza slowly passing and trailing its red drip" and "[t]he whiz of limbs heads stone wood iron high in the air." The vignette ends with yet another powerful image in which the terror of death is associated with choking and muteness:

> Again gurgles the mouth of my dying general . . . . he furiously waves his hand,
> He gasps through the clot . . . . Mind not me . . . . mind . . . . the entrenchments.

As the general's throat becomes clotted with blood, the choppy rhythms—in this first-edition version of the couplet—mimic the sounds of his gagging. Whitman, whose brother Andrew suffered for several years from probable tuberculosis of the throat, was certainly familiar with these sounds. The scene once more points up the poet's near-obsession with the fantasy of thoracic strangulation (like "the fakes of death" in section 26), which he seems to have conceived as the ultimate death-terror.

These scenes of violent death are succeeded, in sections 34 through 36, by two extended nationalistic episodes of death and heroism, both based on popular accounts, which Whitman transforms into poetic myth. Demonstrating his proclivity for the sort of "patriotic gore" that may have suited the temperament of the 1850s, he lingers over the details of carnage and death agonies. In section 34 (probably the weakest section of "Song of Myself") the persona proposes (in a line added in 1867) to "tell what I knew in Texas in my early youth"—that is, the bloody massacre at Goliad, Texas, in 1836. In that year, at age seventeen, Whitman would have been as old as many of the raw recruits who perished at the Battle of Goliad. His decision to tell about Goliad rather than the better-known story of the Alamo was a shrewd political choice. "In terms of tragedy and strategical catastrophe," says Thomas L. Brasher, "the Goliad massacre outweighs the fall of the Alamo. 'Remember Goliad' should be substituted for 'Remember the Alamo.'" Indeed, "Remember Goliad" became the battle cry of General Sam Houston's Texas army and later became a campaign slogan when Houston, then a senator from Texas, was prominently mentioned as the presidential nominee of the nativist Know Nothing Party.[48] As the editor of the *Brooklyn Daily Eagle* from 1846 to 1848, Whitman favored the vigorous prosecution of the (unsanctioned) war against Mexico, attacked Horace Greeley and others who opposed the war on moral grounds, boasted that the war was justly popular with the American "common people," and advocated the annexation of that part of Mexico that lay north of the Rio Grande (southern Mexico apparently being too full of Mexicans for its successful assimilation into white America). In one editorial Whitman (who would later gain fame as a poet of compassion) declared that he panted for the day when "the vengeance of a retributive God should be meted out" to the Mexican soldiers who had, in a confrontation, killed four American soldiers.[49] But section 34 of "Song of Myself" is ahistorical; it never identifies the locale in which the action occurred or provides any details about the battle. Instead, it focuses on the slaughter of the young American irregulars who are idealized as native-born, white "American young men," like those whom the poet extols in his unpublished political tract "The Eighteenth Presidency!" and in "Song of the Broad-Axe" (both 1856), and, later, in his Civil War poetry and prose—and in the Whitman persona. Of these Texas volunteers (only about a dozen were actually Texans), section 34 declares:

> They were the glory of the race of rangers,
> Matchless with horse, rifle, a song, a supper or courtship,
> Large, turbulent, brave, handsome, generous, proud, and
>     affectionate,
> Bearded, sunburnt, dressed in the costume of hunters,
> Not a single one over thirty years of age

The 1855 version of the poem announces as its subject "the murder in cold blood of four hundred and twelve young men" on a day marked by a "jetblack sunrise"—a reference to the burning of the bodies of the slain Americans after the battle. According to the poem's exaggerated account, apparently derived from the popular press, the "rangers," surrounded by an enemy army "nine times their number" and their ammunition exhausted, negotiated an honorable surrender with the promise of safe conduct, but not until they had killed 900 enemy troops! (The entire Mexican force numbered about 1,200.) The passage relates that they were betrayed by the Mexican officers and ruthlessly slaughtered but that each American soldier fought doggedly until death. Unmentioned in the poem is the presence of American women and children at the base, for whom General Santa Anna provided safe conduct.[50] The American contingent was actually made up of 412 untrained young men, commanded by brevet-Captain James W. Fannon Jr.—the heroic "colonel" of Whitman's poem. Fannon was, in fact, a Georgia adventurer who had run sea blockades to smuggle slaves from Cuba and had traded slaves in Texas. The sequence of misadventures leading up to the massacre, says Clarence Wharton, the historian of the battle, would be altogether comic if it were not so tragic.[51] Whitman lingers over the deaths of the young white Americans at the hands of a dark-skinned enemy, their bodies burned on a "First-day morning"—a Quaker term that invests the American dead with an aura of martyrdom. As he would do a decade later in some of the *Drum-Taps* poems, he singles out a representative dying soldier—this one a seventeen-year-old who has supposedly bloodied three of the foe in the general slaughter—as a prototype of all the martyred soldiers who, by their sacrifice, are said to have gained immortality.[52]

Sections 35 and 36 are a breathtaking reconstruction—again based on secondary sources—of the 1779 battle off Fishborough Head between the British frigate *Serapis* and the smaller American frigate *Bonhomme Richard*. Once again the poet concentrates not on the battle itself but on its terrible aftermath.[53] His grandmother's father, Captain John Williams, had, in fact, served under Admiral John Paul Jones, the hero of the battle in Whitman's (generally accurate) account. Section 35 focuses lovingly on "my little captain," the intrepid Scottish naval genius John Paul Jones—"no tougher or truer." The persona assumes the role of an (unseen) observer who watches the British warship *Serapis* close with the American frigate *Bonhomme Richard* until the two ships touch side to side. The *Bonhomme Richard* receives devastating artillery fire to its decks and its artillery pieces, and many of its crew are killed. Whitman illuminates the scene by the flames of the burning ships and the light of the full moon and the "mournful stars," the celestial luminaries seeming to sympathize with the victims of the horrid slaughter taking place on the sea below them. The contrast between the horrors of battle and the patriotic sacrifice for liberty is dramatized in olfactory terms as well, by juxtaposing the stench of rotting bodies with the sweet fragrances wafted from the seashore. Against this background, the passage focuses on the idealized "little captain," serene, bright-eyed, his voice attesting to his inspirational life force. After hours of savage fighting, his ship taking on water and left with only three serviceable guns, Jones composedly intones the memorable words, *"We have just begun our part of the fighting."* And the remaining crew of the *Bonhomme Richard* board the *Serapis* to accept its surrender.

Section 35 serves, in effect, as a prologue to the sensuous and death-saturated description of carnage that makes section 36 a high-water mark in *Leaves of Grass* and, indeed, in all of English-language poetry.[54] Although Whitman had never witnessed any military or naval actions, section 36 conveys a sense of first-hand observation. Its structure and drama, its intense musicality, and its chiaroscuro contrasts between the beautiful and the grim indicate the influence of operatic and symphonic music and of American landscape and seascape painting on Whitman's poetry.[55] Against the backdrop of midnight stillness, lit by the flames of the burning ship that is rocked by the soothing waves, Whitman displays the casualties of battle and of the primitive medical practice before the advent of anesthesia and asepsis, when amputation was virtually the only known method to save the lives of men with damaged extremities. We see and hear the casualties of war—"the corpse of the child that served in the cabin, / The dead face of an old salt with long white hair and carefully curled whiskers"; "formless stacks of bodies by themselves . . . dabs of flesh upon the mast and spars"; "the hiss of the surgeon's knife and the gnawing teeth of his saw, / The wheeze, the cluck, and the swash of falling blood . . . the short wild screams, the long tapering groans." Whitman's words confer upon these anonymous sailors an aura of sainthood. Recalling their heroism and the horrors he has witnessed, the persona cries out, "these so . . . these irretrievable." These four words refocus our attention from the battle action to its witness-persona and his inventor—the aspiring national poet. The past, we know, is never fully (or accurately) "retrievable," even by the most acute witness or by the best mind. But by his act of poetic reconstruction Whitman has, in a sense, retrieved and reshaped a vital moment in American mytho-history. The incident is also "irretrievable" because the witness-persona can never wholly recapture the intense excitement aroused in him in the moments that he witnessed the awesome carnage. No artistic reconstruction can evoke the ultimate terror of such an experience; no words can adequately describe it. The ultimate experience of dying remains forever "irretrievable" to the living.

Like Hawthorne, Melville, and Poe, Whitman knew the terrible toll that is exacted from the artist who ventures too close to the terrors of death and the blackness of the soul. Poe's voyager to "the ultimate dim Thule" of death returns disoriented and maddened. Melville's Ishmael risks his sanity by looking too long into the fire of his own dark thoughts. Hawthorne's Ethan Brand destroys himself when he can no longer endure his frightening introspections. Similarly, the Whitman persona becomes overwhelmed by despair and emotionally drained through his compulsive empathy with the suffering and the dying. "O Christ!" he cries out, "my fit is mastering me!" In this state of disoriented self-torment that his medical contemporaries might have identified as brain fever, he "absorbs" and suffers the miseries of the most wretched beings—young and old prisoners, the mute and helpless beggar with outstretched hat (a tellingly painful sight to the articulate persona who wears *his* hat as he pleases, indoors or out), the handcuffed mutineer, and the cholera victim. Whitman himself was apparently haunted by his memories of the cholera epidemics that devastated New York in the 1840s and as late as 1854.[56] A more abject human being can scarcely be imagined than the dying cholera victim with whom the persona identifies—typically an indigent, helpless, lethally contagious immigrant, who, in the last stages of the disease, is ashen-skinned, wrinkled, bleary-eyed, shrunken, and repulsively foul-smelling:

> Not a cholera patient lies at the last gasp, but I also lie at
>     the last gasp,
> My face is ash-colored, my sinews gnarl . . . . Away from me
>     people retreat.

But his profound despair (like his other intense excitations) eventually exhausts him and drains him of all emotion and eventually, as a consequence, allows him to regain a state of calm and equanimity—the psychic balance that was deemed a prerequisite for achieving the state of clairvoyance. He is thus able, as he says, to "rise extatic through all," to become what Ronald Wallace calls a self-resurrected Christ figure.[57] He acknowledges that his zealous empathy for the miserable and the dying has temporarily distorted his outlook and made him forget the indestructibility of his spirit and his centrality in the cosmic order. Having survived "the fakes of death" (section 26) and his agonizing identification with the legions of the dying (sections 33–37), he once again becomes secure in the thought that the universal "law" of goodness and amelioration will always prevail. Identifying with Christ once again, he declares, "*our* swift ordinances are on their way over the whole earth [emphasis added]." Recalling Christ's resurrection from "the grave of rock" and experiencing a vision in which he sees "the corpses rise . . . the gashes heal . . . the fastenings roll away," he regains his equanimity and his perspective. Like a Christ figure who has momentarily forgotten his bond with humanity, his divinity, and his place in the cosmic plan, he is astonished that he could ever have looked "with a *separate* look on my own crucifixion and bloody crowning [emphasis added]" or that he could have disregarded the divine "law" that governs the universe. Recovered now, he feels re-empowered to absorb universal truths and to utter them.

A collage of images describes the persona who now imagines himself to be a superman at the head of "an average ongoing procession" of the democratic masses moving forward on the road of evolutionary amelioration and toward an awareness of their own worth and their eligibility for immortality. (Since he was neither a philosopher nor a divine, Whitman felt no need for doctrinal consistency.) Having "resum[ed] the overstaid fraction" of positive outlook that he had temporarily abandoned while he was grieving for the suffering and the dead and once again "replenished with supreme power," the persona boldly resumes his divine place in the cosmos:

> I remember . . . . I resume the overstaid fraction,
> The grave of rock multiplies what has been confided to it . . . . or
>     to any graves,
> The corpses rise . . . . the gashes heal . . . . the fastenings roll away.
>
> I troop forth replenished with supreme power, one of the endless
>     procession [across North American states and cities] . . . .
> Inland and by the seacoast and boundary lines . . . . and we pass
>     boundary lines.
> Our swift ordinances are on the way over the whole earth,
> The blossoms we wear in our hats are the growth of two
>     thousand years.

Whitman-Christ wearing a two-thousand-year-old blossom in his hat as he passes the "boundary lines" of life and death is an effective symbol of resurrection. In the context of the above passage, those "blossoms" are the growths, or outgrowths, of the tomb of Christ—first among the persona's principal avatars. Whitman had used the image of "tomb-blossoms" in a prose sketch a decade earlier, and he would use it affectingly a few years later in "Scented Herbage of My Breast," where the grave-herbage once again becomes the symbol of resurrection. With deliberate ambiguity, the above poetic lines speak of "*our* swift ordinances," as though Christ and the Whitman persona (the two are pictured as spermatic buddies in the 1860 lyric "To Him Who Was Crucified") had in unison annunciated the "law" of self-fulfillment, universal progress, and transcendence. By altering the age of those hat blossoms in 1867 from the original "two thousand years" to "thousands of years" Whitman muted the specifically Christian context of the passage.

## 4

The more than three hundred lines that follow in sections 39 through 48 compose the ideological core of "Song of Myself." They portray a mythic hero modeled on Walt Whitman but raised to the level of a "teacher-redeemer,"[58] who attracts lovers and disciples. His words, "simple as grass," appeal to the noblest intuitions of the democratic masses. His spiritual essence is projected by his presence and even by his glances. And, like the hands of a deity or a mesmeric therapist, the touch of his fingertips appears to cure the sick. The "magnetic healer" J. R. Newton, whom Mark Twain credited with having cured his future wife of her chronic neurasthenia, made just such claims for his healing powers, and Whitman himself suggested that his presence and his touch had benefited the sick and dying in the Civil War hospitals.[59] The persona now attracts people by his "charm" (a term used by mesmerists to designate personal magnetism and hypnotic powers) and—like an Egyptian deity—by the fragrance that exudes from his body. He is characterized by his "adhesiveness" and his "fluid and attaching character"—sticky terminology that implies bonding with his fellows. In this connection it may be observed that the author of a religious medical text that Whitman apparently read maintains that human sweat is a medium that can transmit one's spiritual essence to others.[60] The extraordinary persona even demonstrates his power to revivify the dying, contravening death by blowing the "grit" of his life force into the most wretched of humans—the impotent, the "drudge of the cottonfields or emptier of privies," and into those who have been given up for dead by their physicians. Utilizing a house-of-life trope, he expresses his intention to rekindle the desire to live and to revive the faith in one's purposeful destiny even in the most hopeless of these beings:

> I dilate you with tremendous breath . . . . I buoy you up;
> Every room in the house do I fill with an armed force . . . . lovers
>     of me, bafflers of graves,
> Sleep! I and they keep guard all night;
> Nor doubt nor decease shall dare lay finger upon you,
> I have embraced you, and henceforth possess you to myself,
> And when you rise in the morning you will find that what I tell
>     you is so.

Although the passage contains few vestiges of the homosexual imagery that characterized its draft version, the promise of resurrection through the persona's inspirational breath therapy in the above lines is all the more meaningful when it is compared to the imagery in Ezekiel 37, wherein the prophet is set down by God in the Valley of the Dry Bones and commanded to prophesy to the dead: "Behold I will cause breath to enter into you, and you shall live"; "I shall put my Spirit in you, and ye shall live." As a latter-day Ezekiel, a *vates* or poet-healer, whose gospel of faith rejects the merely "supernatural" as of "no account," the persona undertakes to wrestle with death itself. Whitman was apparently untroubled that biblical accounts picture resurrection as a cataclysmic event that does not jibe with his own version of personal imperishableness and steady cosmic progression.

Whitman commented that although the various religions and churches had become outdated and "do not satisfy the appetite of the soul," they must nevertheless be treated with "decent forbearance. Mean as they are when we have ascended beyond them, and look back, they were doubtless the roads for their times,—Let us not too quickly despise them; for they have sufficed to bring us where we are."[61] "All forms of religion," he observed, "are but mediums, temporary, yet necessary, fitted to the lower mass-range of perception of the race—part of the infant school—and that the developed soul passes through one or all of them, to the clear homogeneous atmosphere above them."[62] The persona illustrates this idea in section 41 by gambling his own divinity against that of all the gods who were ever worshiped and (as the precursor of a new religion) outbidding them all. And once more combining sexuality with spirituality, he shifts his image to picture himself as a benevolent and priapic god of his own devising—a god whose genitalia ("my life-lumps") are discharging "the stuff of more arrogant republics":

> By my life-lumps! becoming already a creator!
> Putting myself here and now to the ambushed womb of
>   the shadows.

Throughout "Song of Myself," it should be observed, the partners in the persona's heroic copulations are neither identifiable women nor the idealized women of traditional poetry; rather, they are vast abstractions such as womankind, the earth, the sea, the heavens, and "the ambushed womb of the shadows," each of whom he suffuses with his "libidinous" "prongs of bright juice." Does that shadowy "ambushed womb" belong to the abstract biological mother of all future generations whom the awesome persona proposes to fertilize (or at least to inspire) with his own seminal words? Whitman's language is troublesome. By describing the womb as *ambushed* he may have intended some sort of analogy with the word *embouchure*, one of whose meanings is the outflow of a river into a delta, and hence a fitting symbol of the birth canal or, more abstractly, a passageway from life to death or from death to life.[63]

Thereafter, as a self-anointed prophet and healer, the persona preaches a bracing sermon to the ordinary "folks"—his doubting and despairing fellow citizens, including the "plentiful little manikins" who are the cogs in the machinery of urban capitalism, and to all those "never to the feast going." He reassures them of his instinctual certainty that they are ultimately as worthy and immortal as he is. His is the greatest of faiths, he tells them—one that encompasses (and, by implication, surpasses) all "worship ancient and modern." They need no "saints and sages" to confirm the truth of his gospel, he tells them; they need only to lead courageous lives, to behold the wondrous world they inhabit, and to look deeply within themselves. To the despairing "disheartened atheistical" skeptics he confesses that his knowledge comes from experience, for he has suffered through just such "unspoken interrogatories" as they have: "I know every one of you, I know the sea of torment, doubt, despair and unbelief," he tells them. In a more thoughtful moment he concedes that he knows only what his observations and his instincts have suggested to him about what may follow death, which he terms the "yet untried and afterward." Nevertheless, he reaffirms his faith that death and the inexorable operation of time will prove "sufficient" to provide a redemptive democratic future for all mankind. His very doubts are cloaked in the language of certainty:

> The past is the push of you and me and all precisely the same,
> And the night is for you and me and all,
> And what is yet untried and afterward is for you and me and all.
>
> I do not know what is untried and afterward,
> But I know it is sure and alive and sufficient.
>
> Each who passes is considered, and each who stops is considered,
>     and not a single one can it fail.[64]

Thus he tries to reassure the masses that the ameliorating operation of the vaguely defined cosmic "law" (the infallible "it" of the above passage) cannot fail the living, no matter how wretched or trivial their lives, nor can it fail the dead, "nor any thing in the earth, or down in the oldest graves in the earth." Nor can it fail those yet unborn, or those living in "the myriads of spheres," he proclaims. (Whether those "spheres" are inhabited by "myriads of myriads" of sentient dead, as the spiritualists might maintain, remains subject to the persona's—or the reader's—interpretation. In an era shaken by religious skepticism but replete with would-be messiahs, Whitman favored his inner voice above all the religious arguments or the "scientific" proofs of "linguists and contenders." In this version of eternity, the dead seem to disappear into some vague fourth-dimensional space-time. By implying in the most generalized terms that the afterlife will be "sufficient" in its "richness and variety," he leaves open the question of whether the expression "what comes afterward" refers to a general improvement in the human condition as the generations succeed one another or to the continued existence, in some other form, of each individual.

With a playful nod to evolutionists and Eastern mystics alike, the persona implies that his own embryo has been "ferried," and apparently rebirthed, through a succession of progressively higher forms from "the huge first Nothing" to the pinnacle of selfhood where he stands now "with my soul," ready to take the next step toward what David Kuebrich calls "divine imminence."[65] In a remarkable dialectic, the "something" that is the persona's essential self appears to have emerged from that "first Nothing" and to have become *embodied* through progressive cycles (the thesis and antithesis) of life and death, of embodiment and disembodiment. In each successive cycle his soul seems to have attained a richer identity and become steadily more godlike. This version of the gospel of perpetual advancement implies, or at least hints, that the flesh has always coexisted with the spirit and the spirit with the flesh, and as the physical body evolves, so does the soul. The passage does not consider whether body and soul have evolved at a comparable rate or whether the soul progresses at an accelerated rate that may eventually negate the role of the body. But the passage does dismiss the Victorian critics who pointed to nature's painful aberrations and cruelties during the course of evolution by saying, "I keep no account with lamentation"; "what have I to do with lamentation?"

Unable to sustain gloomy thoughts for very long, the persona now appears delighted with his present life and receptive to death—cheerfully looking forward to the advent of his "old age superbly rising! Ineffable grace of dying days!"—a sentiment repeated in many of the lyrics composed during the poet's last two decades. As a self-declared decoder of the hieroglyphics that are embedded everywhere in nature, he asserts that even "the dark hush" of death has cryptic meanings that he may be able to read during his present life or during some later phase of his existence. Thus, he interprets the stars that he sees at night through his "scuttle" as auguries of an ever-expanding universe in which "there never can be stoppage." He appears willing to die, certain that his soul will continue to evolve until he becomes eligible to meet—on equal terms and in a "fitly appointed" rendezvous, in a "few quadrillions of eras, a few octillions of cubic leagues"—"the great Camerado, the lover true for whom I pine."

His spirit appears to be impelled on its perpetual journey to divinity by an urge that is reminiscent of Saint Augustine's dictum that God had so made humanity that "the inherent gravitation of our being is toward Him."[66] But because he wants to be seen as a feisty American democrat, the persona boasts that he (or his perfected self) will agree to meet God only as an equal. A fragmentary notebook entry reads: "If I walk with Jah [*sic*] in Heaven and he assume to be intrinsically greater than I it offends me, and I shall certainly withdraw from Heaven—for the soul prefers freedom in the prairie or the untrodden woods—and there can be no freedom where . . ." (here the entry breaks off). Even if he were to become God and master of the known universe, he boasts, he would not be satisfied with that status but would aspire higher still.[67] Like Moses glimpsing the Promised Land, the unquenchable persona ascends a hill to catch a Pisgah-sight of the eternal life to which he aspires.

> And I said to my spirit, When we become the enfolders of those
> orbs and the pleasure and knowledge of every thing in them,
> shall we be filled and satisfied then?

To which his spirit replies in a quaint figure of speech, "No, we level that lift and pass and continue beyond." This oddly mechanical image seems to depict the persona's soul being hoisted through the infinite spheres by means of a block and tackle (a reminder that Whitman was involved in house building in the 1850s) or, alternatively, that his spirit will be hoisted through the spheres by a "lift"! (A prototype steam-driven elevator was exhibited at the Crystal Palace during the 1853 World's Fair in New York City.) On the Romantic assumption that unsophisticated minds are naturally attracted to the truth, the priestly persona appears confident that children and "roughs," mothers, and laborers are best attuned to the gospel embodied in *Leaves of Grass*. To illustrate this principle, he offers his "dear son"—presumably a representative disciple, one of the common people—his scriptural Bread of Life, saying, "Here are biscuits to eat and here is milk to drink." And he challenges this young precursor of future generations to be a "bold swimmer" and thus to overmatch him. Unfortunately, the natatorial metaphor loses some of its force when we recall that Whitman himself was a weak swimmer whose specialty, he admitted, was floating.

## 5

In sections 47 through 52 the persona takes his ceremonial leave of the reader and prepares for his death. In these closing sections of the poem, he resembles a Christlike master, leaving messages of faith and love before departing the mortal scene and eventually dissolving into eternity. Nevertheless, his departure is not intended to sever his connection with the living as he and his book venture into eternity, for he gives notice to coming generations that he will forever be there in spirit (and in print) to articulate their highest aspirations and destinies: "I am the tongue of you," he proclaims, asserting that his words will continue to "itch at your ears till you understand them." He feels inspired by the thought that his book, and through his book his memory, will forever endure among the living, for as the poet Joseph Brodsky reminds us, "it is precisely the appetite for this posthumous dimension which sets one's pen in motion."[68]

Once again the persona asserts his status as an interpreter of a world that is filled with divine emblems. Wherever he looks, he says, he finds "letters from God dropt in the street," each one a clue to the divine order and each one accessible to those with liberated minds. Apparently satisfied that he can discern the hand of God in the profusion of symbols that fill his world, he appears willing to abstain from further speculation:

And I call to mankind, Be not curious about God,
For I who am curious about each am not curious about God,
No array of terms can say how much I am at peace about God
  and about death.

I hear and behold God in every object, yet I understand God not
  in the least,
Nor do I understand who can be more wonderful than myself.

Like some of his pious contemporaries, Whitman did not entertain the idea of a personal god. He did not (like George Herbert) yearn for a god to batter his soul into submission or (like James Thomson) desire a god who would "hound" him until he believed. To know God, he felt, we must first know ourselves. He accepted the Deist tenet that nature is "the font of all that is good in the universe and that mankind should never be downgraded in the interest of the supernatural."[69] As the reformer Henry

Clarke Wright wrote in 1863, "HUMAN NATURE! . . . stands out in the very front of the great picture of creation, as the most beautiful and command-ing object. As we can know nothing of God except through his manifes-tations, we naturally regard the Human as the most perfect manifestation of the Divine."[70] And the concept that each man and woman must seek the truth by following his or her own pathway—a fundamental assump-tion in *Leaves of Grass*—was forcefully stated in the years immediately preceding its publication by the radical sexual reformer Stephen Pearl Andrews, a fellow Brooklynite, who asserted that "individuality is the fundamental and indispensable principle of the universe." Not only does it furnish "the 'best image of the Infinite' that the finite mind is capable of perceiving," Andrews maintained, "but it is the foundation of all ra-tional law and justice."[71]

The four concluding sections of the "Song of Myself" are, in effect, a ritual enactment of the persona's death, his physical dissolution, and his implied resurrection. Behaving as though he were a cosmic force, he greets death as an equal, in a fraternal tone and with a bittersweet em-brace. By personifying death, he softens his anticipation of their impend-ing confrontation. In the same way, Emily Dickinson softens the shock of her imagined death by personifying death as a gentleman who has come to squire her on a carriage ride to the grave. "As to you death, and you bitter hug of mortality," warns the Whitman persona, "it is idle to try to alarm me." Always fascinated by the drama of his own birthing—his physical birth, his spiritual birth, and his poetic birth—Whitman depicts the process of dying (in section 49) as though it were yet another birth-ing. The persona calls death an "accoucheur," or male midwife, and, in a voyeuristic fashion, pictures himself propped up against the "sills of the exquisite flexible doors," which are the metaphoric "outlet" of life and death, while he watches death bring forth the dying as though he were observing the parturition of liberated souls and marking "the outlet" and "the relief and escape." Harold Bloom observes that Whitman's double-barreled imagery renders death "indistinguishable from Orphic Eros, a release that is fulfillment," since "neither we nor Whitman know precisely whether he is talking about a womb or a tomb."[72] But the ambiguity is intentional. For Whitman there can be no birth without death and no death without birth, and both are mediated by Eros. Love is an ever-present solvent in his treatment of death as it is in his treatment of life.

The imagery of birthing in these lines implies that the soul is reborn—or rebirthed—through death. In what appears to be a deliberate pun, the persona consigns his own "discharged" body (the corpse deprived of its life-giving electrical "charge"?) to the "corpse-cleaners," confident that his "real" spirit-body is being launched to "other spheres." Repeating the allegation that he has undergone many rebirths as his spirit was "ferried" through its advancing stages, he acknowledges that each mortal life, including his own, is a product of the "leavings of many deaths."

Still, if the persona is to triumph over death, he must make a final attempt to storm death's fortress; to conquer death and attempt to divest death of its mystery. An early British critic thus interprets what he calls Whitman's "sovereign dogma":

> Uncompromising realist that he is, he sees clearly enough that
> death is one of Nature's central facts,—a fact too which seems
> to give the lie to his optimism, to bar its further progress, to
> turn its triumphant advance into a disastrous retreat. If the joy
> of his heart is to lead him to final victory, he must recognize that
> Death is the key to Nature's fortress, that as such it can neither
> be masked nor outflanked, and that if he is not to retire from it in
> confusion he must storm its terrible stronghold. And storm it he
> does with all the passionate energy of his vehement nature. He is
> not content to acquiesce in death, to speculate about it, to hope
> the best from it. He sees the futility of half-measures. He must
> "rush" the heights of death with the force and elan of unconquer-
> able joy. He must find a deeper joy in death than in anything else
> in Nature.[73]

In his final encounter with death, however, the persona does not precisely "'rush' the heights of death"; rather, he makes a shamanlike descent into the depths of death's realm, into "the valley which was full of dry bones" on which the Lord promised Ezekiel He would bestow the breath that would revivify their flesh, hope, and national identity. The persona undertakes a final sortie into death's dark valley to wrest death's secret. But death still withholds its secret from its would-be celebrant. Death remains impenetrable, yielding no intelligible sign or sound. The sounds in death's realm are muffled, the persona finds; the sights obscured by darkening particulates. The fitful "sparkles" of the moon reveal a rotted landscape. In a bizarre example of synesthesia, the twilight seems to be "soughing," or mumbling, its unintelligible secrets. In vain the persona implores the "sparkles" to illuminate the mystery of decay and rebirth. But in this "muck" of dead bodies, the bones utter only the meaningless "gibberish of the dry limbs." Even "the grass of graves," whose meaning the persona had undertaken to translate in section 6, reveals nothing. Frustrated that his excursion into death's realm has revealed no secrets, the persona cries out:

I hear you whispering there, O stars of heaven,
O suns . . . . O grass of graves . . . . O perpetual transfers and
    promotions . . . if you do not say anything how can I say
    anything?

Of the turbid pool that lies in the autumn forest,
Of the moon that descends the steeps of the soughing twilight,
Toss, sparkles of day and dusk . . . . toss on the black stems that
    decay in the muck,
Toss to the moaning gibberish of the dry limbs.

Despite this apparent failure to unlock death's secret, the persona clings to the faith that even death's domain, if it could be properly explored, would eventually yield the secret of perpetual life.

Having failed to secure the secret of mortality during his foray into the netherworld, the persona then "ascend[s] from the moon," which has also been associated with the cold realm of death, but whose "ghastly glitter" nevertheless reflects the sun—the source of physical life.[74] In a final epiphany, the persona pictures himself making an astonishing leap of faith—high enough to gain a sunlit view of all creation. This Spinozan overview of eternity seemingly affords him the perspective he needs to confirm that death is part of nature's purposeful plan and to see that "the ghastly glimmer [of death] is noonday sunbeams reflected." From his exalted vantage point death and evil appear to be only transient elements of an overarching, beneficent plan. In a rather tortured figure of speech, he declares, "I debouch to the steady and central from the offspring great or small." Literally, to *debouch* is to flow as from a narrow channel to a broader one, like a river emptying into a delta or bay. And the term *offspring* most plausibly alludes to the plentiful "springboards" from which the soul can be launched on its "steady and central" voyage through eternity. *Leaves of Grass*, too, is such a springboard from which emanations from the poet's soul will forever be launched into the hearts of men and women to convey the "steady and central" truth of his gospel.

Finally, as though he were emerging from the trance that has transported him to the deepest realm of death and thence into the empyrean heavens for a glimpse of the universe, the persona awakens, "wrenched and sweaty," from his dream state. Still thwarted because he cannot articulate what he *feels* to be the final truth about death and its role in the cycle of existence, he utters a series of staccato clauses whose breathless tension testifies to his frustration at the inadequacy of language:

> There is that in me . . . I do not know what it is . . . but I know
>   it is in me . . . .
>
> I do not know it . . . . it is without name . . . . it is a word unsaid,
> It is not in any dictionary or symbol.
>
> Something it swings on more than the earth I swing on,
> To it the creation is the friend whose embracing awakens me.
>
> Perhaps I might tell more . . . . Outlines! I plead for my brothers
>   and sisters.
>
> Do you not see O my brothers and sisters?
> It is not chaos or death . . . . it is form and union and place . . . it
>   is eternal life . . . it is happiness.

And as though he were making a last desperate effort to convince his readers by sheer oratorical fiat that eternity is their best bet, that last line in the 1860 edition virtually shouts at the reader: "it is HAPPINESS."

In an 1855 anonymous review, in which he refers to himself in the third person, Whitman reassures readers that happiness, like "perfection" is an attainable goal for those who avoid "the preaching and teaching of others, and mind only these words of mine."[75] Immanuel Kant defined happiness as "the state of a rational being existing in the world who experiences through the whole of his life whatever he desires or wills." Kant judged the immortality of the soul to be "a postulate of pure practical reason." Like Whitman, he linked happiness, immortality, and moral law (key terms in Whitman's writings), maintaining that the "infinite process" of immortality "is possible only if we presuppose that the existence of a rational being is prolonged to infinity, and that he retains his personality for all time. That is what we mean by the immortality of the soul. The highest good is therefore practically possible, only if we presuppose the immortality of the soul. Thus immortality is inseparably bound up with the moral law."[76] And of course, Whitman does presuppose the immortality of the soul.

But as he concludes his hopeful gospel, the persona remains painfully aware that he can offer his "brothers and sisters" only "outlines," or what he elsewhere calls "faint clews and indirections." His animated tone reveals that he is still frustrated by an incomplete understanding of death and by his inability to explain its meaning. But having tested, in what he famously called his "language experiment," the power of human speech to convey his intimations concerning life and death, he sticks to what he *feels* must be so—his faith in the cycles of eternal renewal and advancement, confirmed both by his worldly experience and by his moments of mystical illumination. After all, why should one so convinced of his divine selfhood, one whose faith "swings on more than the earth I swing on," be stymied by the inadequacy of language to convey intangible ideas? Why should he be vexed by the limitations of mortal argument? "Song of Myself" was designed to inspire its readers with an awareness that immortality and a purposeful universe are as real as the events in their daily lives. And Whitman's satisfaction with having fulfilled his mission as well as any mortal poet can do is expressed in his seemingly flippant, but deadly serious, disclaimer: "Do I contradict myself? / Very well then . . . I contradict myself; / I am large . . . I contain multitudes." He refuses to be judged by conventional logic or by the limitations inherent in language. Looking back on his masterpiece after a score of years, Whitman declared that "in certain parts, in these flights . . . I have not been afraid of the charge of obscurity . . . because human thought must leave dim escapes and outlets." Through all his trials, as Ivan Marki observes, Whitman kept his faith and never compromised his identity.[77]

In sections 51 and 52, which conclude the poem, the persona takes his final leave of the reader and embarks on the mystic road that will lead him to "the next fold of the future." As he does in the rousing ending of "Song of the Open Road" (1856), he sounds a call for companions to join him along the uncharted path that he is about to follow, hailing the "listener up there" (perhaps one born generations later) to accompany him or to surpass him. Before visibly departing he waits "on the door-slab" of the house of life to be joined by anyone who "will soonest be through with his supper"—that is, the Bread of Life, the gospel of freedom and infinitude. Unlike Emerson, who sought companions whose minds were attuned to his own rarefied thoughts,[78] the democratic Whitman persona seems content to "concentrate toward them that are nigh . . . to walk with me." He invites the "listener" to "look on my face while I snuff the sidle of evening"; metaphorically, at least, he is inhaling the welcome aroma of death and observing the "last scud of day," that is, the twilight of his impending departure that "coaxes" him toward "the vapor and the dusk" of physical disintegration and toward the triumph of the spirit. As the departing persona slowly fades from view, he invites the reader to examine his cloud-borne face as the "plenum of proof" of his triumphant selfhood and as the symbol of eternal hope. (Alternatively, the reader could turn back to Whitman's frontispiece portrait in the 1855 edition and—applying the techniques of physiognomy and phrenology—make his or her own diagnosis of its features.) The ostensibly dying Whitman persona seems willing to exchange his mortal state for another condition, fully determined to remain an active participant in the cosmic mystery, able to influence the lives of the generations that will survive his passing. He leaves, not with a whimper but a decided bang:

> I too am not a bit tamed . . . . I too am untranslatable,
> I sound my barbaric yawp over the roofs of the world.

The "barbaric yawp" that he sounds defiantly, like the "*ya-honk*" of the wild gander in section 14, is a primordial utterance from the heart of nature, whence his inspiration is derived. Summoned by a hawk—a shamanistic messenger—to slough off his mortality, the persona loiters affectionately in the mortal sphere, ready to go but reluctant to loosen his hold on his earthly life or to relinquish the "gab" that is his ultimate connection with humanity. But ultimately he surrenders to physical dissolution and transmutation into the elemental air and soil and grass so that his diffusing spirit can pervade the whole world. "I depart as air [afflatus?]," cries the persona of the thirty-six-year-old poet, as though he were enjoying the imagined act of divesting himself of his mortal body. For it is only his corruptible body that is mortal, and therefore expendable; it is his body that must be abandoned to facilitate the setting forth of his spirit. "Unless the individual survives the mutation of matter," said Whitman's erudite friend Daniel G. Brinton, "the universe is pointless."[79] This is Whitman's view, too. "I shake my white locks at the runaway sun," his persona exclaims joyously. "I effuse my flesh in eddies and drift in lacy jags." One can almost envision the famous Whitman beard being transformed into a lacy cloud that moves across the heavens to remind us of his abiding presence. Like the fertility god Osiris, whom the ancient Egyptians considered the king of the dead,[80] he bestows his spirit-self on the earth, the grass, the human heart, and the universe. The poet bestows himself throughout "Song of Myself," Lewis Hyde observes, on anyone who will have him, as bridegroom, lover, friend, or mentor. It is not surprising that even in death he makes a gift of himself to everyone as a bestower of health, well-being, and inspiration.[81]

> I bequeath myself to the dirt to grow from the grass I love,
> If you want me again look for me under your bootsoles.
>
> You will hardly know who I am or what I mean,
> But I shall be good health to you nevertheless,
> And filter and fibre your blood
>
> Failing to fetch me at first keep encouraged,
> Missing me one place search another,
> I stop some where waiting for you.

The persona, who throughout "Song of Myself" is charged with translating "the converging objects of the universe," appears to be undergoing a major transformation: the would-be *translator* of life's mysteries takes his place in the cosmos to become one of the *translated.* In the spiritualist sense of that word, he has entered the realm of immortality, where he remains forever "untranslatable." Rather than disappear, however, he becomes diffused into a sort of spirit-matter that permeates air, soil, water, cloud, and all living things. This diffusion is a brilliant trope for the perpetual changes he (or his soul) will undergo. But in whatever state he may be, he (or his essence) will continue to filter and fiber *your* blood and remain alive in you as a vital—perhaps sentient—force. As Jacques Derrida explains, it is only "'in us' that the dead may speak, that it is only by speaking *of* and *as* the dead that one can keep them alive."[82] Or as Whitman describes the phenomenon in "So Long!" the persona of his dead self will become "immersed" in you, and thus be perpetuated in you.

## 2

# "Great Is Death"

## *Leaves of Grass* Poems, 1855

I

The closing lines of "Song of Myself," which describe the imagined diffusion of the dying persona into air and earth and convey his promise to "stop somewhere waiting for you" are printed on a left-hand (verso) page in the 1855 folio edition of *Leaves of Grass*. Facing them are the opening lines of "A Song for Occupations" in which the persona appears to keep his promise as his spirit seemingly springs forth through the "cold types" and the "wet paper" of the poem to address his fellow citizens. As though appearing from beyond the grave, he encourages the working people (his presumptive audience) to acknowledge their latent dignity, and he embraces them as his democratic equals with an enthusiasm that borders on sexual excitement:

> Come closer to me,
> Push close my lovers and take the best I possess,
> Yield closer and closer and give me the best you possess.
>
> This is unfinished business with me . . . . how is it with you?
> I was chilled with the cold types and the cylinder and wet paper
> between us.
>
> I pass so poorly with paper and types . . . . I must pass with the
> contact of bodies and souls.

That last line illustrates Emerson's dictum that "not by literature or theology, but only by rare integrity, by a man permeated and perfumed with the airs of heaven—and with the manliest and womanliest enduring love—can the vision [of immortality] be clear to a use the most sublime." And these qualities certainly characterize the Whitman persona.[1] "A Song for Occupations" is permeated, particularly in its 1855 version, by a subtext of death. Its stunning catalogues of occupations and crafts, their tools and skills, appeal to the American "workmen and workwomen" to recognize their own potential greatness. During this era in which the labors of skilled craftsmen provided a measure of personal satisfaction, the poet seeks to assure them that further satisfactions await them when their mortal lives have ended. Resuming the theme of happiness with which he concludes "Song of Myself," the persona offers them neither doctrine nor moralizing but rather the assurance that "life upon the appleshaped earth and we upon it. . . . surely the drift of them is something grand."

"A Song for Occupations" is followed by "To Think of Time," Whitman's first full-dress poem on the theme of death—a poem that is populated by the dead and their corpses. (Untitled, like all of the poems in the 1855 edition, it was called "Burial Poem" in 1856, and given its present title in 1871.) At the heart of the poem are the persona's fascination with the dead, his latent terror of death, and his desire to discover how a better understanding of death and decay might afford him a measure of emotional stasis. With its repeated death motifs and phrases and its shifts in rhythm and voice, the poem reads as if Whitman's musical contemporaries Berlioz and Liszt had inspired a poetic rhapsody on death. Its opening lines (which lack both subject and verb) announce that the poem is, in fact, a meditation. Fourteen of its first sixty-two lines begin with the words "To think":

> To think of time . . . to think through the retrospection,
> To think of today . . and the ages continued henceforward.

As he does in "Song of Myself," Whitman defines time both as a means to measure our daily activities and as an indicator of the infinitude of our existence. As the persona absorbs "all that retrospection" of the past, he downplays life's sorrows and defeats and considers the satisfactions of day-to-day existence. Time, he concludes, works in our favor, regardless of our circumstances. And as he does in "A Song for Occupations," he draws analogies between the satisfactions of the past and those of the present and extrapolates the likelihood of continued satisfactions in any life to come. Intent on demonstrating that death is not to be feared, he poses three critical questions by which to measure one's fear of the grave, addressed as much to himself as to the reader:

> Have you guessed you yourself would not continue? Have you
> dreaded those earth-beetles?
> Have you feared the future would be nothing to you?

Given the Whitman persona's faith in personal survival, these questions may appear to be merely rhetorical. But latent in their wording is his struggle against a lingering fear that mortal existence could possibly be followed by an eternal "nothing." The fearful possibility that dying leads to nothingness rings like a tocsin throughout the poem. The emotional responses that the persona develops to these questions are designed to persuade us—and himself—that death is not "nothing" and to validate his belief in immortality. The poem's principal argument for immortality is its grand analogy between the earth's inexhaustible capacity to renew its sumptuous vegetation and a corresponding potential for universal spiritual renewal.

The poem introduces a vignette picturing death among the lowly; its opening lines could have been written by young William Cullen Bryant, the American poet Whitman most admired:

> Not a day passes . . not a minute or second without an
> accouchement;
> Not a day passes . . not a minute or second without a corpse.

The word *accouchement* (like *accoucheur* in section 49 of "Song of Myself") repeats the familiar concept that birth and death are equally parturitions into another state of being. "To Think of Time" dramatizes this idea in a vignette that pictures the humble deathbed scene of a unnamed person of unspecified sex. The scene has an immediacy that suggests the poet's first-hand observation of deathbeds. In the first half of the nineteenth century, particularly in rural areas such as the Long Island where Whitman grew up, participating in the death watch and preparing the dead for burial were still revered as family and community duties. "When a death occurred," it has been noted, "the community acted. The family of the deceased washed him, laid him out and prepared him for burial. There were women in the community who functioned as 'layers out of the dead,' but they only helped the deceased's family in their task, they did not do it for them." In our era, when dying has become increasingly depersonalized and commercialized, we may have forgotten that the presence of family and friends as a loved one lay dying was once considered a sacred obligation and that attending a deathbed was deemed to be an "instructive" privilege of high "moral value."[2] Nowadays, says Philippe Ariès, "death is often sanitized out of society into institutions." Whitman's practice of sitting by the deathbeds of the dying soldiers during the Civil War may hark back to the importance formerly placed on these observances. The vignette records the physician's somber expression, the family's vigil, the odor of camphor in the room, the final touches and kisses bestowed on the dying person by the loved ones, then the twitching of the expiring body and, finally, the setting in of rigor mortis. The scene is devoid of sentimentality or terror. What the persona presumably beholds through his preternatural powers of observation—a sight invisible to uninitiated mortals—strikingly illustrates the poet's belief in the possibility of an unbroken continuity of consciousness in life and death:

> Then the corpse-limbs stretch on the bed, and the living
>     look upon them,
> They are palpable as the living are palpable.
>
> The living look upon the corpse with their eyesight,
> But without eyesight lingers a different living and looks
>     curiously on the corpse.

The spirit of the deceased individual appears to the persona as a vague, immaterial form or essence—what the poem calls "a different living." This postmortal and out-of-body manifestation of the deceased looks down "curiously" upon its cast-off carnal body—a curious relic of its just-concluded mortal existence. Given the persona's knack for "becoming," or identifying with, the individuals he observes, one can imagine that he has momentarily "become" the deceased entity and that he shares its out-of-body experience. The spirit-essence of the deceased person appears no longer constrained by the limitations of space or mobility as it floats freely above the corpse that is lying on the bed. Some persons who claim to have had a "near-death experience" report that they, too, "floated" above the hospital beds in which their "corpses" lay, but in a different (ectoplasmic?) state in which their new insubstantial "body" could even pass through the physical bodies of living persons.[3] This minidrama of death and transfiguration is Whitman's graphic answer to the rhetorical question that he had previously posed: "Have you guessed you yourself would not continue?" A somewhat similar explanation of this phenomenon occurs in a massive tome by the Brooklyn spiritualist Andrew Jackson Davis: "Could you but turn your gaze from the lifeless body, which no longer answers to your look of love; and could your spiritual eyes be opened;" Jackson says, "you would behold—standing in your midst—a form, the same, but more beautiful, and living! There is great cause to rejoice at the *birth* of the spirit from this world into the inner sphere of life."[4] (Throughout *Leaves of Grass* Whitman pictures death as a birth, or rebirth.)

A dirge-like intermezzo that links the cycles of seasonal renewal to the cycles of human life marks the introduction of the poem's centerpiece—the description of the funeral of a Manhattan workman. An introductory couplet on the universality of death echoes Bryant's "Thanatopsis." Given Whitman's early admiration of the "Thanatopsis" style and his later praise of Bryant for treating death "as a natural fact," this literary echo is hardly an accident:

> Slowmoving and black lines creep over the whole earth . . . . they
> never cease . . . . they are the burial lines,
> He that was President was buried, and he that is now President
> shall surely be buried.[5]

Although memorial poems like Shelley's "Adonais," Arnold's "Thyrsis," and Tennyson's "In Memoriam" celebrate notable, or at least respectable, men and employ elaborate poetic machinery, America's self-designated poet of democracy rejected such practices in favor of eulogizing a destitute forty-one-year-old omnibus driver, whose austere funeral is financed by the contributions of coworkers and friends. Whitman was well acquainted with such drivers on Manhattan's Broadway, as he recalls in *Specimen Days*. He fraternized with them, sometimes joined them as they plied their routes, visited them in hospitals when they were injured, and occasionally contributed money to aid them or to help defray the costs of their funerals. He was attracted to them, as he was to other rugged young workingmen, by their colorful ways, their native intelligence, and possibly by their sexual allure. Cataloging the harsh work routine of the poem's stage driver in the driver's own jargon, Whitman makes him exemplify the humble and despairing men and women to whom this funerary poem is addressed.[6] The short tribute to this non-hero characterizes him a "goodfellow" who was "freemouthed, quicktempered," a brawler, and a womanizer—hardly a suitable subject for the traditional elegy. The poem describes the driver's corpse being brought to the cemetery for burial in winter, under a "gray discouraged sky overhead" (the pathetic fallacy again). Given the urban setting, we may assume that the driver's burial did not occur in one of the wayside cemeteries romanticized by the older poets but that his modest and impersonal interment took place in one of the urban cemeteries that had become available to the poor in the second quarter of the nineteenth century. It is also likely that the corpse was prepared for burial by an undertaking establishment, six of which had been established in Suffolk and Queen's Counties alone by 1860.[7] "He is decently put away . . . . is there anything more?" challenges the persona, thus mocking the elaborate ritualization of death but once again raising the frightening specter that there may *not* be "anything more" beyond the grave. A taunting question like "is there anything more?" challenges us to balance our sense of loss for those we have loved against our desire to believe that death does not mark the extinction of the soul and of personal identity.

The final two-thirds of "To Think of Time" (sections 5 through 9— some 100 of the poem's 153 lines in the original version) constitutes a plain-spoken appeal to the masses to have faith that there is indeed a life beyond the grave and that such life must needs be "satisfactory"—a term often repeated in the first edition of the poem. (References to the satisfaction associated with death were subsequently deleted from the poem, along with sizable portions of the original text.) The persona's preoccupation with the expected "satisfaction" he will find in death expresses his yearning for a postmortal state of spiritually enhanced values, beyond good and evil, but it also demonstrates his suppressed uncertainty and the important role of wish-fulfillment in his thinking.

> The vulgar and the refined . . . . what you call sin and what you
>     call goodness . . to think how wide a difference;
> To think the difference will still continue to others, yet we lie
>     beyond the difference.

Here the reader is challenged to identify both the "we" who will "lie be-yond the difference" and the nature of that "difference." Is the persona identifying with the dead (the "we") and speaking as though he has be-come privy to their secret? His words can possibly be construed that way. In ringing monosyllables that proclaim "what will be will be well—for what is is well," he reiterates his faith that postmortal existence must prove at least as satisfying as our mortal lives have been. His implied promise to the masses is that death means more than an abstract immor-tality or the mere avoidance of personal annihilation; his promise em-bodies the assurance that one's selfhood—the unique character that one develops during a lifetime—cannot be "diffused" or annihilated during whatever cycles of one's existence may follow the Biblically allotted three score and ten. In emotionally charged words he tries to assure the reader that the universe is not purposeless, that he is "well-considered" and that one's core identity (the "Myself" or "Yourself!") will remain inviolable and will endure through time.

> You are not thrown to the winds . . you gather certainly and
>     safely around yourself,
> Yourself! Yourself! Yourself for ever and ever!

Having perhaps surmised that this argument is not altogether convincing because it is not readily demonstrable (the preservation of one's personal identity following death was hardly a unanimous position among theolo-gians), Whitman once again retreats to what might be called his fail-safe position by invoking what "Song of Myself" terms "the same old law." The rather nebulous "law," mentioned over one hundred times in *Leaves of Grass,* assumes the existence throughout nature of an innate urge to-ward perfection—manifested in humans as a moral force that operates both within us and beyond us. Whitman's melding of the nineteenth-century belief in progress with elements of popular religion and "heredi-tary science" reminds us how deeply he was influenced by the quasi-religious theories of physiological and moral reform promoted by the publishing firm of Fowler and Wells, which distributed this first edi-tion of *Leaves of Grass* and, in 1856, covertly published the second edition.[8] The "law of promotion and transformation," the poem explains, operates through time to advance not only the "great masters and kosmos" (terms with which Whitman characterizes his own persona) and the "heroes and do-gooders" but also the "drunkards and informants and mean persons." "All is procession," the poet affirms in "I Sing the Body Electric" (1855): "The universe is a procession with measured and beautiful motion," and "each has his or her place in the procession." And the poem of "Faces" (1855) predicts a time when all humans will have been "unmuzzled" of their animalistic traits and will have acquired their proper godlike visages.[9]

"[T]here is strict account of all," the speaker insists in "To Think of Time"; both life and death are purposive and beneficial to all. Ten times in the course of a seven-line catalogue the poem hammers home the assertion that even the least valued persons "are not nothing"—the ignorant, the wicked, the "common people," the cholera victims, prostitutes, "atheists," and (in keeping with the racialist theories of the time) those who are members of "inferior" races are all subject to the process of ongoing cosmic advancement. In a sort of circular reasoning, the persona explains that his faith in the workings of "the present and past law" is confirmed by his intuitions and his dreams. Apparently persuaded that the dreams of poets and visionaries are conduits for the "law" of mortality and transcendence, he four times repeats the clause "I have dreamed." Linking his own eternal destiny to that of the mass of mankind, he cheerfully assures them that whatever happens in death and the afterlife is sure to satisfy his own desires. Still, he so belabors the idea that death will provide him with "satisfaction" that he betrays his anxiety about what death may actually bring him. "I shall go with the rest. . . . we have satisfaction," he asserts. "And I have dreamed that the satisfaction is not so much changed . . . and that there is no life without satisfaction." "I shall go with the rest, / We cannot be stopped at a given point . . . that is no satisfaction; / To show us a good thing or a few good things for a space of time—that is no satisfaction." However, the cruel and senseless deaths that Whitman witnessed during the Civil War apparently motivated him to delete these tendentious assertions of "satisfaction" and to substitute, in 1871, a "philosophical" couplet declaring "that the purpose of the known life, the transient, / Is to form and decide identity for the unknown life, the permanent." Indeed, Whitman continued to depict death as an outgrowth of life and to insist that the quality of one's postmortal existence depends, in no small measure, on the development of the physical and moral character nurtured during one's lifetime. He seemed convinced that the quality of a democratic society depends on its producing a cadre of physically developed moral exemplars and visionaries—what he calls a "breed of the best"—who will inspire the masses to understand, and to pursue, their potential for better lives here and in the hereafter.[10]

But the persona's confidence is pierced by disquieting moments in which he fears that he may have misread the book of life and death, and that if his expectations were to prove wrong his mortal life would culminate in the dreaded nothingness that Paul Tillich calls "the darkness of the no more."[11] Two millennia earlier, the poet-philosopher Lucretius had described just such a mood of frightened despair: "When in life each man pictures to himself that it will come to pass that birds and wild beasts will mangle his body in death, he pities himself; for neither does he separate himself from the corpse, nor withdraw himself enough from the outcast body, but thinks that it is he, and as he stands watching taints it with his own feeling."[12] And two centuries before the appearance of *Leaves of Grass*, the poet John Dryden had described the feeling of agonizing uncertainty concerning the nature of the afterlife. Betrayed and facing death, the hero of one of his tragedies declaims:

> Distrust and darkness of a future state
> Make poor mankind so fearful of their fate.
> Death in itself is nothing, but we fear
> To be we know not what, we know not where.[13]

When he is momentarily stunned by the thought that death may bring him neither "satisfaction" nor continuity, the Whitman persona protests bitterly against the possibility of annihilation, but still clings to his belief that no such fate could befall *him:*

> If otherwise, if all these things came but to ashes of dung;
> If maggots and rats ended us, then suspicion and treachery
>     and death.
>
> Do you suspect death? If I were to suspect death I should die now,
> Do you think I could walk pleasantly and well-suited toward
>     annihilation?

The rhetorical questions in the second couplet are not far removed from a sentiment uttered by Mahatma Gandhi. "Both birth and death are great mysteries," said the Mahatma. "If death is not a prelude to another life, the intermediate period is a cruel mockery."[14] But Whitman's lines are whimsical, if not paradoxical. How can the persona admit the possibility of his annihilation and, at the same time, depict himself as "well-suited"—well dressed and fitted for robes of glory in the afterlife? His mortal body may be perishable, but he seems to believe that his essential self remains impervious to decay. Observe the relevance of the "well-suited" persona and the grass as symbols of immortality to the familiar words from Matthew 6:28–30: "And why be anxious about clothes? Consider how the lilies grow in the fields; they do not work; they do not spin; yet I tell you, even Solomon in all his splendor was not attired like one of them. If that is how God clothes the grass in the fields, which is there today and tomorrow is thrown in the oven, will he not all the more clothe you?"

Whitman generally makes his case for immortality in *Leaves of Grass* in one of three ways: by describing the grandeurs of nature and the known life and extrapolating from them the possible grandeurs that may follow in the unknown life; by asserting the validity of the persona's intuitions into immortality, often augmented by episodes of epiphany and illumination, like that in section 5 of "Song of Myself"; and by describing a leap of faith, like that of "A Noiseless Patient Spider" (1868). William James, who admired Whitman's healthy world view, suggests that the best recourse in confronting the contradictory evidence regarding humanity's eventual destiny might be to make such a leap. (Like many *fin de siècle* intellectuals who were disturbed by the challenge of scientific rationalism to their faith in personal immortality and who sought idealistic alternatives, James eventually became a devotee of spiritualism.) "To Think of Time" reflects the poet's continued struggle to dispel his troubling doubts concerning a future life. But his underlying faith remained strong, and he was never in serious danger of lapsing into skepticism or a permanent state of despair. So we cannot accept at full value the persona's melodramatic declaration that "if I were to suspect death I should die now," for few people of Walt Whitman's robust constitution have ever perished because they feared that they might not be immortal. Arch-skeptic Mark Twain went so far as to say that "there may be a hereafter, and there may *not* be. I am wholly indifferent about it. If I am appointed to live again, I feel sure it will be for some more sane and useful purpose than to flounder about for ages in a lake of fire and brimstone for having violated a confusion of ill-defined and contradictory rules said (but not evidenced,) to be of divine institution. If annihilation is to follow death, I shall not be *aware* of the annihilation, and therefore shall not care a straw about it."[15]

Unlike twentieth-century existentialists who are said to have looked squarely into the eye of the *nada* and accepted it philosophically, the persona stifles his outcry against the possibility of an eternal nothingness and, in a sudden change of tone, lustily reasserts his faith in the existence of a satisfactory continuum, capping his statement of acceptance with a bold metaphysical pun. Responding to his own rhetorical question, "Do you think I could walk pleasantly and well-suited toward annihilation?" he declares,

Pleasantly and well-suited I walk,
Whither I walk I cannot define, but I know it is good,
The whole universe indicates that it is good,
The past and the present indicate that it is good.

This jaunty affirmation implies that the persona has achieved a stay against doubt: he now feels confident of his immortality and believes himself eligible to take his place in humanity's endless procession toward perfection. Still, his expression of certainty is tautological. In effect he says that he *is* certain of eternal life because he *feels* certain of eternal life. The governing clauses of the poem's two final stanzas—"I swear I see" and "I swear I think"—indicate that the supposedly visionary persona is still scanning the phenomenal world for emblems and analogues that will confirm his intuitions of spiritual continuity. The sensuous penultimate stanza declares:

I swear I see now that every thing has an eternal soul!
The trees have, rooted in the ground . . . . the weeds of the
    sea have . . . . the animals.

But the welter of abstract nouns in the poem's final stanza weakens its immediacy, creating the impression that the persona is no longer addressing a working-class audience but that he is waxing "philosophical."

I swear I think there is nothing but immortality!
The exquisite scheme is for it, and the nebulous float is for it,

and the cohering is for it,
  And all preparation is for it . . and identity is for it . . . and life
  and death are for it.

As the poem closes on a bracing note of affirmation, the persona appears to have drawn a magic circle of bright and confident words around himself—a protective incantation to repel the specter of doubt and the possibility of annihilation. And Whitman, who closed each successive edition of *Leaves of Grass* with lines in praise of death, closes the 1856 edition with this very "Burial Poem."

2

"To Think of Time" hints that the vision of immortality came to the poet in a dream. Uniquely among Whitman's poems "The Sleepers" probes the subconscious and takes its form from the unstructured dream process. As James E. Miller Jr. observes, the poem opens and closes with fragmentary images connected by the dream mode, "juxtaposed scenes of death and love, of brutal destruction and sympathetic attachment," which "serve as commentaries of each other."[16] The fusion of the persona's dreams with those of the other dreamers (the subconscious merging of the *I* and the *you*) is an effective and elegant tour de force. Like the three poems that precede it in the first edition, this powerful lyric is steeped in fantasies of death. Originally untitled, the poem was called "Night Poem" in the 1856 edition, "Sleep-Chasings" (a title that conveys the fitful nature of sleep) in the 1860 edition, and given its present title in 1871. Like the visionary persona in the massive catalogue of "Song of Myself," section 33, the sleeper persona enters freely into the thoughts and feelings of men and women of the past and the present, his imagination liberated during sleep to roam through the realms of time and space, life and death. In some respects he resembles a clairvoyant who contacts the spirits of the living and the dead, travels without hindrance through the world of dreams, identifies with and "becomes" the other dreamers, heals them, and makes them aware of their potential greatness and their eligibility for immortality. He enters into the dreams of other sleepers and he shares *his* dreams with them, so that, in a sense, their identities seem to merge. His dreams, which are initially pleasant, give way to nightmares of torment and dying, and his intrusion into the tragic dreams of the other dreamers induces ever-intensifying cycles of despair. But Whitman does not conclude any of his major poems on a negative note. And so, two-thirds of the way through "The Sleepers," the persona's tormenting dreams suddenly cease, and they are unexpectedly replaced by luminous visions of sleeping humanity flowing (or dreaming that they are flowing) toward well-being and happiness. As the poem draws to a close, its sleepers appear to have absorbed the persona's healing dream-visions into their own dreams; and in their dream within a dream they become freed from pain and return to the homes of their hearts' desires. The poem's sudden shift in mood and structure occurs without warning, giving the impression that the poet has combined two or more disparate draft poems into this larger poem, the sort of radical revision he is known to have made in some other poems.

"The Sleepers" begins *in medias res,* when the persona is already immersed in his open-eyed clairvoyant dream, "lost to myself"—his rational self replaced by his subconscious dream self. The constraints that govern waking relationships do not apply in this midnight world. He feels "confused" as he bends "with open eyes over the eyes of the sleepers"— "ill-assorted," "contradictory." But the sight of his fellow dreamers renews his conviction that the "law" of amelioration operates indiscriminately on behalf of the living and the dead, the lover and the beloved, the murderer and "the murdered person," the rejected, the drunkard, the onanist, and the insane. As we have seen, Whitman is fond of picturing the transitions between life and death as paired birthings in which infants are born into mortal life while the dead are born into yet another life. Thus, the persona's dream-vision reveals some dreamers passing through the "gates" of the world of dreams into a vague hereafter while the newborn pass through other "gates" into the known life. But his dream also reveals an unceasing flow of misery and hope:

> The wretched features of enuyees, the white features of corpses,
>     the livid faces of drunkards, the sick-gray faces of onanists,
> The gashed bodies on battlefields, the insane in their strong-
>     doored rooms, the sacred idiots,
> The newborn emerging from gates and the dying emerging
>     from gates,
> The night pervades them and enfolds them.

Then, in a "fit" that is "whirling me fast," the dreamer-persona—like a clairvoyant healer—goes from sleeper to sleeper, reads their thoughts, shares their dreams, and in this inspired dream-state soothes them and heals them:

> I stand with drooping eyes by the worstsuffering and restless,
> I pass my hands soothingly to and fro a few inches from them;
> The restless sink in their beds . . . . they fitfully sleep.

During this phase of his dream-trance, he imagines himself capable of gaining a godlike perspective on the universe, viewing the world first from a celestial height, then probing beneath the earth to glimpse the realm of the dead. He delves "deep in the ground and sea" to view "the shadowy shore" that all the living are destined to cross. He delights in the beauties hidden throughout the universe. And, as his dream state intensifies, he discovers that he has become what he calls the "ever-laughing" pet of a "gay gang of blackguards with mirthshouting music and wild-flapping pennants of joy!" The poem describes this "gay gang" as "nimble ghosts, "or "journeymen divine," who "cache and cache again deep in the ground and sea" all sorts of "douceurs"—hidden sources of delight and beauty that, significantly, include the beauty of death. In a trial version of this passage, the poet wrote, "I think ten million supple wristed gods are always hiding beauty in the world—burying it every where in every thing—and most of all in spots that men and women do not think of and never look—as Death and Poverty and Wickedness—Cache! and Cache again! all over the world and heavens that swathe the earth and in the waters of the sea—They do their jobs well; [*sic*] those journeymen divine."[17] The delightful dream-companions, with their phallic "wild-flapping pennants of joy," who appear to surround the dreamer-persona, anticipate the coteries of masculine dream-companions in the death fantasies of some "Calamus" poems. At another level, the "journeymen divine" who guide the persona through the world of dreams may be construed as his own expanded faculties, or the "secondary personality," of his own creative imagination.[18] Spiritualists might have identified the "gay gang" as spirit-guides in the realm of the dead who, in this extraordinary fantasy, are welcoming the dream-persona of Walt Whitman into their domain. Dreams, of course, can serve as a medium of wish fulfillment. Many of her subjects told Elisabeth Kübler-Ross, a researcher of paranormal phenomena, that they had undergone a death experience in which they were led through the realm of death by guardian angels, or "guides," who introduced them to their deceased relations and friends, and brought them through a passageway or gate (the sort of symbol Whitman so often associates with the "passage" to death) to catch a glimpse of the god of their choice![19]

In a later phase of his dream, the persona merges with and "becomes" the very dreamers he is looking at. Thus he shares the dreams of both a bride and her male lover. In this sexual fantasy, the lover seems to melt into the darkness (traditionally associated with death), permitting the persona, in turn, to become the bride's surrogate lover. We cannot tell whether the persona has subconsciously destroyed the lover in order to replace him, but in his dream the lover's disappearance triggers a vision in which he pursues the lover and searches for him in the realm of death by means of his sonarlike powers:

My hands are spread forth . . I pass them in all directions,
I would sound up the shadowy shore to which you are journeying.

The despondency triggered by the despairing dream of the abandoned bride and her lost lover initiates a descending spiral of terrifying nightmares. One disturbing dream revisits the trauma that had accompanied the onset of adolescence—the "flooding" of sexual desire and the shame induced by masturbation or by the involuntary nocturnal emissions—the spermatorrhea that sexual reformers deplored as debilitating and sinful. No wonder the dreamer-persona complains of sexual exhaustion, lamenting that "my sinews are flaccid." As he relives this guilty memory he feels himself descending "my western course" toward death. (Whitman excluded this passage from the final edition of *Leaves of Grass* because it could have proved objectionable at a time when America's public censor Anthony Comstock had threatened to jail the civil libertarian Ezra Heywood for daring to reprint sexually explicit passages from *Leaves of Grass*.)[20]

The persona's nightmares become increasingly traumatic. Imagining himself to be the very shroud that covers a buried body, he cries out in despair that even the most sordid mortal existence is preferable to the obscurity of death:

It seems to me that everything in the light and air ought to
    be happy;
Whoever is not in his coffin and the dark grave, let him know he
    has enough.

In another nightmare he beholds the drowning of "a beautiful gigantic swimmer swimming naked through the eddies of the sea" only to be dashed against the rocks and borne out to sea—a swimmer with a "white body," "undaunted eyes," "a courageous giant . . . in the prime of his middle age." This swimmer's death is all the more poignant when we recognize that his physical attributes strikingly resemble those recorded in the various self-descriptions of the six-foot tall, fair-complexioned, keen-eyed, thirty-six-year-old Walt Whitman who, in the prime of *his* middle age, boasted (in poetic passages, prefaces, and self-written reviews) of his perfect body, his perfect health, and his love of swimming. Although it is possible that the poet had witnessed such a drowning, the poem's swimmer is a surrogate of the Whitman dream-persona as he imagines his own death by drowning. This vision of death by water is consistent with various passages of *Leaves of Grass* in which the persona "becomes" a garroted concertgoer, a mashed fireman, an incinerated widow, a disembodied "Whitman," or another drowning swimmer. The dream-persona's nightmare then spirals farther downward (in a possible reworking of a newspaper report) as he delves into his past to recall his helplessness when he supposedly witnessed a ship foundering offshore one frosty, moonlit night, its passengers drowning and he able only to wring his fingers and to "help pick up the dead and lay them in rows in a barn" the next morning.[21] By juxtaposing the drowning of the Whitman-like swimmer with the drowning of the helpless ship's passengers one can perceive the emotional depth of the persona's fantasy of his death by drowning. The tragic dream veers again from the personal into the quasi-historic past as the persona envisions the grieving specter of General Washington, defeated at the Battle of Brooklyn in 1776, as he gazes upon the field of dead soldiers who had been entrusted to his command; and in another vision he sees the weeping general bidding farewell to his adoring officers when the war is over. Then, with a sad nostalgia for the vanished world of childhood innocence, the persona recalls his mother's account of a visit by a "red squaw," a Native American woman of "wonderful beauty and purity," at a time when the mother was herself still a pubescent girl, and he shares her sense of loss as though her pain was his own. (Both *Leaves of Grass* and Longfellow's *Song of Hiawatha* were published in 1855, during an expansionist era when indigenous Americans were being uprooted and their lands devastated, and the theme of the vanishing noble Indian had become a clichéd literary apologia for national expansion.) This bacchanalia of self-torment concludes when the tormented persona reaches a nadir of despair. He "becomes," in rapid order, the betrayed and rebellious slave whose brother, sister, and "woman" have been sold down river where slavery is harshest. Finally he "becomes" a sort of vengeful Moby Dick, a deadly "vast bulk" incapable of forgiving past wrongs—the personification of the satanic element that seems to have both repelled and attracted the poet.

To the reader's surprise, the dream-poem and the dreamer-persona undergo an abrupt change. The blithe mood of sections 7 and 8 of the poem (roughly its last third) differ in style, temperament, and outlook from the preceding six sections. The persona has entered into a pleasant dream-world where he beholds visions of plenty and regains his emotional equilibrium. The dark nightmare world dissipates as he is suddenly "overwhelmed" by an epiphany of "something unseen . . . an amour of the light and air." He responds joyously to this unexpected contact. "I have an unseen something to be in contact with them also," he announces merrily. During this inspired moment the persona feels an equal and reciprocal relation to the cosmos, perhaps even fancying a libidinal contact with it. (The "contact" reference was deleted from the final edition.)[22] These concluding sections depict an evolutionary parade of human souls—"the homeward bound and the outward bound"—into whose dreams of being "restored" and made whole again the persona enters. He beholds them being "averaged now"—becoming specimens of perfected humanity. The "now" during which the dreamers are transformed is ambiguous. Not only does it signify the "now" in which the persona's dream occurs, but it is also the "now" in which the poet-persona recreates his dream. More objectively, it is the eternal and abiding "now" in which this ameliorative process is forever working. Two short catalogues describe the dreams he shares with this endless procession of life's winners and losers—fugitives and poor immigrants (mostly Western Europeans) who in their dreams are "flowing" toward their childhood homes. Dreamers whose wretched fates are related in the earlier sections of the poem—"the beautiful lost swimmer, the ennuyee, the onanist, the female that loves unrequited, the moneymaker," the sick, "the midnight widow, the red squaw, / The consumptive, the erysipalite, the idiot, he that is wronged"—reappear in the closing sections as they become healed and perfected. In "the dim night of dreams," the persona explains, sleep has "restored them," made them beautiful, and brought them peace. But the world of "The Sleepers" is only the persona's dream world; and within this dream the sleepers are gravitating toward peace and perfection. As he often does, Whitman pairs physical improvement with spiritual development:

> The myth of heaven indicates the soul;
> The soul is always beautiful . . . . it appears more or it appears
>     less . . . . it comes or lags behind,
> It comes from its embowered garden and looks pleasantly on
>     itself and encloses the world;
> Perfect and clean the genitals previously jetting, and perfect
>     and clean the womb cohering,
> The head wellgrown and proportioned and plumb, and the
>     bowels and joints proportioned and plumb.
>
> The soul is always beautiful,
> The universe is duly in order . . . . every thing is in its place,
> What is arrived is in its place, and what waits is in its place;
> The twisted skull waits . . . . the watery or rotten blood waits,
> The child of the glutton or venerealee waits long, and the child
>     of the drunkard waits long, and the drunkard himself waits long,
> The sleepers that lived and died wait . . . . the far advanced are
>     to go in their turns, and the far behind are to go in their turns,
> The diverse shall be no less diverse, but they shall flow and
>     unite . . . . they unite now.

This vision of an ongoing process of physical and spiritual perfectibility once again invites the question of how the upgrading of the carnal and corrupt body serves to advance the development of the immortal soul. Traditional religionists have sometimes contended that the body must be disciplined or subdued as a means of liberating the soul from the tyranny of the flesh. The poet who declares in "Song of Myself" that he doesn't mind contradicting himself sometimes implies that the soul is identical with the body (hence the body is to be nurtured) and at other times implies that the body is somehow distinct from the soul (hence it is ultimately disposable). But Whitman, like many contemporary reformers, respected physical culture as a component of spiritual nurture, assuming that developing a healthy body promotes spiritual well-being. In demonstrating his artistic and spiritual eligibility to be his nation's poet, Whitman boasted of his own superb body. "I do not believe that any one possesses a more perfect or enamoured body than mine," he declares in "Excelsior" (1856). The manner in which physical development nurtures spiritual development remains vague in his writings, but he puts his own spin on the contemporary vogue of attaining moral and spiritual refinement through improving one's physique. The moral-spiritual "law" of amelioration he implies in "Faces," operates by gradually erasing humanity's animalistic traits and, in "a score or two of ages," making people more godlike. The process is said to apply to everyone but operates differently and at a different pace with each individual:

> The Lord advances, and yet advances:
> Always the shadow in front . . . . always the reached hand
>     bringing up the laggards.

These predictions of eventual physical perfectibility in the first and second editions of *Leaves of Grass* obliquely echo St. Augustine's assertion that following the Christian Resurrection all crippled, deformed, and aborted bodies will become whole and perfect.[23]

The sonorous and cadenced catalogs in sections 7 and 8 of "The Sleepers" describe a procession of affectionately paired sleepers—"the Asiatic and the African," "the European and the American," male and female, parent and child, scholar and teacher, slave and master as they "flow hand in hand over the whole earth from east to west as they lie unclothed" and as they become "averaged." Their dreams merge with the persona's own dream of universal love in which "the suffering of sick persons is relieved" and the "unsound throat," the consumption, rheumatism, and paralysis that ravaged the Whitman family eventually disappear. The vision ends on a triumphant note:

> The swelled and convulsed and congested awake to themselves
>     in condition,
> They pass the invigoration of the night and the chemistry of
>     the night and awake.

And yet, to borrow Langston Hughes's phrase, this vision is ultimately "a dream deferred." For in flowing "from east to west" the sleepers are moving symbolically from life to death. Indeed, traveling "from east to west" is hardly the fastest route by which to return them to the lands of their European origin. One recalls, perhaps with a shock, that this dream prophecy is not intended to be fulfilled in a few human lifetimes but only "in a score or two of ages." Nevertheless, if the poem's sleepers have become "invigorated" by the dream they shared with the persona, the dream itself may have enabled them to confront their own lives—and their deaths—with greater courage and nobler aspirations. Likewise, "The Sleepers"—the poem itself—may continue to inspire readers with a stronger sense of their physical and spiritual potential.

The metaphor of sleep necessarily implies an awakening. The sleeper's dream state complements his waking state. The persona's declaration upon awakening from his dream that "I will stop only a time with the night . . . and rise betimes" may simply mean that Walter Whitman Jr., as a representative American, will awaken early ("betimes") from his slumber to go about his daily affairs. But the assertion that he will "arise betimes" can also indicate his faith in a destined rebirth. For in its archaic usage, "betimes" means "at the right time" or "at the appointed time." The awakening from sleep has long served as an emblem of Christian resurrection. Thus Jonathan Edwards declared that just as "this sleep is an image of death that is repeated every night; so the morning is the image of the resurrection; so the spring of the year is the image of the resurrection that is repeated every year."[24] "The Sleepers" ends with the persona's awakening from the amniotic realm of dreams "in which I lay so long" and by which "I have been well brought forward by you"—the "you" (personified as Mother Night-Sleep-Death) who had enfolded him and has now liberated him. This reappearance of the mother figure and the reference to her once again exemplifies Whitman's use of birth imagery to describe the transitions from life to death and from death to life. "The Sleepers" fittingly concludes with the persona's address to the mystic Matriarch of the World of Dreams and Death who is his muse and whom he desires to revisit in further excursions into the world of dreams:

> I will duly pass the day O my mother and duly return to you;
> Not you will yield forth the dawn again more surely than you
>    will yield forth me again,
> Not the womb yields the babe in its time more surely than I
>    shall be yielded from you in my time.

The last two lines of the poem's original conclusion, which were deleted in the final edition, reiterate the poet's faith in a cyclical journey of birth, death, and renewal that everyone must undertake on the cosmic road to perfection.[25]

### 3

The last three poems of the 1855 edition of *Leaves of Grass* are suffused with thoughts of death. The mythobiographical vignette of the boy-poet's nurture, "There Was a Child Went Forth," concludes when, at the onset of puberty, he beholds several symbols of death—the purity of twilight with its strata of colored clouds, and the "long bar of maroon-tint" gleaming "solitary" at the horizon's edge, the beckoning sea with its "tumbling waves," and the outbound schooner heading seaward. The optimistic little preachment "Who Learns My Lesson Complete" declares that the persona is immortal, "as every one is immortal"; for "seventy years" is not "the time of a man or woman, / Nor [is] seventy millions of years." And "Great Are the Myths" (later excluded from *Leaves of Grass*) celebrates the persona's zestful delight in the "myths" he associates with all phases of existence—youth, age, the world, the self, language, truth, democracy, goodness, and the soul—and concludes the 1855 volume of *Leaves of Grass* with a solemn tribute to death:

> Great is death . . . . Sure as life holds all parts together, death
>   holds all parts together;
> Sure as the stars return again as they merge in the light, death
>   is as great as life.

# 3
## "The Progress of Souls"
### Leaves of Grass, 1856

The second edition of *Leaves of Grass* (1856) was published as an octavo volume that included all twelve poems of the 1855 edition and twenty-four new poems. Fowler and Wells, the publishers of popular books and periodicals devoted to phrenology, water cure, health and sexual reforms, and a variety of "practical" subjects, issued the volume covertly, because, as one of the firm's officers wrote to Whitman, they wanted to "insist on the omission of certain objectionable passages."[1] (They later relented.) Whitman's relationship with these publishers had a notable bearing on the outlook, the language, and the design of the second edition, and on Whitman's approach to his intended audience.

The 1856 "Poem of the Wonder of The Resurrection of the Wheat" (renamed "This Compost" in 1871) is ideologically and thematically related to the 1855 meditation "To Think of Time." Both poems show the persona struggling against the fear that death may prove to be no more than a meaningless annihilation, and both show him striving to maintain his faith in some form of spiritual regeneration.[2] "This Compost" is a two-part invention. Its first sixteen lines (as numbered in the final version of *Leaves of Grass*) reveal the persona's reaction to the unnerving prospect of ultimately becoming no more than a piece of "foul meat" that is consigned to the earth and thus being betrayed "where I thought I was safest." By fixating on the possibility that after his burial nothing will be left of him but terminal fertilizer, he becomes repelled by the earth's very luxuriance and bounty. His fear of coming in contact with what he fancies to be an infectious earth filled with rotted materials and corpses takes on a paranoid tone, radically different from the affectionate tone the persona had used while contemplating the grass-covered graves in "Song of Myself." He appears confounded that the same grassy earth that swallows up "distempered corpses" can, paradoxically, "be alive with the growths of spring." How can this earth, the source of health and sustenance, digest "all the foul liquid and meat" that have been buried in it, he wonders. In this terrified mood he decides to avoid all contact with the earth:

> I withdraw from the still woods I loved,
> I will not go now to the pastures to walk,
> I will not strip the clothes from my body to meet my lover the sea,
> I will not touch my flesh to the earth or to other flesh to
>     renew me.

Yet this rejectionist mood does not last. In one of those abrupt shifts that characterizes almost all of Whitman's poems that begin with a de-spairing view of his world, the persona's revulsion against decay and pes-tilence is replaced in the second part of the poem by a sudden revelation that the same earth that is the repository of offal and death is simultane-ously the inexhaustible source of health and fruitfulness—a theme akin to the Ceres myth. The persona first exclaims, "Behold this compost! behold it well!" But then he perceives the earth's cyclic regeneration and renewal as symbols of the miracle of existence and the deathlessness of the human spirit. Then (in the imagery of birthing that often occurs in those poems that are concerned with death) he sensuously enumerates the emergent growths—the grass, the trees, "the yellow maize-stalk," and the newborn animal young—that flourish because this same earth has accepted and transformed the deposits of "infused fetor." In the highly allusive line that gave the poem its original title and that underscores Whitman's faith in some form of resurrection, the poet celebrates "the resurrection of the wheat [that] appears with pale visage out of its graves." The resurrected wheat imagery invites comparison with Paul's sermon in 1 Corinthians 15, in which the wheat symbolizes the promise that the dead shall be raised on the day of resurrection:

> But now is Christ risen from the dead, and become the *firstfruits* of them that slept. . . . But some man will say, How are the dead raised up? and with what body do they come? Thou fool, that which thou *sowest* is not quickened, except it die. And that which thou sowest, thou sowest not that body which shall be, but *bare*

*grain, it may chance of wheat,* or some other grain. . . . So also is the resurrection of the dead. *It is sown in corruption, it is raised in incorruption.* It is sown in dishonor, it is raised in glory; it is sown in weakness, it is raised in power. It is sown a natural body, it is raised a spiritual body.[3]

Paul's words make clear that the seed grain is, through God's grace, qualitatively different from the plant that grows from it. As one theologian interprets the passage, "God raises that grain of wheat into a glorious body, infinitely finer than that which is buried; but it is another body, such as it pleases God to give." This interpretation implies that it is not the body buried in the grave that is raised but some sort of spirit body.[4] In changing the poem's title from "Poem of Wonder at the Resurrection of the Wheat" to "This Compost," Whitman muted the specifically Christian implications of the earlier title. And over the years, he also muted other implied references to traditional religion in *Leaves of Grass.*

The "compost" trope is rich in implication. In words that form a bridge between the persona's nearly hysterical outburst of distrust in the cyclical workings of nature and his expressions of faith in the existence of a spiritual continuity, he voices his astonishment at the earth's transformative powers: "What chemistry!" he exclaims. How marvelous that the sea that "lick[s] my naked body all over with its tongues . . . will not endanger me with the fevers that have deposited themselves in it" and that of all the fruits that grow "none will poison me"; "that when I recline on the grass I do not catch any disease, / Though probably every spear of grass rises out of what was once a catching disease." Both *compost* and *chemistry,* as Whitman uses these terms, incorporate the ideas of the cyclical transformation and renewal and of the earth's power to bring goodness and life out of corruption and death. Although *compost* familiarly designates decomposing vegetable matter mixed with earth and used as fertilizer, Whitman extends the definition to include the mixture of earth and human carrion: "This is the compost of billions of premature corpses," he declares in a grisly line that was suppressed in 1867. He also uses the words *compost* and *chemistry* to illustrate the concept that the forces that support life and the forces of decay are interdependent and reciprocal; they are nature's synthesis of opposites—the thesis and antithesis of its grand continuum. The persona's fears that the earth is infectious recall the once widely held theory of miasma (still relied upon by some physicians in the Civil War era), according to which the vapors and effluvia of rotting vegetable and animal matter debilitate and poison human beings and cause such deadly diseases as typhus and yellow fever. (Miasma, we may recall, was responsible for the physical decline and the ultimate extinction of the aristocratic family in Poe's "The Fall of the House of Usher.") The importance of "chemistry" as a factor in the earth's cyclical renewal was explained by the pioneering chemist Justus Liebig, one of whose books on chemistry the poet had reviewed. Liebig uses the word *metamorphosis* to define the process of "fermentation, or putrefaction," the active principle in composting, which involves the simultaneous breakdown and transformation of life forms through the rearrangement of "elementary particles."[5] In Whitman's hands the earth's "chemistry" becomes an effective metaphor for the science and mystery of metamorphosis— the eternal cycle in which life moves forward through death and decay, and death, in turn, nurtures the never-ending renewal of life. Composting can also symbolize the process of purifying the soul from corruption. In another sense, composting can imply the poet's gift of transforming the most common and repulsive matter into the stuff of inspired poetry, for as Anna Akhmatova observes, much verse does really grow from rubbish.[6] The imagery of composting remained meaningful to Whitman. Following the Civil War, when he was haunted by the bodies of the thousands of unidentified soldiers rotting in makeshift graves, he invoked the transforming power of what "This Compost" calls their "infused fetor" (the foul-smelling miasma rising from their corpses) to "perfume" his poems and to "make [the soldiers'] ashes to nourish and blossom" and to "fructify all with the last chemistry." And some years later he rebutted Thomas Carlyle's antidemocratic critique of American society with an astonishing trope drawn from the same source. The "kosmic antiseptic power" of renewal inherent in the American earth and in American democracy, he assured Carlyle, will ultimately prove capable of absorbing its "morbid collection" of flawed citizenry and corrupt institutions. "Nature's stomach," he declared, will digest the corrupt elements of American politics and social institutions and transform them into a genuine democracy.[7]

"This Compost" reflects Whitman's ongoing struggle to wrest a faith in immortality and possible reincarnation from his latent, if generally sublimated, fear of obliteration and decay. Having seemingly subdued his terror of death by the end of the poem, the persona embraces the fruitful earth as the symbol and guarantor of the never-flagging cycle of life, death, and rebirth. It was widely believed in Whitman's day that scrofula, a form of tuberculosis affecting the lymph glands, could be caused by too-frequent pregnancies, but Whitman maintains that Mother Earth remains forever the undiminished acceptor of mortal leavings and the perpetual source of abundant life. In a tone of triumphant irony, the persona demands ("Song of Myself," section 22), "Did you fear some scrofula out of the [earth's] unflagging pregnancy? / Did you guess the celestial laws are to be worked over and rectified?" But as "This Compost" concludes, the persona remains awestruck—he uses the word *terrified*—by the earth's inexhaustible bounty, convinced that its perpetual cycles of renewal are sufficient evidence that death is a vital phase in the perpetual renewal of life:

> Now I am terrified at the Earth, it is that calm and perfect,
> It grows such sweet things out of such corruption,
> It turns harmless and stainless on its axis, with such endless
>     succession of diseased corpses,
> It distils such exquisite winds out of such infused fetor,
> It renews with such unwitting looks prodigal, annual sumptuous
>     crops,
> It gives such divine materials to men, and accepts such leavings
>     from them at last.

## 2

Several popular pseudosciences are relevant to Whitman's writings in the 1850s, not only because he used some of some of their techniques and terminology to color his poems but also because of their claim to span the gap between the known and the unknown, between the material and spiritual worlds, was widely acknowledged. Thus, Emerson could say that mesmerism (the "mental" science of hypnosis and mental conditioning) "confirmed the unity and connection between remote points, and as such was excellent criticism of the narrow and dead classification of what passed for science." Many of these pseudosciences were rooted in what Orson S. Fowler termed "hereditary science." (Whitman owned a copy of Fowler's *Hereditary Descent*.) Basic to many pseudosciences was the Lamarckian premise that by following a prescribed physical and mental regimen individuals could improve themselves and transmit their improved condition to their progeny. Whitman, who sought to develop an overarching, or what he termed an "omnient," approach to science,[8] found these semisciences serviceable. The 1856 edition of *Leaves of Grass* not only has the outward appearance of a Fowler and Wells self-help manual but it also reflects some of the firm's ideologies.[9] The handsomely produced volume is the most popularistic edition of the poems. Some of its new poems picture the Whitman persona as a teacher-confessor who adopts the pose of a guru addressing a working-class crowd that is eager to take his hand and hear his reassurance that they, as self-reliant Americans, are eligible for physical and spiritual advancement. Operating immeasurably to Whitman's advantage in these poems is his deliberately ambiguous use of the pronoun "you"—the "you" to whom many of the new poems are addressed. Sometimes the "you" designates the American masses who are assumed to be listening to the inspired poet who has assumed the guise of a folk-orator. Sometimes the "you" seems to imply a single listener whom the persona addresses as an equal, an intimate friend, or a lover. And often the "you" refers interchangeably, and even indistinguishably, to both the individual and the mass. Whitman often chooses to make no clear distinction between the many and the one.

"Poem of You, Whoever You Are" ("To You, Whoever You Are") is a compendium of the 1856 volume's reformist doctrines. The persona urges his uninitiated compatriots, who are "walking the walks of dreams," to realize that they, too, are eligible to achieve their true selfhood: "Your true soul and body appear before me," he asserts. By learning to trust their own instincts as distinct from secondhand ideas, he tells them, they can "find themselves eternal" and able to master "the throes of apparent dissolution." In an intimate gesture, as both lover and guru, he places his hand on a representative "you" and whispers that he alone perceives and celebrates his or her potential greatness. Whitman certainly knew of Karl Ludwig Reichenbach's theory according to which "sensitives" were able to receive the emanations of *odyllic* force (somewhat akin to magnetism and/or light) that supposedly flows from the bodies, particularly the heads, of humans.[10] Likewise, the persona claims to see a nimbus—like that which adorns the crowns of saints, angels, and the deity in medieval and Renaissance paintings—glowing from the head of each American, however humble. Therefore he promises that his poems will portray the divinity that is inherent in each of them, that he "will paint no head without its nimbus of [the] gold-colored light" that streams "from the brain of every man and woman," "effulgently flowing forever." "The mockeries are not you," he encourages them. The real "you" may be thwarted by adverse conditions—false beliefs, empty routines, fashionable disguises, drunkenness, and "premature death." But the persona assures them that he sees through their masks and "mockeries" and that no physical or moral taint can hide their ultimate worth from him:

> I sing the songs of the glory of none, not God, sooner than I sing
>     the songs of the glory of you . . . .
> Master or mistress in your own right over Nature, elements, pain,
>     passion, dissolution.

The ameliorative "law," he maintains, operates for everyone, permitting men and women, no matter how wretched their lives may appear, to develop during their lifetimes and beyond this life, to take responsibility for their lives and their afterlives, to work out their defects, and, in the process, to nurture the true "what you are."

> Through birth, life, death, burial, the means are provided,
>     nothing is scanted,
> Through angers, losses, ambitions, ignorance, ennui, what you
>     are picks its way.[11]

The conclusion of "To You, Whoever You Are" seeks to instill faith and self-trust in the American populace of the 1850s, including the most wretched of them. Its heady visionary promise of a better life in this world and the next is the high-water mark of Whitman's optimism.

The sixteen-line "Faith Poem" (much revised in 1871 as "Assurances") is a credo: fifteen of its lines begin with the clause "I do not doubt." It is predicated on the idea that every being is eligible to progress toward divinity. In fact, declares its persona, his own soul tells him that a universal spiritual democracy operates in the "majesty and beauty" that are "latent in any iota of the world," in the least of creatures—in "trivialities, insects, vulgar persons, slaves, dwarfs, weeds, rejected refuse." He revels in the conceit that his limitless self may, in "millions of years," develop into an interstellar phenomenon; the infinitude of the universe, he feels, is mirrored in him. And in an oblique reference to the pseudosciences of physiognomy and phrenology he repeats the claim he had made in "Faces," that he can discern the character of his fellow creatures beneath the masks they present to the world. "Faith Poem" posits the existence of an indwelling principle (here called "inherences") that impels each person forward in this life and beyond. The expression of this principle is noteworthy because it exemplifies Whitman's developing philosophic dualism. Each person, he implies, is endowed with a spiritual faculty (the "I am") that coexists with the mortal consciousness of the individual and that prompts him or her toward spiritual fulfillment:

> I do not doubt interiors have their interiors, and exteriors have
>     their exteriors, and the eyesight has another eyesight, and the
>     hearing another hearing, and the voice another voice,
> I do not doubt that the passionately wept deaths of young men
>     are provided for, and that the deaths of young women and the
>     deaths of little children are provided for . . .
>
> I do not doubt that whatever can possibly happen, any where, at
>     any time, is provided for in the inherences of things.

In 1871, when Whitman had become much less the poet of the body and its worldly delights and more distinctly "the poet of the soul," he added a line that emphasizes his enduring belief that death is a vital component in the cycles of personal and universal evolution: "I do not think Life provides for all and for Time and Space, but I believe Heavenly Death provides for all."[12]

Whitman's implication in "Song of Myself" that he is equally the poet of the body and the poet of the soul may suggest that he consistently affords equal importance to the body and the soul. Yet this assumption is contradicted in his many attempts to develop an ideological synthesis that could embrace all phases (or stages) of existence. And given the unlikelihood of resolving the problem before him, contradiction is inevitable. Thus the brief 1856 lyric "Poem of Remembrances" ("Think of the Soul") plainly states that the body is *less* than the soul, its chief purpose being to prepare the soul for the next phase of its eternal journey: "I swear to you that body of yours gives proportions to your soul somehow to live in other spheres." That "somehow" highlights the underlying uncertainty in this vaunted assumption, based essentially on the persona's feelings. And "I swear" is a term that the poet sometimes uses interchangeably with "I dream" or "I guess." "I do not know how [this transformation] may come to be," the persona asserts, "but I know it is so." A declaration, later deleted from "Song of the Open Road" clearly articulates the assumption that the body is subordinate to the soul: "The body does not travel as much as the Soul, / The body has just as great a work as the Soul, and parts away at last for the journeys of the Soul."

A sympathetic interpretation of Whitman's proposed body-soul relationship is offered by Edmund Holmes, an early admirer of *Leaves of Grass*, who contends,

> [t]he soul that is "included in the body" necessarily dies in the hour of death, and the soul that dies in the hour of death is (obviously) a mere function of the body—in other words, as soul it is non-existent. But the soul that escapes into the larger world of death assimilates itself to its new environment and expands its being up to the illimitable limits of existence. The language that Whitman uses about the soul is certainly perplexing and self-contradicting, but whenever the deeper philosophy of his heart asserts itself, his philosophy undergoes a singular change. Instead of identifying the soul with the body, he sends it abroad till it becomes coterminous with the Universe.[13]

Holmes, however, like Whitman himself, skirts the knotty problem of how the postmortal soul can be "coterminous with the Universe" and nevertheless maintain the distinctive identity and independence that it has supposedly brought forward from its mortal state, as seems to be implied in many of these poems. The body-soul dualism in the earlier editions of *Leaves of Grass* ultimately gave way to an almost exclusive emphasis on the soul in the poems that Whitman wrote after the Civil War.

Two important poems elaborate on the principle pervading the 1856 edition, that one's future existence is determined in no small measure by one's mortal character. "Song of the Broad-Axe," in which Whitman contrasts "the hell of war, the cruelty of creeds" and the martyrdom of innocents in the feudal era to the democratic individualism and freedom he attributes to America's pioneers, enthusiastically proclaims the influence of one's mortal character upon the sort of afterlife that one will enjoy:

> Muscle and pluck forever!
> What invigorates life, invigorates death,
> And the dead advance as much as the living advance,
> And the future is no more uncertain than the present,
> And the roughness of the earth and of man encloses as much as
>     the delicatesse of the earth and of man,
> And nothing endures but personal qualities.

"A Song of the Rolling Earth" ("Poem of the Sayers of the Words of the Earth" in the 1856 edition) shows the persona once again posing as a translator of the earth's words, declaring that "amelioration is one of the earth's words" and that nature's clues are audible to those who listen attentively. And the earth's message, he tells all who will listen, is the heady news that the magnificence of the universe is theirs for the taking—"each man to himself, and each woman to herself"—if only they lead forthright lives:

> Whoever you are! you are he or she for whom the earth is
>     solid and liquid,
> You are he or she for whom the sun and moon hang in the sky,
> For none more than you are the present and the past,
> For none more than you is immortality.

A forceful, if rather awkward, stanza from "Song of Providence" hammers home the thesis that the conduct of one's earthly life shapes the spiritual destiny of every man and woman:

> The Soul is of itself,
> All verges to it—all has reference to what ensues,
> All that a person does, says, thinks, is of consequence,
> Not a move can a man or woman make, that affects him or her
>     in a day, month, any part of the direct life-time, or the hour
>     of death, but the same affects him or her onward, afterward
>     through the indirect life-time.

Whitman's concept of the "law," or what he sometimes calls "prudence," has elements of the classical idea of karma. "According to the orthodox [Buddhist] theory, karma simply means the conservation or immortality of the inner force of deeds, regardless of the author's physical identity. Deeds, once committed, good or evil, leave permanent effects on the general system of sentient beings, of which the actor is merely a component part."[14] Thus "Song of Prudence" states that each person must test every action by the reaction of the soul, because "whatever satisfies souls is true . . . The soul has that measureless pride which refuses every lesson but its own." These poems escape the trap of extreme subjectivism only by maintaining a firm bond with the material, workaday world. Nevertheless, the idea of following the dictates of one's soul is based on the attractive, but questionable, premise that human instincts are invariably benevolent. However, modern history illustrates the grievous consequences that may ensue when the intuitions of self-conceived great leaders override their sense of humaneness.

The 1856 "Clef Poem" (later truncated to form "On the Beach at Night Alone") is a fascinating affirmation of the persona's faith in his own immortality and a preview of the satisfactions he anticipates in the life to come. As he walks on the beach one starlit night he is overwhelmed by an inspirational "thought of the clef [or clue] of the universes, and of the future." The "thought" takes the form of an anthropocentric analogy between the familiar satisfactions he has known as a mortal being and the enhanced satisfactions that he may experience in the afterlife. Nevertheless, he questions whether any future existence could prove to be better than "the life of my body." "What can the future bring me more than I have?" . . . "Do you suppose I wish to enjoy life in other spheres?" But these musings are only a preamble to another faith-based affirmation of his own personal indestructibility:

> I do not know what follows the death of my body,
> But I know that whatever it is, it is best for me,
> And I know that whatever is really Me shall live just as much
>     as before.

Wishfully, he fantasizes about the satisfactions of the afterlife: "I suppose I shall have myriads of new experiences—and that the experiences of this earth will prove only one out of my myriads."[15] Unable to predict "what follows" "the death of my body," he vows to accept whatever may come in the hereafter, confident that he will "enjoy good housing" then. Wisely avoiding the pitfall of many contemporary religionists, who drew a virtual map of the hereafter, he declines to describe the nature of his postmortem "housing" or to speculate as to what sort of spirit-body he may eventually inhabit. Many of his contemporary immortalists, as R. Laurence Moore points out, "provided very concrete and detailed portraits of the after-life," and the spiritualists outdid them all. For them, says Moore, "spirits retained the discrete characteristics of their earthly personalities, although it was widely believed that after a long passage of time they lost contact with earth."[16] Although the 1856 "Clef Poem" offers few specifics about the persona's envisioned afterlife, it does spell out his expectation of preserving his identity through whatever changes his indestructible self may undergo. Characteristically, he articulates the hope that in the life to come he will continue to enjoy the reciprocated love of young men and old men and motherly women. In a striking (if somewhat juvenile) analogy between the divine nurture of Mother Earth and whatever nurture may await him in an afterlife, he speculates,

> I am not uneasy but I am to be beloved by young and old men,
>     and to love them the same,
> I suppose the pink nipples of the breasts of women with whom I
>     shall sleep will touch the side of my face the same,
> But this is the nipple of a breast of my mother, always near and
>     always divine to me, her true child and son, whatever comes.

"Clef Poem" may be construed as an exercise in wish fulfillment—an emotional bulwark against the misgivings concerning the nature of love and death that appear to have troubled Whitman at this stage of his life. The male and female lovers who inhabit an imagined and amorphous afterworld represent a dream of being compensated in some future time for the boons that mortal existence may have denied him. "Here I grew up," declares the persona, apparently in no hurry to find out what joys or terrors may lurk beyond the curtain of mortality.

While calmly contemplating the starry night and the sea, the solitary persona experiences an epiphany. During this enchanted moment, he exclaims, "I believe I have this night a clew through the universes," / "And

I believe I have this night thought a thought of the clef of eternity"—a momentous intimation that seems to penetrate his "body and soul." This vision reinforces his faith that life and death are a continuum of experience and that "a vast similitude interlocks all"—every phase of animate and inanimate existence: "All the substances of the same, and all that is spiritual, upon the same . . . . All souls—all living bodies, though they be ever so different, *or in different worlds*" (emphasis added). (That "similitude" interlocking mortal experience and whatever may follow is a striking illustration of what Whitman calls the "law.") Playfully speculating that he may "be eligible to visit the stars" in this life, or in the lives to come, he tempers his enthusiasm with the thought that he may nevertheless find nothing more "mystic and beautiful" in his future existence than what he has known on earth. He refuses to accept the thought that the identity he has developed in the known life will be obliterated or changed into something qualitatively different in any postmortem existence. Indeed, the 1856 version of "Clef Poem" succeeds in being both a fascinating exercise in fantasy and a vital representation of Whitman's thoughts about immortality and the life-death continuum. In retaining only the two introductory lines and the last eleven lines of "Clef Poem" in 1867 to create "On the Beach at Night Alone" Whitman expunged the poem's self-questioning about the possibility of an afterlife but preserved the terse but brilliant analogy, "A vast similitude interlocks all," that affirms a faith in immortality consistent with his later pose as a guru of death.

### 3

Three major poems that first appeared in the 1856 edition—"Poem of Salutation" ("Salut au Monde!"), "Poem of the Road" ("Song of the Open Road"), and "Sun-Down Poem" ("Crossing Brooklyn Ferry")—describe visionary journeys in which the persona reaches out to masses of people in order to proclaim the infinitude of the soul and to demonstrate his boundless empathy. In the first of the two "movements" of "Salut au Monde!" the persona undertakes a clairvoyant journey beyond the limitations of space and time. He imagines himself circumnavigating the earth, as though he were aloft in a balloon, naming, as he passes by, the continents, oceans, and nations he beholds below him. However, he does not individualize the people he sees; they are usually identified only by a name or by a national trait. Because the persona appears to be physically distant from these peoples, observing them only from aloft, the poem lacks the immediacy of the persona's two extensive dream-journeys in "Song of Myself," sections 15 and 33. His mental journey in "Salut au Monde!" is apparently induced by a mesmerist who (serving as his Muse) takes his hand, hypnotizes him, and stimulates his clairvoyant powers. The mesmerist's spell enables the persona to relate all the "gliding wonders" he beholds during his trance. And as though the persona were pregnant with the terrestrial globe, the mesmerist demands, "What widens within you, Walt Whitman?"—"What cities, climes, peoples?" To which the mesmerized persona replies that he is aware of absorbing latitudes, longitudes, and the very solar system where "the sun wheels in slanting rings and does not set for days." A few years before the appearance of *Leaves of Grass,* an American mesmerist had explained that mesmerism was a scientific method for discovering the continuity between mind and spirit—between the conscious and the unconscious states.[17] And the persona's conscious and unconscious states in "Salut au Monde!" do appear to be integrated in the dream-vision that follows. The litany of continents, bays, oceans, mountain ranges, and peoples that he sees and mythic figures he conjures up in this almost two-hundred-line cluster of catalogs is redolent of the atlases and source books that Whitman had been reading.[18] The persona's globe-girdling journey is interspersed with affecting glimpses of suffering and images of violent death, dying, and resurrection. As he observes the "navigators of the world," for example, he grieves for those who drift helplessly in storms, "some with contagious diseases." He beholds "the battle-fields of the earth [where] the grass grows upon them and blossoms and corn." And on a rugged sea coast he beholds "the burial-cairns of Scandinavian warriors" from which "the dead men's spirits when they wearied of their quiet graves might rise up through the mounds and gaze on the tossing billows, and be refreshed by storms, immensity, liberty, action."

Midway in "Salut au Monde!" occurs an intriguing catalog—an eclectic grouping of deities that illustrates how Whitman adopts Emerson's principle that all religious inspiration stems from a single divine source. Having seemingly mastered time and space, the persona travels back to mythic antiquity where he beholds an array of his avatars—gods, holy men, and bards. In view of the declaration in the 1855 preface that the old order of priests and prophets is destined to be succeeded in America by an order of poets it is hardly surprising that "Salut au Monde!" should depict "the succession of priests on the earth"—the "avatars in human form" in whose line of succession the persona has positioned himself as an oracle and "exhorter." His images of the tragic deaths of the young, manly gods—avatars all—are particularly poignant.

> I see the place of the idea of the Deity incarnated by the
> avatars in human form,
> I see the spots of the successions of priests on the earth,
> oracles, sacrificers, brahmins, sabians, llamas [sic], monks,
> muftis, exhorters,
> I see where druids walked in the groves of Mona, I see the
> mistletoe and vervain,
> I see the temples of the deaths of the bodies of gods, I see the
> old signifiers.[19]

> I see Christ once more eating the bread of his last supper, in
> the midst of youths and old persons,
> I see where the strong young man, the Hercules, toiled
> faithfully and long, and then died,
> I see the place of the innocent rich life and hapless fate of
> the nocturnal son, the full-limbed Bacchus,
> I see Kneph blooming, dressed in blue, with the crown of
> feathers on his head,
> I see Hermes, unsuspected, dying, well-beloved, saying to
> the people, *Do not weep for me,*
> *This is not my true country, I have lived banished from my*
> *true country—I now go back there,*
> *I return to the celestial sphere, where every one goes in*
> *his turn.*

The tragic deaths of these ancient gods prefigure their resurrection. Christ, at his last supper, awaiting the death that will translate him from Man to Living God, appears, surrounded by his disciples, in a tableau possibly inspired by Bertel Thorvaldsen's impressive statuary group *Christ and His Apostles,* to which Whitman was strongly attracted when it was shown at New York's 1853 Crystal Palace Exhibition.[20] The lines describing the classical gods were taken (some nearly verbatim) from Count Constantin Volney's *Ruins, or Meditations on the Revolutions of Empires* (1791), which features representative heroes of various civilizations and faiths. But Whitman reworked this once-popular material to produce a powerful evocation of immortality and transcendence. According to myth, Hercules, the epitome of physical and moral perfection, had been mistakenly presented with a poisoned cloak by his wife, and sensing his impending death he ordered his funeral pyre so that his resurrected spirit could join the other gods on Mount Olympus. Bacchus was the god of grapes and honey whose fermentation and transformation into wine and mead symbolize resurrection, not unlike "the resurrection of the wheat" in "This Compost." And, according to myth, Bacchus (whose picture, along with those of Hercules and the satyr Silenus hung, in Whitman's modest boardinghouse room) is said to have transcended death and returned from his fatal dismemberment stronger than before.[21] Kneph, the blue-colored creator-god of Egyptian myth, was also associated with resurrection. A nineteenth-century French archaeologist explained that Kneph's "journey to the lower hemisphere appears to symbolize the evolution of substances, which are born to die and be reborn." The neo-Platonist Porphyry called Kneph the "creator of the universe"; a father of the Church characterized him as the "Divine intellect, which was the Demiurge of the world, giving life to all things"; and the poet Petrarch called him the "unmade and eternal deity."[22] But it is Hermes, the fabled inventor of the lute and, according to Homer and Hesiod, the patron god of eloquence—the *ur*-poet in the succession of inspired bards—who is the most impressive of these avatars. Hermes is a striking symbol of immortality—a messenger of the gods, who leads the way from life to death. Of him Karl Kerényi says, "It is as a god of Kabeirian mysteries that Hermes is ithyphallic and a guide of souls . . . the messenger and herald between the realm of souls and the realm of the born." The pairing of the phallic figure Hermes and Silenus is said to represent the sources of life, Hermes's "spiritual aspect [co-existing] on friendly terms with the animal-divine aspect" associated with Silenus. Indeed, Hermes's taming of the animal world can be interpreted as the taming of the animal nature within each human being.[23] "Salut au Monde!" calls Hermes "well-beloved." by the people in much the same way that Whitman describes his own persona as "well-beloved, close held by day and night" as he wanders about "the

States," "the stalwart and well-shaped heir" of all predecessor bards.[24] Hermes's allusion in the above passage to "the celestial sphere where every one goes in his turn" is decidedly romantic. For although Greek gods, whenever they chose, could return to the "celestial spheres" that were reserved for their exclusive use, the Greek masses dreaded the prospect of what they believed to be a shadowy, joyless existence in the afterlife.[25] Those "celestial spheres where every one goes *in his turn*" are more compatible with Whitman's or Bryant's democratic imagery of death as the peaceful transition from life than with anything that might have appealed to most ancient Greeks.

The first ten sections of "Salut au Monde!" (in the final edition) are largely composed of anaphoric, first-person lines (more than eighty of them beginning with the words, "I see") in which the persona records his impressions during his far-ranging mental journey. In sections 11 and 12, which conclude the poem, the persona, having circumnavigated the globe, is back on American soil and salutes "all the inhabitants of the earth," seemingly without distinction, and delivers a sermon to them. He extends his democratic greetings to all people—prisoners, scoundrels, "the menials of the earth," slaves and slave masters, helpless women and children, and "the male and female everywhere," although one may sense a touch of Anglo-European pride in his singling out for the highest praise the "brotherhood," "constructiveness," and "industry of my race." He names dozens of lands and cities, wishing their inhabitants "health to you! good will to you all, from me and America sent!" Wherever they may be and whoever they may be, he assures them, they participate in the same essential divinity:

> Each of us inevitable,
> Each of us limitless—each of us with his or her right upon
>     the earth,
> Each of us allowed the eternal purports of the earth,
> Each of us here as divinely as any is here.

Although he proclaims a belief in universal advancement, the persona offers the darker-skinned peoples—including the "uncouth" Bedouins, the "plague-swarms in Madras, Nankin, Kabul, Cairo," Mexican peons, dwellers in the Arctic regions, the "Hottentot with clicking palate," the "wooly-hair'd hordes," and the "human faces with the fathomless ever-impressive countenances of brutes"—only second-class tickets on the cosmic road to perfection. This is most evident in the poem's final version:

> I do not prefer others *so very much* before you either,
> I do not say one word against you *away back there* where
>     you stand,
> You will come forward *in due time* to my side.
>     [emphasis added]

For many centuries theological debates had raged in Europe about the eligibility of non-European peoples to enter into the Kingdom of Heaven. Johann Kaspar Lavater, in his influential *Essays on Physiognomy* (1778), illustrated the idea of racial superiority by sketching faces of non-Europeans that showed a greater brutishness than the faces of Germanic peoples, because, he reasoned, the latter were more closely fashioned in God's image. And although the persona of "Salut au Monde!" seems to make an exception of the "dim-descended, black, divine-souled African . . . superbly destined, on equal terms with me!" (the Noble Savage who was a staple of popular culture), the poem is tainted by nineteenth-century racial attitudes.[26] In assuming that nature advances all peoples—but at different rates—Whitman expresses a view that was sanctioned by the United States government and espoused by many white reformers. Bryant's *New York Evening Post*, nominally a liberal Free-Soil paper, argued that before the Negro could achieve equal status with the whites in the Western States he would have to "take those primary lessons in civilization which his race has never yet mastered" and alleged that "the superior intelligence and advantages of the whites" would block blacks from achieving self-reliance and independence.[27]

Having explored "every shore" as he circled the earth before landing on home territory, the persona, in keeping with the folksy tenor of the 1856 edition, embraces all his "brothers, sisters, lovers" everywhere in the world, declaring that "I find my home wherever there are any homes of man."[28] In the 1860 edition, the poet added the statement, "I think some divine rapport has equalized me with them," thus signaling his democratic empathy with all humanity. And in a four-line stanza added in 1860 the persona sends the peoples of the world a sign that his immortal self will be "in sight forever" to welcome all men and women. Thus the poem that begins with the mesmerist's cry, "O take my hand Walt Whitman!" ends with the persona's high-five gesture—"I raise high the perpendicular hand, I make the signal."

A similar gesture concludes "Song of the Open Road, "in which the persona offers to take the hand of his "eleve," "or "Camerado," in order to launch him or her along the timeless road of existence. Whether it is described as a "public road," a "long brown path" or a city street in this impressive and affecting poem of more than 220 lines, the road is a complex of metaphors for the route that each one must find to achieve self-realization. It leads (in words that prefigure Whitman's "old age poems") toward the "sublime old age of manhood or womanhood . . . flowing free with the delicious near-by freedom of death" and toward spiritual growth. Each journey, we are assured, is unique: "not I—not God—can travel this road for you." Like the "men of subdued minds and conquered passions" described in the Bhagavad Gita, Whitman's "traveling souls" may even aspire to become "godly pilgrims" and enter upon the "never-failing" Brahminic path "that leads to supreme happiness." "The procession of time," as Frederick William Conner explains, "was destined never to arrive at a final resting place, but to be forever on the march, finding a new goal beyond each one attained."[29] Following an episode of spiritual enlightenment that the preternaturally sensitive persona experiences at the beginning of the poem, he discovers that embedded in the road—the macrosymbol for life's path that each of us must choose to pursue—are countless microsymbols, analogous to the flower in the crannied wall or the blade of grass. "From the living and the dead," says the emblem-deciphering persona to the road, "I think you have peopled your impassive surfaces, and the spirits thereof would be evident and amicable with me." Whitman trusts to sensory data to reveal higher truths. "A knowledge of [emblematic material] images," says, Perry Miller, "would be a knowledge not of spiritualized commonplaces but of truth acquired in the only place where, after Locke, it was possible to find it, in sensible experience. To understand the relation of image to truth would be nothing less than to make one's calling and election sure." More bluntly, Jonathan Edwards declared that "EXTERNAL THINGS are intended to be IMAGES of things spiritual and divine."[30] And Whitman's "road" does indeed appear ready to divulge its secrets to the persona through his Kantian double consciousness—his capacity to absorb and to process both practical knowledge and spiritual data. The persona assures those traveling the road that they, too, may eventually learn "to know the universe itself as a road, as many roads, as roads for traveling souls." Once possessed of such knowledge they may even aspire to become enlightened seers. Whitman's road is a palimpsest of possibilities. It may even lead the journeyer on a path to behold the effulgent image of God (like Dante in the *Paradiso*)—to meet Whitman's supreme "Camerado" on equal terms.

Some of the many avenues to self-realization lead to death and beyond. In the poem's second half, the persona emerges once again as a prophetic speaker who relates the truths he has absorbed along the road of his life. He claims to have experienced the elevated state of awareness (like that which Richard Maurice Bucke calls "cosmic consciousness") that allows him to proclaim "the certainty of the reality and immortality of things, and the excellence of things." But this sort of wisdom, the poem cautions, cannot be taught or "passed from one having it to another not having it," because it is "of the soul." Each must discover it alone. Social and material advances along this road are interpreted as harbingers of individual spiritual advancement—"the progress of souls." Conversely, spiritual progress necessarily implies social and material advancement. Nevertheless, even though the persona seems confident that his journey will turn out well, he does not hazard a guess about his destination or about the road's terminus. He does, however, make one of the strongest affirmations in all of *Leaves of Grass* that every soul is indestructible and that it will persevere toward its unfailing destiny:

All parts away for the progress of souls,
All . . . falls into niches and corners before the processions
    of souls along the great roads of the universe.

Of all the progress of the souls of men and women along the
    grand roads of the universe, all other progress is the needed
    emblem and sustenance.
Forever alive, forever forward,
Stately, solemn, sad, withdrawn, baffled, mad, turbulent,
    feeble, dissatisfied,
Desperate, proud, fond, sick, accepted by men, rejected by men,
They go! they go! I know that they go, but I know not where
    they go;
But I know that they go toward the best—toward something
    great.[31]

Like similar affirmations in *Leaves of Grass* that are rooted in personal feelings, the speaker uses the expression "I know" more or less interchangeably with "I feel" or "I dream." Avoiding explanations, dogma, and logic, he is content to be the mystic drummer who leads this hopeful parade along the open road, testing the validity of his assumptions in the alembic of his own feelings.

4

The third poetic journey, "Crossing Brooklyn Ferry," is the masterpiece of the 1856 edition and the only extended depiction of the postmortem persona in *Leaves of Grass*. In the poem the persona hovers above the East River long after he has shed his mortal body, but the reader never learns what sort of "body" he now possesses. Indeed, he seems to be almost a disembodied consciousness, still endowed with the powers of perception, memory, and sympathy. Like the mortal persona, he can still experience beauty, libidinal urges, and a desire for companionship. Yet how this seemingly disembodied entity can experience the thoughts and sensations that scientists tell us are processed by the perishable brain and the nervous and endocrinal systems of mortal beings is never clarified. If the dead no longer have the bodily functions that they had in life, asks a critic of immortality, how can they exercise *physical* memory or experience the same feelings as do the living?[32] And if one's soul could survive without the body, declares the skeptic Corliss Lamont, it would necessarily be deprived of all bodily sensations and functions. The sort of physiologically rooted consciousness exhibited by the persona in "Crossing Brooklyn Ferry," he would argue, cannot exist independent of the (biological) sensory organs. Although the combination of disembodiment and memory, or disembodiment and sensual perception, appears to be unlikely, if not impossible in scientific terms, the disembodied Whitman persona's chief bond to the living in "Crossing Brooklyn Ferry" is precisely his retention of those seemingly unimpaired mental functions. Nevertheless, the poem's premise that one's mortal faculties may be retained following death was consistent with the reasoning of such spiritualists as Andrew Jackson Davis, who declared rather floridly: "Believe not that what is called death is a final termination to human existence, nor that the *change* [from life to death] is so entire as to alter or destroy the constitutional peculiarities of the individual . . . but believe righteously, that death causes as much *alteration* in the condition and situation of the individual as the *bursting* of a rose-bud causes in the condition and situation of a flower."[33] Such vexing inconsistencies of interpretation become moot, however, when we realize that Whitman was not so much concerned with ideology or scientific probability as with projecting the glowing imagery of a scenario of his own perpetual continuity.

The dead persona's retention of his unimpaired mental and emotional faculties is, of course, a masterpiece of wish fulfillment. For *mind* and *soul*, it has been pointed out, are not "substantial" words referring to things that can be objectively demonstrated, but because they are essentially verbal constructs they *can* be imagined and described. And in this sense, they can be conceived and realized by the artist.[34] Whitman's difficulty in portraying a postmortal self and a postmortal milieu was hardly unique. Unlike some religious thinkers, he did not separate his Self into its before-death and its after-death manifestations but stressed the continuity of his personality. The rationale by which he endows the supposedly dead persona with mortal attributes in "Crossing Brooklyn Ferry" is very close to the reasoning of many contemporary spiritualists and religious idealists. "If the religious ideas expressed by many spiritualists tended to dissolve the personality of God," says R. Lawrence Moore, "they had not similar effects on the concept of human individuality. [These concepts] maintained a firm insistence on the uniqueness of the individual soul before and after death."[35]

An intriguing modern interpretation of the sort of consciousness that Whitman attributes to the disembodied persona is contained in John Hick's essay "The Survival of the Disembodied Mind." Hick ventures the idea that one's postmortem perceptions may be comparable to the visions one sees in dreams. Any possible state of consciousness in the afterlife, he conjectures,

> will be mind-dependent, and will be formed out of mental images acquired during one's embodied life. These will include images of one's own body as seen by oneself and of a surrounding material environment. The result will, from the experient's point of view, be the perception of a "real" and solid world in which he exists as a bodily being. The world may however differ from our present world in the kinds of way in which the sequence and arrangement of events in our dreams is liable to differ from that of wak-

ing life by exhibiting on occasion discontinuities and all sorts of sudden elisions and transformations. For the laws of the post-mortem world will not be those of physics but of psychology, since our survival (according to the hypothesis we are considering) will be of a psychological rather than a physical survival.

Hick also conjectures that in such a state the deceased may be able to conjure up images of touch, taste, smell, and even images of the three-dimensional world. The raw materials from which they might fashion mental images, he concludes, are the memories of their mortal selves and of their mortal desires, halfway between "a private-mental-world picture and a bodily-resurrection picture." In cautiously (and apprehensively) applying Hick's speculations about the interaction of the sentient dead with the sentient living (the core motif of "Crossing Brooklyn Ferry") it is well to remember Hick's caveat that postmortal "dreams" can demonstrate only a limited consciousness of life-formed experiences, and (in contradiction to Whitman's assumption that the soul continues to develop through all the stages of its existence) that the souls of the dead have no further options for growth. And even though the shadowy figures beheld in this dream-death might possibly appear to be vivid, Hick warns, they may, after all, be only delusions.[36] Whitman's sentient postmortal persona is essentially a poetic creation, and it may be unwise to expect his version of life beyond death to jibe with any explanation based on logic, theology, or science.

The persona of "Crossing Brooklyn Ferry" is presented as an immortal spirit with a local habitation somewhere above the route of the poet's beloved Fulton Ferry—a reborn and fully conscious inhabitant of an ideal postmortal world.[37] In this elevated state of being, he appears to be visionary and immune to mortal affliction but still endowed with curiosity and compassion and the ability to utter truths. Although ostensibly dead, he retains recognizable mortal characteristics, empathizing with everyone he beholds, longing for followers and lovers, confessing the "dark patches" of misery and doubt that link him to all living men and women, and recalling the affectionate thrill of eying the "young men" in public places and feeling the "negligent leaning of their flesh against me as I sat." In his mortal state, the persona had liked to "sit and look out" at the world and its ways as an observer "both in and out of the game"; and now, in this free-floating state of "psychic migration,"[38] he can still observe, enjoy, and reach out to the living—or at least he can imagine that he is doing so. And because Whitman consistently links his personal identity and his life force to the preservation of his voice (Terry Nathanson has said that Whitman is defined by his voice),[39] the elegance of the (presumably dead) persona's voice is evidence of his enduring identity.

As a meditation on life, death, and immortality "Crossing Brooklyn Ferry" maintains a unity of drama and doctrine. The poem's action, like that of a classic drama, takes place in the span of a single day, from the dawn until the factory fires become visible at night, and it occurs in a limited space over the East River from which the persona observes the ongoing spectacle below him and yearns to convince the living that the qualities that ennoble life also ennoble death. Of immortality Whitman had declared, "that to pass [mortal] existence is supreme over all, and what we thought death is but life brought to a higher parturition."[40] And this is the lesson that the compassionate persona wishes to impart to the living of all generations, to convince them that the emotional tug that drew him to them when he was alive still ties him to them in the "now" of his postmortal state and will remain tied to the living "ever so many generations hence":

> Flood-tide below me! I see you face to face!
> Clouds of the west—sun there half an hour high—I see you also
>     face to face.
>
> Crowds of men and women attired in the usual costumes, how
>     curious you are to me!
> On the ferry-boats the hundreds and hundreds that cross,
>     returning home, are more curious to me than you suppose,
> And you that shall cross from shore to shore years hence are more
>     to me, and more to my meditations, than you might suppose.

The "flood-tide" of mortality, the clouds in the western sky, and the transit of the Charonlike ferry are all images representing the passage from life to death. Beholding the passengers' "curious" costumes, the persona envisions the time when, like him, they will have shed their earthly "costumes" for a more spiritual habiliment. They also appear "curious" to him because he longs to know the destiny of each of "you who shall cross from shore to shore." And may we not assume that, as he writes the poem, the mortal poet remains "curious" about his own postmortal destiny?

Whitman again illustrates the proposition that "a vast similitude interlocks all" in "Crossing Brooklyn Ferry" by enumerating "the similitudes of the past and those of the present." The "impalpable sustenance" that nourished the persona's spirit during his mortal tenure appears to be still nourishing him in his translated state. The sights that inspired him then still "dazzle" his eye—seagulls weaving effortlessly in the air, shimmering waves, colorful boats, and the shifting light patterns in the sky and on the water. Philosophers and poets have often equated truth and beauty, and if they are right, the persona's undiminished sensitivity to beauty would appear to validate the truth of his vision. In his own version of the Great Chain of Being, Emerson remarks that "a man of thought is willing to die, willing to live: I suppose because he sees the thread on which the beads are strung, and perceives that it reaches up and down, existing quite independently of the present illusions."[41] In Whitman's variation of this trope, the sights and sounds of the varied world that the persona sees below him become "glories strung like beads" along the golden chain of being that forever links him to the generations of the living and dead:

> The impalpable sustenance of me from all things at all hours of
>     the day,
> The simple, compact, well-joined scheme, myself disintegrated,
>     every one disintegrated, yet part of the scheme,
> The similitudes of the past and those of the future,
> The glories strung like beads on my smallest sights and hearings,
>     on the walk in the street and the passage over the river,
> The current rushing so swiftly and swimming with me far away,
> The others that are to follow me, the ties between me and them,
> The certainty of others, the life, love, sight, hearing of others.

The river's "current" conveys Whitman's duplex vision of time. To the living, time appears as a series of discrete events. But the presumably immortal persona perceives time not only as we mortals do but also as the eternal and immeasurable flow of the universe. This double perspective permits him to comprehend the limitations of the mortal condition and to reach out to the living while measuring their destinies in terms of infinity. Corliss Lamont points out that the assumption by Platonists,

Buddhists, and Hindus that the soul has a prior existence (like Whitman's "float") enables them "to avoid entrapping the soul in durable time by postulating a pre-existence with no beginning whatsoever."[42] The persona, no longer feeling trapped in "durable time"—since he also exists in another "time" that has no beginning and, presumably, no end—can say to the living that "time nor place—distance avails not, / I am with you, men and women of a generation, or even many generations hence," and he can inspire them by a sort of perpetual spiritual outreach:

> What is more subtle than this which ties me to the woman or
>     man that looks at my face?
> Which fuses me into you now, and pours my meaning into you?

The persona pictures himself infusing his "meaning" into those yet unborn during the "now"—the timeless moment of the poet's imagination or (looked at objectively) the moment when the reader discovers the truth embodied in *Leaves of Grass.* The poem's "now" designates both the moment in which the living poet reaches out to his contemporaries and the eternal "now" in which the persona perpetually inspires future readers. The "now" also constitutes an emotional haven for the poet himself—an imaginary postmortem milieu in which the persona can envision himself serene and free from mortal disappointments.

As he watches the worldly spectacle from above, the persona once again reminds the generations of passengers of his enduring presence: "Consider you who peruse me, whether I may not in unknown ways be looking upon you"; the "you" again encompasses both the mass of humanity and the individual who is reading "Crossing Brooklyn Ferry." As a social critic, Walt Whitman was deeply concerned with what sort of Americans the future would produce. Hence the ectoplasmic persona reminds the yet-unborn generations of Americans that "I considered long and seriously of you before you were born" and that he may be "as good as looking at you now, for all you cannot see me." His declaration that he will continue to be an object of regard for all living generations, who will "look back at me because I look forward to them" is one of several such statements in *Leaves of Grass.*[43] He speaks of "myself disintegrated . . . yet part of the scheme," a condition that should render him visible through an exercise of the creative imagination; yet in this mythic realm of the everlasting "now" his words and his abiding presence seem destined forever to reach out to generations of readers. Even "when he exists in the past tense," says Stephen Railton, "he's very much alive to his readers. This is Whitman's characteristic definition of immortality."[44] According to Stephen A. Black, Whitman conceives of an interlocking literary and personal immortality. "[D]eath seems beautiful to Whitman," Black declares. "The most convincing assurance of immortality Whitman can find accompanies the idea that the poet's soul can merge with the poems and thus outlive his body. . . . At the same time death promises him relief from various guilts about the perversities uncovered during poetic journeys—and so he falls half in love with death's easefulness."[45]

Despite Whitman's characteristic dualism, he wisely avoided describing the mechanism by which the body is joined to, or integrated with, the soul. But, unfortunately, as the coda of the 1856 version of "Crossing Brooklyn Ferry" attests, he yielded for a moment to an unfortunate impulse to explain the linkage between the objective-material world and the subjective-spiritual world. The result, as the following lines testify, is an anomaly.

> We realize the soul by you, you faithful solids and fluids,
> Through you color, form, location, sublimity, ideality,
> Through you every proof, comparison, and all the suggestions
>     and determinations of ourselves.

Superficially, the lines illustrate the familiar principle that a spiritual element inheres in all material things and that each object in the material world is a cryptic indicator of something spiritual. However, a literal reading of these lines reveals that Whitman was toying with the notion that the mind—or, more precisely, the brain—is an alembic that distills (and, by implication, combines) the sensory data derived from the material world and the influxes of spirit. He phrases this conjectured process of assimilation, oddly enough, in terms of the pseudoscience of phrenology. The words *color, form, location, sublimity, ideality,* and *comparison* in the above lines, are all phrenological terms that designate purported segments, or "faculties," of the brain, each "faculty" said to be responsible for processing specific material or immaterial stimuli. Sublimity and ideality were credited by phrenologists with absorbing and transforming influxes of the spirit and intimations of immortality from the raw data of the material world into exalted thoughts, insights, and inspiration. By flirting with the notion that intimations of spirituality and immortality are processed by the brain's phrenological "faculties," Whitman risked falling into a trap like that of Réné Descartes, who, in attempting to integrate material and spiritual elements, had located the soul in the brain's pineal gland. Of course, Whitman may have included these bizarre terms in an effort to placate Fowler and Wells, the covert publishers of the second edition, or because he liked their "scientific" ring. In any case, he had second thoughts about these aberrant lines, eliminating them altogether in 1871.[46] His later poems keep the body-soul connection deliberately vague, essentially by ignoring the role of the body. But in evaluating "Crossing Brooklyn Ferry," this loveliest of lyrical fantasies about personal immortality, it would be capricious to insist on physiological accuracy or ideological consistency.

# 4
## *"So Long!"*
### *Leaves of Grass,* 1860

I

The third edition of *Leaves of Grass* (1860) celebrates death equally with life and, like the second (1856) edition, it can be read as a manual of faith. W. C. Harris proposes that the edition be viewed as a sort of bible, designed to spread Whitman's bracing word in the fashion of the active Bible societies of his day. And, like most editions of the Bible, the poems are divided into numbered sentences rather than stanzas.[1] The exciting drama in which the persona imagines himself dead and happy while his spirit still maintains an empathetic contact with the living (the premise of "Crossing Brooklyn Ferry") resonates in several of the poems that first appeared in this volume. One brief lyric, for example, announces that "death, the future, the invisible faith, shall be conveyed" by a new breed of spirit-mediums who will proclaim throughout the land the abiding personal existence of the departed. And in "Apostroph" (a sixty-five-line poem that appears only in the 1860 edition) Whitman seems tempted to take his place among the teachers of the "invisible faith":

> O mediums! O to teach! to convey the invisible faith!
> To promulge real things! To journey through all The States! . . .
> O purged lumine! you threaten me more than I can stand![2]

The "invisible faith"—a recognizable synonym for spiritualism—is predicated on a belief in the abiding personal existence of the "departed." Whitman seemed pleased to be accepted by the spiritualists as one of their own; in fact, he reprinted a review from the *Christian Spiritualist* that acknowledged his "mediatorial nature," together with Emerson's, and named him among the upcoming "mediums" of the age. Although he attended a séance several years later and dismissed the practice as "humbug,"[3] hints of his affinity to spiritualism are scattered throughout *Leaves of Grass*. Widely popular in America, spiritualism appropriated elements from the teachings of Emanuel Swedenborg, Charles Fourier, popular reform movements, and the "socialist" experiments of the period, and, in turn, exerted a powerful influence on religious and reform movements. Whitman's interest in spiritualism was not unusual, for by 1851 there were an estimated 150 circles in the Brooklyn area.[4] "Modern Spiritualism," said John Humphrey Noyes in 1870, "has been the great American excitation" from which all modern "socialisms" have "debouched." His book *Bible Communism* (1848) defined the chief tenets of "The Age of Spiritualism" and its gospel of "Perfectionism," maintaining that "the world is full of symptoms of the coming of a new era of spiritual discovery," "that man has an invisible organization that is as substantial as his body," and that the world will eventually be governed according to "God's righteousness, and not self-righteousness."[5] In anonymously reviewing his own poems, Whitman (referring to himself in the third person) said that "his scope of life is the amplest of any yet in philosophy. He is the true spiritualist. He recognizes no annihilation, or death, or loss of identity. He is the largest lover and sympathizer that has yet appeared in literature."[6] Like many of the spiritualists, Whitman imagined the possibility of building ideological bridges between intuitive belief and modern science.

A faith in immortality pervades the poem "Unnamed Lands," in which the persona meditates upon the countless millions who have died and disappeared into obscurity through the ages—peoples ranging from those with the "oval countenances, learned and calm" (the ideal Germanic type, according to the pseudoscience of physiognomy) to "the naked and savage" peoples the poet consigns to the end of the evolutionary chain. "Are those billions of men [and women] really gone?" demands the poem. Have their lives been useless? The awkward but uncharacteristically explicit reply stresses his belief that humans carry with them into the afterlife the character and personality that they have developed during their mortal years:

> I believe of all those billions of men and women that filled the
>     unnamed lands, every one exists at this hour, here or elsewhere,
>     invisible to us, in exact proportion to what he or she grew from
>     life, and out of what he or she did, felt, became, loved, sinned,
>     in life.

The persona speculates that these vanished individuals and nations may still exist somehow without having lost their identities: "I suspect their results curiously await in the yet unseen world—*counterparts of what accrued to them in the seen world* [emphasis added]." And he remarks coyly: "I suspect I shall meet them there," the words "I suspect" indicative of a tempered curiosity rather than a certainty concerning what "results" may "curiously await" him in the "unseen world." He is "curious" not only about the relations between the living and his dead self but also about how his altered self will be received by those *he* will meet in the "unseen" realm of death. And may not those dead souls be "curiously" waiting to find out what sort of postmortal Walt Whitman *they* will encounter in the hereafter?

Intimations of immortality and transfiguration are also the theme of "Leaves of Grass" sequence numbers 15 and 16, which illustrate Whitman's tendency to express his belief in an afterlife by drawing an analogy between the glories of the known life and the implied glories of a life to come. In number 15 (later titled "Night on the Prairies") the persona finds himself alone at night, "filled with great thoughts of space and eternity." Awestruck by nature's grandeur, he finds that he is able to "absorb [thoughts of] immortality and peace," to "admire death and test propositions," and to contemplate the possibility of his own blissful death. Relating the wonders he beholds in the evening sky to the wonders he may yet behold in his future existence, he reasons that just as some stars remain invisible to his unaided sight, so there must be splendid undiscovered realms of existence beyond the known life. "O! I see now that life cannot exhibit all to me, as the day cannot," he exclaims; "I see that I am to wait for what is exhibited by death." "Leaves of Grass 16" (later titled "The World below the Brine") compares the brutish "dumb swimmers" and the "sluggish existences" that inhabit the primitive undersea world and the sea change from their world to the superior world of civilized humanity. And then the analogy is extrapolated to indicate the quantum change that he conjectures will occur across the countless eons in the change from mortal existence to the life in "other spheres." In a fragmentary notebook entry that parallels "The World below the Brine," Whitman observes "that our immortality is *located* here upon earth—that we are *immortal*—that the processes of refinement and perfection of the earth are in steps, the least part of which involves trillions of years—that in due time the earth beautiful as it is now will be as proportionately different from what it is now, as it now is proportionately different from what it was in its earlier gaseous or marine period, uncounted cycles before men and women grew. That we shall be here, proportionately different from now and beautiful. That the Egyptian idea of the return of the soul after a certain period involved a beautiful . . . nature . . . mystery."[7]

Whitman speculates about the afterlife in several poems that originated, in whole or in part, during the 1856–1859 period. "Proto-Leaf" (later "Starting from Paumanok"), the long quasi-autobiographical introductory poem of the 1860 edition,[8] notes the personal and ideological "convulsions" that have gone into the shaping of the poet's credo, and it affirms his conviction that there is a spiritual dimension in every aspect of the material world. The poem hints that the material and immaterial (unseen) worlds coexist within a cosmic-spiritual matrix and that both worlds yield clues to the nature of that matrix.

> I will make the poems of materials, for I think they are to be the
>     most spiritual poems,
> And I will make the poems of my body and of mortality,
> For I think I shall then supply myself with the poems of my Soul
>     and of immortality.

From what he conceives to be his central position at the hub of the concentric universes—the seen and the unseen—the persona seemingly absorbs the emanations that flow inward to him from all persons and phenomena and, in turn, enable him to become the spokesman from whom these truths radiate outward. By locating the persona at the center of a boundless and timeless world, the poet makes him an abiding presence in the lives and in the deaths of the men and women of all generations. His centrality and his capacity to perceive and to interpret the cryptic clues embedded in every rock and plant and every mortal creature are his defining attribute in such poems as "Song of Myself" and "Song of the Open Road." He delights in reading the "prophetic spirit of materials shifting and flickering around me, / Wondrous interplay between the seen and unseen . . . Extasy everywhere touching and thrilling me." "Proto-Leaf" records a defining visionary moment during which the persona beholds the successive generations of American "masses" as they "debouch" on the Western lands, "projected through time," and providing "for me an audience interminable." As these "millions" of Americans march past the immortal persona they turn "backwards or sideways toward me to listen, with *eyes retrospective towards me* [emphasis added]."

"Proto-Leaf" stresses Whitman's determination to compose poems of death and immortality that "will show that nothing can happen more beautiful than death," that the quintessence of "the body and the mind . . . adheres and goes forward, and is not dropt by death," and that the interplay of life and death occurs in a "compact" time frame. But indicative of the poet's ongoing effort to define the key terms of his argument, the poem again blurs the distinction between "body" and "soul" and, more critically, between "mind" and "soul." During our mortal span, the poem implies, the body and the soul are coextensive and coterminal, and the body serves as a mirror of the soul:

Was somebody asking to see the Soul?
See! your own shape and countenance—persons, substances,
    beasts, the trees, the running rivers, the rocks and sands . . .
Behold! the body includes and is the meaning, the main
    concern—and includes and *is* the Soul;
Whoever you are! How superb and how divine is your body, or
    any part of it. [emphasis added]

Although Whitman appears to treat the cohabiting soul and body evenhandedly in this rather pantheistic passage, he also implies that this partnership of equals will be terminated at death when the physical body is sloughed off. For the body, which is the seat of physical pleasure, carries the seed of death. The poet who had also assured his readers in "I Sing the Body Electric" that the body *is* the soul here seems to shift his perspective as he informs them, in rather prosaic language, that following their demise the soul will abandon its carnal body to become clad in a "real" body—possibly the insubstantial "astral" body of the spiritualists—while preserving its essential identity and its responsiveness to human stimuli:

Of your real body, and any man's or woman's real body, item for
    item, it will elude the hands of the corpse-cleaners, and pass to
    fitting spheres, carrying what has accrued to it from the moment
    of birth to the moment of death.

A more personalized version of this concept occurs in "To One Shortly to Die," one of the cluster of short "Messenger Leaves" poems. There the tender persona, seated like a priest at the bedside of an unidentified expiring individual, absolves him or her "from all except yourself—*that* is eternal." (My italics stress that it is precisely one's selfhood—one's identity and spiritual essence—that Whitman presumes to be indestructible.) The abandoned body becomes worthless, like the slag that remains after the pure ore has been extracted. But once liberated from the physical body, the persona declares, the soul will persevere in its eternal quest. Whereas some poems had defined the persona's selfhood in terms of the splendid body that coexists with his immortal soul, Whitman now dismisses the body with the contemptuous remark that "the corpse you will leave will be but excrementious." Nevertheless, he assures the dying person that "there is nothing to be commiserated" about dying. Displaying the celebrated Whitman bedside manner that will manifest itself in the military hospitals during the war years, the persona congratulates the dying person because "I am with you" as the "sun bursts through in unlooked-for directions." These words seem to hint that the persona (like the god Hermes) is well acquainted with spirit-journeys from life to death. In the course of *Leaves of Grass* he makes, or imagines that he makes, several such excursions.

"A Song of Joys" is a virtual piñata of the "joys" that the persona, or Whitman himself, has experienced directly or vicariously—each "joy" accorded a separate stanza. Throughout the poem the persona rejoices in his sense of infinitude and his conviction that his immortal soul is always gleaning spiritual satisfactions. (In lines added to the poem in 1871, the persona even anticipates "[p]rophetic joys of better, loftier love's ideals, the divine wife, the sweet, eternal, perfect comrade.")[9] But the poem also illustrates how the persona thrills to the scenes of the violent death that he conjures up, like those of the "mashed fireman" and the deadly naval battle in "Song of Myself." In "A Song of Joys" he relives such brutal moments as those of "the strong-brawned fighter . . . thirsting to meet his opponent"; "soldiers dying in battle without complaint"; "the savage taste of blood" and the "gloat[ing] so over the wounds and death of the enemy"; the "joys" of imagining the wounded whale's agony during a whale hunt, when it feels "a lance driven through his side, pressed deep, turned in the wound." The persona's "joys" range from those of the violent aggressor to the bittersweet and masochistic "joys" of victims and martyrs. He seems to relish imagining how "men die and fall and not complain!"; "the joy of suffering . . . popular odium, death, face to face! / To mount the scaffold, to advance to the muzzles of guns with perfect nonchalance! / To be indeed a God!" This array of purported joys implies that to savor life fully he must exclude no experience, neither shame nor pain, neither rejection nor ignominy, nor the ecstasies of a dying god, nor death itself. But the supreme "joy," the poem stresses, is meditating on death and imagining the feeling of one's soul being liberated from the constraints of mortality: The following lines, although couched in general terms, depict a joyous epiphany in which the persona anticipates the moment of dying, when his physical satisfactions will give way to the pure delights of the soul. Like the aborted passage in "Crossing Brooklyn Ferry," the following explanation (or revelation) of the interaction between body and soul contains trace elements of spiritualism and the "mental science" of phrenology:

> O the joy of my Soul leaning poised on itself—receiving identity
>     through materials, and loving them—observing characters and
>     loving them;
> O my Soul, vibrated back to me, from them—from facts, sight,
>     hearing, touch, my phrenology, reason, articulation, comparison,
>     memory and the like;
> O the real life of my senses and flesh, transcending my senses
>     and flesh;
> O my body, done with materials—my sight, done with my
>     material eyes;
> O what is proved to me this day, beyond cavil, that it is not my
>     material eyes which finally see,
> Nor my material body which finally loves, walks, laughs, shouts,
>     embraces, procreates.

A feeling of well-being "of my senses and flesh" seems to convince the persona that his soul is well prepared for its mystical transcendence. He imagines the moment of his death when, "done with my material eyes" and, "done with materials," he can look at the world through the eyes of his spirit. ("From the [mortal] eyesight," says the 1855 preface, "proceeds another eyesight.") Then (like the dead person in "To Think of Time"),

he will look down on his discarded corpse by means of his spiritual eye-
sight.

> O Death!
> O the beautiful touch of Death, soothing and benumbing a few
> moments, for reasons;
> O that of myself, discharging my excrementious body, to be
> burned, or rendered to powder, or buried,
> My real body doubtless left to me for other spheres,
> My voided body, nothing more to me, returning to the
> purification, further offices, eternal uses of the earth.

The phrase "for reasons" recurs a dozen times in *Leaves of Grass* and al-
ways indicates that something mysterious, something not subject to logic
or scientific proof, is happening. But despite all the poetic fervor in the
above lines, the poet shows signs that he is not fully convinced by his own
vision of death and transfiguration. By qualifying his assertion that his
"real body" will be preserved for "other spheres" with the word *doubtless,*
he still appears to be steeling himself against those persistent doubts that
the ultimate victory of his "impregnable" soul may be only a joyous dream.

2

None of the poems added to the 1860 edition mirror Whitman's fascina-
tion with death with the sweep and emotional intensity of "Out of the
Cradle Endlessly Rocking" and "As I Ebb'd with the Ocean of Life."
"Out of the Cradle Endlessly Rocking" is framed as a "reminiscence" in
which the persona perpetually relives, or reimagines that he relives, his
portentous adolescent initiation into the mysteries of life and death that,
in turn, inaugurated his career as a poet. This Wordsworthian myth-
poem relates how the wondrous boy, the avatar of the bardic Whitman,
magically absorbs the secrets of Eros and Thanatos and is thus initiated
as America's poet of death. Robert D. Faner has called it "an opera with-
out music," its verbal recitatives and arias influenced by Italian opera;
and, like many melodramatic operas, it is a story of love, separation, and
death.[10] A lyrical prologue re-enacts the boy-persona's emergence from
the amniotic world of his mother's womb, his being "struck from the
float" of the genetic pool of life, and his setting forth in the month of

May—the late springtime that marks the divide between childhood and adolescence—to examine the wonder-filled world around him. (As it does in "The Sleepers," the amniotic imagery suggests that the entire poem takes place in a world of fantasy or dreams.)

The emotions of the "outsetting bard" are awakened by the lush and rhythmic song of the nesting he-bird. The wonder child (or the reminiscing middle-aged persona into whom he has developed) translates the song that the bird sings to his mate into a carol of joyous love and, later, translates the song the bird sings after the disappearance of his mate into a carol of "unsatisfied love" that reverberates with grief and lamentation.[11] The poem thus builds upon a venerable literary tradition. From the ancient Greeks to Whitman's contemporaries, poets treated birdsong as the encoded voice of nature to whose meanings the poet alone is privy. In the 1880s, an English reviewer observed that "Shelley's skylark pours forth harmonious madness of joy, Keats's nightingale seems to be intoxicated with passionate yearning, but never before has a bird poured forth to a poet a song so capable of stirring the depths of emotions in the heart, so heart-breaking indeed in its intensity of grief, as that of the lone singer 'on the prong of a moss-scalloped stake, down among the slapping waves.'"[12] The persona recalls (or imagines) that even as a child he had identified his own latent song with the song issuing from the bird's "trembling throat," for he addresses the bird as a "demon, singing by yourself—projecting me." In later editions he speaks of "demon or bird." For the bird is his inspirational "demon"—the voice of nature sent to awaken his poetic powers. As Padraic Colum pointed out, "Whitman surely was aware when he gave that strange name to the bird that the demon in tradition is the spiritual power beyond our own soul that prompts to extraordinary manifestations."[13] And it is in reference to this "demonic" power that the boy-persona addresses the bird:

Bird! (then said the boy's Soul,)
Is it indeed toward your mate you sing? or is it mostly to me?
For I, that was a child, my tongue's use sleeping,
Now that I have heard you,
Now in a moment I know what I am for—I awake,
And already a thousand singers—a thousand songs, clearer, louder, and more sorrowful than yours,
A thousand warbling echoes have started to life within me,
Never to die.

Once again Whitman overlays time frames so that the magic moment of the man-child's awakening coincides with the moment when the adult poet-persona is inspired to write this poem of love and death. He interprets the mockingbird's songs of love and mourning, "the meanings of which I, of all men, know" and "have treasured every note," as nature's sanction to write poems of love and loss. Nevertheless, the wonder child (or the man he becomes) realizes that the bird's song can furnish only a part of the lesson that he must learn if he is to "utter" great poems of life and death. The child-persona becomes aware that if he is to become a poet whose words encompass death and immortality, nature has yet to grant him the "the word final—superior to all." The poem's original title, "A Word out of the Sea," highlights the fact that not until the man-child receives that longed-for "word out of the sea," seemingly spoken to him alone by the sea-mother, can he be initiated into the mysteries that will enable him to become the vatic poet whose music resonates with the mysteries of life and death. And the mature Whitman, contrasting his own work to that of his contemporary versifiers who wrote "tearful harp or glib piano" tunes about life's superficies, did indeed consider himself to be such a cosmic poet.[14] The bird's lament seemingly imparts the mysteries of love and grief to the Long Island wonder child. But before he becomes eligible to evolve into America's master poet, he has to be initiated into the knowledge of death. As he stands at the sea's brink beneath a "yellow and sagging moon" that seemingly sympathizes with "the sweet hell" within his bosom, he feels a frustrated awareness that something is lacking to complete his knowledge, an "unknown want" that will reveal "the destiny of me." He is eager to feel the erotic thrill and the joyous terror of the forbidden world of death. Hence he cries out to the sea,

> O give me some clew!
> O if I am to have so much, let me have more!

Time and space become conflated at this moment, for "the dusky demon aroused" in the youth's imagination on the Long Island shore has yet to reveal the "clew" that still "lurks in the night *here* somewhere." (That last phrase—emphasis added—occurs in the 1881 edition, when "demon" was changed to the more obvious "messenger.") The locus of the *here* is not a defined point, since it may allude to the mature poet's never-ending struggle to interpret the sea's "lurking" clue and the still impenetrable mystery of death.[15] Hence the poet conjures up the scene in which his youthful self stands by the seashore and beseeches the "old crone," the amniotic ocean of life, the sea goddess of creation and destruction, to give him the ultimate word, the "word, final, superior to all," that he hopes will unlock the mysteries. And, miraculously, that word is seemingly vouchsafed to him as the sea whispers "the low and delicious word DEATH / And again Death—ever Death, Death, Death."

The boy-persona has imagined that he hears the sea intone the cryptic word *death,* thus seemingly granting him—and the poet—the clue to the most profound of nature's mysteries. But an important passage in the 1859–1860 version of "Out of the Cradle Endlessly Rocking," which was later deleted, differs significantly from the poem's final revision by clearly articulating the persona's inability to construe the sea's "message." Haunted by the fear that what he has seen and heard may be only an illusion, and doubtful that he has made contact with the true voice of nature or that he has comprehended the sea's runic message—if, indeed, there ever was such a message—he implores the sea to grant him a further clue to what he has supposedly seen and heard:

> O a word! O what is my destination?
> O I fear it is henceforth chaos!
> O how joys, dreads, convolutions, human shapes, and all shapes,
>     spring as from graves around me!
> O phantoms! you cover all the land, and all the sea!
> O I cannot see in the dimness whether you smile or frown
>     upon me;
> O vapor, a look, a word! O well-beloved!
> O you dear women's and men's phantoms![16]

These excluded lines may reflect Whitman's depressed mood in the late 1850s. If so, they imply that the mature poet-persona still fears that such clues as the "message out of sea" may be only deceptive "phantom" clues to the mystery of existence. At this juncture the beleaguered persona appeals to the "dear women's and men's phantoms," the shapes in the dimness that "spring as from graves around me." If the "phantoms" are not mere illusions, could they possibly be the vision of spirit messengers of the dead vainly trying to impart the secrets of the grave and the meaning of death to this "outsetting bard"? In this context, the lines that follow (in all editions) voice the persona's passionate appeal to the sea and to the dear "phantoms" to reveal death's final secret:

> A word then, (for I will conquer it,)
> The word final, superior to all,
> Subtle, sent up—what is it?—I listen;
> Are you whispering it, and have been all the time, you sea-waves?
> Is that it from your liquid rims and wet sands?

In the poem's original version, the sea's utterance of the ambiguous word *death* in reply to the man-child's plea for "the key, the word up from the waves" occurs when the persona is experiencing his worst fear—the fear that his ultimate "destination" may indeed be "henceforth chaos" and a meaningless death. Read in the light of the poem's final version, this ambiguous passage in which the sea reiterates the word *death* may easily be interpreted as a confirmation of the persona's faith that death embodies the promise of renewal and perpetuity. However, the use of the present tense in the line, "Are you whispering it, and have been all the time, you sea waves?" intimates that the adult poet-persona is still trying—and will forever try—to decipher the sea's message. In 1881, when Whitman was intent on being recognized as the poet of "heavenly death," he canceled the troublesome 1860 passage about his feared "destination," thus giving the poem a positive slant.

The man-child's demand for a further clue seemingly elicits the sea's intimate answer, couched in lines of supernal beauty that rock to the very rhythm of the sea. Eros and Thanatos seem to merge in the sea's imagined response, which is accompanied by the gentle waves that provide the persona with a measure of adolescent bliss (heightened in the later version in which the sea "laves" him all over):

> Answering the sea,
> Delaying not, hurrying not,
> Whispered me through the night, and very plainly before
>   daybreak,
> Lisped to me constantly the low and delicious word DEATH . . .
> But edging near, as privately for me, rustling at my feet
> And creeping thence steadily up to my ears,
> Death, Death, Death, Death, Death.

The adult persona appears to relive the child's mysterious initiation as all "through the night" of his dreams and memories he hears the sea "hissing" and "lisping" the word *death*. Nevertheless, the sea's answer remains shrouded in vagueness, since it can be understood as either terrifying or comforting. The sea's language, it has been suggested, was never meant to be intelligible speech in the first place, but rather nature's *ur*-speech or the pre-language with which nature communes with transcendental minds like that of the nascent poet-persona.[17] As such it remains open to a broad range of interpretations and conjectures.

The 1860 version of "Out of the Cradle Endlessly Rocking" illustrates the persona's recurrent doubts concerning his ability to understand death. As Richard Chase observes, the poem "begins with the sense that all life is a mode of death, and flowers with the perception that all imagination is a mode of our sense of death." Hence, Chase reasons, there can be only one answer to the demands of the boy's soul for a "clue" to life and inspiration.[18] The poem's argument does indeed appear to be circular, since for Whitman death pervades everything. Readers of the poem's final version may reasonably conclude that by "absorbing" the bird's song and the sea's whispered word the boy-persona has been initiated—and through him the poet-persona is perpetually being initiated—into death's mystery. "My own songs awakened from that hour," declares the persona retrospectively of the moment of cosmic enlightenment when the sea seemingly repeated "the low and delicious word DEATH" and launched his career as a singer of "clearer, louder, more sorrowful" songs. David Kuebrich interprets the word from the sea as an indirect communiqué from God or Heaven, so that the sea's mystic word can be read as a confirmation of the persona's faith that death implies an afterlife of the soul.[19] Still, we can only wonder whether the enchanted boy—or the cosmos-poet, for that matter—ever fully comprehends what the sea means by its runic whispers of the word *death*. If the poet, or the poet-persona, knows he withholds the secret from the reader.[20] The repeated "word out of the sea" remains only a faint clue that the mature bard (at least in the poem's final version) chooses to interpret as an invitation to probe ever deeper into the mystery of death. Stephen A. Black explains that the reiterated word *death* that the man-child seems to hear all through the night "takes on some of the quality of what psychoanalysts call 'magic words,' words that give their speaker a sense of omnipotence and the illusion that he controls the thing named."[21] So that even if the "word out of the sea" remains cryptic and ultimately indecipherable, the persona can still find comfort because his imagined communion with the heart of nature has provided him with a buffer against the terror of death.

The passage excluded from "Out of the Cradle Endlessly Rocking" links that poem to "As I Ebb'd with the Ocean of Life," the eloquent depiction of a crisis in which the persona is again overcome by the fear that his faith may be meaningless and that he has deluded himself into thinking that he can ever hope to translate nature's words.[22] The persona's profound alienation culminates when his despair brings him to the brink of physical death. This experience, however, is followed by intimations of his recovery and his ultimate transcendence. The persona, as Black points out, hears "incompatible voices" of doubt and affirmation, those that articulate "the idea that the self is immortal and infinite" and those that affirm that "the knowledge that the self exists in nature and is, according to all rational evidence, mortal and finite."[23] The persona's conflicting feelings of hope and gloom—and Whitman's unsettled doubts about penetrating nature's mysteries—are mirrored in the titles that Whitman gave the poem. Its final title "As I Ebb'd with the Ocean of Life" clearly implies despair and waning hope. Yet the poem originally appeared in the *Atlantic Monthly* in 1859 with the hopeful title "Bardic Symbols," identifying Bard Whitman as a decipherer of nature's clues. As if to confirm the poem's positive orientation, Whitman made it the lead poem in the upbeat "Leaves of Grass" sequence in the 1860 edition. In 1867, he retitled the poem "Elemental Drifts"—a sort of metaphysical pun that expresses the persona's desire to "impress others" with his mastery of the cryptogrammic "drifts" that pervade the universe.[24] Moreover, the poem's ending implies that even after its speaker has endured an agonizing disconnect with nature, and after he has abased himself to the level of elemental sand and ooze, he still aspires to translate the sea's mysterious hymns of death.

The sterile landscape pictured at the beginning of this "auto-elegy"[25] serves as the objective correlative of the persona's devastated mood. On an "autumn day" he walks endless miles along the barren Long Island seashore and (in another example of the pathetic fallacy) hears what he interprets to be the sea's "sobbing dirge" for the dead, for the empty lives of his fellow beings, and also for the cooling of his own inspirational fire. He is wracked by the fear that his words no longer stem from his creative selfhood but reveal only a hollowness at the core of his being and a severed contact with the universe. He fears that the sea no longer "rustles" at his feet to reassure him, but, having ebbed, "the fierce old mother" only cries for her "castaways." The detritus thrown upon the barren shore and the windrows of capriciously driven sand seem to mimic his sense of divorcement from nature. He feels a tug-of-war between his "eternal self" and "the spirit that trails in the lines underfoot"—grim indicators of his quest to find meaning in an ostensibly meaningless universe. While struggling against despair, unwilling to concede that his life is purposeless, he walks the desolate shore "with that eternal self of me, seeking types" and "likenesses," which are his spiritual counterparts, analogs of what he labeled the "vast similitude that interlocks all" and that he later calls "eidolons."[26] But he remains "fascinated" (that is, hypnotized) and depressed by his grim surroundings, still seeking a clue to confirm his hope that his life is meaningful. But nature offers no intelligible clue. The "impalpable" sea breeze seems devoid of inspirational afflatus. The sea's "dirge" sounds like "the voices of men and women wrecked." He feels spiritually dead, "baffled, balked . . . oppressed with myself that I have dared to open my mouth," and terrified at the thought that the "blab" of his "insolent" (later changed to "arrogant") poems may not have emanated from his true self. Like a Byronic hero, he cries out that nature is "taking advantage" of him, that the winds are mocking him with their "distant ironical laughter . . . till I fall helpless upon the sand . . . because I was assuming so much, / And because I have dared to open my mouth to sing at all." Unable to understand anything he sees or touches, he is reduced to seeking a kinship with the sea's lowly "bubbles" and the "little washed-up drift of the sea."

Brought to the verge of existential death by his crisis of faith in this seemingly inert world of nature's castoffs—a world of virtual death—he is almost willing to concede that nature's awesome powers and seeming uncaringness have defeated him. Yet he cannot do so, for he feels a kinship even with these "lowliest shreds," these "little corpses" of the sea's jetsam. He cannot bring himself to surrender, for he sees these "elemental drifts" or "types" as "likenesses" of himself, sharing the divinity that exists within him and inspiring his faith in a meaningful universe. And so he utters a childlike prayer to be permitted once again to hear the clear voice of nature:

You oceans both! You tangible land! Nature!
Be not too rough with me—I submit—I close with you,
These little shreds shall, indeed, stand for all.[27]

Having abased himself by identifying with the lowliest objects, he entreats "fish-shaped" Father Paumanok (Long Island personified) to bestow a paternal kiss that will reconnect him with nature and permit him to inhale the breath of inspiration and to decipher "the secret of the wondrous murmuring I envy, / For I fear I shall become crazed if I cannot emulate it, and utter myself as well as it." Many scholars have identified Father Paumanok with Whitman's own father, whose daily kiss "onward from childhood" is memorialized in "Starting from Paumanok" and whose body had lain moldering in the Long Island earth since *Leaves of Grass* first appeared. If we assume that Father Paumanok represents Father Whitman, then may he not be imagined as a Lazarus figure who, the persona hopes, will "breathe" to his poetic soul the secrets from beyond the grave?

However glum his mood, the persona cannot surrender his faith that the sea will once again restore the inspiration that will enable him to become nature's intermediary voice for suffering humanity ("me and mine"):

> Ebb, ocean of life, (the flow will return,)
> Cease not your moaning, you fierce old mother,
> Endlessly cry for your castaways—but fear not, deny not me,
> Rustle not up so hoarse and angry against my feet, as I touch you,
>     or gather from you.
>
> I mean tenderly by you,
> I gather for myself, and for this phantom, looking down where we
>     lead, and following me and mine.

Even in this state of despair, he clings to his faith in the ultimate goodness of existence and his faith that from this world of seeming death there must emerge a possible resurrection. And this would-be interpreter of nature's symbols perceives nature vouchsafing a seeming response to his pleas: The prismatic ooze issuing from his mouth and staining the bleak shore is a token that his radiant words will endure.

> (See! from my dead lips the ooze exuding at last!
> See—the prismatic colors, glistening and rolling!)

Ultimately, he interprets the sea's message, "buoyed hither from many moods, one contradicting another"—and thus mirroring his own moods—

to mean that beneath the seeming turbulence and chaos of life there exists an undercurrent of hope and transcendence. Just as sea casts up its jetsam of despair, so she casts up tokens of hope, such as a "limp blossom or two." (In "Song of Myself," we may recall, the persona expresses his enduring hopefulness by wearing a two-thousand-year-old blossom in his hat.)

> Musing, pondering, a breath, a briny tear, a dab of liquid or soil;
> Up just as much out of fathomless workings fermented and thrown,
> A limp blossom or two, torn, just as much over waves floating,
> drifted at random;
> Just as much for us that sobbing dirge of Nature,
> Just as much, whence we come, that blare of cloud-trumpets.

In this brightened mood the persona chooses to interpret the "sobbing dirge of nature" as compassionate music that hints that nature is ultimately concerned about her children. And those "cloud-trumpets" that seem to have originated "whence we come"—that is, from the heart of nature—betoken life's perpetual parturitions of the living and the dead; their hopeful sound is also the objective correlative of a "force within" and of the persona's inextinguishable faith.[28] Compare "The Mystic Trumpeter" (1872), in which the speaker asks an unseen celestial trumpeter to "sing my soul, renew its languishing faith and hope," and to play "hymns to the universal god from universal man." Nevertheless, at the conclusion of "As I Ebb'd with the Ocean of Life" the persona has not yet overcome his fears that nature's signals may be mixed, and so he utters a final prayer for reassurance to an unknown, and possibly capricious, god or world-force, humbling himself like a bit of sea-chaff tossed on a barren shore: "Whoever you are—we too lie in drifts at your feet," he says.[29]

### 3

The 1860 *Leaves of Grass* introduces two memorable sequences of love poems. "Enfans d'Adam" (later "Children of Adam") is a group of sensuous lyrics centered on the persona's heterosexual reproductive drive. "Calamus," which includes some of the most self-probing lyrics that Whitman wrote, is a sequence of moving homoerotic poems marked by a profound undercurrent of introspection and pervaded by thoughts of death.

The principal motif of "Children of Adam" is that of species continuity. When the Word becomes Flesh, Hegel declares, the individual is born, and that is the beginning of the individual "finitude." And when the individual dies that "finitude" ceases and he becomes part of the universal *zoe*. The historian of religion Karl Kerényi makes a similar distinction between the two concepts of mortal existence: the *bios* life, by which term he refers to the individual life that terminates with death, and the *zoe* life—the unbroken thread of existence that runs through the *bios* life of a species but is not terminated with the death of an individual.[30] In "Children of Adam," the *zoe*-force, the agency of species continuity that connects the generations, is manifested in the Adam persona by what he calls "the semen of centuries." This mysterious electrical essence courses through the veins of the poems' idealized breeder, firing him with the urge to mate with "athletic" and sexually charged women in order to create an ideal progeny of Whitman-Adams and their athletic Eves. He conditions himself for the ideal fatherhood needed to perpetuate the "immeasurably long" species life and to perpetuate his soul according to the rules propounded by the physiological and sexual reformers of the day.

> After me, vista!
> O, I see life is not short, but immeasurably long;
> I henceforth tread the world, chaste, temperate, an early riser,
>     a gymnast, a steady grower,
> Every hour the semen of centuries—and still of centuries.[31]

The Victorian novelist and essayist Samuel Butler remarked wryly that a chicken is merely an egg's way of creating another egg. By transmitting "the semen of centuries," Whitman-Adam, the heir designate of the primal Adam, becomes, in turn, the avatar and the *zoe*-transmitter of future Adams. "Children of Adam" highlights Whitman's belief that the sexual drive coexists with the urge for spiritual transcendence, and that the two seemingly disparate urges nurture one another. His *zoe*-continuity thus becomes the instrumentality of spirit-continuity.

In the first "Children of Adam" poem (later titled "To the Garden the World") the Adam persona, "anew ascending" and resurrected after his "slumber" of five thousand years by "the revolving cycles, in their wide sweep," reenters the garden of this world, the "quivering fire" of his sexuality burning within him, "for reasons, most wondrous." This image of

Whitman-Adam as the successor to, and a possible reincarnation of, the Biblical Adam was not unprecedented. A seventeenth-century Muggletonian tract—reprinted in the nineteenth century—relates that a London commoner in 1650 declared himself "to be God Almighty, and that he was the Judge of the Quick and the Dead; and that [like the persona of the 'Children of Adam' poems] he was the first *Adam* that was in that innocent State, and that his Body had been Dead this Five Thousand Six Hundred and odd Years; and now he was risen again from the Dead, And that he was that *Adam Melchisadek* who met *Abraham* on the Way and received Tithes of him."[32] Although Whitman-Adam is accompanied by his Eve in this poem, his mating urge throughout this suite of poems is not directed at any specific flesh-and-blood woman but to a generic female mate—an amorphous sexual other. Nor does the Adam persona's declared sexual appetite for women necessarily reflect that of the poet himself who, in the words of his younger companion Peter Doyle, was never "bothered up by a woman." Indeed, the Adam persona's urge to inseminate women illustrates the antic, and strikingly sexist, eighteenth-century notion that the semen contains a fully formed microcosmic human being that "unfolds" during pregnancy, while the ovum essentially supplies the nutriment to nurture it.[33] In "A Woman Waits for Me" ("Enfans d'Adam" 4) the persona, posing as "the robust husband" of legions of impregnable women, praises "the deliciousness" of his sex drive and anticipates "perfect men and women out of my love-spendings," the latter term a euphemism for the seminal discharge. He vows to engender "bully breeds of children yet" upon generations of women who are "athletic in their own right." Henry C. Wright, a well-known marriage "clinician" and reformer, explained the principle thus: "Progress, not pleasure is our aim . . . the purest enjoyment is indeed designed to be experienced in intercourse when prompted solely by love and desire for offspring." Similarly, in a flurry of imagery the persona explains that his "madness amorous" and his phallic exertions are intended to bestow, distill and infuse entire "pent-up rivers of myself" in some undifferentiated female "you" in order to beget the babies who, in their turn, will mature and give birth to the sort of "perfect men and women" that America sorely needs. Although Whitman would later question whether America lacked "the gift of perfect women fit for thee . . . the mothers fit for thee,"[34] he fashioned the Adam persona as a sort of deathless ("unchanged") *zoe*-god, who forever wanders the nation seeking eligible and willing mates in whom to implant the primal *zoe*-seed of ideal manhood and womanhood and of species and personal immortality. His Adamic quest for ideal sexual partners seemingly transcends generations and eras. No eligible woman appears to be safe from the lust of this mythic sexual athlete:

> Death indifferent—Is it that I lived long since? Was I buried
>   very long ago?
> For all that, I may be watching you here, this moment;
> For the future, with determined will, I seek—the woman of
>   the future,
> You, born years, centuries after me, I seek.

Throughout the "Enfans d'Adam" poems the persona's "mystic deliria" links his "spermatic" urge to his creative urge; and, not surprisingly, his seminal discharge becomes a trope for his powers of utterance. Whitman underscores this linkage in a notebook entry that declares that a new American literature "can only be generated from the seminal freshness and proportion of new masculine persons," such as his idealized self.[35] Similarly, while the Adam persona is in the throes of sexual passion, he aspires to contact the world of the spirit. Like many modern poets who have followed his lead, Whitman portrays sexual ecstasy as a foretaste and a possible concomitant of spiritual transcendence. The persona yearns (whether in this life or the next):

> To ascend—to leap to the heavens of love indicated to me!
> To rise thither with my inebriate Soul![36]

And he thrills at the thought of being physically dead and disembodied and yet, in some new manifestation of himself, feeling the excitement of making passionate love to a mortal woman.

The forerunner of "Calamus," a group of forty-five intimate love poems, was an unpublished "cluster" of a dozen love poems, collectively titled "Live Oak, with Moss," vaguely resembling an Elizabethan sonnet sequence. Whitman dispersed these verses, which have been called the "proto-leaf" of the "Calamus" poems, throughout the published version of the "Calamus" suite, apparently to soften or to disguise their overt homosexuality.[37] The extent to which these love poems also function as poems of death is borne out by an intriguing notebook entry: "A Cluster of Poems, Sonnets expressing the thoughts, pictures, aspirations, &c / To be perused during the days of the approach of Death." A basic assumption of the "Calamus" poems is that the love of comrades—which Whitman also calls *"fraternite"* or "adhesive" love—will somehow bridge the gap between the present life and the unknown and wished-for life. "Adhesive" love implies a blending of brotherhood, (male) sexual love, and pure affection, often culminating (for the persona, at least) in a mystic experience.[38] Whitman's pairing of love and death in a vague ambiance of spirituality has obvious affinities to certain tendencies in Romantic literature or opera. However, unlike these art forms, in which the object of the persona's desire is some well-defined man or woman, "Calamus" portrays the persona's love perturbations without once describing a lover or "significant other" and rarely hinting at the lover's response to the persona's overtures. Some "Calamus" poems record the persona's attempts to resolve his recurring doubts about immortality by linking love and death. Always reluctant to concede that death could mean spiritual extinction, he again invokes the tautological argument that immortality must exist because he and so many of his fellow humans yearn for it. Had not Immanuel Kant proposed that God offers immortality to mankind in order "to secure the happiness which their moral nature demands," and that the great moral law—Kant's categorical imperative—demands immortality for its proper fulfillment?[39] Still, despite its affirmations, "Calamus" also depicts several crises of faith. For example, the crisis described in "Calamus 7" ("Of the Terrible Doubt of Appearances") is comparable to that in "As I Ebb'd with the Ocean of Life" in which the persona acknowledges that from his "present point of view" he can see "only apparitions and the real something has yet to be known." "Calamus 7" expresses his fear that the ever-shifting nature of appearances threatens to destroy his faith:

> . . . the uncertainties after all,
> That may-be reliance and hope are but speculations after all,
> That may-be identity beyond the grave is a beautiful fable only.

But rather than address this crisis of faith in ideological terms, the persona bypasses any theoretical discussion by declaring himself "indifferent" to death and "satisfied" with things as they are because "He ahold of my hand has completely satisfied me." This quasi-sexual clasp of hands seems to trigger a mystical moment that "satisfies" the persona and allays his doubts about death and reality. A similar conjunction of Eros and Thanatos occurs in "Calamus 17" ("Of Him I Love Day and Night"). There, having dreamt that his lover was reported dead, the persona searches throughout the land for the lover's burial place, finding only empty houses filled with spiritually dead beings. If he were to lack faith in a meaningful existence, he concedes, he, too, would be one of the living dead. And viewing this landscape covered with graves, he belittles the significance of formal burial sites. In midcentury America, architecturally designed cemeteries filled with elaborate monuments to the dead had become icons of popular culture. But the persona appears willing to spurn cemeteries and to leave his own body" to the "corpse-cleaners," trusting that his soul will persevere no matter how his body is disposed of. In lines reflecting his certainty of the postmortem destinies of himself and his lover, he declares:

> And if the memorials of the dead were put up indifferently
>     everywhere, even in the room where I eat or sleep, I should be
>     satisfied,
> And if the corpse of one I love, or if my own corpse, be duly
>     rendered to powder, and poured into the sea, I shall be satisfied,
> Or if it be distributed to the winds, I shall be satisfied.[40]

For if death is latent in every phase of life, he reasons, so must the promise of life be latent in death. Ironically, three decades after writing these lines, when his own death was near, the poet ordered a costly mausoleum for himself and his family in Camden's Harleigh Cemetery.

In some "Calamus" poems the persona fancies that *Leaves of Grass*—the book itself, or even the "Calamus" lyrics—will become an embodiment of his imperishable self and serve as his passport to immortality. "Calamus 3" ("Whoever You Are Now Holding Me in Hand") declares that the persona's spirit has been transmuted into *Leaves of Grass* but cautions the reader against presuming to penetrate his final mystery by reading his printed words. In a vivid, and possibly orgasmic, fantasy, he conjures up the picture of a rendezvous with an unknown reader when he or she is alone with a copy of *Leaves of Grass* and a postmortem manifestation of the Whitman self, as a passionate bisexual lover of men and women, suddenly springs from the pages of the book to embrace the reader. Savoring the encounter as though it were occurring at the present moment, the persona cries out,

> Here put your lips upon mine I permit you,
> With the comrade's long-dwelling kiss, or the new husband's kiss,
> For I am the new husband and I am the comrade.

Stimulated by the thought that love and death will remain intertwined throughout the soul's timeless existence, the persona playfully conjures up an alternative fantasy of postmortem spiritual affinity and sexual intimacy in which *Leaves of Grass*—the mystic embodiment of the poet—is nestled against the warm flesh of a reader who loves him for his self and for his book:

> Or, if you will, thrusting me beneath your clothing,
> Where I may feel the throbs of your heart, or rest upon your hip,
> For thus, merely touching you, is enough, is best,
> And thus, touching you, would I silently sleep and be carried
>     eternally.

Thus he imagines himself nestled against the hip or the bosom of a mortal lover or—to change the image—in a state of postmortem babyhood in which he lies at the breast of the mother who, in poem after poem, ambiguously personifies both the life-giver and the death-receiver. But readers must be on the alert for Whitman's verbal playfulness. Although the invitation to "thrust" the ambiguous "me" (his self? his book?) beneath one's clothing may indeed be a sensual fantasy, it can also have a factual basis. The "Calamus" poems were composed in the late 1850s, after the appearance in 1856 of the second edition of *Leaves of Grass,* a compact volume that was almost a "pocket book," small enough perhaps to be "thrust" into the breast pocket or hip pocket of the reader's garment.

The drama of imagining himself to be dead but still sentient and eagerly sought after by lovers is played out in "Calamus 45" ("Full of Life Now"), the last poem of the "Calamus" sequence. There the forty-year-old poet, boasting that he is "full of life now" and "full of affection" pictures himself enjoying a tête-à-tête with a reader centuries after his physical death. In this scenario his "always living" self leaps from the pages of *Leaves of Grass* to embrace a living man or woman in an encounter of mutual ecstasy. The poet, who longed to make universal brotherhood the norm in civil society, addresses a representative reader, yet unborn, in an intimate tone that once again hints that even in death his passionate self may "materialize" in the presence of the living reader.[41]

> When you read these, I, that was visible, am become invisible;
> Now it is you, compact, visible, realizing my poems, seeking me;
> Fancying how happy you were, if I could be with you, and
>     become your lover;
> Be it as I were with you. Be not certain but I am now with you.

To "ascend to the atmosphere of lovers" into a purer love that may exist in the realm of death represents a fantasy escape from the vagaries of mortal (and probably homosexual) love. Thus "Calamus 38" ("Fast Anchor'd Eternal O Love") expresses the persona's desire to reach this stratospheric realm of idealized homosexual love, where, "disembodied, or another born," he will encounter "the ethereal, the last athletic reality, my consolation." The attainment of perfect love, it appears, must await the transition to perfect death. An even more intriguing love-death fantasy is "Calamus 4" ("These I Singing in Spring") which combines the themes of male bonding and *Waldeinsamkeit* (forest solitude) with a bittersweet evocation of an ideal world of the dead. The poem's solitary persona imagines that he has passed through the "gates" of an arboreal dream world where he joins "a silent troop" of male companions—the transfigured spirits of friends he has known or imagined—who embrace him with an acclaim and affection greater than the mortal Whitman could ever have known. In this woodland Elysium the poet's transfigured alter ego dispenses lilacs and sage and the leaves of the pine, laurel, and wild oak to each companion as a token of his affection. But to "him that tenderly loves me, and returns again never to separate from me" he tenders the calamus root, a token of male bonding and, possibly, of immortality.[42] As a symbol of homosexual love-death the calamus lends the poem a certain Wagnerian flavor. Rather than trusting to political engagement, the Whitman persona expresses the hope that the combined workings of death and love will ultimately resolve the contradictions between individualism and democracy. In the years preceding the Civil War, when political action may have seemed frustrating to him, Whitman—

like some of his utopian contemporaries—projected the resolution of his troubles and the problems facing civil society into an idealized world situated in some possible future.

The most striking poem of love and death in the "Calamus" sequence, "Calamus 2" ("Scented Herbage of My Breast"), has been called "a condensed nocturne, a symbolic descent into the realms of death and the unconscious."[43] It is Whitman's variation of the Osiris myth, which, in some of its versions, tells of grass growing from the breast of the dead Egyptian god whose name was synonymous with the forces of goodness and vegetation. After Osiris is slain by his evil brother, according to the myth, and segments of his dismembered body are buried in different places, each burial site becomes a place of worship. When his sister Isis has gathered his bodily parts he is resurrected as a god and copulates with her in order to perpetuate their divine dynasty. In "Scented Herbage of My Breast" the Osirislike Whitman persona celebrates "the scented herbage"—the "tomb-leaves, body leaves, growing above me, above death"—issuing not only from Osiris, but those that will issue from the breast of his buried self. The sweet perfume exuded by the "herbage" sprouting from the lifeless body is (consistent with Egyptian mythology) a token of divinity. The grave-herbage imagery also serves as an effective metaphor for all of Whitman's death-saturated poetry or as D. H. Lawrence remarked hyperbolically, "Walt's great poems are really huge fat tomb-plants, great rank graveyard growths."[44] In a Chinese box of metaphors, the poem's herbage "becomes" the fragrant leaves of grass, the pages of the poet's book, the token of universal adhesive love issuing from the persona's heart, and a joyous symbol of his immortality:

> Yet you are very beautiful to me, you faint-tinged roots—you
>     make me think of Death,
> Death is beautiful from you—(what indeed is beautiful, except
> Death and Love?)
> O I think it is not for life I am chanting here my chant of
>     lovers—I think it must be for Death,
> For how calm, how solemn it grows, to ascend to the atmosphere
>     of lovers,
> Death or life I am then indifferent—my Soul declines to prefer,
> I am not sure but the high Soul of lovers welcomes death most,
> Indeed, O Death, I think now these leaves mean precisely the
>     same as you mean.

Stephen J. Tapscott explains that Whitman's imagery of "spiritual and vegetable generation" is particularly effective because "the Egyptian thanatology does fit, even closer than Christianity, the main tenets of death and immortality. For the Egyptians, all the dead become Osiris, participating in his essence in a future of perfect democracy."[45] The persona conflates times and eras, simultaneously assuming the roles of the dead god and of the mortal poet who looks into the future and beholds the countless generations who will savor his perpetually fresh tomb-leaves—*Leaves of Grass,* the product of *his* breast—and be enchanted and invigorated by them. And he expresses the hope that these leaves will in time reveal the secret of death.

Among the imagined comrades who may, in this life or the next, become the persona's lovers is Death itself. Just as the persona had implored a "word" from the sea to explain the cosmic order in "Out of the Cradle Endlessly Rocking" and begged the elements for encouraging signs in "As I Ebb'd with the Ocean of Life," so in "Scented Herbage of My Breast" he coaxes his lover Death to confide its ultimate secret, which he aspires to translate for humanity:

> Through me shall the words be said to make death exhilarating,
> Give me your tone, therefore, O Death, that I may accord with it,
> Give me yourself—for I see that you belong to me now above all,
>     and are folded together above all—you, Love, and Death are,
> Nor will I allow you to balk me any more with what I was
>     calling life,
> For now it is conveyed to me that you are the purports essential.

By "according" with Death the poet-persona would create the music of death. "According," in this context, implies striking a harmonious chord from the heart—the *cor*—of the persona and the heart of Death. In pleading with Death to "give me yourself," he expresses a wish that thrums like a tragic ostinato throughout the "Calamus" poems and through much of *Leaves of Grass.* Whitman, who had earlier declared himself to be "the poet of materials" no less than "the poet of the soul," here identifies death as "the real reality" that waits "behind the mask of materials" and "will one day, perhaps, take control of all" and "will perhaps dissipate the entire show of appearances." Although these words may disguise the fear that death will obliterate the individual life and all sensation, they seem intended to convey the idealist concept that mortals do not yet inhabit the "real" world as well as the conventional religious idea that the known world is a staging area that is anterior to the "real" world. Indeed, these words are a signpost of the ongoing shift in the poet's ideology that culminates in the poem "Eidòlons" (1876) and the later prose writings—a steady de-emphasizing of the material world and an emphasis on the ideal, nonmaterial world.

Following "Calamus 45," the concluding "Calamus" poem in the 1860 edition, is a simple line drawing of the sun, its beams radiating boldly, half submerged beneath the waves, half risen above the horizon line. Here is the final ambiguity of the "Calamus" sequence. Is the sun setting beneath the ocean of death, one wonders, or is it rising into the daylight of life?

## 4

The 1860 edition of *Leaves of Grass* is designed so that "Proto-Leaf" ("Starting from Paumanok") serves as its summarizing introduction and "So Long!" serves as its coda and formal leave-taking. Preceded by several death-tinged poems, some reprinted from the earlier editions, "So Long!" constitutes the volume's formal farewell to the reader and dramatizes the persona's imagined farewell to life.

Some time between 1857 and 1860 Whitman considered composing "another Death Song? Death Song with prophecie's [*sic*]." That proposed death song became the poem "So Long!" which Allen Ginsberg, in a gust of enthusiasm, called a "desperado farewell" by "the old soldier, old sailor, old writer, old homosexual, old Christ poet journeyman, / inspired in middle age to chaunt eternity in Manhattan,"[46] The poem is a three-part recitative: Verse paragraphs 1 to 11 in the final edition summarize the causes to which the poet has dedicated his life; verses 12 through 17 form an intermezzo that dramatizes the persona's impending "passing" and voices his many farewells to the world as he "hovers just short of a definite dissolving that would leave his body available to being represented but not to be presented directly."[47] The last four verses—for which the poem is justly famous—depict the deceased persona's imagined intimacy with the living reader and voice his final good-bye to his readers and to his book. The poem's informal title "So Long!" is defined by Whitman as "a salutation of departure, greatly used among sailors, sports, & prostitutes— the sense of it is *till we meet again*—conveying an inference somewhere, some how [*sic*] they will doubtless meet—sooner or later."[48] Although the poem's title suggests a tone of democratic familiarity, the poem belongs to the venerable tradition of the poet's farewell to his book. It avoids the impersonality of the classical *envoi*, however, its passionate leave taking "being especially effective because of the association of mortality and closing." Indeed, the concluding verses depicting the persona's impending death have been called a kind of emotional "performance theater."[49]

The poem begins as the persona, like a dying prophet, utters a series of "announcements"—verbal seeds that, long after his demise, will flower into a future-perfect America. He is confident that his prophetic words will some day be reified in "what comes after me." He prophesies an America endowed with great institutions, populated by athletic and "natural persons," and bound together by universal "adhesiveness": "I announce greater offspring, orators, days, and then depart," he declares theatrically. He declares, with a dash of patriotic oratory, that he had resolved early in his career to "raise my voice jocund and strong with reference to consummations." These sociopolitical "consummations" summarize many of the evolutionary and reformist causes that are expanded upon in such works as "Song of the Broad-Axe" and *Democratic Vistas*. They embody no revolutionary programs and call for no immediate social or political actions. Rather, they trust to the passage of time and the workings of the cosmic "law" to provide for the gradual dying out of the flawed masses and the emergence of "a hundred millions of superb persons." A long series of statements, many of them beginning with the words "I announce," recapitulates the principles that supposedly have guided the persona's mortal career, among them the ideals of individualism, "immortality, the body, procreation, hauteur, prudence," adhesiveness, and fraternity. And for each of these principles, he announces "at this moment I set the example" for future generations. Just as "To Old Age" (one of the 1860 "Messenger Leaves" poems} describes old age as the slow and steady voyage on "the estuary that enlarges and spreads itself grandly as it pours in the great sea" of death, so the ostensibly dying persona in "So Long!" foresees the day when the democratic masses will be ennobled by a liberating spiritual consciousness that enables them to accept death serenely and to make an easy "translation" from mortality to whatever existence may follow:

*So long!*
I announce a life that shall be copious, vehement, spiritual, bold,
And I announce an old age that shall lightly and joyously meet
    its translation.

Satisfied that he has completed his mortal obligations, the persona prepares to exit from the mortal scene.

Now acting as his own valetudinarian, the persona eulogizes himself in the sort of florid style that a contemporary orator might have used in delivering the poet's obsequies. One can almost hear him thinking that *this* is the sort of tribute I should like to hear at my own funeral. Having bequeathed the best of himself to future generations and having seemingly taken leave of mortality, the persona now celebrates the drama of his impending "translation" to an immortal spirit whose words and image will continue to inspire generations of readers. Sensing his impending demise ("It appears to me I am dying"), he cries, "Now throat, sound your last! / Salute me—salute the future once more. Peal the old cry once more."[50] Then poised on the brink of eternity and sounding his final "so long!" he imagines himself dead and "screaming electric" words that will instill his mysterious spirit-essence into future generations. Despite the living poet's gnawing doubts about the survival of his words, the dying persona proclaims his faith in their enduring and unflagging inspirational efficacy, and thus he illustrates the poet Joseph Brodsky's perspicacious remark, "of course, a writer always takes himself posthumously."[51]

Particularly intriguing is the hint of butterfly imagery as the persona anticipates his spirit moving "swiftly on, but a little while alighting." Whitman made the butterfly the signature icon of the 1860 edition. Preceding "Starting from Paumanok," the volume's opening poem, and following "So Long!," the volume's closing poem, is the line drawing of a butterfly perched on the index finger of a half-closed left hand, apparently ready to take flight for the unknown, much as Whitman's celebrated spider launches itself from its little promontory into the unknown. And, of course, there is the famous photograph of the seated Whitman with a (paper) butterfly perched on his finger. Whitman may have known that butterfly wings on ancient Greek statuary represent the psyche, for as Karl Kerényi points out, uniquely "in Greek the butterfly has the same name as the soul," the word *psyche* having originally designated the soul and only later designated the butterfly.[52] As a symbol of death and transfiguration, the butterfly is affectingly described by the immortalist Elisabeth Kübler-Ross, who anticipates her own death arriving as "a warm embrace" and declares in words that Whitman might have admired:

*When we have passed the tests we were sent on Earth to learn, we are allowed to graduate. We are allowed to shed our body, which imprisons*

*our soul the way a cocoon encloses the future butterfly, and when the*
*time is ripe we can let go of it. Then we will be free of pain, free of*
*fears, and free of worries . . . free as a beautiful butterfly returning*
*home to God . . . which is a place where we are never alone, where*
*we continue to grow and sing and dance, where we are with those*
*we loved, and where we are surrounded with more love than we can*
*ever imagine.*[53]

For Whitman, too, the butterfly symbolizes the passage to death, which
he addresses as "the translateress" and "the finale of visible forms."[54] Like
the closing lines of "Song of Myself," in which the persona bequeaths
himself "to the dirt, to grow from the grass I love," the lines signaling
the departing persona's self-bestowal in "So Long!"—"Sparkles hot, seed
ethereal, down in the dirt dropping"—are also framed in seed-sprouting
imagery to indicate the belief in a spiritual resurrection. And like the
herbage growing from the breast of the dead Osiris that, according to
myth, is transformed into armed men, the words of the dying persona in
"So Long!" also seem destined to sprout into "troops out of me rising"—
the "athletic" and poetic men and women who will inhabit a future
America. Although desiring to retain his mortal voice for as long as he
possibly can, the persona seems eager for whatever transformation his
"passing" may bring:

> So I pass—a little time vocal, visible, contrary,
> Afterward, a melodious echo, passionately bent for—death
>     making me undying,
> The best of me then when no longer visible—for toward *that* I
>     have been incessantly preparing. [emphasis added]

He finds comfort in the thought that when he has become "no longer
visible" he will still enjoy the bittersweet pleasure of being mourned by
generations of readers and lovers yet unborn. But, as Henry Staten ob-
serves, the expectation of being remembered is subject to an uncertain
outcome, because the living can only *imagine* whether, or how, future gen-
erations may love them or grieve for them:

> The flaw in the libidinal logic of the desire to be mourned
> for lies, of course, in the fact that the dead cannot enjoy the trib-
> ute of grief that their death occasions: a serious flaw, but one that

may be overcome in several ways. We are, after all, in the realm of intertwining fantasy and "reality." Even if one submits to death, it is always possible to drink in anticipation, imaginatively, the pleasure of being grieved [for], and once the pleasure is tasted, the actual dying can be postponed into the indeterminate future."[55]

It is no wonder that the serenity with which the persona appears ready to accept his death and his readiness to abandon the known life become tempered by the cool breeze of doubt and that he seems reluctant to take his leave just yet. Oliver Wendell Holmes is reported to have said, "we may love the mystical and talk much of the shadows, but when it comes to going out amongst them with the hand of faith, we are not of that excursion."[56] After all, earthly life hasn't been altogether unpleasant for the poet or his persona, and it still promises unexplored joys. So that even as he voices his readiness to depart this life, he still withholds his final good-bye as long as possible. This reluctance to abandon the material world is expressed in the aborted 1860 poem "Apostroph" where the persona cries out: "O Death! O you striding there! O I cannot yet!" And like an old-style thespian taking his final-final curtain call after a long career, the persona in "So Long!" strikes a melodramatic pose with knees bent, arms extended, voice raised in a last tremulous good-bye before he retires:

What is there more, that I lag and pause, and crouch extended
    with unshut mouth?
Is there a single final farewell?

Then, as though he were about to tell a ghost story, the ostensibly dying persona warns the reader that he may at any moment materialize before his or her eyes. In a stunning necrosexual fantasy, the eternally virile, eternally seductive spirit of the dead Whitman persona appears to ready to couple with a living reader of unspecified gender. This is the closest approach to picturing an afterlife of sensual bliss in *Leaves of Grass*. In scenes of startling sexual intimacy, the five brief concluding stanzas (lines 48 to 71 of the final version of "So Long!") depict the ostensibly dead, but eternally passionate, persona approaching the living reader in such guises as mentor, comrade, and ardent lover. Acting more boldly toward the reader than the flesh and blood Whitman might have dared, the disincarnate persona announces, "From the screen where I hid,

I advance personally." Mystically integrated into his ever-living volume of poems, and seemingly aroused by the contact of his electric spirit with that of the reader who holds a copy of the poems in his or her warm hand, he becomes the reader's spirit-lover. As we know, Whitman generally avoided describing the afterlife; he conceived of it neither as an everlasting bacchanalia nor as what Robert Louis Stevenson derided as "this fairy tale of an eternal tea party."[57] But Whitman here invents a scene in which his book and his persona, the past and the present, sensation and spirit merge in a death fantasy that takes on a life of its own. In words charged with tremulous emotion and in short, choppy phrases that mimic the persona's hard breathing, the ostensibly dead persona cries out:

This is no book,
Who touches this, touches a man,
(Is it night? Are we here alone?)
It is I you hold, and who holds you,
I spring from the pages into your arms—decease calls me forth.

O how your fingers drowse me!
Your breath falls around me like dew—your pulse lulls the
    tympans of my ears,
I feel immerged from head to foot,
Delicious—enough.

The passage has intriguing ramifications. At one level, the persona's imagined encounter resembles a passionate assignation. As his lover slumbers after their lovemaking, his (her?) pulse "lulls the tympans of my ears." (In a "Children of Adam" poem the persona recalls lying in bed with his lover's arm beneath his head and hearing the sound of "little bells last night under my ear.")[58] His exclamation, "Enough! O deed impromptu and secret!" suggests the possibility of a troubled Victorian conscience following a surreptitious assignation. At another level, the persona's behavior may be likened to that of the cabalistic figure of the *gilgul,* the wandering and disembodied soul of a dead person that enters and possesses the body and soul of a living person.[59] In a more elevated sense, the persona's action may represent the godlike act of infusing the persona's inspirational powers into a living subject; in James M. Cox's apt phrase, "the words of the poet will die into and become the flesh of the reader."[60]

That the above passage represents both a physical and a spiritual union with his reader/lover is confirmed by the persona's strange feeling of being "immerged from head to foot" during their union. *To immerge* means literally to dissolve or to disappear into a homogenized liquid, and this choice of words suggests the completeness of the persona's sexual and spiritual union with the reader. Even though this weighty term appears rather jarring in the context of a simply worded passage, the concept of immergence was particularly significant to some of the century's religious revisionists, who contended that it was a more accurate term than the word *baptism*. In this light the above passage may be construed as a mutual baptism—the spirit of the living reader is being baptized by, or merged into, the spirit of the deceased Whitman persona, while the persona's spirit undergoes a reciprocal renewal through its immersion into the spirit of the living reader. Some internal evidence exists for interpreting this act of immergence as one of reciprocal baptism. In "Song of the Answerer" (1856), the persona poses as "the Answerer," a godlike being, whose "word is decisive and final, / Him they accept, in him *lave*, in him perceive themselves, as amid light, / Him they *immerse*, and he *immerses* them [emphasis added]."[61] However, Whitman's verbal game play leaves one hard-pressed to draw a dividing line between the sexual and the spiritual elements of the passage. In accordance with his practice, he does not identify the "significant other" in the persona's ghostly union. Granted, it may be anyone, real or imagined. But if we choose to view the persona as an inspired being who exults in his own potential godliness—a stance he assumes in several poems—may he not be expressing a dramatic yearning to amalgamate with a Being that is infinitely greater than himself? May he not be seeking a union with a spiritual "spouse"[62] by dissolving, or "immerging," into the very godhead and thus becoming part of the divine essence—the central idea in "Passage to India"? Given the boldness of this fantasy, may not the persona be envisioning that as he dissolves into his divine lover, his divine lover is reciprocally dissolving into *him*, while his spirit retains its identity, and *he* becomes God—the God he aspires to meet and to surpass, according to certain passages in "Song of Myself"? Must we necessarily assume that his partner in this imagined merging, or immersing, is a mortal being? In fact, a startling 1860 lyric pictures the persona walking as a companion to Christ, both of them "saturat[ing] time and eras, that the men and women of races, ages to come, may prove brethren and lovers as we are."[63] And we might compare Whitman's bold imagery, for example, to this venerable hymn by Isaac Watt:

> Jesus, the vision of thy face
> Hath overpowering charms!
> Scarce shall I feel death's cold embrace,
> If Christ be in my arms.[64]

In *Leaves of Grass* Christ appears as the persona's chief avatar—a figure who shares many affinities with the idealized Whitman persona. The poet apparently shared Elias Hicks's interpretation of Jesus as an embattled outcast who struggled against false doctrines and whose eloquence exhibited "the force of his power to exalt and inspire—to inflame" the human spirit.[65]

The persona's final farewell in "So Long!" is expressed in a lofty but subdued stanza that serves as a coda to the poem and as a *vale* for the 1860 volume. As the persona prepares to exit his mortal life, his eyes focused on "the unknown spheres" and his head crowned by a saintly aura, he takes his gentle and solemn leave of the reader, bestowing—like a departing god—a final blessing. The stanza is quoted from the 1860 version:

> Dear friend, whoever you are, here, take this kiss,
> I give it especially to you—Do not forget me,
> I feel like one who has done his work—I progress on,
> The unknown sphere, more real than I dreamed, more direct,
>     darts awakening rays about me—*So long!*
> Remember my words—I love you—I depart from materials,
> I am as one disembodied, triumphant, dead.

Although he is still trying with his final breath to persuade the reader—and himself—that his vision of the eternal life may be "more real than I dreamed" his use of the simile in the last quoted line—"*as* one disembodied, triumphant, dead"—serves as a gentle assurance that the poet and his vibrant alter ego are still very much alive, still clinging to the satisfactions of *this* world, and still playing the most subtle of death games and word games with the reader. Whitman's spirit is less than eager to depart for the eternal realms where it may (or may not) be merged into the godhead. One suspects that he would prefer to have it both ways—to be "O, living always, always dying."⁶⁶

Whitman modified the poem's haunting final stanza in 1871 in order to reflect an expanding sense of himself as a prophetic poet, steeped in the traditions of Eastern mysticism. For the declaration, "I feel like one who has done his work—I progress on," in the 1860 version, he substituted the lines, "I feel like one who has done his work for the day to retire awhile, / I receive now again of my many translations, from my avataras ascending, while others doubtless await me."⁶⁷ For the phrase "I depart from materials," he substituted "I may again return." This revision implies that the persona's supposed demise represents something more than the simple transition from the mortal life to a stage beyond death. The reference to his "avataras ascending" suggests that the persona is about to undergo one more transition in an unending series of spiritual promotions that characterize the soul's ever-evolving existence.⁶⁸ In this context the persona's ascending avataras may also imply that his soul is advancing to ever-higher stages toward a supreme godhood and, in terms of the sacred writings of the East, that he is "raising himself to an equality with the Supreme One." The Hindu god Krishna has been described as "the eighth and most important of the incarnations of Vishnu—who in his character of Preserver of mankind was said to descend to earth in certain earthly forms (*avataras*) for the purpose of protecting and extending his religion."⁶⁹ Whitman's 1871 language implies some sort of parallel between Krishna's sacred mission and the persona's perceived mission to demonstrate his divine potential and to proclaim the potential divinity of all humanity. The revised final stanza implies that when the persona has completed his mortal tenure, he will die, saintlike, in the realm of purity, only to emerge as another manifestation of the Whitman self. Instead of speaking of him as being "reborn" or "reincarnated," the term "rebecoming" may be more consistent with Buddhist belief, which maintains that "in these other 'worlds' rebecoming is not a matter of being born as a baby but rather of the stream of personal consciousness, which from the point of view of an earthly observer terminates in death, continuing in another environment." If we choose to take our clue from this explanation, we can assume that in the course of the Whitman persona's series of "existences," he will "arise, in Buddhist terms, at the breaking up of the body after dying in a good bourn, a heaven world."⁷⁰

# 5
# "Come Sweet Death!"

## The *Drum-Taps* Poems, 1865–1866

There was indeed a long foreground to Whitman's sympathetic service in Washington's military hospitals. The prose sketches he wrote as a young man were filled with compassionate scenes of suffering and dying; he had possibly assisted victims of a New York City cholera epidemic; and in the years preceding the Civil War he had often visited the hospitalized firemen and omnibus drivers who suffered frequent, and often fatal, injuries. From the early 1850s onward, he visited hospitals in Brooklyn and New York, familiarizing himself with the patients' injuries and ailments, becoming an amateur critic of medical practice, and developing an admiration for the young doctors who attended the patients. "I suppose that I learned to nurse suffering humanity and not to be afraid of wounds, or manifestations of pain by nursing the sick or injured stage drivers," he recalled.[1] Something in his nature made him bond and empathize with suffering and dying men. He was drawn to deathbeds in the New York and Washington hospitals in no small measure by the opportunities they afforded him to observe the ways in which men endured pain and faced death. Thus, after the outbreak of the Civil War, when hundreds of injured and dying soldiers were being shipped to the New York hospitals on a contract basis with the army, he visited many of them and listened to their accounts of the military actions in which they had participated. And, in at least a couple of instances, he wove elements of their stories into the poems he incorporated into the seventy-two-page collection of war poems that he published in 1865 as *Drum-Taps.*[2] For more than two critical years, during the war and after, Whitman served as a volunteer visitor in Washington's military hospitals, where he befriended ailing and dying soldiers, comforting them, bringing them the small gifts and items they requested, writing letters for them, sometimes nursing them, and even intervening on their behalf with the medical staff. Occasionally, he claimed, he had dressed their wounds. And sometimes for a period of days he sat beside a dying soldier as he clung to life. These activities found literary expression in different forms. Whitman recorded his immediate reactions to the sufferings and deaths of soldiers in occasional newspaper dispatches, generally intended to rally support for the troops or raise funds for his hospital labors. He wrote letters to the families of injured or dying soldiers. And he filled little improvised pocket notebooks, "jotted down on the spot," with his impressions of wartime Washington, the hospital milieu, and the ailing soldiers. These notebooks, he said, "brief[ed] cases, persons, sights, occurrences in camp, by the bedside, and not seldom by the corpses of the dead." A selection of these notebook entries, published in a little volume as *Memoranda During the War* (1876), reprises these scenes of battles, carnage, and "the countless phantoms of those who fell and were hastily buried by wholesale in the battle-pits" or buried (many of them unidentified) in national cemeteries or improvised battlefield cemeteries. *Memoranda* chronicles the courage and equanimity of the hospitalized soldiers in their hours of suffering or dying—traits that profoundly impressed Whitman and buoyed his faith in the heroic character of America's young men. *Memoranda* is one phase of the task that Whitman had undertaken—to record the spirit of the war and to demonstrate that the soldiers had passed his test for moral character. Their calm and bravery in the face of suffering and dying sustained his belief that a nation's moral fiber can be measured by "what it thinks of death, and how it stands personal anguish and sickness." Writing in the corrupt, go-getting postwar "Gilded Age" of President Grant, he warned that "in the mushy influences of current times, the fervid atmosphere and typical events of those years [1861–1865] are in danger of being totally forgotten."[3] And he was determined that the trauma of the war years not be forgotten. (Many of these impressions were also incorporated a decade later in his informal autobiography, *Specimen Days*.)

The crowning literary achievement of Whitman's war years, of course, is the group of more than fifty poems that he assembled in *Drum-Taps* and *Sequel to Drum-Taps*. Central to the collection is the wartime Whitman persona, one of the greatest inventions in American literature. The poet's exposure to the realities of war made a profound impression on him and inspired an outpouring of poetry, for after he had been in Washington only a few months—by July 5, 1863—he could declare, "I intend to move heaven & earth to publish my 'Drum-Taps' as soon as I am able to get around."[4] But because of the wartime shortages of paper he was unable to do so until 1865. Unfortunately, when the "Drum-Taps" poems finally appeared in slender volumes and again when they were reprinted in the 1867 edition of *Leaves of Grass*, their cumulative impact was severely diminished by Whitman's ineffective organization: he mingled the death-scented poems of suffering and heroism with such unrelated pieces as "Pioneers! O Pioneers!" and "A Broadway Pageant," the latter celebrating a parade of Japanese emissaries down Manhattan's Broadway.[5] William Michael Rossetti's selected English edition of *Poems by Walt Whitman* (1868) rearranged the war poems into "clusters" that highlighted the prevalence of death,[6] and Whitman followed his example in the *Leaves of Grass* edition of 1871, which helped to set the model for the present arrangement. Some textual changes to the *Drum-Taps* poems that Whitman made in subsequent editions of *Leaves of Grass* also tended to weaken their impact. From the brief dedicatory lyric "Shut Not Your Doors to Me Proud Libraries" he later deleted the declaration that *Drum-Taps* is "a book I have made for your dear sake, O soldiers! / And for you, O soul of man, and you, love of comrades," thus muting its emphasis on the persona's "calamus" and spiritual bonding with the soldiers living and dead. But in 1871 he added lines to the poem (subsequently also deleted) that were intended to highlight his image as his nation's death-singer whose wartime poems express the concept of a "flowing, eternal Identity . . . and accepting exulting in Death, in its turn, the same as life." Of the soldiers, he declares, "for them I have lived, in them my work is done."[7]

In a January 5, 1865 letter to his staunch friend and publicist William Douglas O'Connor, Whitman boasted that the still unpublished *Drum-Taps* was "more perfect as a work of art" than the three preceding editions of *Leaves of Grass* because it was better adjusted in its "proportions and passions" and more "under control." Even though the letter was possibly intended as a rough draft of a self-advertisement, it sheds a valuable light on what the poet intended to achieve in his war poems:

> But I am perhaps mainly satisfied with Drum-Taps because it
> delivers my ambition of the task that has haunted me, namely, to
> express in a poem (and in the way I like, which is not at all by

directly stating it), the pending action of this *Time and Land we swim in,* with all their large conflicting fluctuations of despair and hope, the shiftings, masses, and the whirl and deafening din, (yet over all, as by invisible hand, a definite purpose and idea) with unprecedented anguish of wounded and suffering, the beautiful young men in wholesale death and agony, everything sometimes as of blood color and dripping blood. The book is therefore un-precedentedly sad (as these days are, are they not?), but it also has the blast of the trumpet and the drum pounds and whirrs in it, and then an undertone of sweetest comradeship and human love threads its steady thread inside the chaos and is heard at every lull and interstice thereof. Truly also, it has clear notes of faith and triumph.[8]

Armed combat has two discrete aspects—fighting and killing.[9] At the outbreak of the Civil War, when Whitman was still living in New York and the distant battles seemed glamorous and the scenes of killing were far away, he was caught up in the romantic fervor at the moment when most Northerners expected their forces to prevail after one or two deci-sive skirmishes—an attitude that changed to bewilderment after the Union armies suffered a series of military reverses. Whitman's initial en-thusiasm for the victory of the "Free States," shadowed by some accom-panying doubts, is expressed in an aborted verse, from which some lines follow:

Welcome the storm—welcome the trial . . .
Come now we shall see what stuff you are made of Ship of
    Libertad
Let others tremble and turn pale,—let them . . .
I welcome this menace—I welcome thee with joy.[10]

Some *Drum-Taps* poems apparently had their genesis in these early days of the war, when the poet was visiting hospitalized soldiers in New York Hospital and other facilities. He perceived even then that the sufferings and deaths of soldiers was a powerful poetic theme. "What a volume of meaning, what a tragic poem in every one of these sick wards!" he ex-claimed. "Yes, in every individual cot, with its little card-rack nailed at the head." And anticipating the way in which the wartime persona would focus on the visage of a single dying soldier in several of the *Drum-Taps* poems, he remarked that "the pale faces, the look of death, the appealing eyes, come curiously of a sudden, plainly before me."[11] However, Whitman's first published war poems—what Jerome Loving calls his "recruitment poems"[12]—are filled with enthusiasm for the war. "Drum-Taps" (later "First O Songs for a Prelude"), the opening poem in *Drum-Taps,* displays a patriotic zeal bordering on jingoism for the fevered spirit of war preparations and expresses his desire to become the war's poet: "Mannahatta a-march—and O to sing it well!" he exclaims. The personified figure of Mother Manhattan, who is tearfully sending her sons—"an arm'd race advancing"—into battle symbolizes Whitman's approval of the proceedings, for these young recruits, he proclaims, are the harbingers of America's great democratic future, the "advancing" race of heroic American young men whose appearance he had forecast in "Song of the Broad-Axe" and in his unpublished political tract "The Eighteenth Presidency!" (1856). The poem catches the very lilt of martial music.

> All the mutter of preparation, all the determin'd arming,
> The hospital service, the lint, bandages and medicines,
> The women volunteering for nurses, the work begun for in
>     earnest, no mere parade now;
> War! an arm'd race is advancing! the welcome for battle, no
>     turning away;
> War! be it weeks, months, or years, an arm'd race is advancing
>     to welcome it.

The enthusiastic but stilted "Song of the Banner at Daybreak" is an elaborate effort to justify the war on patriotic-ideological grounds. It is a sort of poetic cantata, with faint echoes of Schubert's "Erl König," arranged for four voices—a child (representing the nation's democratic spirit); a father (the straw man representing those reluctant to enter into the spirit of the war}; the Banner (the spirit of wartime patriotism); and the Poet (Whitman's alter ego), who announces his intention to become the war's bard, declaring that his is not the spirit that "lashes its own body to terror and death, / But I am that which unseen comes and sings, sings, sings." In an act of virtual self-anointing, the Banner hails the Poet as the spokesman of the forty million Americans: "O bard! in life and death supreme, / We, even we, henceforth flaunt out masterful, high up above, / Not for the present alone, for a thousand years, chanting through you, / This song to the soul of one poor little child." That child, representing the patriotic soul of America, acknowledges the poem's poet-persona as the nation's "masterful" bard—a bold gesture of wish fulfillment. And when the Banner sings of "demons and death . . . and a pleasure new and ecstatic," one can sense the allure that violence and death sometimes held for Whitman. The persona declares his readiness to defend the American "idea," which still remains "out of reach, an idea only, yet furiously fought for, risking bloody death, loved by me."[13] What exactly this national "idea" might be—whether the preservation of the Union, the defeat of slavery, the promotion of democracy, or some other principle—is never clarified in this bombast. But the "idea," in the context of the poem, definitely embodies the popular concept that the war will somehow promote national unity—Hegel's principle that "by arousing the passions of solidarity and transcendence, *war makes nations,* or at least revives and refreshes them."[14] Thus before he left for Washington Whitman had already positioned himself as America's wartime poet-designate.

The inability of the New York–based Whitman to find an appropriate poetic voice is evident in "The Centenarian's Story." The poem is intended to demonstrate what Whitman elsewhere calls the "peerless, passionate, good cause"—the patriotic dedication to the democratic ideal that even in the face of defeat presumably runs like an unbroken thread through America's history. The poem's central figure, an ancient veteran of America's War for Independence, watches the drilling of young volunteers in Brooklyn's Washington Park and tremulously recalls the Battle of Brooklyn, which had occurred on that very site—a holding action in which General Washington's troops were "terribly thinned" by enemy fire. The old veteran recalls seeing "the moisture gather in drops on the face of the General," who "wrung his hands in anguish." But he also recalls Washington's defiant look as he resolved to snatch victory from the jaws of this temporary setback, just as the North, it was assumed, would quickly turn its early defeats into victories. Nevertheless, the poem is an artistic failure because it is so far removed from the war's essential action and because the (still unformed) wartime Whitman persona is characterized only as a passive bystander listening to an elderly observer summon up his memories of an earlier war.

Whitman's continuing search for a poetic persona who would be both an emotionally engaged participant in the war and its literary interpreter to the American people is evident in the poem "Eighteen Sixty-One," in which the figure of the persona combines three images—an archetypal Northern soldier, the American nation, and a Whitmanlike archetype—into a single figure. "I repeat you, hurrying, crashing, sad, distracted year," he exclaims. The manly self-image he wishes to project is not that of "some pale poetling seated at a desk lisping cadenzas piano," he asserts, but that of "a strong man erect, clothed in blue clothes, advancing, carrying a rifle over your shoulder, / With well-gristled body and sunburnt face and hands . . . your sinewy limbs clothed in blue." This composite image of the soldier-poet bears an unmistakable likeness to the self-portraits—strong, sinewy, sunburnt, and prematurely gray ("well-grizzled"?)—that Whitman had depicted in his anonymous self-reviews and in some passages of *Leaves of Grass.*[15] Still undeveloped, however, is the image of the assertive and compassionate persona who, as participant and active observer, is the center and focus of the best *Drum-Taps* poems.

The poet's life changed dramatically after he visited his wounded brother George, a captain in the Fifty-first New York Volunteers, at Falmouth, Virginia, where the aftermath of General Burnside's ill-advised attempt to break through Confederate lines at the Battle of Fredericksburg presented him with the horrifying spectacle of unburied corpses and heaps of severed limbs—an experience that, he wrote to his mother, represented "three days of the greatest suffering I ever experienced in my life." Some of these scenes of death and carnage found their way into *Drum-Taps.* The poet was once again thrust into the midst of wounds and death when he accompanied a medical team bringing the casualties from Fredericksburg to Washington. He was shocked to see the wounded and the dead lying unattended in the open air on the long steamer trip or in open railroad cars.[16] Despite his enthusiasm for the Northern cause when the war broke out, he had serious doubts about prosecuting the war once he moved to Washington and beheld the war's horrors close up. Prior to the war his attitude had been ambivalent. Like many liberal journalists in the 1840s and 1850s, he had expressed a revulsion toward hanging and capital punishment, but during the conflict with Mexico he published articles calling for bloody reprisals against the Mexican leaders, even suggesting that "an excursion to the South" (i.e., Texas) might be "fun" for some young men.[17] But after having seen some of the war's horrors early in 1863, he reportedly exclaimed to the Reverend William

Channing, a Unitarian minister then residing in Washington, "I say stop this war, the horrible massacre of men." Channing calmed him, saying "You are sick; the daily contact with these poor maimed and suffering men has made you sick; don't you see that the war cannot be stopped now? Some issues must be made and met." Later, a friend observed that Whitman had apparently come to accept the war as "a struggle that had to go on until some conclusion was reached." He was able to do so by making a distinction between what he called "the Nation," in whose essential unity he had long believed, and what he derided as the "secession-slave-power."[18] Still, throughout the war his deep-seated feelings of revulsion against the bitter reality of the war contended with his sense of patriotism. As he told his mother, "one's heart grows sick of war, after all, when you see what it really is—every once in a while I feel so horrified & disgusted—it seems to me like a great slaughter-house & the men mutually butchering each other—then I feel how impossible it appears, again, to retire from this contest, until we have carried our points—(it is cruel to be so tossed from pillar to post in one's judgment)."[19] Despite whatever dissatisfactions he may have felt about the war's misconduct, its brutality, and the ill-treatment of the injured soldiers, Whitman's dedication to the preservation of the Union ultimately made him accept the war as a necessary sacrifice. His dedication to those whom he regarded as the war's primary victims—the wounded and dying soldiers, many of them adolescents—was a response driven by his compassionate nature. And by observing their quiet bravery as they endured pain or as they lay dying he was able to establish the centrality of death in his poetic rendering of the war. The war positioned him—and through him his poetic persona—in the military hospitals and on the field of battle where death was the grimmest reality. In turn, he made death the core of his wartime poems. Throughout his remaining lifetime he felt that his service to the soldiers had strengthened his position as the poet of death.

In January 1863 Whitman decided to remain in Washington, obtained work at the Army Paymaster's office, and immediately commenced his program of visits to the city's military hospitals—a practice he continued through the war years and for some time after the war ended. Summing up his activities during those terrible years, he claimed to have visited from eighty thousand to one hundred thousand soldiers, Northerners and Southerners, in camps and hospitals—a recollection skewed by the vagaries of memory, for that awesome number is equivalent to his having made contact with about eighty or ninety *new* patients each calendar day over a three year period. Even so, his record of many hundred hours is very impressive.[20] He served countless hospitalized soldiers with as great a measure of sacrifice as could be expected from any noncombatant and at a terrible cost to his physical and emotional health. The primitive and often negligent medical care that he witnessed in the military hospitals, particularly during the war's early years, was a source of pain and aggravation. Moreover, he agonized over the thousands of dead soldiers—particularly the many unidentified disappeared, who were buried in battlefields or by obscure waysides. One feels the pathos of his cry, "the dead, the dead, the dead—*our dead*—or South or North ours all, (all, all, all finally dear to me)."[21] Attending the soldiers—most of them unsophisticated young farm boys or city laborers, the sort of men to whom he had long been attracted—sapped his energies, but the practice met some of his psychological needs. With many of these soldier boys he developed an intimacy somewhere between that of a lover and a father. Nor should we overlook the deeply compassionate "maternal" streak in Whitman's nature.[22] Robert Leigh Davis, whose study of Whitman's wartime service examines the female element in persons who devote their energies to hospital work, believes (as do some earlier critics) that "Whitman's therapeutic perspective is shaped by a self-conscious homosexual sensibility." However, this "sensibility" is best seen as one component of his fatherly-motherly-comradely devotion to the soldiers.[23] His compassion for the hospitalized boys was tempered by a genuine humanitarianism and a sense of patriotic duty. Therefore, caution should be exercised in assuming a predominantly erotic motivation in Whitman's wartime service. There is an imbalance, for example, in Paul Zweig's declaration that "Whitman's self, bathed in the erotic, fed on suffering; it lived off the helplessness of a dying generation. No wonder these 'contradictions' tore him apart and finally helped to make him sick."[24] Indeed, Whitman's constant exposure to disease and death and the anguish of having to outlive so many of the soldier boys whom he had attended and who were young enough to be his sons would have sufficed to cause his deep emotional distress and physical breakdowns.

As a frequenter of the military hospitals, a journalist, and a poet, Whitman felt a compelling motivation to document what he saw of the war and to preserve the tragic and heroic milieu of those painful days in prose records and in *Drum-Taps*. Like many of those who later survived twentieth-century holocausts, he feared that the bravery and the agonies he had witnessed would go unrecorded or be misinterpreted with the passage of years. And, like them, he felt compelled to record and to preserve his memories of these events—to be the war's memorialist. By focusing the reactions to the war's trauma in the consciousness of the persona, the poems serve both a personal and a political function. They speak for the war's dead and for its inarticulate young soldiers, but they also speak for the man whose presence had touched the lives of so many soldiers. Because Whitman understood the war's literary potential, he set himself the task of translating the suffering, the chaos, the grief, and the heroism of the war into poetry, observing in 1864 that the war's events "would outvie all the romances in the world & most of the famous biographies and histories to boot."[25] Yet few *Drum-Taps* poems deal directly with battles or mass carnage; they do not illustrate the kind of on-the-spot war reportage that one finds, for example, in the embittered World War I poems of Wilfred Owen and Siegfried Sassoon or depict the waves of assaulting and dying troops as do such novelists as Leo Tolstoy, Eric Maria Remarque, or Konstatine Simonov. Whitman acknowledged that composing war poems on such a grandiose scale was beyond his capabilities. "My experiences on the field have shown me that the writers catch very little of the atmosphere of a battle," he said. "It is an assault, an immense noise, somebody driven off the field—a victory won: that is all. It is like trying to photograph a tempest."[26] He came to realize that his literary forte was "photographing" the more intimate scenes, narrowing his focus to picture a small incident or an individual dying or dead soldier.

Whitman's initial difficulty in writing poetry about the war's turmoil and slaughter is demonstrated by the draft of an unpublished poem, preserved in an 1862–1863 notebook, which contains elements of both "The Artilleryman's Vision" and of the brilliantly achieved "A March in the Ranks Hard-Prest, and the Road Unknown." Some details of the draft version may have originated in New York when hospitalized soldiers related tales of their terrifying battle experiences. The draft shows Whitman still struggling to develop the right persona and the right tone with which to report the war. The grim details and the cry of revulsion at the war's brutality in the draft poem may also have stemmed from Whitman's witnessing the heaps of severed limbs when he first went to the front at Falmouth, Virginia, and from his having viewed the aftermath of the Battle of Chancellorsville, in May 1863, where masses of wounded and injured soldiers lay on the ground, illuminated by torchlights. That horrid sight elicited his terse, embittered comment that "the wounded are getting to be common, and people grow callous." But he felt duty bound to prevent the American public from becoming indifferent to the war's casualties. Of the Battle of Chancellorsville he observed: "a thousand deeds are done worthy to write never greater poems on—and still the woods on fire—still many not only scorch'd—too many unable to move are burn'd to death. . . . Then the camp of the wounded—O heavens, what scene is this? Is this indeed *humanity*—these butchers' shambles?"[27] His intense reactions to these gut-wrenching scenes of violence and carnage kept him from achieving the objective distance from which he could translate these events into disciplined poetry. As illustrated by a chaotic draft poem, which verges on hysteria and preachment in describing scenes of violence he had witnessed or about which he had been told, Whitman had not yet developed the needed perspective from which to compose effective war poetry or found an effective voice for his wartime persona. The manuscript poem opens as a bloody battle is in progress and contains more vivid details of actual fighting than any published *Drum-Taps* poem. It is far more grim and gory than "The Artilleryman's Vision," to which it is related. The draft records "the groans of the wounded, the sight of blood . . . The position of the dead, some with arms raised, poised in the air, / Some lying curl'd on the ground—the dead in every position. . . . Some of the dead, how they turn black in the face and swollen."

> Then, after the battle, what a scene! O my sick soul! How
>     the dead lie,
> The wounded—the surgeons and ambulances—
> O the hideous hell, the damned hell of war [*sic*]
> Were the preachers preaching of hell?
> O there is no hell more damned than this hell of war
> O what is here? O my beautiful young men! O the beautiful hair,
>     clotted! the faces!
> Some on their backs with faces up & arms extended.[28]

Abandoning his efforts to depict the broad sweep of battle, Whitman fashioned well-wrought poems whose scenes of limited focus are filtered through the lens of the compassionate persona. Only a few poems describe the pain-wracked bodies of the injured or the mangled corpses of the dead, and none report any soldier's outcry against going unwillingly into the dreaded night of death. Most are devoted to the individual dying or dead soldiers with whom the persona experiences an intimate mystic communion. Through this lens they seem to attain an ineffable beauty and serenity. And in order to heighten the illusion of intimacy, the persona "spotlights" their faces and their eyes. Reading these scenes of the persona's loving devotion could have nourished the hopes of the wartime public that their ailing or dying sons and brothers had been comforted by a sympathetic attendant (like Whitman) at their side. Whitman had long been fascinated by the "language" of photography, and some of the poetic techniques he developed in these poems range from close-ups to panoramas. Indeed, photographers had became ubiquitous during the war, taking pictures not only of battle scenes but also of soldiers living and dead to be sent to families or to local newspapers.[29] The reverential close-ups of dying soldiers in some of Whitman's poems endow their subjects with almost-visible halos—a practice that could help to comfort a public hopeful that *their* dead may have died peaceably.

The twenty-five lines of "A March in the Ranks Hard-Prest, and the Road Unknown"—a masterpiece of compressed agony—demonstrate that the poet had found his proper voice and his ideal persona as an ambulatory witness and healer. Its four balanced sections, each viewed from a clearly defined camera angle, center on the acute sensibilities of the persona, who appears—rather ambiguously—as a soldier or a medic. The first section pictures the remnant of a decimated army unit arriving at night at a country church that serves as a makeshift hospital. In the second section, the hellish scene inside the church is illuminated by flickering torches. Whitman had in fact been reading Dante's *Inferno,* which he praised for its "great vigor, a lean and muscular ruggedness, no superfluous flesh" and a style "so gaunt, so haggard and un-rich, un-joyous."[30] His own style in "A March in the Ranks" is correspondingly terse.

> Shadows of deepest, deepest black, just lit by moving candles
>     and lamps,
> And by one great pitchy torch stationary, with wild red flame
>     and clouds of smoke,
> By these, crowds, groups of forms vaguely I see, on the floor,
>     some in pews laid down,

At my feet more distinctly a soldier, a mere lad, in danger of
   bleeding to death, (he is shot in the abdomen,)
I stanch the blood temporarily, (the youngster's face is white
   as a lily).[31]

In the third section the persona sweeps his lens in a panoramic survey of
the ghastly scene to capture the bodies of the living and the dead; sur-
geons operating in the dim, flickering light amid the sickening smells of
ether and blood; "the glisten of little steel instruments"; and "the crowd
of bloody forms" lying on planks or stretchers or on the bare ground out-
side the church building, "some in the death spasm sweating." Then, in
the closing six lines he conflates past and present, experience and undying
memory into a speech act. In "Song of Myself," section 36, we may recall,
the persona, having imprinted the details of "an old-time sea-fight" on
his memory, exclaims, "These so, these irretrievable." In the same way,
the persona in "A March in the Ranks" takes mental photographs of these
scenes and exclaims, "These I resume as I chant," so that the scenes be-
come embedded in his memory and in his poem. Finally, before he re-
sponds to the orders to resume the march down the endless "road un-
known" we see the healer-persona "bend to the dying lad" whose bloody
wound he had earlier dressed and whose anxieties he had apparently
calmed. With "his eyes open, a half-smile he gives me," the persona re-
cords. "Then the eyes close, calmly close, and I speed forth in the dark-
ness." That "half-smile" of the dying soldier marks the ritual bonding
between the persona and his dying soldier-"son." His empathetic inter-
action with one lily-faced soldier lad, whose marble-like visage suggests
that of a saint who has died for a sacred cause, mythologizes Whitman's
devotion to thousands of soldiers, and transfigures both the representa-
tive soldier and the persona. Perhaps by observing the calm with which
so many soldiers faced the end and by composing these poems, it has
been suggested, Whitman was able to salvage his own sense of humanity
and individuality in these trying days.[32]

The pallid, dying soldier of "A March in the Ranks" has a counterpart
in "Vigil Strange I Kept on the Field One Night," a passionate poem in
which Whitman again singles out an individual soldier fatally injured in
battle. Those who died in the military hospitals were generally buried
with some measure of military honors and religious observance, but the

task of burying a soldier on, or adjacent to, the field of battle was generally assigned to military burial squads, who had to dispose of the dead unceremoniously and as hastily as possible.[33] "The slain of higher condition, 'embalmed and iron-clad,'" observed Oliver Wendell Holmes, "were sliding off on the railroad to their far homes; the dead of the rank and file were being gathered up and committed hastily to the earth."[34] In "Vigil Strange I Kept on the Field One Night" the persona assumes the role of a veteran combatant who is obliged to leave an injured soldier lying on the field in order to rejoin an ongoing battle. When he returns at nightfall, he finds the soldier dead—"Found you in death so cold dear comrade, found your body son of responding kisses, (never again on earth responding,) / Bared your face in the starlight." A related lyric ("Look Down Fair Moon") invokes the "sacred moon with its "unstinted nimbus floods" to bathe the faces of "the dead on their backs with arms toss'd wide"—faces that are "ghastly, swollen, purple." The heavenly light appears to transfigure the soldier and make him holy. The soldier-persona's "vigil wondrous and vigil sweet here in the silent night" refers not only to his tearless all-night watch over the dead soldier (his grief is beyond tears) but to his observance of two revered Christian traditions—the deathwatch and the laying out of the body for burial. This anonymous soldier lying on an unnamed battlefield becomes an effective synecdoche for the legions of soldiers who died and were unceremoniously or ignominiously disposed of, many in unmarked graves, during the haste of battle. Of the three hundred thousand soldiers who were buried in the various military cemeteries, said Whitman, "more than half of them (and that is really the most significant and eloquent bequest of the War) lie in graves marked 'unknown.'"[35] *Memoranda During the War* records his grief for the thousands of these unknown soldiers, many of whom perished on lonely roadsides, or were drowned, or vanished unaccountably. Wars everywhere are characterized by their missing in action, and the American Civil War is among the most tragic examples in this respect. The poem cries out to be read as a memorial for all the soldiers who died alone or without proper burial or whose fates remained unknown to their loved ones. The persona's burial of the young soldier represents a ritual act of symbolic closure for the nation's unknown dead, here reverently buried, mourned for, and remembered by one who loved them. As the attentive and loving persona observes this death vigil (the word *vigil*, rich in sacred connotations, occurs eight times in the twenty-six-line poem) and as he provides an honorable burial for the unknown soldier, whom he addresses as "my comrade" and "my son," he becomes the surrogate for all the loving parents, siblings, and comrades of the dead in whose stead he has performed these traditional burial rites that celebrate the sacredness of existence.

Much of *Drum-Taps,* as M. Wynn Thomas has noted, assumes a "ritualistic and liturgical character."[36] Enshrouding and burying the soldier's body transforms this death, and by extension the deaths of countless soldiers, into a sacred action in which grieving families and friends, symbolically at least, could find a measure of surcease. Wrapping a soldier's body in an army-issue blanket and burying him in a shallow grave on or near the battlefield was sometimes a necessary practice, particularly when the troops were under fire. During the earlier phases of the war, when there was no adequate ambulance service, vast numbers of soldiers were abandoned to die on the field of battle.[37] When viewed against such a background, the persona's deed is particularly touching, but it is far more than a simple act of mercy. "I faithfully loved you and cared for you living," says the persona to the dead soldier, and voicing the hope of personal immortality, he adds, "I think we shall surely meet again." Attention has been drawn—perhaps overdrawn—to the "strange combination of compassion and arrogant assertion through which 'my son' becomes Christ buried by the poet/god just as the dawn announces not the son's resurrection, but that of the poet/god transformed."[38] But in laying out the soldier's body the persona has performed a selfless act and observed a hallowed ritual that commemorates the sanctity of death. Philippe Ariès provides a context to help us understand that

> the laying out of a body is a traditional rite; however, its meaning has changed. Formerly the purpose was to arrange the body in a position representing that era's ideal image of death, that of a recumbent effigy, its hands crossed, waiting for its life in the afterworld. It was in the Romantic era that men discovered the special beauty that death imposed on a human face, and the purpose of the final solicitude was to free this beauty from the death agonies that spoiled it . . . to retain an image of death—a beautiful corpse, but a corpse.[39]

An observation by Thomas Lynch, who is both a poet and a professional undertaker, also helps us interpret the persona's actions. "The bodies of the newly dead," cautions Lynch, "are not to be regarded as debris nor remnant, nor are they entirely icon or essence. They are, rather, changelings, hatchlings of a new reality that bear our names and dates, our images and likenesses. . . . It is wise to treat such new things tenderly, carefully, with honor."[40] By "the rising sun" the persona deposits his "son" in "his "rude-dug grave" and concludes his "vigil for comrade swiftly slain." And like so many scenes of the war, this "vigil I never forget" becomes inscribed in the persona's memory and, as Whitman would hope, in the memory of his nation.

The ultimate distillation of soldiers' dying is compressed into a sacred moment, when the persona gazes close-up at the faces of a trio of dead soldiers. The fifteen lines of "A Sight in Camp in the Daybreak Gray and Dim" strip away the trappings of war to focus on the faces of three dead soldiers, seemingly beatified in death. Emerging at dawn to "walk in the cool fresh air the path near by the hospital tent," the persona beholds the forms of three dead soldiers, wrapped in drab army-issue blankets, who are about to receive burial. Since these soldiers had been cared for in a military tent hospital, we may assume that their modest funerals will be conducted by members of the United States Sanitary Commission, who registered and marked their graves. As Gary Laderman explains in his study of nineteenth-century death practices, "burial rites for those who died in the hospitals for most of the conflict included the registration of the death, the placement of the corpse in a coffin with some form of written identification, a small military escort from the hospital to the grave, the presence of an army chaplain to perform a brief service, the firing of arms, the playing of the 'Dead March' if a band was available (a fife or drum would do if not), and the erection of a board at the grave site." Whitman himself described the procedure in these unpublished lines:

> The graves with slight boards, rudely inscribed with the names,
> The front of the hospital, the dead brought out, lying there so still,
> The piece of board, hastily inscribed with the name, placed on
>     the breast to be ready,
> The squad at the burial, firing a volley over the grave.[41]

Whitman sharply criticized the medical treatment that the soldiers received in some of the military installations he visited and decried the procedures followed by hospital personnel and by some individual physicians.[42] Although the war would bring about countless innovations in medical care and medical technology, military doctors were often negligent or were still committed to unorthodox or obsolete practices. And, as Whitman recorded, the bodies of the dead were often handled unceremoniously, even callously. Although *Drum-Taps* does not dwell on such matters, its author was attentive to the way hospitals treated their dying soldiers. He recorded his impression of one such death, that of a soldier endowed with "a perfect specimen of physique," going into "convulsive spasms," being chloroformed by a physician, fanned by nurses, prayed over by "a religious person," and watched by a "crowd" of doctors, nurses, students, and soldiers—"then welcome oblivion, painlessness, death. A pause, the crowd drops away, a white bandage is bound around and under the jaw, the propping pillows are removed, the limpsey head falls down, the arms are softly placed by the side, all composed, all still,—and the broad white sheet is thrown over everything." Of one makeshift military hospital he remarked, "Death is nothing here. As you step out in the morning to wash your face you see before you on a stretcher a shapeless extended object, and over it is thrown a dark gray blanket—it is the corpse of some wounded or sick soldier of the reg't, who died in the hospital tent during the night." "A Sight in Camp" does not tell how the three anonymous soldiers—covered by brown blankets as they will soon be covered by the brown earth—died or how they will be buried. (Many soldiers received only temporary, makeshift burials; some bodies were later reburied.)[43] The poem focuses solely on the three faces that, in the persona's mind, become sacred icons of the thousands of soldiers who died in obscurity.

As the solitary persona sequentially removes "the ample brownish woolen blanket, / Gray and heavy blanket, folding, covering all" from the face of each dead solder, he beholds faces made beautiful by death and studies each face to decipher the essential character of the once-living man. (In the 1855 poem "Faces" Whitman had diagnosed the characters of the citizens he passed on the streets by employing the techniques of physiognomy and phrenology.) Removing the first blanket, he beholds the face of a grizzled veteran:

Curious I halt and silent stand,
Then with light fingers I from the face of the nearest the first
  just lift the blanket;

Who are you elderly man so gaunt and grim, with well-gray'd
    hair, and flesh all sunken about the eyes?
Who are you, my dear comrade?

Then with a mingling of paternal/maternal affection and the "calamus"
love that pervades his feelings for all the "sweet boys" he befriended and
nursed, he removes the blanket from the second member of the trio, ex-
claiming piteously, "and who are you my child and darling? / Who are
you sweet boy with cheeks yet blooming?" And next to these two figures
made holy in death lies the third soldier whose face, he thinks, resembles
that of the crucified god:

Then to the third—a face nor child nor old, very calm, as
    of beautiful yellow-white ivory,
Young man I think I know you—I think this face is the face of
    the Christ himself,
Dead and divine and brother of all, and here again he lies.

In both "Song of Myself" and "To Him Who Was Crucified" (1860) the
persona had imagined himself as Christ's companion and confidant, but
here he beholds with astonishment, alongside the bodies of two dead
soldiers, the imagined incarnation of a soldier-Christ. The poem is a
stunning exercise in wartime myth making.

As a hospital volunteer Whitman wrote hundreds of letters for the dis-
abled and often half-illiterate soldiers. Many were written to inform
family members that a son or husband had died and that Whitman had
kept a watch at the bedside of their loved one. Thus, for example, he
wrote a letter "about the last days of your son" to the family of Erastus
Haskell of Company K, 141st New York Volunteers, whose physical de-
cline he had followed as the boy lay dying. "I am only a friend, visiting the
wounded and sick soldiers (not connected with any society—or State),"
he wrote to make clear that he was not employed by, or associated with,
the Christian Commission or any church or government agency. "Many
nights I sat in the hospital by his bedside till far into the night . . . the
lights would be put out—yet I would sit there silently, hours, late. . . . I
shall never forget these nights, it was a curious and solemn scene, the sick
and wounded lying around in their cots, just visible in the dimness, & the
dear young man close at hand lying on what proved to be his death

bed."[44] The grieving families treasured these affecting letters, often a family's only record of a soldiers' last hours. In the poem "Come up from the Fields Father" Whitman tries to picture how such a gloomy missive might have been received by the family of one such soldier. He does so by transforming his persona into an unseen spirit-presence who hovers over the family's farm, transported there, one assumes, by the electrical magic of the words contained in his letter. Some contemporary mediums advertised that their healing powers could be transmitted with the words they wrote—the very paper and ink that they used—and a somewhat similar fiction underlies the poem's assumption that some manifestation of the persona's self has been transmitted with, and embodied in, this letter.[45] In a melodramatic style, "Come up from the Fields Father" pictures an Ohio farm where the harvest-ready fields and orchards display the ever-renewed plenitude of nature and form a backdrop to the family's receipt of the letter announcing the loss of a son and brother. As an empathetic, if invisible, witness to the family's grief for a boy that they, and he, had loved, the mediumistic persona views the family's horrified reaction. His voice merges with that of the stricken mother whose only wish now is to be with her son in death and whose intense grief epitomizes the pain felt by thousands of mothers who have received letters announcing the loss of their sons.

> Open the envelope quickly,
> O this is not our son's writing, yet his name is sign'd,
> O a strange hand writes for our dear son, O stricken mother's
>   soul!
> All swims before her eyes, flashes with black, she catches the
>   main words only,
> Sentences broken, *gunshot wound in the breast, cavalry skirmish,*
>   *taken to hospital,*
> *At present low, will soon be better.*

Having witnessed the boy's decline in a military hospital, the letter-writing persona interjects a silent comment:

> Alas poor boy, he will never be better, (*nor may-be needs to be*
>   *better,* that brave and simple soul,)
> While they stand at home in the door he is dead already,
> The only son is dead. [emphasis added]

The death of the soldier continues to resonate in the hearts of those who loved him. "The son does not die in any single instant—neither in the hospital, nor in the hospital letter," observes Robert Leigh Davis. "Instead he dies many times, and it is one of those deaths Whitman represents in the poem, his death to his mother." And the false hope entertained by the soldier's sisters that he may still be alive only indicates that they are trying to defer the shock they will feel when their brother's death is later confirmed.[46] The poet's determination that the war's deaths shall forever reverberate in the memories and the hearts of the American people is a major aspect of *Drum-Taps*.

Whitman did not mind conveying the impression, in *Drum-Taps* and in later semiautobiographical writings, that as he moved through the hospital wards his presence and his touch had a curative efficacy, claiming with some satisfaction that his personal magnetism had revived many "faint & lonesome" soldiers who had given up hope of physical recovery. "[T]hey and I are too near each other," he explained; "there is no time to lose, & death and anguish dissipate ceremony here between my lads & me." And he observed with considerable pride that "the doctors tell me I supply the patients with a medicine which all their drugs & bottles & powders are helpless to yield."[47] The poetic distillation of his hospital labors among the ailing and dying soldiers is "The Wound-Dresser." The title is itself something of a pun. It not only identifies the persona as one who dresses the wounds of the hospitalized soldiers—and Whitman himself remarked that "I have some cases where the patient is unwilling anyone should do this but me"[48]—but it also casts him as a dresser of his nation's wounds, a pose he elaborated upon in his later writings about the war. Whitman was in his mid-forties when he composed "The Wound-Dresser," but in order to achieve the needed artistic distance from which to picture the war's tragic scenes he introduced the poem's persona as "an old man" who relives his wartime service as a wound-dresser. A decade after publishing the poem, Whitman transferred the original epigraph to the *Drum-Taps* volume to the introductory stanza of "The Wound-Dresser," thereby fusing the images of the wartime persona and the living poet who had dedicated his life and his poetry to his nation's wounded.

(Arous'd and angry, I'd thought to beat the alarum, and urge
    relentless war,

But soon my fingers fail'd me, my face droop'd, and I resign'd
    myself,
To sit by the wounded and soothe them, or silently watch the
    dead.)[49]

Whitman knew that the high death rate among the troops, particularly in the early years of the war, was largely attributable to poor sanitation and to crude and inept medical practice. Many doctors still believed in the efficacy of "laudable pus" and rarely used the readily available bromine and carbolic acid to cleanse wounds. Moreover, a frightening toll was taken by malaria, hospital fevers, and diarrhea, and a diet consisting largely of army biscuit, beans, and salt meat further imperiled the recovery of the injured and wounded.[50] In a later poem the persona admits that he is continually haunted by nightmares of his "land's maim'd darlings," of the "regiments so piteous, with your mortal diarrhoea, with your fever." Years later, as he bitterly recalled, "O God! that whole damned war business is about nine hundred and ninety-nine parts diarrhea and one part glory."[51]

Strangely enough, "The Wound-Dresser" portrays the persona as an ambulatory physician who is engaged solely in dressing wounds. Judging by his duties and his rounds of walking from bedside to bedside, the persona's conduct in this poem most closely resembles that of a "walker," a term then applied to the junior physicians or interns. Senior physicians generally performed surgeries and supervised hospital personnel. The medical historian Richard Shryock points out that "the greatest part of (so-called) nursing duties in the military hospitals were performed by convalescing soldiers who lacked training, aptitude, and strength to do the work," and who consequently wrought great damage. Thus Whitman notes that one soldier was killed by an overdose of laudanum prepared by "an ignorant ward master" and another by a dose of "lead muriate of ammonia, intended for a wash for his feet." When the army brought in women "nurses," mostly untrained motherly women whose venues were restricted to a single ward and whose duties were chiefly menial, it specified that they be "strong, middle-aged, and plain of appearance."[52] The "walkers"—or junior physicians—were assigned much of the wound dressing. Whitman had recorded his attraction to the youthful "walkers" at New York Hospital in his "City Photographs" series early in 1862.[53] In "The Wound-Dresser," the elderly narrator relives his role as a dresser, moving "in dreams' projections" from one critically wounded patient to another. He recalls the very kinesthetic "feel" of the experience as he moves "with hinged knees" (a repeated phrase) from bed to bed: "I onward go, I stop"; "On, on I go." Most of his patients have sustained wounds to the limbs. In that distant era before the general use of antibiotics, when few doctors practiced sterilization, wounds to the extremities frequently became infected or gangrenous, and so proved fatal to the patient. As the persona compulsively relives these heart-rending scenes, he invites the reader to witness his ministrations and to "follow without noise and be of strong heart." Whitman's language is economical and bleak:

> Bearing the bandages, water, and sponge,
> Straight and swift to my wounded I go,
> Where they lie on the ground after the battle brought in,
> Where their priceless blood reddens the grass the ground,
> Or to the rows of the hospital tent, or under the roof'd hospital,
> To the long rows of cots up and down each side I return,
> To each and all one after another I draw near, not one do I miss,
> An attendant follows holding a tray, he carries a refuse pail,
> Soon to be fill'd with clotted rags and blood, emptied, and
>    fill'd again.

As he moves from bed to bed the persona stoically dresses the soldiers' wounds to the head, side, shoulders, and limbs; many of them are amputations. Doctors frequently ordered the removal of injured extremities as a life-saving procedure to avoid the possibility of gangrene and fatal infection. (Nevertheless, the infections often persisted and proved fatal.) Meanwhile, the persona barely manages to control his empathy with the soldiers' suffering.

> I am faithful, I do not give out,
> The fractur'd thigh, the knee, the wound in the abdomen,
> These and more I dress with impassive hand, (yet deep in my
>    breast a fire, a burning flame.)

Although the poem does not reflect the nature of Whitman's service during the war, it epitomizes his dedication to these young men and boys, many of whom were on the verge of dying from their injuries or from the consequences of poor medical practice. His letters to his mother and his wartime dispatches to the New York press reveal how profoundly these deaths affected him and how deeply involved he became in the soldiers' struggles with death. They are filled with wonderment at the calm and fortitude that his "sons" displayed as they faced death. "Mother," he wrote, "you can have no idea how these sick & dying youngsters cling to a fellow, & how fascinating it is, with all its hospital surroundings of sadness & scenes of repulsion & death." Armory Square Hospital, where he visited frequently, he said, "contains by far the worst cases, most repulsive wounds, has the most suffering & the most need of consolation." The doctors, who appreciated his efforts, he said, give him "room," and "I am let to take my own course."⁵⁴ Dozens of these suffering and dying soldiers are named in Whitman's letters, in *Memoranda During the War,* and in *Specimen Days.* For example, he records his interaction with a young New York man, wounded in the knee and dying of diarrhea and blood poisoning, who asked him to read a passage from the New Testament about Christ's crucifixion and resurrection: "He ask'd me if I enjoy religion. I said, 'Perhaps not, my dear, in the way you mean and yet, may-be, it is the same thing.' Oscar behaved 'manly.' The kiss I gave him as I was about leaving he return'd four-fold."⁵⁵ And yet, aside from brief allusions to the nature of their wounds or their physical condition, the soldiers on the persona's tour of duty in "The Wound-Dresser" are never named and never individualized. Nor does the persona interact with them; the anguish he feels is internalized. They appear only as so many suffering bodies and faces whom the "walker"-persona attends, but this very anonymity permits Whitman to represent them as examples of what he calls the vast "army of the wounded." The literary tactic of preserving the soldiers' anonymity, which Whitman uses throughout the *Drum-Taps* poems, affords him the artistic control to make these scenes vivid and representative of the suffering sustained by the ailing and dying soldiers he observed or attended. And by portraying these almost generic inhabitants of a nightmarish world, "The Wound-Dresser" can focus on the interior drama of the saintly wound-dresser as he tends them—those with fractures and festering wounds, the soldier with the amputated hand lying on his pillow "with curv'd neck and side-falling head," the soldier wounded in his side who has only "a day or two more" to live and whose wasted frame and "yellow-blue" countenance are symptomatic of the onset of death from gangrene. To a soldier with a head wound, the persona murmurs internally, "poor crazed hand tear not the bandage away," thus illustrating Whitman's observation that quite a few of the badly wounded and infected soldiers became crazed by pain (in this era when the symptomatology of pain was poorly understood).[56] Still the fictive wound-dresser attends the helpless soldiers while suppressing any outward sign of his own emotional distress:

> I am firm with each, the pangs are sharp yet unavoidable,
> One turns to me his appealing eyes—poor boy! I never knew you,
> Yet I think I could not refuse this moment to die for you, if that
> would save you.

That last line internalizes the very words that mothers everywhere have spoken to their ailing children. Whitman's "feminine" side was noted by several of his contemporaries. He told a friend in 1863, "I think sometimes to be a woman is greater than to be a man—is more eligible to greatness, not the ostensible article, but the real one." And the next year the feminist prison reformer Eliza Farnham named Whitman as one of the very few "great men of this feminine order of mind," thus classing him among the most advanced thinkers of the era.[57] No wonder that as the walker-persona observes the agonizing death spasms of a soldier who has been wounded in the neck, he utters this internalized prayer for mercy to Mother Death:

> Hard the breathing rattles, quite glazed already the eye, yet life
> struggles hard,
> (Come sweet death! be persuaded O beautiful death!
> In mercy come quickly!)

Whitman confessed that the "lingering and extreme suffering from wounds or sickness seem to me far worse than death in battle. I can honestly say that the latter has no terrors for me, as far as I myself am concern'd." Observing that the human imagination tends to exaggerate the terror of death, he testified that he had not encountered one instance in which a dying soldier "met death with terror," and he concluded that to the dying death was generally "a welcome relief and release."[58]

"The Wound-Dresser" has an "envelope" structure. It begins and ends with acts of remembrance. At its beginning the now elderly persona—intent on making sure that the war's sacrifices are not erased by the passing of time—tells young children who have no active memory of the war of the nation's sacrifice and of his own. The poem's ending establishes the persona's destiny (and that of Whitman himself) to relive the bittersweet experiences of the wound-dresser and to keep alive the memory of those agonizing days. As M. Wynn Thomas says, Whitman remained "preoccupied with the problem of providing an appropriate personal and emotional memory out of the war."[59] In an impressive display of pathos, the poem comes full circle by merging Whitman's personal recollections of the hospitals with the agonizing thoughts of the poem's walker-persona. The lines show the persona forever fated to relive the hospital scenes in an everlasting present, and they enshrine the image of a healer-persona whose "soothing hand" has comforted the sick and whose presence has calmed the dying.

> Thus in silence in dreams' projections,
> Returning, resuming, I thread my way through the hospitals,
> The hurt and wounded I pacify with soothing hand,
> I sit by the restless all the dark night, some are so young,
> Some suffer so much, I recall the experience sweet and sad,
> (Many a soldier's loving arms about this neck have cross'd
> and rested,
> Many a soldiers kiss dwells on these bearded lips.)

## 2

The venerable establishment poets—Longfellow, Lowell, Whittier, and Bryant—wrote movingly about the war, but they were not witnesses to its carnage. Herman Melville, who did visit the Army of the Potomac in order to observe the suffering of the soldiers at first hand, highlighted the ironies of battle and fate in his *Battle-Pieces and Aspects of the War* (1866).[60] But as one who was saturated in the war's spirit of carnage and death, of hysteria and elation, Whitman felt that he alone had emerged as the war's authentic poet. Thus in "Spirit Whose Work Is Done" he beseeches his wartime Muse—the "spirit of the hours I knew, all hectic red one day, but pale as death next day"—to infuse him with her electric "currents," which will authenticate his words as those of the war's poet:

Touch my mouth ere you depart, press my lips close,
Leave me your pulses of rage—bequeath them to me—fill me
    with currents convulsive,
Let them scorch and blister out of my chants when you are gone,
Let them identify you to the future in these songs.

And in the impassioned lyric "Pensive on Her Dead Gazing" the persona imagines that he can hear "the Mother of All"—the spirit of life and death—plead with the earth, the trees, the mountainsides, and the rivers to cherish and to preserve the essences of the war's Missing in Action, whose bodies lie in unmarked graves and in unknown and unhallowed places, so "that they may live" in "unslaughter'd vitality."[61] Just as "This Compost" assumes that the earth, through its divine chemistry, accepts human leavings and transforms them into new life essences, so "Pensive on Her Dead Gazing" beseeches the earth to process the sweet exhalations—the "fragrance" emanating from the soldiers' graves—into the mystic afflatus that will invigorate American democracy and permeate these poems.

My dead absorb or South or North—my young men's bodies
    absorb, and their precious precious blood,
Which holding in trust for me faithfully back again give me
    many a year hence . . .
Exhale me them centuries hence, breathe me their breath, let not
    an atom be lost,
O years and graves! O air and soil! O my dead, an aroma sweet!
Exhale them perennial sweet death, years, centuries hence.

The exhalations from the soldiers' burial sites—like the leaves growing from the breast of Whitman-Osiris in "Scented Herbage of My Breast"—reiterate Whitman's abiding faith in the essential goodness of the cycle of life, decay, and rebirth. The soil leavened by the blood of the war's dead in the "endless vistas" of America's North and South, and hence made sacred, is also the subject of "To the Leaven'd Soil They Trod," the hymnlike poem that concludes *Sequel to Drum-Taps.*

Several elegiac poems written at the close of the war also express Whitman's lasting empathy for the war's dead. "How Solemn as One by One" shows the persona probing beneath the impassive visages in the

ranks of returning soldiers to discern beneath each facial mask the inde-
structible soul "as great as any . . . waiting secure and content, which the
bullet could never kill." Whitman still viewed these soldiers as archetypal
"American young men"—the best hope for America's democratic future.
Observing one contingent of the two hundred thousand homeward-
bound Union soldiers parading through the streets of Washington, many
of them feeble and disabled, Whitman expressed his admiration for what
he considered their quintessentially "weatherbeaten" American look and
their "unmistakable Western physiognomy and idiom."[62] In "Dirge for
Two Veterans" the persona pictures himself standing on a Washington city
curbside among a group of mourners and witnessing a "sad procession"—
a cortege for two soldiers, father and son, both killed in action and for
whom "the double grave awaits." He hears the bugles and drums, each
drumbeat striking him "through and through." Unlike the exhilarating
drumbeat of "Beat! Beat! Drums!" that at the beginning of the war had
rallied able-bodied men to abandon their work and enlist in the Union
armies, the nine richly cadenced stanzas of the "Dirge" are written (in
Whitman's own phrase) in the slow, steady rhythm of "a strong dead-
march." And as the persona, by the light of the rising moon, watches the
coffins of the two veterans "passing to burial," the rude music inspires
another prayer for the all the war dead.

"Lo, Victress on the Peaks" dedicates Whitman's "cluster" of war
poems—with their depictions of "night's darkness and blood-dripping
wounds, / And psalms of the dead"—to Mother "Libertad," the spirit of
American freedom. And "Old War-Dreams" rehearses the persona's (and
possibly Whitman's own) recurring nightmare of moving impassively
"through the carnage" and "gather[ing] the heaps." Each of its stanzas
ends with the refrain, "I dream, I dream, I dream."

> In midnight sleep of many a face of anguish,
> Of the look at first of the mortally wounded, (of that
>    indescribable look,)
> Of the dead on their backs with arms extended wide,
>    I dream, I dream, I dream.

However, "Ashes of Soldiers" (which Whitman later placed in the "Songs
of Parting" section of *Leaves of Grass*) records a happier dream in which
the persona beholds "the slain elate and alive again, the dust and debris

alive." In this dream, the "phantoms of the dead" who are "Invisible to the rest henceforth become my companions, / Follow me ever—desert me not while I live." In a line that fuses the senses of sight, sound, and taste, he declares that the living are dear to him, "but sweet, ah sweet, are the dead with their silent eyes" who fill his dreams. He craves the blessings of these dead, imploring them to make *him* their voice and to let the exhalations from their corpses perfume his words. And he invokes the soil of battlefields, "the wordless earth, witness of war and peace," leavened with the bodies and blood of the war's dead, to be his muse, to make him a "fountain" whose ever-living words will moisten "the ashes of all dead soldiers South or North."

Finally, the six incomparable lines of "Reconciliation" encapsulate Whitman's cherished identity with the war's dead and his wish to be a peacemaker. They express his faith that love and death are congruent elements that will humanize mankind and will ultimately abolish the very memory of war and inaugurate the reign of peace. The idea of reconciliation, mythologized in the poem's first four lines, is translated in its closing couplet into a magnanimous speech-act. Whitman had repeatedly declared his love for all soldiers, and here, as the persona bestows a comradely kiss on his representative dead enemy, he takes his place as his nation's poet-reconciler.

*Reconciliation*
Word over all, beautiful as the sky,
Beautiful that war and its deeds of carnage must in time be
    utterly lost,
That the hands of the sisters Death and Night incessantly softly
    wash again, and ever again and again, this soil'd world;
For my enemy is dead, a man divine as myself is dead,
I look where he lies white-faced and still in the coffin—I draw
    near, and lightly touch with my lips the white face in the
    coffin.[63]

### 3

Of Whitman's crowning wartime poem, "When Lilacs Last in the Dooryard Bloom'd," the British critic John Bailey declared more than seven decades ago: "No great man has ever wept in a nobler elegy, all the nobler because it has in it so much more than the death of one man, as much indeed of nature as of man, as much of life as of death."[64] Of the vast poetic outpouring of grief that followed the assassination of President Lincoln only "Lilacs" has sustained the dual status of a popular favorite and an artistic classic. Neither Bryant's "The Death of Lincoln" (in which God takes Lincoln to his bosom) nor Melville's "The Martyr" ("For they killed him in his kindness, / And their madness and their blindness, / And his blood is on their hand") nor even James Russell Lowell's impressive "Ode Recited at the Commencement to the Living and Dead Soldiers of Harvard University" combines the scope, the sweep of personal and national anguish, the powerful myth making, and the consummate artistry of "Lilacs." No other poetic commemoration of the war so exaltedly embraces the mystery of death, both in terms of national tragedy and as a record of one man's progression through despair, mourning, and a resolution of his own and his nation's anguish.

Probably the closest approach to Whitman's intention in "Lilacs" at the time he completed the poem is afforded by John Burroughs's *Notes on Walt Whitman* (1867), parts of which were actually written by Whitman, and whose whole manuscript was overseen by him.[65] The statement stresses the poem's pictorial brilliance, its underlying musicality, and its focus on "the central thought of death."

The main effort of the poem is of strong solemn and varied music; and it involves in its construction a principle after which perhaps the great composers must work—namely, spiritual auricular analogy. At first it would seem to defy analysis, so rapt is it and so indirect. No reference whatever is made of the mere facts of Lincoln's death; the poet does not even dwell upon its unprovoked atrocity, and only occasionally is the tone that of lamentation; but, with the intuitions of the great art, which is the most complex when it seems the most simple, he seizes upon three beautiful facts of Nature, which he weaves into a wreath for the dead President's tomb. *The central thought is of death,* but around this he curiously twines, first the early blooming lilacs which the poet may have plucked the day the dark shadows came; next the song of the hermit thrush, the most sweet and solemn of all our

songsters, heard at twilight in the dusky cedars; and with these
the evening star, which as many may remember, night after night
in the early part of that eventful spring, hung low in the west
with unusual and tender brightness. These are the premises
whence he starts his solemn chant.

Burroughs and Whitman emphasize that death is the poem's vital core,
declaring that "no other opportunity but a vast ensanguined war, and a
personal movement in it, like Walt Whitman's, as consoler, confidant,
and most loving support to hundreds of wounded men, most of them
very young, could have drawn in that unprecedented manner on the soul
for sympathy and pity." And a possible note of self-praise asserts that
Whitman's "soul met these demands, and fully responded to them." The
Burroughs/Whitman summary does much to clarify the poem's meaning
and its artistry:

> The [poem's] attitude, therefore, is not that of being bowed
> down, and weeping hopeless tears, but of singing a commemora-
> tive hymn in which the voices of Nature join, and [the music] fits
> that exalted condition of the soul which serious events and the
> presence of death induce. There are no words of mere eulogy, no
> statistics, and no story or narrative, but there are pictures, proces-
> sions, and a strange mingling of darkness and light, of grief and
> triumph, now the voice of the bird, or the drooping lustrous star,
> or the sombre thought of death, then a recurrence to the open
> scenery of the land as it lay in the April light, "the summer ap-
> proaching with richness and the fields all busy with labor," pres-
> ently dashed in upon by a spectral vision of armies with torn and
> bloody battle-flags—and again of the white skeletons of young
> men long afterward strewing the ground. Hence the piece has
> little or nothing of the character of the usual productions on such
> occasions. It is dramatic, yet there is no development of plot, but
> a constant interplay, a turning and returning of images and senti-
> ments.[66]

The emphasis on the musicality of the "Burial Hymn," as "Lilacs" was
sometimes known, suggests its affinity to a tragic symphonic tone poem
insofar as any verbal art can approximate such music. Whitman's elegy

is obliquely related to the tradition of what has been called nineteenth-century "mortuary music." Beginning with the *marcia funebra* of Beethoven's Third Symphony, Romantic composers like Liszt, Wagner, Chopin, and Bruckner developed a virtuoso music of personal lamentation. The poem also has nuances of the Romantic operas that Whitman loved.[67]

Some fifteen years after the war Whitman wrote a poem mocking his detractors' claims that his "chants" had "forgotten art, / To fuse within themselves its rules precise and delicatesse," but boasting that his poems—like the Rocky Mountains themselves—were not "formless wild arrays" but responses to nature's creative impulse.[68] Far from unfamiliar with English poetry, he probably knew some of the great elegies that had preceded his. "I don't ignore the old stock elements of poetry," he remarked, "but instead of making them main things, I keep them away in the background, or like the roots of flowers and trees, out of sight."[69] For "Lilacs" has some definite affinities with the tradition of the English elegy and its formalized lament for the death of a great or esteemed personage and such classical conventions as the grieving poet's surrender to the inexorable sway of death. Moreover, the English elegists had demonstrated the flexibility of form and language that is possible within the elegiac mode. Of the major devices customarily associated with the classical elegy, Whitman omitted two important ones: employing classic mythological trappings (although, as we shall see, he invented a powerful mythology of his own) and bestowing a name on the poem's deceased subject. Among the elegiac conventions that he included are the announcement of the subject's death; a eulogy for the dead man; the pathetic fallacy in which nature sympathizes with the poet's grief; the placing of flowers on the bier; a funeral procession with its many mourners; a confession that the poet's grief has rendered him emotionally impotent; and an antiphonal interplay between the poet's grief and that of his nation.[70] In contrast to traditional practice, the martyred president who is the true subject of the poem is never named, never described, and never directly addressed. Although the poem contains a striking episode describing the mystical bonding between the poet's spirit and that of the doomed president, it claims no personal relationship between the poet and the president. Whitman's wartime notebook entries and his newspaper dispatches do indeed praise Lincoln for his calm, for his wisdom in the face of adversity, and for his mastery of a trying situation. And in lines as terse as Lincoln's Gettysburg Address, Whitman later wrote:

This dust was once the man,
Gentle, plain, just and resolute, under whose cautious hand,
Against the foulest crime in history known in any land or age,
Was saved the Union of these States.[71]

This praise resembles Emerson's estimation of Lincoln as "a plain man of
the people . . . a man without vice . . . a miracle of Providence," which
had designated him as the unique leader for his times.[72] As a poet who
identified the spirit of the war with the spirit of democracy, Whitman
could not memorialize Lincoln as though he were an aristocratic person-
age; Lincoln must somehow represent all the war's dead. "When Lilacs
Last in the Dooryard Bloom'd" identifies him only as the figure in the
draped coffin, as the "Western fallen star," and as "the "wisest, sweetest
soul of all my days and lands" to whose "dear sake" the poem is dedicated.
The Lincoln of Whitman's poem is an abstract national hero, the first
among equals, representative of the legion of the dead who were felled
in a sacred war that the poem never names—a war without geography
or historical details or place names, as though its locus were the poet's
own "dreams' projections." It identifies none of the cities where Lincoln's
funeral train stopped on its 1,662-mile roundabout journey across the
Northern states. Nor does it describe the magnificent presidential rail-
road carriage, which had been converted to a funeral car in which the
embalmed body in its magnificent coffin lay in state on a catafalque
and was exhibited before an estimated one million mourners in a quasi-
political effort to solidify support for the Union.[73] Nor does the "Burial
Poem" ever mention the interment of the hero-president—a standard
feature in the elegy. We can only hypothesize that the president's burial
on May 4, 1865, may have coincided with that mystic moment in section
14 of the poem when the poet's spirit intones its incomparable tribute to
death.

Like the "ample, brownish, woolen blanket" that covers the dead in
some of the *Drum-Taps* poems, the poem's unidentified "coffin carrying
a corpse to where it shall rest in its grave" is also a pall of anonymity and
serves as a symbol of all the war's unknown dead. Whitman never de-
scribes the president's body, even though huge crowds in major popula-
tion centers viewed the embalmed and cosmeticized corpse, dressed in a
frock coat and white shirt, as it lay in state in its ornate black metal casket.
Many susceptible viewers even assumed that the body was preternaturally

impervious to decay because the facial features remained impressively lifelike many days after the assassination. In fact, the face was regularly made up by skilled cosmeticians to hide the ravages of death. Whitman knew that when poor soldiers died, they were generally buried in military cemeteries near the hospitals or in makeshift graves on the battlefields. The slain sons of the well-to-do were often embalmed (an art perfected during the war by skilled entrepreneurs) and shipped home in metal caskets to be buried in a cemetery close to the family home. During the train stops on its twelve-day journey, the president's corpse lay in state in its casket, the head propped on a pillow; and despite the best work of the embalmer who accompanied the body on its journey to its burial at Springfield, Illinois, the face began to take on a "leaden" hue.[74] In this most impressively structured poem of his career, Whitman took from history only those elements that served his artistic needs.

Such poems as "To Think of Time," "This Compost," and "Out of the Cradle Endlessly Rocking" show the persona testing the meaning of mortality essentially in terms of his own death. But since "Lilacs" is a national poem, the persona's mourning must also exemplify the nation's confrontation with death. "Lilacs" conflates his progress toward an accommodation with death with his nation's need for surcease and reconciliation, so that the poem is designed, in Paul Zweig's words, to serve as a "soothing myth of death—an instrument of healing for the nation and for himself."[75] "Lilacs," in fact, can be read as an exemplary history of one man's mourning, tracing the persona's grief work from the emotional chill when he first learns of the president's slaying to his stupor and verbal impotence, and thence to his "letting go" through his mystic immersion in the mystery of death, and finally his acceptance of death as a redemptive force.[76] Intertwining personal and national grief, the poem culminates as the persona regains the prophetic voice that had been muted by grief and his vision of a future prosperous America that the horrors of war had obscured. War is sometimes viewed as a "blood rite" or a "collective high"—a purgative experience that creates the feeling that a nation is being redeemed and strengthened by the blood shed by its choicest young men, an event whose aftermath is an (often deluded) sense of national renewal and rebirth.[77] Emerson implies as much in his comment that "one whole generation might consent to perish, if by their fall, political liberty, a clean and just life could be made sure to the generations that follow."[78] And Lincoln enunciates a similar principle in his address at the dedication of the Gettysburg National Cemetery when he praises the silent Union dead "who gave their lives that the nation might live." Although Whitman consistently criticized the war for its irrational slaughter of young men on the battlefields and in the hospitals, he designed "Lilacs" as a palliative and conciliatory document, and as such only one of its sixteen sections describes the terrifying carnage that characterized the war. The war's end had nurtured a desire for national reconciliation and national unity, for a new morality, and for an industrialized democracy inspired by a spirit of brotherhood and sisterhood. "Lilacs" postpones describing the horrors of the war that so upset Whitman to its penultimate section, where the persona views them "askant"—out of the corner of his eye, as it were. The poem blunts the chaos and terror of the war by focusing on one archetypal death, on one personification of grief work, and on the awesomeness of death itself.

In the poem's celebrated opening lines, April ushers in a symbolic "trinity" of death and renewal—the return of the planet Venus, the reappearance of the lilacs, and the recurring memory of the beloved president. The rocking rhythm, the repetitions, and the short breath units in the opening lines mimic a religious chant—a common feature in elegiac poems:

> When lilacs last in the dooryard bloom'd,
> And the great star early droop'd in the western sky in the night,
> I mourn'd, and shall mourn with ever-returning spring.
>
> Ever-returning spring, trinity sure to me you bring,
> Lilac blooming perennial and drooping star in the west,
> And thought of him I love.

The distraught persona's staccato outcries in the poem's second stanza reflect the intensity of his grief and his sense of personal loss.[79] For as Jacques Derrida says, "we cannot discuss mourning without taking part in [se faire part de] death, and first of all one's own death"; it is not only Lincoln but what Derrida calls "the him in me" that Whitman mourns. Henry Staten affirms that "what motivates the classical project of transcendence of mourning at the deepest level is the fear not of the loss of object but the loss of self."[80] Thus the persona's grief work begins with his admission that his grief for the dead (and ultimately for himself) has rendered him impotent:

O powerful western fallen star!
O shades of night—O moody, tearful night!
O great star disappear'd—O the black murk that hides the star!
O cruel hands that hold me powerless—O helpless soul of me!
O harsh surrounding cloud that will not free my soul.

The lilac, thrush, and planet (or star) motifs are repeated, with varia-
tions, throughout the poem as affecting symbols of death and renewal.
The perfumed and "miraculous" lilac bush, "with heart-shaped leaves of
rich green" may indeed have been blooming in April 1865 on the Long
Island farm where the poet was born. The persona's anguish and his sense
of personal loss may be represented by his breaking off a "sprig" of the
lilac bush—an act that has been represented as "a castrative act of mourn-
ing."[81] This sprig of deciduous lilac, symbolic of eternal renewal, may be
included in the mass of flowers that the persona will bring, "with loaded
arms," to decorate the graves of the war dead (section 7). The hermit
thrush, said to be singing in praise of death in its "secluded recesses," is
another symbol of hope and resurrection—an icon that was often etched
into the gravestones of New England cemeteries, and, like the butterfly
that adorns the opening and closing pages of the 1860 edition of *Leaves
of Grass,* a representation of the flight of the soul after death.[82] Like the
poem's persona who keeps to himself in order to work out his private
grief, the bird—his alter ego, his "brother," an aspect of his "I am"—is
pictured as "shy and hidden," "withdrawn to himself," while it secretly
rehearses its hymn in praise of death. In choosing the thrush to represent
the voice of nature and to echo his *own* voice, Whitman selected the
bird whose song has been recognized as "the most beautiful bird song in
America."[83] The song of the thrush embodies the allure that death has
always had for the persona, who interprets it as the "[s]ong of the bleed-
ing throat, / Death's outlet song of life, (for well dear brother I know, / If
thou was not granted to sing thou would'st surely die.)" And "the black
murk that hides the star" represents the pall of personal and national grief
that has temporarily obscured the star, which the persona identifies with
the spirit of the president and with which, in section 8 of the poem, he
holds communion.

Sections 5 through 7 of "Lilacs" picture the Lincoln funeral train on its
circuitous journey across a springtime landscape replete with images that
represent both death and renewal. For the poet and for the grieving na-
tion, the progress of the train across the face of the land constituted a rite

of passage.[84] The poem's train moves across fields where violets spot "the gray debris." Violets are cheering indicators of springtime renewal, but the "debris" from which they grow has a tragic connotation. (Section 15 of "Lilacs" speaks of "the debris and debris of all the slain soldiers of the war"; and "Ashes of Soldiers" identifies *debris* with the bodies of the dead soldiers.) The train passes blossoming trees and "endless grass" and fields of "the yellow-spear'd wheat, every grain from its shroud in the dark-brown field uprises"—all saluting the martyr-chief with the earth's brilliant display of seasonal rebirth. The striking image of the saluting wheat is reminiscent of Whitman's wheat-resurrection imagery in "This Compost" and also invites comparison with Emily Dickinson's poem "Because I Could Not Stop for Death" in which the "gazing grain," in a bold reversal of the normal subject-object relationship, appears to be saluting the passing dead.

The Lincoln funeral train stopped in Northern cities, where vast crowds viewed the president's body as it lay in state. They expressed their grief for the fallen chief through torchlight processions, oratory, hymns, and tolling bells. In the popular mind the body had assumed the status of an icon, both as the man who had saved the Union and as a representative corpse of the war's fallen soldiers. The rituals and ceremonies surrounding Lincoln's coffin served to keep alive the mourning nation's affectionate relationship to the departed president, for funerals, as Thomas Lynch says, "are the way we close the gap between the death that happens and the death that matters."[85] By decking the deceased president's coffin with armloads of roses and lilacs—nourished perhaps by the compost of the dead—the persona observes a convention the of the classical elegy. (In "Lycidas" John Milton names a dozen flowers that mourners should bring to the tomb of the dead scholar.) But the persona's internalized tribute (his innermost thoughts are set off by parentheses) makes clear that this symbolic gesture is intended to honor not Lincoln alone but, symbolically, to decorate the graves of "all of you"—all the known and unknown dead soldiers wherever they may be buried. The flowers are also a tributary offering to Death itself:

(Not for you, for one alone,
Blossoms and branches green to coffins all I bring,
For fresh as the morning, thus would I chant this song for you
    O sane and sacred death.

All over bouquets of roses,
O death, I cover you over with roses and early lilies,
But mostly and now the lilac that blooms the first,
Copious I break, I break the sprigs from the bushes,
With loaded arms I come, pouring for you,
For you and the coffins all of you O Death.)

In a well known poem, Theodore Roethke apologizes for daring to eulogize his dead student with the lines, "I, with no rights in this matter, / Neither father nor lover."[86] One might also question by what "rights" Whitman dared to become Lincoln's self-appointed elegist, since he was neither a friend nor a colleague of the president, and with whom he is not known to have exchanged a single word. Of course, he had admired Lincoln from afar and was generally favorable toward him in his dispatches to the *New York Times;* later, in *Specimen Days,* he claimed that as the president rode through the streets *he* recognized and acknowledged Whitman.[87] But the fantasy world of "When Lilacs Last in the Dooryard Bloom'd," where reality and "dreams' projections" coalesce, is not governed by historicity or even by probability. And so, by an amazing act of the creative imagination, Whitman dispels the appearance of having intruded on the solemn observances by inventing a mythic encounter (in section 8 of the poem) in which the persona's spirit and the spirit of the still-living president silently commune throughout one magic night a month *prior to* Lincoln's assassination. In this scenario the intuitive persona observes the brilliant "western star" as it is "sailing the heavens" above his Long Island "dooryard." He identifies the star as the personification of Lincoln's prescient spirit, mystically aware of its impending tragic fate and signaling its gloomy forebodings to the persona who, as is evident in many poems, is adept at reading natural and supernatural signs. In this elaborate dramatization of the pathetic fallacy, the persona beholds the portentous star shining sadly, its beams directed at him. Of all the mortals to whom the brilliant Lincoln star might have appeared, it chooses to commune its fatal augury to the Whitman persona, seemingly bending down to him to impart its runic secret, while the other stars, like so many mourners, look on in wonderment. During this enchanted meeting the persona "stood on the rising ground in the breeze in the cool, transparent night"—his transfigured night—and received a premonitory intimation of the April 15 assassination. What better "rights," then, could any poet claim for undertaking such an elegy than to have communed spirit to spirit with the ill-fated president? The persona's night-long mystic vigil ends as he sadly contemplates the grieving star-spirit descending its western course toward the realm of death:

> As the night advanced, and I saw on the rim of the west how
>     full you were of woe,
> As I stood on the rising ground in the breeze in the cool
>     transparent night,
> As I watch'd where you pass'd and was lost in the netherward
>     black of the night,
> As my soul in its trouble dissatisfied sank, as where you sad orb,
> Concluded, dropt in the night, and was gone.

Although the Lincoln star's "netherward" course carries it into the regions of blackness and death, we must remember that "the western orb sailing the heavens" also symbolizes the interplay of death and life, for Whitman identifies it as the "ever-renewing star" that gleams boldly each springtime, the Venus-star, the star that the Greek elegist Bion designated the symbol of life and of nature's rebirth.[88]

As Jeffrey Steele observes, "Whitman portrays poetic grief work as a progressive recovery of artistic control. By shrinking his grief to a manageable moment in time, the poet begins the dedication of his poetry to the process of mourning. The shift is facilitated by the ritual offering of poetic images to death."[89] So, in the next stage of his grief work, and in conformity with the conventions of the classical elegy, the persona proceeds to decorate the president's tomb. The pictures that he proposes to "hang on the walls, / To adorn the burial-house of him I love" (sections 10–12) represent his visions of a postwar America blessed with peace and plenty. Everywhere lush nature is pictured putting forth plants and grasses. There are pictures of prosperous farms and populous cities, and of workmen wending their way homeward from workshops and from factories with their "stacks of chimneys." These idealized images soften the harsh reality of the rapidly industrializing American landscape; thus, as Leo Marx observes, paying "the most direct, wholehearted tribute to this industrialized version of the pastoral ideal."[90] One picture that the poet bestows depicts the sun, the symbol of material and spiritual plenitude, as it makes its westward progress one April day across the "varied and ample land," thus mimicking the progress of human life from birth to death. "[T]he yellow gold of the gorgeous, indolent, sinking sun burning, expanding the air" and the impending sunset symbolize the fulfilled life, culminating in the advent of peaceful death. In the stanza that follows, the sonorous first line and the three following five-stress lines with their spondees ("just-felt," "soft-born") express a delight in life that gives way (in two lines of flowing hexameters) to the welcoming of "the coming eve delicious" and the all-enveloping death it will bring:

> Lo, the most excellent sun so calm and haughty,
> The violet and purple morn with just-felt breezes,
> The gentle soft-born measureless light,
> The miracle spreading bathing all, the fulfill'd noon,
> The coming eve delicious, the welcome night and the stars,
> Over my cities shining all, enveloping man and land.

The sun is said to be "a central image in Egyptian funeral symbolism, where the eye of Osiris is represented as the sun and is the symbol of the resurrection and salvation of both the dead man and the risen Osiris." Jonathan Edwards's typology characterizes "the rising and setting of the sun [as] a type of the death and resurrection of Christ."[91] And Whitman's "old age" poems employ the images of twilight, starry nights, and approaching darkness to express his patient readiness for death and his felt certainty of immortality.

However, the two most impressive bequests that the persona bestows on "the large sweet soul that has gone" are distinctly personal ones. First, like an Egyptian god, he bestows his exhalation—his breath-afflatus—to "perfume the grave of him I love"; that is, he dedicates the song he is now singing, "When Lilacs Last in the Dooryard Bloom'd," as monument to the president and to the war dead. Similarly, Yevgeny Yevtushenko begins his memorial poem "Babi Yar," commemorating the thousands of Jews slain in Kiev during World War II and ignominiously buried in the gully of Babi Yar, with the words "There are no monuments over Babi Yar" and dedicates his poem as a monument to them. But in addition to this incomparable gift of song that arises from his soul, the persona proposes to "warble myself," that is, to bestow and dedicate *himself*—his divine

selfhood—to the memory of all the dead. And, indeed, Whitman dedi-
cated much of his remaining life to preserving the memory of the presi-
dent, the war, and all its casualties.

Following this episode, the persona finds himself in the dusky woods,
where, for the third time, he encounters the thrush, which he calls a
"wondrous singer" and his "dearest brother," and which, like him, is said
to be endowed with a "voice of uttermost woe." The "Hermit Thrush
Solitary Thrush," Whitman wrote in a manuscript note on birds, is "very
secluded"; its "song is a hymn—real seriously sweet"; "it is the bird of the
solemn woods & of nature pure and holy."[92] The persona is prepared to
undertake his descent into the realm of death, but before he does so he
must conclude his period of mourning and attain the serenity in which
his mind is open to inspiration. He must end his fixation on "the long
black train" and on the black cloud of grief "enveloping me with the rest."
This is Emily Dickinson's "letting go." For "normal mourning, too, while
it lasts," says Freud, "absorbs all the energies of the ego."[93] Once the per-
sona has attained a state of calm, the song of his spirit can join with the
song of the bird to sing "Death's outlet song of life." Whitman's careful
language makes clear that the persona's encounter with the thrush oc-
curs as an enchantment or a dream-vision. In declaring that "the charm
of the [bird's] carol rapt me," the persona affirms that he is under a spell,
for in nineteenth-century usage the words "charm" and "rapt" were asso-
ciated with the mesmerized or hypnotic state. The voice of the bird,
which is the voice of nature, and the voice of the poet, who is his na-
tion's inspired singer, can now unite in a mystic harmony to chant their
incomparable hymn of welcome to death. Their celebration of death, as
James E. Miller Jr. phrases it, "paradoxically bestows birth—a rebirth into
a spiritual life" during which the persona's voice, which had been muted
by grief, is restored.[94]

As the persona prepares to descend into the mysterious dark swamp to
meet death face to face, as it were, he senses that he is being accompanied
by two dim presences—the "thought of death," a representation of the
grief and loss experienced by death's living survivors, and by "the sacred
thought of death," his conviction that death is a necessary element of the
cosmic plan. That these mystic companions are phantoms—the shadowy
projections of the persona's own thoughts—is made clear by the poet's
use of similes in which the persona describes himself "*as* walking" with
these dim figures, "*as* with companions."

Then with the knowledge of death as walking one side of me,
And the thought of death close-walking the other side of me,
And I in the middle as with companions, and as holding the
    hands of companions,
I fled forth to the hiding receiving night that talks not,
Down to the shores of the water, the path by the swamp in
    the dimness,
To the solemn shadowy cedars and ghostly pines so still.

The swampland he enters to hear the bird's carol is a realm of darkness and decay, but, paradoxically, it is also a lush source of primal life, of the vast oozy composts that generate perpetual renewal. The "shores of the water," "the hiding receiving night," and the "cedars and ghostly pines" are all images suggesting that he has descended into the spirit-realm of death. Helen Vendler views the swamp as "a distinctly watery underworld . . . doing duty for Hades, for the realm of the ghosts and the shades," and for the mythic realm of death that Whitman sometimes associates with the watery realm of the sea.[95] But like Whitman's image of the "compost" and like Thoreau's image of the primal mud surrounding Walden Pond that teems with emergent life during the springtime thaw, Whitman's swamp represents a place of metamorphosis—a realm in which death and decay perpetually nurture life and renewal.

Once the mystic threesome has descended into the swamp's recesses the enchanted persona hears (and silently intones) the bird's carol in praise of Death. In the 1871 edition, the seven quatrains of birdsong were captioned *"DEATH CAROL"* and were italicized, thus conferring upon them the status of an extended aria or, as the poet calls them at the poem's close, a "powerful psalm in the night." The heart of the "psalm," born of Whitman's having witnessed the prolonged and painful deaths of soldiers, is a prayer beseeching *"lovely . . . soothing . . . delicate death"* that when she *"must indeed come"* to each person, to *"come unfalteringly,"* that is, unaccompanied by prolonged suffering. Death is pictured as the *"coolembracing"* Mother Sea who (ideally) gently folds all of us to her bosom— the sea whose soothing "undulations" are an anodyne for mortal pain and whose chartless pathways are the implied roads to eternal life. The "carol" endows death with an almost physical intimacy as the persona anticipates the "feel," the very sensation, of his own eventual embrace by Mother Death, *"the soul turning to thee O vast and well-veil'd death, / And the body gratefully nestling close to thee.*" The rich musicality of the "Death Carol" and its melding of iambs, dactyls, anapests, and spondees into a seamless lyric constitute one of the highest achievements in our poetry and have made it a favored text for many composers.[96]

Death Carol

*Come lovely and soothing death,*
*Undulate round the world, serenely arriving, arriving,*
*In the day, in the night, to all, to each,*
*Sooner or later delicate death.*

*Prais'd be the fathomless universe,*
*For life and joy, and for objects and knowledge curious,*
*And for love, sweet love—but praise! praise! praise!*
*For the sure-entwining arms of cool-enfolding death.*

*Dark mother always gliding near with soft feet,*
*Have none chanted for thee a chant of fullest welcome?*
*Then I chant it for thee, I glorify thee above all,*
*I bring thee a song that when thou must indeed come, come*
  *unfalteringly.*

*Approach strong deliveress,*
*When it is so, when thou hast taken them I joyously sing the dead,*
*Lost in the loving floating ocean of thee,*
*Laved in the flood of thy bliss O death.*

*From me to thee glad serenades,*
*Dances for thee I propose saluting thee, adornments and feastings*
  *for thee,*
*And the sights of the open landscape and the high-spread sky*
  *are fitting,*
*And life and the fields, and the huge and thoughtful night.*

*The night in silence under many a star,*
*The ocean shore and the husky whispering wave whose voice I know,*
*And the soul turning to thee O vast and well-veil'd death,*
*And the body gratefully nestling close to thee.*

*Over the tree-tops I float thee a song,*
*Over the rising and sinking waves, over the myriad fields and the*
*    prairies wide,*
*Over the dense-pack'd cities all and the teeming wharves and ways,*
*I float this carol with joy, with joy to thee O death.*

The poet prays that his carol, like the waves of the sea or the currents of the air, may "undulate" throughout the world to comfort and strengthen all those who must confront death. Death, says the carol, is to be welcomed no less than birth, knowledge, joy, or love. If death is accepted on these terms, says David Kuebrich, then Lincoln's death, too, may be finally understood as "ultimately neither a personal nor a national tragedy."[97]

The persona's tribute to death as a "cool-embracing" mother coexists with his anguished awareness that death also operates as a senseless destroyer. As Stephen E. Whicher says, the thrush's song succeeds only temporarily in "weaving a veil of life-illusion over the same hard truth and so easing it for us."[98] Inevitably, the portrayal of death as a gentle mother is supplanted, in the following section (section 15), by the persona's tormented "panoramic vision"—the phrase "I saw" is repeated fifteen times—triggered by his memories of the war as a merciless slaughterhouse. As though he were reliving a soundless nightmare, he beholds "askant" through the battlefield's smoke the "bullet-pierced bodies of soldiers," the "white skeletons of young men," and the "debris and debris of all the slain soldiers in the war."

Although both the soothing death carol and the terrifying death panorama are centered in the persona's imagination they need not be interpreted as separate actions that occur in discrete time frames. Like many a romantic opera in which an aria conveys one mood or situation while the accompanying orchestral music and the background action convey a contrasting mood or situation, the bird's exuberant death-hymn, we may assume, takes place in the persona's mind *concurrently*, and perhaps jarringly, with his "long panoramic vision" of the war's carnage. In a sense, the visions may be said to be superimposed on one another. But unlike music, drama, or film, which lend themselves to the simultaneous depiction of contrasting actions or moods, the limitations of poetry required Whitman to relegate the carol of the bird and the vision of the battlefields to successive sections of the poem, thus permitting the reader to conclude that the persona's retrospective impressions of these events occur sequentially. But Whitman was intent on stretching the limits of the poetic medium by creating an *illusion of synchronicity and simultaneity*—a sort of "counterpoint" between the buoyant "thought of death" in section 14 and the grim "knowledge of death" in section 15. The overlay of contrasting events and moods in the two sections highlights the contradictions and the complexity of the persona's recollections and the intensity of his warring feelings of horror, despair, hope and elation in regard to death. Section 15 clearly explains that the persona has experienced the exultation of the bird's song "while" (i.e., *at the same time as*) he beholds "askant" (or from the corner of his eye) a grim, "long procession of visions" of the war in which death appears not as the embracing mother but as an agent of random and merciless slaughter.

In section 6 of "Song of Myself" the persona had proclaimed his faith that the dead who lie beneath the grass "are alive and well somewhere"; but "Lilacs" avoids such an explicit statement concerning the destinies of those who died in the war. Nevertheless, Whitman was aware that postwar America needed words that could promote closure and reconciliation. The Methodist bishop who conducted the funeral service at Lincoln's tomb pronounced that very message: Lincoln's iconic body, he declared, had traversed the land on its awesome journey on a mission of reconciliation. Pleading for unity in an hour when the nation was still stunned by tragedy, the clergyman observed, "far more eyes have looked upon [the visage of] the departed [president] than ever looked upon the face of any other departed man. . . . The deepest affections of our hearts gather around some human form, in which are incarnated the living thoughts and ideas of a passing age." Lincoln's funerary journey, the bishop concluded, had served as a symbol to unify the nation.[99] "Lilacs" was intended to serve a similar purpose—to memorialize the war and its fallen, to personalize the nation's grief, and to honor the deceased president as an icon of national unity. Hence, following its grim details, section 15 ends with the consolatory message that death has immunized the war's dead from further suffering:

But I saw they were not as was thought,
They themselves were fully at rest, they suffer'd not,
The living remain'd and suffer'd, the mother suffer'd,
And the wife and the child and the musing comrade suffer'd,
And the armies that remain'd suffer'd.

The lines are intended to assuage the nation's pain; but Whitman may have been too deeply immersed in his terrible memories of the war to temper his message with the overt promise of an afterlife.

In section 16, which concludes the poem, the persona emerges from his dream state. Like the dreamer-persona of "The Sleepers," he "passes" from the mystic night of his dreamworld into the daylight world of waking consciousness, but he preserves his memories and his dreams—his ghostly "retrievements out of the night." Though he is still traumatized by his clinging memories, his waking marks the completion of his formal mourning for the "lustrous" president and the fallen soldiers. As the war's poet, he dedicates himself to preserve these "retrievements" in his memory and, through his writings, to secure them in his nation's memory. The poem ends on a tragic-wistful note. The "echo arous'd in my soul" by the song of the thrush still resonates in his mind, but now it produces apprehension as well as calm. As the lilac, the star, and his swamp companions once more appear before him, he pays a final tribute to "the sweetest, wisest soul of all my days and lands" for whose "dear sake" he has composed this poem.

The end of the Civil War marked the close of an era. And although Whitman may not have intended it that way, "When Lilacs Last in the Dooryard Bloom'd" serves as an elegy for the bygone days that had inspired the poet—in the first three editions of *Leaves of Grass*—to create a luminous vision of hope for the American people, articulated by and embodied in the persona of the quenchless, democratic Whitman persona. Coincidentally, only a few months after Whitman completed his great elegy, John Greenleaf Whittier published "Snow-Bound," the era's most popular poem of wistful longing for a vanished world of American innocence. At the conclusion of "When Lilacs Last in the Dooryard Bloom'd" the persona is alone, recapitulating his bittersweet memories of Lincoln and of "the dead I loved so well." Henceforth, death would become the most important subject of Whitman's poetry, often focused inward as he contemplated the imminence of his own dying. The more important of his later poems, such as "Prayer of Columbus" and "Passage to India," are elegies to himself as he prepares for his final spirit-journey to the unknown realm that may lie beyond mortality.

# 6

# "Sweet, Peaceful, Welcome Death"

## *Leaves of Grass*, 1867–1892

I

In the years following the war Whitman's body became weakened by many organic ailments, and as his zest for an active life diminished his poetry became increasingly absorbed with death. In 1873 the poet suffered a stroke that left him with hemiplegia on his left side. Unable to retain his federal employment, he moved to Camden, New Jersey, where he lived with his brother George's family until 1884, when he purchased the modest frame house on Mickle Street in a working class neighborhood— the house in which he died in 1892. His later poems tended to be less virile and more consciously "philosophical" than the earlier ones; many were written in welcome anticipation of his own death. The expressions of delight in his physical body and in the joys of the turbulent world around him that characterize the persona in the earlier poems—including poems about death—steadily diminished. As he gained, or affected, a new serenity, his later poems rarely depicted the tug of war between his sensual and spiritual selves that so energized his earlier work. Essentially these poems display the calm and spirituality of his later years. His poetic powers, though still formidable, had declined. He concurred with his physician-friend Richard Maurice Bucke's charitable assessment, a year before his death, that his poetry had undergone a "tremendous drop . . . but that drop occurred in the early 60's. Since then you have held your own and today your verse has as great, as wonderful subtlety and charm as it ever had."[1]

Although one religious scholar has referred to Whitman's postwar productions as "the poems of [his] radiant period," primarily because of their emphasis on the mystery of death, M. Jimmie Killingsworth calls Whitman's 1866–1876 years "a decade of revision," and Roger Asselineau labels these years a time of "self-censorship" during which Whitman toned down or excluded a number of passages from his earlier poems, including some that more boldly revealed his sexual orientation and his episodes of self-doubt.[2] Whitman's poetic output flagged: In addition to the *Drum-Taps* poems, only thirteen minor poems were added the 1867 edition of *Leaves of Grass*. However, he experienced some impressive bursts of creativity in the late 1860s and during the 1870s, and he had occasional flurries of inspiration in the 1880s. Moreover, his recognition as a poet of death was strengthened during the postwar years by several events. John Burroughs's laudatory little book *Notes on Walt Whitman as Poet and Person* (in which Whitman had a decisive hand) was published in 1867 to bolster the sales of the 1867 edition of *Leaves of Grass*. Whitman gained an entrée to the pages of the prestigious *Galaxy* magazine, which published a number of his poems as well as two installments of *Democratic Vistas,* a major critique of American society.[3] The next year William Michael Rossetti's edition of poems selected from *Leaves of Grass* brought Whitman's work to the attention of a broader British audience. The complaint by a British reviewer that Whitman was "always mystical—always democratic—always speaking in praise of ghastly death" was overbalanced in 1870 by an anonymous but passionate defense written by his astute English admirer Anne Gilchrist, who observed that "living impulses flow out of these [poems] that make me exult in life, yet look longingly towards 'the superb vistas of Death.'" And in the following year, the prestigious *Westminster Review* published an appreciative essay in which the young Irish literary critic Edward Dowden praised Whitman as a true original and recognized the centrality of death in his poetry. Dowden grasped the importance of personality in Whitman's value system, observing that "he clings to his identity and his consciousness of it, and will not be tempted to surrender that consciousness in imagination by the attraction of any form of *nirwana.* Death . . . is a name to him full of delicious tenderness and mystery, not without some elements of sensuousness curiously blended with it." Admitting that he cannot altogether comprehend "the nature of Whitman's religious faith," Dowden insightfully observed that "the chief thing to bear in mind is that Whitman cares less to establish propositions than to arouse energy and supply a stimulus."[4] Such encouragement may have fueled the ever-increasing emphasis on death in Whitman's poems. Asserting in the preface to the 1872 edition of *Leaves of Grass* that "old ecclesiasticism" had been too "long in its dotage," Whitman proposed a new democratic theology that "prepares the way for One indescribably grander . . . New Theology . . . lusty and beautiful . . . [the] final science of God—what we call science being only its minister. . . . And a poet of America (as I said) must fill himself with such thoughts, and chant his best out of them."[5] Several of Whitman's postwar poems and prefaces are expressions of this "new theology" in which the development of the soul and a readiness for death are essential elements.

This later phase of Whitman's poetry was auspiciously inaugurated in October 1868, when the London *Broadway Magazine* published five impressive lyrics about the journey of the soul following physical death: "Whispers of Heavenly Death," "A Noiseless Patient Spider," "The Last Invocation," "Darest Thou Now O Soul," and "Pensive and Faltering." "Whispers of Heavenly Death" records an auditory and visual epiphany in which the persona senses the rebirth—the "parturition"—of some unknown soul that is progressing from life to death. As he observes the "flickering stars" and the mournful "cloud masses" overhead, he is inspired by the thought that he can hear nature whispering to him that another soul is "ascending" and that he is witnessing "some solemn immortal birth, / On the frontier to the eye impenetrable, / Some soul is passing over." "Pensive and Faltering" sounds the keynote for many of the later poems, recording the persona's "faltering" speculation that the soul will enjoy an uninterrupted continuity in life and death and that mortal life is a staging area for a higher state of existence. It also demonstrates Whitman's steady drift toward a philosophical idealism that here borders on spiritualism:

> Pensive and faltering,
> The words *the Dead* I write,
> For living are the Dead,
> (Haply the only living, only real,
> And I the apparition, the spectre.)

Many of the later poems depict the persona's conscious self accompanied on its postmortal journey to eternity by his "soul" or his "fancy"—terms that apparently designate the purest embodiment of his creative imagination. According to this dualistic vision, the self and the soul will be paired in death, but somehow they will remain distinct. For example, the self addresses his soul in "Darest Thou Now O Soul" as though the self were both identical with and distinctive from the soul. The poem announces the persona's readiness, as the mortal "ties loosen," to quit his earthly mooring for his—and his soul's—imagined journey to the "inaccessible land" where there are no constrictions of time, space, or human fallibility and where there is no "darkness, gravitation, sense, nor any bounds bounding us":

> Then we burst forth, we float,
> In Time and Space O soul, prepared for them,
> Equal, equipt at last, (O joy! O fruit of all!) them to fulfil O soul.[6]

These lyrics do not clarify the distinction between the "we" or the "us" who seem to be paired, yet remain discrete, in the imagined afterlife. If the soul is an intangible essence that is impervious to death, and if the mind or the consciousness, as is generally assumed, has a physiological basis that ceases to function at the moment of death, then the reader is left to ponder what may be the nature of the disembodied self that accompanies the immaterial soul on its transcendent journey. Whitman imagined a postmortem self that retains recognizable vestiges of his mortal personality and that appears to tag along with (or perhaps merge with) his soul in the next world. The fear that had surfaced in earlier poems—that death may be only the eternal nothingness—has now become sublimated into a faith in an afterlife during which elements of the conscious (mortal) identity are somehow preserved. Although the persona fancies himself destined to live in an idealized postmortem world, he appears to be in no hurry to begin his journey there. Beneath the many proclamations of his readiness to embark from the earthly shore, one can sometimes hear the whistling of a boy who is afraid to dip his foot into the chilly waters of doubt. Thus while praying to be wafted "tenderly" through the exit door of the house of life, he complains (in "The Last Invocation") that "Strong is your hold, O mortal flesh, / Strong is your hold O love."[7] Indeed, these "carols" of parting, like so many sea chanties, seem intended to cheer the persona's "passage" from this known world into what Whitman sometimes called "the Invisible World."[8]

The best known of these 1868 poems, because of its daring simile and its "calamus" provenance, is "A Noiseless Patient Spider." An 1862–1863 notebook contains a draft version of the poem in which "the Soul,

reaching, throwing out for love," like a spider leaping to connect its fila-
ment to a distant support, seeks to make an intimate "connection" with
a passing stranger. Apparently not having succeeded, the persona defers
the accomplishment of such a "connection" to a postmortem future in
which he anticipates being wafted to "waiting oceans of love! yearning
and fervid! and of you sweet souls perhaps for the future, delicious and
long: / But Dead, unknown on this earth—ungiven, dark here, unspoken,
never born: / You fathomless latent souls of love—you pent and unknown
oceans of love!"[9] While retaining the draft poem's essential metaphor of
outreach, Whitman fashioned the superb lyric in which the spider's leap
from its "little promontory" to affix its "gossamer thread . . . somewhere"
now represents the solitary persona's envisioned leap of faith from the
known life to a spiritual anchorage in an uncharted existence:

> A noiseless patient spider,
> I mark'd where on a little promontory it stood isolated,
> Mark'd how to explore the vacant vast surrounding,
> It launch'd forth filament, filament, filament, out of itself,
> Ever unreeling them, ever tirelessly speeding them.
>
> And you O my soul where you stand,
> Surrounded, detached, in measureless oceans of space,
> Ceaselessly musing, venturing, throwing, seeking the spheres to
>     connect them,
> Till the bridge you will need be form'd, till the ductile anchor hold,
> Till the gossamer thread you fling catch somewhere, O my soul.

The published poem is a striking statement of Whitman's faith in im-
mortality. Scientists had found no evidence that the individual life could
continue after the body expires, and the negative impact of science upon
religious belief was shocking to many nineteenth-century intellectu-
als. Friedrich Engels notes that many world-famous scientists in the
1870s, fearful of pursuing materialist science to the conclusion that physi-
cal death is final, turned for affirmation to spirit-rappings, "magneto-
phrenological miracles," and other irrational solutions.[10] But a Unitarian
minister demonstrated that "A Noiseless Patient Spider" could be inter-
preted in terms of the pro-immortality argument then being widely pro-
moted by the liberal clergy. He saw the poem as a testament of Whit-

man's own faith in immortality, the proof of which is not "ascertainable by any known means." He paraphrased the poem thus: "If every effort to fasten a definite theory on some solid support on the other side of the gulf [of death] fails, venture forth on the naked line of limitless desire, as the spider escapes from an unwelcome position by flinging out exceedingly long and fine thread and going forth upon it sustained by air." In the absence of verifiable proof of a future life, the minister reasoned, there always remains a universal will to believe in, and a craving for, a satisfying existence beyond death.[11]

Two milestones in Whitman's poetry of death were the publication in the *Atlantic Monthly* in 1869 of "Proud Music of the Sea-Storm" (later "Proud Music of the Storm") and the publication in 1871 of the 120-page booklet *Passage to India*, which, together with *Democratic Vistas*, was later bound into the fifth edition of *Leaves of Grass*. The lengthy "Proud Music" is a splendid example of Whitman's ability to capture the cadences of nature and of human speech. In a dream that has the weight of a manifesto, the poem's persona beholds a vision of "the Almighty leader [who] now for once has signal'd [to Whitman] with his wand," and he hears a grand mysterious diapason communicating directly to his soul "the clew I sought so long." Some higher power, he now feels, has charged him to go forth and write "Poems bridging the way from Life to Death." The *Passage to India* booklet assembles death-oriented poems from earlier editions and a number of memorable postwar poems into what Whitman labeled "clusters." Its title-page epigraph celebrates the voyage of the persona's soul "[t]hrough Nature, Time, and Space," singing not of "Life alone" but of "Death—Many Deaths." The brief lyric "Now Finalè to the Shore" pictures the poet as a "Voyager" or "old Sailor" loosening his moorings and launching forth from the known life across the uncharted ocean of death. The volume's closing poem "Joy, Shipmate, Joy!"—another lyric of the "self" launching his boat ride to death and beseeching his "soul" to accompany him as partners, lovers destined to abide together through eternity—prompted another contemporary clergyman to remark, "I know of nothing in all literature to match the sweet, grand things that Whitman has written about death. This one [poem] you can place beside Tennyson's *Crossing the Bar*"[12]—the most popular soul-launching lyric in all of English poetry. The imagery of setting sail for death, which Whitman so frequently employs, is related to a well-established tradition in American painting. The American landscape painter Thomas Cole had "made the boat on the water a recognized symbol for the passage from life to death in his second landscape cycle, *The Voyage of Life* (1840)." And Whitman long remembered a remark made by an officer during the war years: "He went out with the tide and the sun's set."[13]

The most ambitious of the ocean-going "carols" in the *Passage to India* booklet is its loosely structured title poem.[14] Here the persona prepares to launch his spirit journey from America's Pacific Coast—itself a mythic place that the poet never visited—to find the mythic "India" of the soul. When Whitman was younger and physically agile, his persona determined to "tramp a perpetual journey" toward the limitless beyond, but once the poet became less physically active, his persona favored the less strenuous imagery of sailing. "Passage to India" initiates the soul's voyage back to "primal thought"—the sacred source of wisdom and spirituality. The poet praises the explorations of the past and the modern triumphs of transportation technology that have succeeded in girdling the world—the trans-Atlantic cable, the transcontinental railroad, and the telegraph. These material achievements lead him to the conclusion that technological advances are indicators of human advancement toward a nobler spirituality, working "in God's name, and for thy sake O soul." According to this reasoning, mechanical energy becomes an "analogue for divine spirit" and material and scientific progress becomes an analog for spiritual advancement.[15] Although "Passage to India" is, in part, a critique of American society, it essentially celebrates the persona's quest for the "India" of the spirit and for his hoped-for transcendence, through time and death, to a state of ultimate wisdom. Whitman commented in 1876 that "all lives and poems" should refer to "the justified and noble termination of our identity, this grade of it, and the outlet-preparation for another grade."[16] "Passage to India" commemorates the persona's imagined "outlet-preparation" for "another grade" of existence as he readies to seek the mysterious God who will be his equal, his companion, his lover, and his ultimate Self. Thus the poem that begins by praising mechanical progress becomes a paean to spiritual progress and the ennobling state of death. In a series of rhythmic anaphoras—lines beginning with the repeated phrase "I see"—the persona scans the American continent, newly crossed by railroads, and envisions the coalescence of America's material culture with the spiritual culture of the mythic East. He regards the many daring explorers and bards of the past who have mapped the world's vast *terra incognita* as his precursors who dreamt of "crossing all seas" and who readied the way for the momentous voyage of *his* soul. Their exploits, like his own, he concludes, have conformed to a cosmic plan, a "purpose vast," which is not yet understood. Contemplating the world's "vast Rondure, swimming in space," he senses that he is on the verge of discovering some "inscrutable purpose, some hidden prophetic intention" that governs the universe. In this moment of inspired musing, when the seas "seem already cross'd" and the universe begins to appear almost intelligible, he feels confident of his honorable place in the succession of visionaries and poets.

From the poem's beginning, the persona is drawn to the "India" of his soul's desiring with its imagined "Towers of fables immortal fashion'd from mortal dreams!"—"fables spurning the known, eluding the hold of the known, mounting to heaven!" In Whitman's customary usage the words *fable* and *myth* are often interchangeable with the word *faith;* and thus the poem's reference to "fables immortal" can perhaps be translated as "faith in immortality." In an anthropocentric way, Whitman envisions an ideal future that is "fashion'd from" his own "mortal dreams." To the "never-happy hearts" of the world's men and women who have become immiserated by their difficult lives on this seemingly "unloving earth," this "cold earth, the place of graves," he offers his bardic visions of amelioration. Like *Democratic Vistas,* which predicts that a class of inspired literati will lead America into a wholesome democratic future, "Passage to India" proclaims that "Finally shall come the poet worthy of that name, / The true son of God shall come singing his songs." Thereafter, "Nature and Man shall be disjoin'd and diffused no more, / The true son of God shall absolutely fuse them." Anticipating his self-portrait as a tragic Columbus figure in "Prayer of Columbus" (1874), "Passage to India" sketches a Whitmanlike Columbus who is scorned, poor, and facing death, but who is certain that his faith and prophecy will be justified "centuries after thou art laid in thy grave":

(Curious in time I stand, noting the efforts of heroes,
Is the deferment long? bitter the slander, poverty, death?
Lies the seed unreck'd for centuries in the ground? lo, to God's
   due occasion,
Uprising in the night, it sprouts, blooms,
And fills the earth with use and beauty.)

The last ninety lines of "Passage to India" (almost a third of its length) are a love song to the persona's soul, the spirit-lover who will accompany him to their mystic India of pure thought and to a union with the Oversoul. Once again, Whitman's dualism teases us to distinguish between the conscious "I" that is setting off for this India and the seemingly distinct "soul" that will accompany him. The problem of assuming that one's immortal state will preserve at least a measure of mortal consciousness (a defining characteristic of the Whitman persona's postmortal self) was pointed out by the biologist J. B. S. Haldane, who argued that "to prove the survival of the mind or soul [after death] as something living and active, we should need evidence that it is still developing, thinking, and willing." Divested of the body, the consciousness "may perish altogether."[17] On the other hand, Whitman's assumption that the soul undertakes its passage to God accompanied by some manifestation of the conscious self is consistent with some religious interpretations of an uninterrupted unity of body and soul. John Williamson Nevin, a spokesman of the German Reformed Church, propounded a radical version of this idea in 1846, declaring that body and soul are "identical in their origin, bound together by natural interpenetration subsequently at every point." Body and soul lead one life, he maintained. "When the resurrection body appears, it will not be as a new frame abruptly created for the occasion, and brought to the soul by outward addition and supplement. It will be found to hold in strict organic continuity with the body, as it existed before death."[18] And in the closing years of Whitman's life some members of the American clergy launched a widespread defense of the doctrine of the immortality of the body.[19] Assertions that body and soul will "interpenetrate" (in the clergyman's words) are more or less consistent with Whitman's assumption that some aspect of the persona's conscious "self" will accompany the "soul" on its journey to eternity.

Impatiently laughing and kissing his soul, and "singing our song of God,"—"thou pressing me to thee, I thee to me, O soul," like a pair of ardent lovers—the Whitman persona readies his departure to the realm of "primal thought": "To reason's early paradise, / Back, back to wisdom's birth, to innocent intuitions, / Again with fair creation." He does not journey toward the God of Western theology but toward an abstract, composite god—Whitman's "Comrade perfect," the source of all the harmonies in the universe, "a moral, spiritual fountain" in which he hopes to bathe perpetually. The journey toward the Spirit Beyond is also a quest to attain the perfected Spirit Within. The godhead toward which the persona is tending is a state of perpetual revelation, exhilaration, and epiphany—a permanent spiritual high. His plea for enlightenment resembles a Vedic prayer: "May that soul of mine, which mounts aloft in my waking hours, as an ethereal spark, and which even in my slumber has a like ascent, soaring to a great distance, as an emanation from the light of lights, be united by profound meditation with the spirit supremely blest, and supremely intelligent."[20] In a burst of ecstasy—unfortunately marred by its stilted "Biblical" language—the persona voices a premonition that his soul—"thou actual Me"—will ultimately become a Creator-God, impervious to death:

> How should I think, how breathe a single breath, how speak,
>     if, out of myself,
> I could not launch, to those, superior universes?
>
> Swiftly I shrivel at the thought of God,
> At Nature and its wonders, Time and Space and Death,
> But that I, turning, call to thee O soul, thou actual Me,
> And lo, thou gently masterest the orbs,
> Thou matest Time, smilest content at Death,
> And fillest, swellest full the vastness of Space.

"Reckoning ahead"—voyaging across the Unknown Sea by dead reckoning—in these inspired moments, he envisions his soul reaching its destination and encountering a friendly, loving God: "the Elder Brother found, / The Younger melts in fondness in his arms." Thus the persona who had once been a fancier of calamus lads now fancies himself a member of the Divine Pantheon where he has become God's favorite Calamus Lad. Impatient to set sail for this India of his dreams, the persona cries out melodramatically, "Passage, immediate passage! the blood burns in my veins!"

The poem's conclusion (section 9) features the persona's imagined sendoff to the "more than India" "where mariner has not yet dared to go," to the mythic realm that lies beyond the "aged fierce enigmas" of good and evil that plague mankind, beyond fallible theorizing and fallible science, a realm where the enlightened soul will finally comprehend the wisdom that lies behind the Vedas and behind the epiphanies of pure inspiration. The "primal thought" for which he yearns is an "India" of perpetual illumination and spiritual equilibrium. However, even as the persona prepares to depart on Death's glorious voyage—in this matchless exercise of wish fulfillment—he still reveals a need to reassure himself that his conjectures are valid and that the projected "journey" will be "safe."

> Sail forth—steer for deep waters only,
> Reckless O soul, exploring, I with thee, and thou with me,
> For we are bound to where mariner has not yet dared to go,
> And we will risk the ship, ourselves and all.

> O my brave soul!
> O farther farther sail!
> O daring joy, but safe! Are they not all seas of God?
> O farther, farther, farther sail!

The mystic faith that pervades "Passage to India" does not settle the questions of whether the persona's visionary journey to attain wisdom and holiness is feasible or where it may ultimately lead.[21] But there can be little doubt that the very act of contemplating this glorious possibility—even with the goal uncertain and his faith subject to moments of doubt—provided Whitman with comfort and a profound sense of satisfaction.

## 2

In the mid-1870s Whitman composed four poetic testaments of faith in which death is the central element. "Song of the Redwood-Tree" (1873) and "Prayer of Columbus" (1874) are, in effect, companion pieces that dramatize the persona's patient and heroic readiness for death. Each features a transparent Whitman surrogate who, on the brink of death, envisions what his life and his death will have contributed to the future of mankind. The lyrical and affecting "Song of the Universal" (1874) and the abstruse "Eidòlons" (1876) constitute the most sustained expressions of philosophical idealism in all of *Leaves of Grass*.

The ambitious and supple "Song of the Redwood-Tree" incorporates two bravura "arias" in which a dryad of the world's most magnificent tree species—the persona's thinly veiled alter ego—chants its readiness to die, confident that it will have helped to usher in a nobler race of Americans. Amid the tumult of woodmen felling the virgin redwood forests in California's Mendocino County, the persona imagines that he hears the dryadic voice of the tree, "its mighty death-chant chanting," and he undertakes to translate it. (Whitman, who had never traveled west of the Mississippi when he wrote the poem, apparently drew descriptive details from published sources.) The tree's "murmuring out of its myriad leaves" thinly disguises the voice of the persona speaking through *Leaves of Grass.* In featuring as its speaker a redwood tree in the process of being cut down, the poet calls attention to his own condition at the time—"cut down" by weakness and grief but apparently strengthened by the belief that he has helped to create a vision of a nobler future for mankind. Like the dying "Indian" who was a staple of popular culture, the redwood tree voices its gratitude for the privilege (painful though it might be) of disappearing from the land to make way for the "higher stage" of (white) society that is destined to take its place. Whitman, like his contemporaries, tended to picture the aboriginal Americans as vanishing from the American scene. "It is consequently not surprising," observes Ed Folsom, "that the most extended poems he wrote about Indians were of them dying."[22] Most contemporary readers would have assumed that the dying redwood tree was a metaphor for the supposedly vanishing "Red Man." And most of them did in fact view America's westward movement as a harbinger of personal and national progress, perhaps unaware of its tragic implications for Native Americans or its environmental havoc.[23] The seemingly cheerful disappearance from the land of the indigenous population to make way for the "white race" was the subject of countless literary productions, including Longfellow's "Song of Hiawatha," Fenimore Cooper's "Indian" novels, Whitman's "Yonondio" (1887), and the "frontier thesis" of Frederick Jackson Turner. Basic to this assumption was the theory of the "stages of society," according to which the darker, and presumably inferior, races and their cruder social formations would inevitably be superseded by a more sophisticated and technologically adept Europeanized society.[24] Like the "good Indian" in a nineteenth-century melodrama, Whitman's tree seems happily resigned to die and to see its fellow trees cut down in order to hasten the arrival of what it calls "the new society proportionate to nature." Having *"grandly fill'd our time,"* sings the tree in its first aria, we *"leave the field for them . . . predicted long, / For a superior race, they too grandly fill their time."* And in its second aria the tree proclaims that with the passage of time *"Nature's long and harmless throes"* will install in *"these virgin lands"* a free people, endowed with an *"average spiritual manhood"* and a *"womanhood divine"*—a people who are *"hardy, sweet, gigantic,"* and *"tower proportionate to Nature."* The tree's cheerful acceptance of death in response to a force that is presumably both national and cosmic—*"(age upon age working in death the same as life)"*—is an example of nationalistic mythmaking. Surely, Whitman knew that what he calls "nature's harmless throes"—if not always red in tooth and claw—could be far from "harmless"; an 1867 notation shows how closely the poem reflects his belief that racial selection is a component of the self-fulfilling evolutionary "laws." Inexorably, he observes, "comes Ethnological Science, cold, remorseless, not heeding at all the vehement abstractions of equality and fraternity . . . and settling these things by evolution, by natural selection by certain races notwithstanding all the frantic pages of the sentimentalists helplessly disappearing by the slow, sure, progress of laws, through sufficient periods of time."[25] Thus the tree's demise illustrates the premise that "to build a grander future" humanity must accept the workings of death as an instrument of selection and of inevitable progress. Each successive social order in its turn, the poem implies, must welcome death as an agency in the continuous process of developing still nobler orders of beings in nobler societies.

"Prayer of Columbus" is a monodrama that (like "Song of the Redwood-Tree") illustrates its hero's readiness for death. The Columbus figure, facing rejection and death following a life of great achievements, remains steadfast in his faith—an impressive surrogate for the paralyzed and pain-wracked Whitman. The poem serves as an apologia and near-elegy for the poet, who was still traumatized by the loss in 1873 of his beloved mother and his sister-in-law, and fearful of losing his life to paralysis and other ailments. Obliquely, it calls attention to his own disappointment in failing to gain a mass audience. Prepared to die, Whitman-Columbus makes a final curtain call that has an old-fashioned melodramatic ring.[26] He appears as a dying and "batter'd, wreck'd old man," still intoxicated by his vision of the "newer better worlds, their parturition," which he has discovered, and he remains eager to seek new worlds. If we accept Emerson's dictum that the birth of a poet is the chief event of half a millennium of human history—and Whitman toyed with the idea that he was *that* poet—we can understand why Whitman donned the Columbus mantle. A quarter of a century earlier, Henry David Thoreau had developed a heroic simile that might have intrigued Whitman by linking Columbus and a vision of immortality. In lamenting the deaths of a shipload of poor Irish emigrants who perished in 1849 when their ship foundered approaching the American shore and whom he was unable to help rescue, Thoreau wrote:

> Why care for these dead bodies? They really have no friends but the worms and fishes. Their owners were coming to the New World, as Columbus and the Pilgrims did—they were within a mile of its shores; but, before they could reach it, they emigrated to a newer world than Columbus dreamed of, yet one of whose existence we believe that there is far more universal and convincing evidence—though it has not yet been discovered by science—than Columbus had of this: not merely mariners' tales and some paltry drift-wood and sea-weed, but a continental drift and instinct to all our shores. I saw their empty hulks come to land; but they themselves, meanwhile, were cast upon some shore yet farther west, toward which we are all tending and which we shall reach at last, it may be through storm and darkness, as they did. No doubt, we have reason to thank God that they have not been "shipwrecked into life again."

Thoreau's observation, that "it is hard to part with one's body, but, no doubt, it is easy enough to do without it once it is gone," anticipates Whitman's poetic reference to the "excrementious" body, said to be sloughed off at death; and Thoreau's prediction that these Irish dead will find a new land in "halcyon days" and "kiss the shore in rapture there" anticipates Whitman's many poems celebrating the soul's voyage to the uncharted regions. Thoreau's reference to "a continental drift and instinct" indicates that he, like Whitman, assumes that the best argument for an afterlife is the supposedly universal sentiment in its favor.[27]

The identification of Columbus with Whitman seemed only natural to the poet and to his friends. After reading an installment of *Democratic Vistas,* Bronson Alcott wrote Whitman a letter in which he called the poet "the American Columbus, whose sagacity has thus sounded adventurously the sea of our Social Chaos and anchored his thought serenely in the newly discovered Atlantides about which the Grecian Plato died dreaming."[28] Following the publication of "Prayer of Columbus," Anne Gilchrist asserted that the person portrayed in this "sacred poem" who had sacrificed his health for a noble cause was indeed "our Columbus, Walt Whitman." Whitman's friend Ellen O'Connor claimed that the poet had "unconsciously put a sort of auto-biographical dash into 'Prayer of Columbus.'" These friends, like many readers in the last quarter of the century, interpreted the poem as the inspired utterance of a great mystic. Whitman's "Columbus" has been compared to Tennyson's "Ulysses," a poem Whitman said "shows the grand master" and which, according to Dr. Bucke, the poet sometimes recited aloud.[29] In both poems an aging speaker gazes at the ocean as he proclaims his abiding faith and his eagerness to serve in his declining days. Tennyson's elderly Ulysses, "made weak by time and fate, but strong in will," still burns "to strive, to seek, to find, and not to yield." But as the product of a poet in his twenties, Tennyson's hero seems more imbued with the Victorian spirit of let-us-then-be-up-and-doing than with what Bishop Jeremy Taylor two centuries earlier had called Holy Dying, which is the chief concern of Whitman's Columbus figure. In Whitman's America, a patient readiness for death was revered as a virtue. Thus the George Washington depicted in Parson Weems's mythobiography was as much esteemed by two generations of readers "for his deathbed patience and submission as for his inability to tell a lie."[30] A patient readiness for death also characterizes the hero of Washington Irving's *Life and Voyage of Christopher Columbus* (1828), from which Whitman drew some of the poem's details. Irving had pictured a dying Columbus, still pleading with the Spanish monarchs to restore him to his position of honor. (Coincidentally, some of Whitman's friends sought in vain to obtain a federal pension to reward the disabled poet for his service in the military hospitals.) Irving's idealized Columbus, his frame shattered, his mind "chilled" by the cold ingratitude of his sovereigns, who have not even reimbursed his monetary outlays, prepares to die: "Having thus scrupulously attended to all the claims of affection, loyalty, and justice upon earth, he turned his thoughts to heaven, confessing himself, partaking of the holy sacrament, and complying with the ceremonies of a devout Catholic . . . he expired with great resignation, on the day of Ascension, the 20th of May, 1506, being about seventy years of age. His last words were, '*In manus tuas Domine, commendo spirito meum.*' 'Into thy hands, O Lord, I commend my spirit.'"[31]

Although Whitman rarely addressed a personal God and had scant regard for ritual, he followed Irving's lead in portraying a Columbus who was prepared to meet death with a clear conscience because he was on the best of terms with his Maker. Whitman's Columbus mirrors Whitman's self-image—a "batter'd, wreck'd old man" who is "venting a heavy heart," uncertain that his cherished enterprises have succeeded. The poem's Columbus figure faces death with the patience of a saint as he utters the passionately cadenced prayer that forms the heart of the poem and that can be read as Whitman's own testament. The Columbus persona declares that he has never lost "faith nor ecstasy" in his God, that he has always responded to "the potent, felt, interior command, stronger than words, / A message from the Heavens, whispering to me even in sleep." In the testimony of Whitman/Columbus that he has been spurred on by his faith to discover new worlds, we can almost hear Whitman himself testify that he, too, has been driven by a higher force to explore new worlds of thought and language. As he explained in 1872, he felt an avowedly "religious" motivation in writing *Leaves of Grass:*

> I fulfilled in that an imperious conviction, and the commands of my nature as total and irresistible as those which make the sea flow or the globe revolve. . . . But what is life but an experiment? and mortality but an exercise? with references to results beyond. And so shall my poems be. If incomplete here, and superfluous there, *n'importe*—the earnest trial and persistent exploration shall at least be mine, and other success failing, shall be success enough. . . . I ventured from the beginning, my own way, taking chances—and would keep on venturing.[32]

However, the Columbus persona's faith as he faces death is momentarily shaken by the fear that his ventures may have been failures. Sensing his "terminus near," his "brain bewilder'd," his "timbers part[ing]," he voices the hope that "haply" (by chance or accident) he will have helped to reform "the brutish measureless undergrowth" of humanity. That statement hardly coincides with the conduct of the historic Columbus toward the indigenous Caribbean peoples, whom he regarded as subhuman and whom he ordered to be enslaved and decimated. But it accords with Whitman's assessment, in *Democratic Vistas,* of the moral disease pervading the American body politic and his hope that his writings will point the way to eventual reforms.[33] Still, the poet uses the voice of "Columbus" to express a lingering fear that his poetic vision and his labors may not have helped to inaugurate the new worlds he has foreseen and that his death may prove meaningless after all. In tormented lines that reflect the poet's difficulties in sustaining his image as an optimistic bard and seer, the Columbus persona questions the fogginess of his visions:

> Is it the prophet's thought I speak, or am I raving?
> What do I know of life? what of myself?
> I know not even my own work past or present,
> Dim ever-shifting guesses of it spread before me,
> Of newer better worlds, their mighty parturition,
> Mocking, perplexing me.

But this momentary crisis of faith is unexpectedly resolved, in much the same fashion that similar crises are resolved in some of the earlier poems, by a sort of deus ex machina—a sudden epiphany during which the persona is miraculously rescued from his despair by nature's visual and aural auguries of hope. His eyes and ears are seemingly unsealed by some higher power, and he senses that his claim to prophetic powers has been validated and his fame assured:

> And these things I see suddenly, what mean they?
> As if some miracle, some hand divine unseal'd my eyes,
> Shadowy vast shapes smile through air and sky,
> And on the distant waves sail countless ships,
> And anthems in new tongues I hear saluting me.

That "hand divine" appears to have unsealed his eyes and strengthened his visions of the future; "shadowy vast shapes" appear as if to escort him through the blessed gates of death. And he seems to hear welcoming "anthems" from nature or the Oversoul, the significance of which is glossed in a passage in an 1860 poem in which the inspired persona discovers that the inspirational "music always round me, unceasing, unbeginning, yet long untaught I did not hear," has suddenly revealed its "exquisite meanings" to him.[34] Whitman's Columbus appears prepared to die in a state of grace, prepared to meet his Maker. During his two remaining decades, Whitman seemed always prepared for his death, ready to meet his Maker (or whatever destiny might await him) on the best of terms.

Another testament of Whitman's faith, deeply moving in its simple language and imagery, is "Song of the Universal." The much-revised poem was composed in response to an invitation from students at the all-male Tufts College to deliver a poem at the college's 1874 commencement. Because of his illness, Whitman could not attend the event; the poem was read by another with unknown success. Although critics have detected Hegelian and Brahminic influences in the poem,[35] Tufts College, it should be observed, was founded by Universalists, and both the poem's title and its message may be construed as gracious nods to a Universalist audience. Its proclamation of faith in the perseverance of the soul and the steady and ultimate triumph of good over evil is congruent with the Universalist creed, which has historic affinities to Spiritualism. Universalism has been defined as "the doctrine that the destiny of mankind is to progress onward and upward forever; that always before man is a chance to develop and that always in man is a power to unfold, always a time and a place in which to grow and always in man a power to respond to the opportunity."[36] Such, generally, was Whitman's faith. He declares in the closing pages of *Democratic Vistas* that "our modern civilization, with all its improvements" is doomed unless it "be confronted and met by at least an equally subtle and tremendous force-infusion for purposes of spiritualization, for the pure conscience, for genuine esthetics, and for absolute and primal manliness and womanliness."[37] The poet's argument resembles "the doctrine of salvation by character" of the Reverend Hosea Ballou, a key figure in the development of Universalism, who maintained that sin is "not an inherited condition, that the human will is free and that ultimately man will learn to conform to the will of God; that the death of Christ was not to pay a debt to God, but to draw men away from sin; that Christ was example and incorporation to lead men to the perfect life; that man would suffer reasonable punishment for violation of all law, but in the end would work in harmony with God." And like Whitman's imagery of the soul's voyage toward divinity, article 5 of the (Universalist) Winchester Profession of Faith proclaims "the final harmony of all souls with God."[38] Divested of their theological language, Ballou's principles harmonize with those articulated in Whitman's postwar poems, one of which envisions "the little that is Good steadily hastening towards immortality, / And the vast all that is call'd Evil I saw hastening to merge itself and become lost and dead."[39]

"Song of the Universal," which the poet calls "a song that no poet yet has chanted," opens on a Universalist note:

> In this broad earth of ours,
> Amid the measureless grossness and the slag,
> Enclosed and safe within its central heart,
> Nestles the seed perfection.

Within the soul of each human being, the poem implies, inheres the urge to perfection, capable of sprouting even under the worst circumstances. Once again Whitman opts for "the soul above all science," maintaining that in the course of evolution "the real to the ideal tends"—a statement implying that our lives are governed by a tendency toward physical and social betterment or that our mortal existence must, in time, be superseded by some form of spiritual existence. And in words that could have been sanctioned by Hosea Ballou, the poet asserts that both the "right" and "what we call evil" will ultimately evolve into a condition of universal goodness and joy—pointedly concluding his stanzas with the word *universal*:

> Forth from their masks, no matter what,
> From the huge festering trunk, from craft and guile and tears,
> Health to emerge and joy, joy universal.
>
> Out of the bulk, the morbid and the shallow,
> Out of the bad majority, the varied countless frauds of men
>     and states,
> Electric, antiseptic, yet cleaving, suffusing all,
> Only the good is universal.

The terms "electric" and "antiseptic" in the above stanzas point to a universal ameliorative force forever operating to purify and improve the human race. In a similar vein, *Democratic Vistas* declares that human corruption is steadily being absorbed and neutralized by "Nature's antiseptic power," and the poem "As They Draw to a Close" (1872) defines "the joyous electric all" as encompassing nature and God, life and death.

Rejecting the "Babel" of doctrines, the third section of "Song of the Universal," the poem hints that inspired seers and poets, who are called "the blest eyes, the happy hearts," may follow "the guiding thread so fine, / Along the mighty labyrinth," and so catch a glimpse of the ideal in "one ray of perfect light, / One flash of heaven's glory." Or, with equal luck, they may chance to hear "from some far shore the final chorus sounding." True poets, the lines imply, may even hope to receive mystic communications from beyond the grave. The final section (some twenty-four of the poem's sixty-five lines) designates America as the destined site of the "scheme's culmination"—a place where, through "deific faiths and amplitudes" and through the working of "immortality" and "love," all men and women may ripen into idealized "spiritual images" (or what the poet later calls "eidolons") of themselves. And, as befits an ode intended to be read before an audience of Universalist clergy and theology students, the penultimate stanza is a prayer for the triumph of goodness within the Divine Plan and a call to sustain the faith on which the poem is predicated:

Give me O God to sing that thought,
Give me, give him or her I love this quenchless faith,
In Thy ensemble, whatever else withheld withhold not from us,
Belief in plan of Thee enclosed in Time and Space,
Health, peace, salvation universal.

Without alluding to any specific dogma, the "[b]elief in plan of Thee" once more assumes the existence of a divinely ordered universe. The declaration that without faith in such a plan life itself could prove to be only "a dream" exemplifies the depth of Whitman's philosophic idealism and could, without difficulty, be deconstructed to imply that the fulfillment of God's plan ultimately hinges on the strength of one's belief in it.

Whitman's prewar poems had derived much of their tension from the poet's efforts to balance material and spiritual values, but his later poems edged closer to Berkeleyan idealism by scanting the material element in favor of the spiritual. The older Whitman even hints that if the ideal world of which he has dreamt is not a reality, then the reality he perceives in the everyday world may be only a dream. "As his conception of the soul widens," says an early critic, "his attitude toward the actual and the ideal undergoes a corresponding change. The infinite possibilities of death begin to disparage the actualities of life. The latter are still conceived of as wonderful and glorious; but Whitman feels that there are "wonders beyond their wonder and glories beyond their glory."[40] The ultimate example of the precedence of the ideal over the tangible in Whitman's later poems is the stanzaic "lecture" by an unnamed (but readily identified) "seer" in the poem "Eidòlons" (1876). The poem's importance to Whitman is indicated by the fact that it is the only long poem he chose to include in the group of introductory "Inscription" poems in the definitive 1881 edition of *Leaves of Grass.* Most of its twenty-one irregular stanzas end with the words "eidòlon" or "eidòlons"—terms indicating phantoms or apparitions, but in this poem specifically referring to images of the spiritual ideal that are presumed to permeate every aspect of existence. And coexistent with these eidolons is what Whitman calls the "Eidòlon-of-Eidòlons," or the Universal Spirit, toward which each soul tends and with which it seeks to unite. The often opaque poem does not develop a closed philosophic system. In fact, only its two introductory stanzas form complete sentences. The remaining stanzas, in which the nebulous eidolons seem to flit before the reader's eyes, are incomplete, as if to stress that our unaided logic and our unaided senses can perceive only what the poem calls "the ostent evanescent"—the world of flickering appearances that vanish before we realize what we are looking at. The poem implies that unless we discover our own eidolon—the mystic ideal-seeking element within us—our unassisted thinking reveals only partial truths. Whitman explained his concept of the "ostent evanescent" in an abortive essay: "[T]he journey of philosophy beginning with Kant brings us to an uncertainty about every thing," he said. "The laws of sight, touch, weight, &c. are dethroned. Materials & material experiences amount to nothing. The realities we thought so absolute are only ostensible and are either scattered to the winds or permitted but a passing & temporary sway." William Sloane Kennedy, an early aficionado of Whitman's writings, simply equated these eidolons with the soul, remarking that "behind all appearance is the soul, the ultimate reality, central and changeless."[41] Two centuries earlier America's ranking idealist Jonathan Edwards had argued, in a similar vein, that the tangible, visible world is chiefly important as an analogy of the "real," or spiritual, world. "The material world, and all things pertaining to it," he said, "is by the creator wholly subordinated to the spiritual and moral worlds."[42] Edwards's "real" world seems not far removed from Whitman's world of eidolons, which the poem identifies as the spiritual images or "phantoms" of an ideal self which each artist, savant, or martyr strives to fashion during the course of a lifetime. The urge to reach these "higher pinnacles," according to the poem, may manifest itself through science, democracy, exploration, or invention, and even be apparent in the "giant trees," rocks, buildings, the earth and the stars that are "swelling, collapsing, ending" during countless eons and thus "sweeping the present to the infinite future." By situating our mortal existence in the "ostent evanescent" Whitman implies that the known world may be only a dark mirror image of the luminous "real" world of eidolons, toward which each soul must strive:

Not this the world,
Not these the universes, they the universes,
Purport and end, ever the permanent life of life,
    Eidòlons, eidòlons.

In its moments of "rapt, ecstatic" inspiration, the poem suggests, the soul may "shape and shape" its "orbic tendencies" toward a higher existence, a divine being. But at the present stage of human development, Whitman explains, taking a modest bow, "the prophet and the bard" remain the truest interpreters of "God and eidòlons." And, once again, death is presented as the necessary intermediary between the known life and the life of pure spirit. The persona feels certain that once he has doffed his carnal body in favor of his eidolon-body—"the body lurking there within thy body"—he will gravitate toward "the real I myself, / An image—an eidòlon." And then he will find the eidolon-mates for whom he yearns. Like Poe's angel Israfel, he will eventually become the Eidolon-Whitman whose holy songs will harmonize with the music of the Eidolon Spheres, "rising at last and floating, / A round full-orb'd eidòlon."

### 3

The 1876 edition of *Leaves of Grass*, Whitman informs his readers, was composed during a period of "grave illness, making this volume "almost Death's book." "*Preface 1876*—Leaves of Grass and Two Rivulets" confirms his change of poetic emphasis from celebrating the active life to celebrating the spiritual life. Using a photographic figure of speech, he expresses a desire to "shift the slides, and exhibit the problem and paradox of the same ardent and fully appointed Personality [i.e., the Whitman persona] entering the sphere of resistless gravitation of Spiritual Law, and with cheerful face estimating Death, not at all as the cessation, but somehow what I feel it must be, the entrance upon by far the greatest part of existence, and something that Life is as much for, as it is for itself." Apparently sensing that his days may be coming to a close and fearful that he would never publish another edition, he added, "I end my books with thoughts, or radiations from thoughts, on Death, Immortality, and a free entrance into the Spiritual World." And in an extended note appended to the preface, he adds that having formerly celebrated the vibrant physical world, his work "still remains to be completed by suffusing through the whole and several, the other pervading *invisible* fact, so large a part (is it not the largest part?) of life here." Still envisioning America as the center from which democratic and spiritual values will "radiate" around the world, he adds that he believes "it is no less than this *idea of Immortality, above all other ideas,* that is to enter into, and vivify, and give crowning religious stamps to Democracy in the New World." He continues to subordinate science to what he calls "a higher fact, the Eternal Soul of Man (of all Else too), the Spiritual, the Religious—which is to be the highest office of Scientism, in my opinion, and of future Poetry also, to free from fables, crudities, and superstitions, and launch forth in renewed Faith and Scope a hundred fold." But despite its tone of passionate advocacy, the 1876 preface is less than persuasive, since it perpetuates the older Whitman's tendency to explain abstractions in terms of other abstractions.[43]

Not surprisingly, several minor poems first published in the 1876 edition stress the perseverance of the soul and dramatize the persona's readiness for what he imagines to be his impending demise. Many of these verses celebrate his passage to realms beyond the known world, where he expects to survive with his identity unimpaired. The volume's dedicatory poem equates the persona's faith in immortality with his faith in the future of *Leaves of Grass,* fantasizing that even "after death" he may "invisibly return" and still be chanting his songs to "some group of mates . . . in other spheres." In the poem "After an Interval" the poet recalls gazing into the starry heavens one midnight in November 1875, inspired by the thought that, like the stars themselves, his book will be "standing so well the test of death and night." The poem "Two Rivulets" once more illustrates the poet's ideological dualism, as the persona and his soul flow together toward "the mystic Ocean" that encompasses "Death and Life, / Object and Subject . . . The Real and Ideal." Not only does the persona feel the lure of death, but it appears that the "yearnful waves!" of the Ocean of Death long to receive *him* and to kiss him with their watery lips. "In Former Songs" also shows death ready to welcome him because his "new Democratic chants" are saturated with the spirit and mystery of death. In a mild musical pun, he remarks that his days, like his "chants," appear to be coming to a "close." And in his "pealing final cry" he proclaims that his steadfast faith (like Martin Luther's "fortress") is his "citadel and tower."

The 1881–1882 edition, chiefly important for establishing the final arrangement of *Leaves of Grass,* contained only fifteen new lyrics, all of them brief. "Thou Orb Aloft Full-Dazzling" sets the tone for the verses that Whitman would compose during the last decade of his life by welcoming his own death and voicing the hope that his mortal life, though circumscribed by invalidism and pain, will continue as long as possible. In the "October" of his life the persona beseeches the life-giving sun to permeate his poems and, in setting, to ease his way to death:

Nor only launch thy subtle dazzle and thy strength for
    these [poems],
Prepare the later afternoons of me myself—prepare my
    lengthening shadows,
Prepare my starry nights.

Yet the benign tone of most of these late lyrics still masks a lingering anxiety concerning death. Witness the frenzied emotion in the persona's imagined foray into the "dim, illimitable grounds" of death in "As at Thy Portals Also Death" as Whitman summons up the haunting memory of his beloved mother lying in her coffin. His ebbing days still produced gnawing doubts about whether his poems would ultimately succeed. Painfully dejected about what he felt to be the "last of ebb, and daylight waning" of his life and prepared to face the worst fate that could befall him—the vanishing of *Leaves of Grass* from living memory—he shored up his psychological defenses by recalling the fate of the legions of unfulfilled "artists greatest of any, with cherish'd lost designs," who had died in obscurity. In this depressed mood, he uttered the tormented cry, "On to oblivion then!"[44]

Having finalized the arrangement of *Leaves of Grass*, Whitman published a supplemental volume of prose and poetry with the autumnal title *November Boughs*. Many of its sixty-four lyrics and what Whitman labeled its "poemets" (for which the poet received small honoraria from various periodicals) were added as an "Annex" to the 1888 edition as "Sands at Seventy." These verses reported his cheerful bearing as he faced physical deterioration—solemn-sweet announcements of his readiness for death, and cheerful expressions of farewell.[45] (Whitman also published a number of undistinguished elegies during these years, brief memorial lyrics, many of them commemorating celebrated personages.)[46] In the prose preface "A Backward Glance O'er Travel'd Roads" (1888), Whitman wrote: "In the free evening of my day I give you reader the foregoing garrulous talk, thoughts, reminiscences," and suggested that, alive or dead, he would ever aspire to talk to the living reader. That sentiment is beautifully developed in the bittersweet *vers de société* masterpiece "After the Supper and Talk."[47] Against the onrush of the ultimate night the poem shows the Whitman figure striving to the very end to preserve his voice—the same "garrulous talk" he had referred to in the introduction to "A Backward Glance"—the "talk" that embodies his life force and his spiritual selfhood. He feels that his words alone will perpetuate him in the mortal sphere. Standing at the "exit-door" of life but loath to leave for the unknown, he clings compulsively to the warmth of human hands, to the music of human voices, and to the sound of his own voice. Although he hopes that his poetic voice will endure into the future, he wishes to prolong his mortal vocal powers as long as he can. In order to achieve dramatic distance, and perhaps to cushion the shock of his impending death, the poet employs a rhetorical device that is rarely found in his poems. He refers to himself in the third person and pictures himself observing from a distance the vanishing figure of the mortal Whitman. His reluctance to depart from the House of Life is expressed in a series of death-related metaphors. And as a master of participials, Whitman constructs a verse that (except for three lines contained within parentheses) forms an uncompleted statement, so that his departure, as he might have wished, seems to be postponed indefinitely:

After the supper and talk—after the day is done,
As friend from friends his final withdrawal prolonging,
Good-bye and Good-bye with emotional lips repeating,
(So hard for his hand to release those hands—no more will
    they meet,
No more for communion of sorrow and joy, of old and young,
A far-stretching journey awaits him, to return no more,)
Shunning, postponing severance—seeking to ward off the last
    word ever so little,
E'en at the exit-door turning—charges superfluous calling back—
    e'en as he descends the steps,
Something to eke out a minute additional—shadows of nightfall
    deepening,
Farewells, messages lessening—dimmer the forthgoer's visage
    and form,
Soon to be lost for aye in the darkness—loth, O so loth to depart!
Garrulous to the very last.[48]

Many short poems relate Whitman's physical decline and his thoughts about dying. When he was sixty-seven years old and had five more years to live, he anticipated the snuffing out of "the early candle-light of [his] old age."[49] "Twilight" depicts the steadily dimming light of his fading years but praises the twilight glow as an abiding source of comfort:

The soft voluptuous opiate shades,
The sun just gone, the eager light dispell'd—(I too will soon be
    gone, dispell'd,)
A haze—nirwana—rest and light—oblivion.[50]

Those twilight colors are "voluptuous" (like the onomatopoeia of the above lines) because they still afford the aging poet a measure of sensuous delight; and they are "opiate" because they ease his pain and dull his physical senses to prepare him for an easier transition to death. Old age, remarked Dr. Oliver Wendell Holmes at about the same time that Whitman wrote these lines, is "that narcotic which Nature administers" to ease our passage to death.[51] In this example of the pathetic fallacy, the poem depicts the fading sun as "eager" to display its light; it, too, wishes to linger as long as possible. The reference to "nirwana" suggests the emancipation from temporal life in a union with eternity, and according to Whitman, the word *oblivion* best reflects "the idea I had in mind."[52] Another poem shows how much he cherished these final years by picturing him as a tree whose "lingering sparse leaves on winter-nearing boughs" (like the verses of his old age) are still precious to him. And he enshrined these twilight days of blissful surrender in one of the most charming anticipations of easeful death in all of English verse—the sensuous and rhetorically dazzling "Halcyon Days":

> Not from successful love alone,
> Nor wealth, nor honor'd middle age, nor victories of politics
> or war;
> But as life wanes, and all the turbulent passions calm,
> As gorgeous, vapory, silent hues cover the evening sky,
> As softness, fulness, rest, suffuse the frame, like fresher, balmier air,
> As the days take on a mellower light, and the apple at last hangs
> really finish'd and indolent-ripe on the tree,
> Then for the teeming quietest, happiest days of all!
> The brooding and blissful halcyon days.[53]

To further illustrate his readiness for death as he entered his eighth decade Whitman revisited the saintlike deaths of two mythic heroes of his youth—James Fenimore Cooper's pathfinder Natty Bumppo and Osceola, the legendary chief of the Seminoles. In *The Prairie* (1827) Cooper had pictured the frail and ancient Natty Bumppo standing erect and with an "air of grandeur and humility" against the backdrop of a remote Western prairie. Having apparently heard the voice of God summoning him home, Bumppo stands at strict attention before his "Commanding Officer," and "with a fine military elevation of the head, and, with a voice that might be heard in any part of that numerous assembly, he pronounces the word—Here!" Whitman, who had recently replaced the oil lamp in his parlor with an electric light bulb, was rereading Cooper's novels. He had long admired Cooper's hero: "I never forget Natty Bumppo— he is from everlasting to everlasting," he said.[54] So, having himself completed the allotted three-score and ten and, being attentive to *his* Maker's call (and having formerly pictured himself in the role of an old soldier in *Drum-Taps*), the ailing Whitman likens his own readiness for death to Natty Bumppo's:

To-day at twilight, hobbling, answering company roll-call,
*Here,* with vital voice,
Reporting yet, saluting yet the Officer over all.[55]

Whitman also depicted the romanticized death of the young Seminole chieftain Osceola, betrayed by his American captors in 1838. The poem pictures a dignified and composed Osceola dying of a broken heart as he dons his full regalia and war paint, smiles, and silently shakes hands with his captors. Then he "fix'd his look on wife and children—the last." The immediate source for this poem was probably a lithograph copy of George Catlin's highly inventive painting of the scene that was hung in the poet's room. Whitman claimed that the poem was based word for word on what Catlin had related to him about the events that inspired the painting.[56]

However, Whitman could not remain impervious to the grimmer aspects of death. His seventieth birthday coincided with the disastrous flood in Johnstown, Pennsylvania, when an upstream dam burst and some 2,200 persons were drowned in the flood waters that swamped this working-class town. Deeply unnerved by the magnitude of the disaster, Whitman composed "A Voice from Death," which appeared on the front page of the *New York World* one week after the tragic event The poem mourns the victims "found and unfound" while praising America's capacity to recover from such a cataclysm. The language with which Whitman acknowledges death as an awesome (masculine?) destroyer is oddly reminiscent of Jonathan Edwards's famous sermon "Sinners in the Hands of an Angry God," whose wrathful deity holds sinful humanity in His hand over the precipice of destruction:

Thou that in all, and over all, and through and under all,
    incessant!
Thou! thou! the vital, universal giant force resistless,
    sleepless, calm,
Holding Humanity as in thy open hand, as some ephemeral toy,
How ill to e'er forget thee!

The disaster jarred the composure of the aging poet, whose sights had been focused on his peaceful departure from life; it made him realize that he had temporarily "forgotten" death's crueler aspect. And it reawakened him to the realization that "wrapt in these little potencies of progress, politics, culture, wealth, invention" were the "silent ever-swaying power" and "the mighty elemental throes" of death, "in which and upon which we float, and every one of us is buoy'd." In sharp contrast to his many poems of benign death, "A Voice from Death" exhibits a rekindled respect for death as a cruel destroyer. In the poem, the personified voice of Death calls attention to a paradox: whether it be manifested as a gentle midwife or as a ruthless destroyer, death is an aspect of the universal law that governs the world. The voice of sudden death asserts that although it may arrive unexpectedly, "in horror and pang," it, too, is "a minister of the Deity."[57] The poem reiterates Whitman's belief that even such dire events as the Johnstown flood must eventually become integrated into the cosmic process of spiritual advancement. In imagery that recalls the hopeful resolution of "As I Ebb'd with the Ocean of Life," "A Voice from Death" predicts that from the very ooze of the flood waters "blossoms and birth [will] emerge."

## 4

By the year 1888 Whitman was sending rivulets of verses, virtual health bulletins in which he reported his ailments and his abiding faith, to the newspapers. The verses related his struggles against "weakness, blindness, more paralysis," irritability, or death's onslaught that would "cut me short for good"; and they expressed the fear that his "daily songs" could become tainted by his "ungracious glooms, aches, lethargy, constipation, whimpering, *ennui*."[58] "A Carol Closing Sixty-Nine" describes "The body wreck'd, old, poor, and paralyzed—the strange inertia falling pall-like round me, / The burning fires down in my sluggish blood not yet extinct, / The undiminish'd faith—the groups of loving friends." There were, in fact, many moments when the poet seemed to his doctors about to breathe his last, and at times death loomed up before him like an ominous specter:

I sing of life, yet mind me well of death,
To-day shadowy Death dogs my steps, my seated shape, and has
   for years—
Draws sometimes close to me, as face to face.[59]

Still he pursued the dream of setting sail, together with his soul, across the sea of death, picturing himself as an "old ship" with sails unfurled and ready to "take to the deepest, freest waters" or as the "eidòlon yacht of me!" destined not on "our concluding voyage, / But outset and sure entrance to the truest, best, maturest."[60] In a gloomier moment the aging paralytic presented what he called a "mirror" image of himself as a beached sailing ship—"an old dismasted, gray and batter'd ship, disabled, done . . . rusting, mouldering." The image was probably inspired by an etching of a beached, decaying sailing ship that hung in the home of Thomas B. Harned, his benefactor and one of his literary executors.[61]

But he could not resist playing little mind games with death, even as his vitality ebbed and he felt "low down." At times he tried to dispel his doctors' gloomy prognoses about his condition. In what may have been a grim jest, the poet, who had long been preoccupied with his chronic indigestion and constipation, speculated in a letter to his last attending physician, Dr. Daniel Longaker, that the energies required to sustain his flagging digestive powers were steadily diminishing but that they were somehow being transferred to his ever-active mind, the better to prepare him, he conjectured, for a future life in some realm of pure thought:

> My great corpus is like an old wooden leg. Possibly (even probably), that slow vital almost impalpable by-play of automatic stimulus belonging to living fiber has, by gradual habit of years and years in me and (especially of the last three years), got quite diverted into *mental* play and *vitality* and attention, instead of attending to normal play in stomachic and muscular and peristaltic use. Does this account for the stomachic non-action, no stimulus? Or what is there in this, if anything?[62]

Still, he cherished his lessening moments of joy and inspiration. "To the Sun-Set Breeze," which Dr. Bucke called a "most subtle, extraordinary little poem," captures those moments when, "alone, sick, weak-down, melted-worn with sweat," the vitalizing afflatus still brings him "occult medicines." The mystic doctor equated that evening breeze at the end of the poet's day with the occasional infusions of "cosmic consciousness," the divine influx that the poet still experienced. Bucke interpreted the poem to mean that at age seventy-one, the closing year of Whitman's life, his visionary powers had diminished, his inner voice had grown fainter, and the "Brahmic splendor" had waned. Whitman, he declared, was bidding good-bye not only to his friends and to his mortal self but to his cosmic consciousness.[63] As if to confirm Bucke's words, "Good-Bye My Fancy," a four-line title poem of the "Second Annex" to the "Deathbed Edition" of *Leaves of Grass* (1891–1892), shows the poet bidding a loving farewell to his "fancy," the shaping spirit of his imagination. A note appended to the poem defines his good-bye as "the salutation of another beginning" but concedes that his "last words" are not "samples of the best" of his utterances. In another brief lyric he deplores the state of his body, now grown "sluggish, aged, cold . . . the light in the eye grown dim," but cheers himself with the thought that all "shall duly flame again," for neither "life, nor force, nor any visible thing" ever disappears. And (in words that anticipate William Carlos Williams's "Spring and All") he affirms that "To frozen clods ever the spring's invisible law returns."[64]

One of Whitman's last known conversations, with his New York hostess Alma Calder Johnston, shows him still focused on the subject of immortality. According to Mrs. Johnston, who came away in tears from her interview with the dying poet:

> We had talked disconnectedly—with eloquent pauses—of immortality, of the indestructibility of things physical and things spiritual; of "things that cohere and go forward and are not dropped by death"; of Death as dissociated with disease as Life is ever dissociated with disease; of Death as feminine, a Strong Deliveress. Yet we were not unmindful of the insight, the comprehension, the experiences, that weakness and pain bring to the Soul, and so accounted valuable a long and intimate acquaintance with Death—a familiar contemplation giving new knowledge of life.[65]

The aging Whitman had attained the status of American guru without a portfolio, and he was credited by some of his enthusiasts with possessing incomparable insights into death and immortality. And they were not alone. Even Algernon Swinburne, who in 1877 had dismissed Whitman as immoral and lacking poetic talent, later concluded that "his views on death are invariably noble" and that he "never speaks so well as when he speaks of great matters—liberty, for instance, and death."[66] Whitman's exchanges with the famed agnostic Robert Ingersoll, who, despite their disagreements concerning the possibility of an afterlife, deeply admired the poet, were covered by the press. Ingersoll, says a biographer, viewed Whitman as a would-be philosopher "who does not know the nature of the ultimate reality—whereas Whitman insists that it is not necessary to know but simply to accept the reflection of God in himself and in all men." "What would this life be without immortality?" the poet demanded of Ingersoll. "What is the world without Divine purpose in all?"[67] Yet Ingersoll, who first read *Leaves of Grass* in 1888, remarked to Horace Traubel shortly before the poet's death: "What a cosmos is that man! He is a vastness of thought and life, studded with stars!" And Whitman claimed to respect Ingersoll's "scientific"—that is, skeptical— approach to immortality. Although he was passionately devout in his faith in some sort of personal continuity beyond death, he claimed to prefer the skepticism of Ingersoll or Burroughs to the rejectionism of disbelievers, on the one hand, and the rigid formulas of the "true believers," on the other. He dismissed those he regarded as high-flown theorists and ridiculed what he called their "*churching* theological" ideas about "the Methodistic Presbyterianistic god" and "all the mysterious humbuggery of what they call heaven." "[I]f these infernal Tom-fools [i.e., ministers] knew more they would be less certain, would know how little is certain, and that the scientific men who are staggered by 'conclusions' give us the wisest conclusion after all. But it is always . . . the least knowing, intuitional, pretending to see the most." He credited scientists with having the proper modesty of opinion. "Of course, we don't know, neither do I know, if other worlds than this are inhabited," he told Traubel. "Yet I am as sure as that we talk about it here together here this minute." Concerning cosmic matters, he admitted, "there are senses in which we do not know—I know and I *don't* know." As to immortality, "the whole matter hinges there," he said. Ultimately, it seems, he regarded immortality as something of a personal matter between himself and the cosmos.[68]

To the very end he remained proud of his achievement as a poet of death. His last known effort at sustained speech, just five days before he died (he had been too faint to speak more than a word or two for some time) was an outburst in what Traubel called "a mandatory tone." If he were able to write "anything more," he told Traubel, "I would compare Tennyson, Whittier and me, dwelling quite a bit on the three ways we each have treated the death subject—Tennyson in 'Crossing the Bar,' Whittier in

'[Burning] Driftwood'—both ecclesiastical, theoretical—and my 'Good-Bye My Fancy'—based, absorbed in, the natural. That that I've just said is quite significant." After a struggle to catch his breath, he added, "But it will bear saying in full: it tells the whole story of 'Leaves of Grass.'"[69] In fairness to Tennyson and Whittier, it should be said that their wistful quatrains announcing their readiness to set out on the sea of death to meet their Maker are hardly more "ecclesiastical, theoretical" than Whitman's later verses. At the time of this final outburst, he had apparently forgotten that he had once compared "Crossing the Bar," "Burning Driftwood," and his own "Now Finalè to the Shore" in a short essay titled "A Death-Bouquet." There he had reiterated his conviction that death is "the greatest subject." The essay likens death to "an invisible breeze after a long and sultry day" that "sets in, at last, soothingly and refreshingly, almost vitally" and sometimes "even appears to be a sort of ecstasy"—a sentiment like the one he expressed in "To the Sun-Set Breeze." And reiterating his antic notion about his physical decline, he had added: "It is a curious suggestion of immortality that the mental and emotional powers remain to their clearest through all, while the senses of pain and flesh-volition are blurred or even gone."[70] How revealing that the dying poet's last words were an emotional defense of his place as the era's premier poet of death, as opposed to the two elder poets whom he regarded as his principal contenders (all three poets died in 1892).

During the closing months of his life Walt Whitman lay in a pitiful and sordid state in the upstairs bedroom in his Mickle Street house. His devoted physician Dr. Bucke described his visit to "the sick room (where a divine man lies dying)." The room was cluttered and filthy; the bed (which had once belonged to Whitman's mother) was rotten and foul-smelling because of the poet's incontinence and his being too set in his ways to permit any changes in his sleeping arrangements. Whitman's intransigence in matters concerning his living arrangements prevented the making of "such changes as seemed absolutely necessary that he might be cared for."[71] Despite the physical ravages he had suffered (a collapsed lung, near deafness, kidney failure, weight loss), the elderly bachelor defied his doctors' predictions of his imminent death. Almost a year before he died he had complained of "a near deathliness which crept subtly, as the day wore on, through all my bones." In December 1891 he suffered a severe physical crisis during which his doctors hourly expected his death. The following February, a month before he died, and during a period of intense suffering, he acknowledged that "one of these mornings I shall be slipping away from you forever."[72] And possibly forgetful that he had once famously compared his proposed leap to immortality to that of "a noiseless patient spider," he switched animals and said, "It would be a satisfaction to know how the cat was going to jump."[73] But he preserved his equanimity to the last. When his devoted housekeeper Mary Davis asked him, during a period of extreme pain, "How goes it, Mr. Whitman?" he replied, "I'm having a hard pull, Mary." "I hope you will pull through all right," she said; and he answered, "It will be all right either way."[74] He died March 26, 1892, having held out against a battery of diseases: chronic digestive ailments, paralysis, pleurisy, pulmonary and abdominal tuberculosis, nephritis, gallstones, cysts, meningitis, and the almost complete collapse of his lungs.[75] Lying immobilized in bed, his last words, addressed to his attendant Warren Fritzinger, were not the prophetic utterances of a dying saint but only a request to have his helpless body turned or lifted again. He had told Traubel that he felt like giving "my body, my corpse" to be dissected after he died and that he was also "disposed" to being cremated. In the meantime, however, he had set aside considerable money and, with the generous assistance of Thomas B. Harned, he was able to order a six-hundred-square-foot tomb—an "Egyptian"-style mausoleum—on what he boasted was the prettiest lot in Camden's Harleigh Cemetery. He had made provisions for members of his family to be entombed there as well.

Whitman had expressed the wish that his death be properly observed. He told an English journalist that he admired the *London Times's* dignified obituaries of statesmen and literary figures, hinting that he would like to receive similar treatment when he died. His ideal write-up, he told a reporter in 1890, would be modeled on "The Carpenter," William Douglas O'Connor's thinly disguised saint's legend about Whitman, which the poet called the best "article" about him ever written.[76] Nevertheless, he might have been pleased by the way the press treated the news of his death. As the most photographed American poet of his generation, his face and his name (if not necessarily his poems) were widely recognized. The press coverage in America and in Great Britain was impressive and often insightful.[77] And the crowd of friends and neighbors who came to view his body, filling his house and the street outside, testified to his popularity and to his status as a celebrity. At least a thousand people, many of them the laboring folk to whom the 1856 edition of *Leaves of*

*Grass* had been addressed, crowded Mickle Street, waiting to view the corpse; thousands more reportedly lined the funeral route to view the passing coffin, and the crowd at the cemetery, it is said, stretched as far as the eye could see.[78]

Some Whitman devotees accepted the poet's death as a momentous event. Thus John Addington Symonds wrote from England that Whitman's "sick-bed, his death-bed, is the seal of the magnetic inspiration he has sent to quicken spiritual life in others," adding that Whitman's "'sublime doctrine' teaches us to live and die."[79] Horace Traubel implied that Whitman had died like a saint. Borrowing Whitman's imagery of twilight and sunsets, Traubel wrote: "He passed away as peaceably as the sun, and it was hard to catch the moment of transition. That solemn watch, the gathering shadows, the painless surrender are not to be forgotten. His soul went out with the day. The face was calm, the body lay without rigidity[!], the majesty of his tranquil spirit remained. What more could be said? It was a moment not for the doctor, but for the poet, the seer."[80] Three days later, in another burst of hagiography, Dr. Bucke, who has been called "the Saint Paul, who spread the word about the departed Messiah,"[81] described the deceased poet in godlike terms in a letter to an English Whitmanite, proclaiming, "*Christ ist erstanden!* More correctly, he is arising." And a few days later John Burroughs noted in his journal that "W. W. is the Christ of the modern world—he alone redeems it, justifies it, shows it divine, floods and saturates it with human-divine love."[82] Bucke's *Cosmic Consciousness* (1901), a collection of case histories of mystic illumination, places Whitman's inspirational faculty second only to that of Christ, asserting that "in no man who ever lived was the sense of eternal life so absolute." At the poet's funeral service Bucke declared (as Whitman's poems sometimes hint) that Death had whispered to Whitman the secret of the hereafter. "With [Whitman] immortality was not a hope but a beautiful dream," said Bucke. "He believed that we all live in an eternal universe, and that man is as indestructible as his Creator. His views of religion have been misunderstood. He was tolerant of the opinions of others, and recognized the good of all religious systems. His philosophy was without limitation of creed, and included the best of every age and clime."[83] And Harned, citing a line from one of Whitman's late poems, declared that the poet gladly welcomed death as the "Usher, Guide, at last, to all," and he, too, testified that the poet had peacefully surrendered to death. "Never did he fear that fatal and certain end," Harned asserted. "Idle, indeed, it was for Death to try to alarm him." The *New York Evening Telegram* shrewdly characterized Whitman's funeral service as a "marriage feast of death."[84]

In a poem dedicated to "W. W." Horace Traubel pictures himself at Whitman's bedside, holding the hand of the dying poet who, with an unspoken "look of bestowal," conferred on him the Whitman mantle.[85] But not long after the poet's death, as Joann P. Krieg has documented, "cracks were appearing in the wall of defense Traubel was trying to build around the Whitman image"—suspicions voiced by critics on both sides of the Atlantic regarding Whitman's homosexuality and his propensity to puff up his own reputation.[86] When Francis Howard Williams, who had taken part in Whitman's funeral service, defended the honor of "the most reviled of poets" in the pages of *Poet-Lore* only five years after Whitman's death by maintaining that the poet had "most fully expressed the truth of immortality," he was already fighting a rearguard action.[87] Traubel prepared an elaborate response to those who impugned Whitman's moral purity, exalting him as an inspired poet with profound insights into death. He culled the pages of *Leaves of Grass* for appropriate passages on death and published these excerpts as *The Book of Heavenly Death, by Walt Whitman* (1904). The now-forgotten volume reprinted only those passages that depict the poet's philosophical acceptance of death, particularly the later poems in which Whitman is optimistic about his ultimate fate. Excluded from the Traubel's collection are all the "Children of Adam" poems (a source of the controversy regarding Whitman's "decency"), the erotic "Calamus" poems, most of the *Drum-Taps* poems, and nearly every passage in which death is associated with violence, terror, and pain. Also excluded are passages that suggest the possibility that death is the end of individual existence or that reveal the poet's uncertainties about death. Traubel's collection presents Whitman as the Good Gray Poet of Immortality and, like Bucke's *Cosmic Consciousness*, promotes the poet's assertion that his utterances were inspired by influxes of divine inspiration. Only with the appearance of Bliss Perry's pioneering objective biography of Whitman in 1906 was the groundwork being laid for the dispassionate study of the poet and his poetry.

5

A memorial coup of sorts was scored by *Harper's New Monthly Magazine*, whose editor, in August 1889, had asked Whitman for a poem to accompany an etching of *The Valley of the Shadow of Death* (1869), a painting by the renowned American landscapist George Inness. The original painting depicts "large rocks, heavy cloud effect with sign of the cross in the sky" and "small rocks right of center"; its warm earth and grass tones, its luminosity and sidelights are typical of the artist.[88] On a low declivity among the brooding mountains may be seen a tiny figure in white, but it is not clear which way it is facing. Whitman, who may never have seen the original painting, submitted the requested poem within a month and received an honorarium of twenty-five dollars. However, the editors cagily withheld publication of the poem, which they called "a mighty legacy from the poet," until the month following Whitman's death. Then they published two of its three original stanzas as "Death's Valley," and hastily sandwiched the etching and the poem into a makeshift space, together with a rather angelic etching of the poet, after a painting by J. W. Alexander, which shows him crowned with fleecy hair and a cloudlike beard (and wearing granny glasses).[89] The poem's first stanza, which the editors chose not to print, concedes that "'tis ghastly to descend that [grim] valley" where so many have entered and which is always ready "for entrance, yours and mine," and whose terrors have been exploited by preachers, painters, poets, and philosophers. The two published stanzas, however, are free of fatalistic implications. Speaking as one who has been a "hoverer of late in this dark valley [of death]," Whitman asserts his "right to make a symbol too." And the symbol he chooses is, appropriately enough, that of Walt Whitman himself—death's preeminent witness and lover:

> For I have seen many wounded soldiers die;
> After dread suffering—have seen their lives pass off with smiles;
> And I have watch'd the death hours of the old, and seen the
>    infant die,
> The rich, with all his nurses and his doctors,
> And then the poor, in meagerness and poverty,
> And I myself for long, O Death, have breath'd my every breath
> Amid the nearness and the silent thought of thee

Professing to be unafraid of death's terrors or its inscrutable mysteries— "struggle, or contortion, or hard-tied knot"—the poet offers instead the idealized vision of death that he had long nurtured. Nearly half a century earlier, in a verse called "Death of a Nature Lover," the fledgling poet had described the sort of solitary death he longed to experience. He desired, he wrote then, to lie prone upon "this glorious earth" in an opening among the trees, while "looking on water, sun, and hill, / As on their maker's face," and, at sunset, he hoped to "step / Down to the Unknown World alone."[90] Despite the intervals of painful doubt that Whitman endured throughout his life, this image was never far from his thoughts. As an ailing old man nearing the end of his days, he recreated in "Death's Valley" a scene that had fired his youthful imaginings. And he offered this welcoming prayer to Death as the ultimate liberator:

> Of the broad blessed light and perfect air, with meadows,
>     rippling tides, and trees and flowers and grass,
> And the low hum of living breeze—and in the midst God's
>     beautiful eternal right hand,
> Thee, holiest minister of Heaven—thee, envoy, usherer, guide at
>     last of all,
> Rich, florid, loosener of the stricture-knot call'd life,
> Sweet, peaceful, welcome Death.[91]

Whitman wrote a number of minor poems after completing "Death's Valley"; but *Harper's* had shrewdly sensed that this poem would make a fitting tribute to the dead poet. Throughout Whitman's career, death had formed an essential core of his poetry, and he had long sought (and has probably attained) the high ground as America's premier poet of death. As the twilight darkened around him and the vitality ebbed from his pain-wracked body, his spirit was still singing the praises of "sweet, peaceful, welcome Death."

# Notes

## Abbreviations

*Corr    *The Correspondence,* ed. Edwin Haviland Miller, 6 volumes (1842–1892), 1961, et. seq.

*EPF    *The Early Poems and Fiction,* ed. Thomas L. Brasher (1963).

*LG    *Leaves of Grass,* Comprehensive Readers Edition, ed. Harold W. Blodgett and Sculley Bradley, 1965 (reproduced as a "Norton Critical Edition," 1975).

LG1855    *Leaves of Grass,* Brooklyn, 1855 (available in facsimile).

LG1860    *Leaves of Grass,* Boston: Thayer and Edridge, 1860 (facsimile, ed. Roy Harvey Pearce [Ithaca: Cornell UP, 1961]).

*LGVar    *Leaves of Grass: A Textual Variorum of the Printed Poems,* ed. Sculley Bradley, et. al., 3 vols. (New York: New York UP, 1980).

*NUPM    *Notebooks and Unpublished Prose Manuscripts.* Ed. Edward F. Grier. 6 vols. (1984).

*PW1892    *Prose Works 1892,* ed. Floyd Stovall, 1964. Vol. 1 contains *Specimen Days,* Vol. 2 contains *Collect and Other Prose.*

UPP    *The Uncollected Poetry and Prose of Walt Whitman.* Ed Emory Holloway. New York: Peter Smith (1932).

WWC    Horace Traubel, comp. *With Walt Whitman in Camden,* 9 vols. covering March 1888 to March 1892.

    *With Walt Whitman in Camden,* vol. 1 (1905; reprint, New York: Rowman and Littlefield, 1961).

    *With Walt Whitman in Camden,* vol. 2 (1908; reprint, New York: Rowman and Littlefield, 1961).

    *With Walt Whitman in Camden,* vol. 3 (1912; reprint, New York: Rowman and Littlefield, 1961).

    *With Walt Whitman in Camden,* ed. Sculley Bradley, vol. 4 (Carbondale: Southern Illinois UP, 1959).

    *With Walt Whitman in Camden,* ed. Gertrude Traubel, vol. 5 (Carbondale: Southern Illinois UP, 1964).

*Volume of the New York University Press edition: *The Collected Writings of Walt Whitman.*

*With Walt Whitman in Camden,* ed. Gertrude Traubel and William White, vol. 6 (Carbondale: Southern Illinois UP, 1982).

*With Walt Whitman in Camden,* ed. Jeanne Chapman and Robert MacIsaac, vol. 7 (Carbondale: Southern Illinois UP, 1992).

*With Walt Whitman in Camden,* ed. Jeanne Chapman and Robert MacIsaac, vol. 8 (Oregon House, Calif.: W. L. Bentlely, 1996).

*With Walt Whitman in Camden,* ed. Jeanne Chapman and Robert MacIsaac, vol. 9 (Oregon House, Calif.: W. L. Bentlely, 1996).

WWBB    Harold Aspiz, *Walt Whitman and the Body Beautiful* (Urbana: U Illinois P, 1980).

WWQR    *Walt Whitman Quarterly Review,* ed. Ed Folsom.

# Introduction

1. *WWC,* 8:334; Horace Traubel, comp., *The Book of Heavenly Death by Walt Whitman* (Portland, Me.: Thomas B. Mosher, 1907), xix–xxiii.

2. Daniel Brinton, eulogy, in *The Walt Whitman Fellowship Papers* (Philadelphia, May, 1892), Unnumbered page.

3. Havelock Ellis, *The New Spirit* (New York: Boni and Liveright, 1890), 111; Robert Ingersoll, "At the Graveside of Walt Whitman," *Conservator* (April, 1892).

4. D. H. Lawrence, "Whitman," in *Whitman: A Collection of Essays,* ed. Roy Harvey Pearce (Englewood Cliffs, N.J.: Prentice-Hall, 1962), 17–23; Padraic Colum, "The Poetry of Walt Whitman," in *Walt Whitman and the World,* ed. Gay Wilson Allen and Ed Folsom (Iowa City: U Iowa P, 1995), 57–58; Fernando Alegría, "Whitman in Spain and Latin America," ibid., 73.

5. *LG,* 276–277.

6. *NUPM,* 3:976; "Preface 1855," *LG,* 715.

7. *NUPM,* 1:60–61.

8. *NUPM,* 1:408, 4:1313.

9. *NUPM,* 6:2097.

10. *NUPM,* 6:2052.

11. *LG,* 690–691. Whitman's alternate reading for "Divine is the body" is "Divine is the Person."

12. "*Preface 1872*—As a Strong Bird on Pinions Free," *LG,* 74–; *NUPM,* 6:2011–2012.

13. *NUPM,* 4:1515–1516.

14. "*Preface 1876*—Leaves of Grass and Two Rivulets," *LG,* 747–795. Whitman's interest in photography is evident in the slide show imagery.

15. *Specimen Days,* in PW1892, 1:259.

16. Walt Whitman, "Diary in Canada," in *Daybooks and Notebooks,* ed. William White (New York: New York UP, 1978), 3:614–615; *UPP,* 261–266, passim; *NUPM,* 3:1185–1186. On Dr. Hunt, see *WWBB,* 47, 257, n. 34.

17. Thayer is cited in Joel Myerson, ed., *Whitman in His Own Time: A Biographical Chronicle of His Life, Drawn from Recollections, Memoirs, and Interviews by Friends and Associates* (Detroit: Omnigraphics, 1991), 303; Helen Price in a memoir included

in Richard Maurice Bucke's 1883 biography of Whitman (Myerson, *Whitman in His Own Time*, 29).

18. *WWBB*, 58–63. On Whitman's supposed feminine side, see chapter 5, below, p. 184 and p. 264, n.22. The superior character of the omnibus drivers is attested by Dr. William B. Drinkard, whom Whitman met at the New York Hospital and who attended him in Washington; see *NUPM*, 2:536.

19. Joseph Jay Rubin, *The Historic Whitman* (University Park: Pennsylvania State UP, 1973), 46.

20. "The Tomb-Blossoms," *EPF*, 94.

21. *EPF*, 9, 24, 28–29.

22. Quoted in Jerome Loving, *Walt Whitman: The Song of Himself* (Berkeley: U California P, 1999), 84.

23. *EPF*, 30–32. The lachrymose tale, "Reuben's Last Wish" (ibid., 110–114) similarly pictures a child who wishes to die in a lovely garden in the presence of God.

24. *WWBB*, 49; *EPF*, 316–317.

25. Elisabeth Kübler-Ross, *The Wheel of Life: A Memoir of Living and Dying* (New York: Scribner, 1997), 147.

26. Harold Bloom, "Death and the Native Strain in American Poetry," in *Death and the American Experience*, ed. Arien Mack (New York: Schocken Books, 1973), 83.

27. See the Whitman genealogy by William Pennypacker in *Walt Whitman: An Encyclopedia*, ed. J. R. LeMaster and Donald D. Kummings (New York: Garland Publishing Co., 1998), 807–812.

28. See David S. Reynolds, *Walt Whitman: A Cultural Biography* (New York: Knopf, 1995) 519; Helen E. Price, "Reminiscences of Walt Whitman" (1919), cited in Myerson, *Whitman in His Own Time*, 282. For Whitman's touching tribute to his mother, "As at Thy Portals Also Death," see *LG*, 497.

29. Martin Henry Blatt, *Free Love and Anarchism: The Biography of Ezra Heywood* (Urbana: U Illinois P, 1989), 86, 142–144, 178; William O. Reichert, *Partisans of Freedom: A Study of American Anarchism* (Bowling Green, Ohio: Bowling Green University Popular Press, 1976), 297, notes that many of the anarchists were also spiritualists. Most of Whitman's comments on spiritualism were unflattering: He called it "gibberish" (*NUPM*, 6:2051; see also *Corr*, 1:143, 206–208).

30. "A Backward Glance O'er Travel'd Roads," *LG*, 568–569; Hyatt H. Waggoner, *American Visionary Poetry* (Baton Rouge: Louisiana State UP, 1982), finds an indebtedness to Milton and Blake; Richard Maurice Bucke asserted that Whitman read several translations of Homer (see Myerson, *Whitman in His Own Time*, 40).

31. Ann Douglas, "Heaven Our Home: Consolation Literature in the Northern United States, 1830–1880," in *Death in America*, ed. David E. Stannard (Philadelphia: U Pennsylvania P, 1975), 46.

32. Lawrence Taylor, "The Anthropological View of Mourning Ritual in the Nineteenth Century," in *A Time to Mourn: Expressions of Grief in Nineteenth-Century America*, ed. Martha V. Pike and Janice Gray Armstrong (Stony Brook, N.Y.: Museum of Stony Brook, 1980), 39–48.

33. April Selley, "Satisfied Shivering: Emily Dickinson's Deceased Speakers," *ESQ: A Journal of the American Renaissance* 37 (1991), 215–217. Selley notes that over

fifty of Dickinson's poems feature deceased narrators and twice that number feature "ambiguous" narrators. On the relation of Lydia Sigourney's voluminous poems of death to Dickinson's, see Burton Levi St. Armand, *Emily Dickinson and Her Culture: The Soul's Society* (Cambridge: Cambridge UP, 1984), 24, 41.

34. *Specimen Days*, in *PW1892*, 1:293. Whitman accompanied Bryant on walks and attended his funeral; see Christopher Beach, *The Politics of Distinction: Whitman and the Discourses of Nineteenth-Century America* (Athens: U Georgia P, 1996), 204.

35. *UPP*, 1:245–246.

36. Arthur E. Briggs, *Walt Whitman: Thinker and Artist*, (New York: Philosophical Library, 1952), 64–65.

37. Richard Maurice Bucke, cited in Reynolds, *Walt Whitman*, 488.

38. "*Preface 1876*—Leaves of Grass and Two Rivulets," *LG*, 746.

39. Whitman, *Daybooks and Notebooks*, 781.

40. *Specimen Days*, in *PW1892*, 1:258–259.

41. On the difficulties of attempting to articulate the nature of the afterlife, see Corliss Lamont, *The Illusion of Immortality* (New York: Frederick Ungar, 1965), 172.

42. "Passage to India," *LG*, 415.

43. Howard Selsam, *What Is Philosophy? A Marxist Introduction* (New York: International Publishers, 1962), 39–40.

44. *NUPM*, 1:408.

45. Briggs, *Walt Whitman*, 95. Whitman's verse "Going Somewhere?" takes its title from a phrase by Whitman's "science friend" Anne Gilchrist, who maintained that all life advances and is purposive.

46. *WWC*, 2:71.

47. Minot Judson Savage, *Life beyond Death* (1899; reprint, New York: G. P. Palmer's Sons, 1905), 66–67; "These I Singing in Spring," *LG*, 118–119.

48. *The Phaedo*, tr. Benjamin Jowett, cited in William Osler, *Science and Immortality* (1904; reprint, New York: Arno Press, 1977), 1.

49. Lamont, *Illusion of Immortality*, 66.

50. Daniel Cohn-Sherbok, "Death and Immortality in the Jewish Tradition," in *Death and Immortality in the Religions of the World*, ed. Paul Badham and Linda Badham (New York: Paragon House, 1987), 24–25; Savage, *Life beyond Death*, 42–45, 59; J. B. S. Haldane, *Possible Worlds and Other Papers* (New York: Harper and Brothers, 1928), 26; Ecclesiastes, 2:11, 9:5; Psalms, 115:17.

51. Harry Staten, *Eros in Mourning: Homer to Lacan* (Baltimore: Johns Hopkins UP), 1; 1 Corinthians, 15:12–19.

52. "Elias Hicks," *PW1892*, 2:640–641.

53. Ralph Waldo Emerson, "Immortality," in *The Complete Writings of Ralph Waldo Emerson* (New York: William H. Wise & Co., 1929), 825–834, passim.

54. Bruce R. Reichenbach, "Buddhism, Karma, and Immortality," in *Death and Immortality in the Religions of the World*, ed. Badham and Badham, 141. For Whitman's treatment of species immortality in the "Children of Adam" poems, see chapter 4, below.

55. David Kuebrich, *Minor Prophecy: Walt Whitman's New American Religion* (Bloomington: Indiana UP, 1989), 22. The quotation is from the poem "To You," *LG*, 233.

56. Charles Darwin, *The Origin of Species,* in *Darwin: A Norton Critical Edition,* ed. Philip Appelman (New York: Norton, 1975), 131; *WWC,* 3:49, 1:101; Whitman, "A Backward Glance O'er Travel'd Roads" (1889), *LG,* 563.

57. Traubel, *Book of Heavenly Death,* xix–xxiii.

58. *WWC,* 6:167.

59. *WWC,* 6:146–147; Clara Barrus, ed., *The Heart of Burroughs's Journals* (1928; reprint, New York: Kennikat P, 1967), 163–164.

60. See Lamont, *Illusion of Immortality,* 176–177, 253.

61. Cited respectively from *WWC,* 6:165, 6:147, 2:71.

62. *Democratic Vistas,* in PW1892, 418–422.

# Chapter 1

1. The Longfellow translation of the *Inferno* (Garden City, N.Y.: Dolphin Books, n.d.), 13. Dante was thirty-five when he wrote the *Inferno.*

2. C. J. Jung, "The Soul and Death," in *Collected Works,* ed. Herbert Read et al. (Princeton: Princeton UP), 8:407, quoted in John Hick, *Death and Eternal Life* (New York: Harper and Row, 1976), 88.

3. Georg Wilhelm Friedrich Hegel, *Encyclopedia,* 1:152–5, quoted in Friedrich Engels, *Dialectics of Nature* (New York: International Publishers, 1960), 164.

4. Edwin Haviland Miller, ed., *Walt Whitman's "Song of Myself": A Mosaic of Interpretations* (Iowa City: U Iowa P, 1989) is a rich collection, by many modern critics, of interpretations and readings of the poem as a whole and of various passages.

5. Jerome Loving conjectures that some of the other poems in the first edition were originally part of an ungainly earlier draft of "Song of Myself," but were later separated (*Walt Whitman,* 198–202).

6. Unless otherwise noted, all quotations in this chapter and in chapter 2 are taken from the first (1855) edition, as they often vary significantly from later versions. For sake of convenience, many passages are identified by the section number assigned to them in the final edition.

7. Richard Maurice Bucke, *Cosmic Consciousness: A Study in the Evolution of the Human Mind* (1901; reprint, New York: E. P. Dutton, 1923), 226–228.

8. At midcentury when dwellings were smaller and beds rarer than they are now, men—often strangers—shared beds for convenience and savings. This note is not intended to preclude other interpretations that the reader may have.

9. *Democratic Vistas,* in *PW1892,* 2:398–399. For contrasting views of Whitman's dualism, see Rufus M. Jones, *Some Exponents of Mystical Religion* (New York: Abingdon Press, 1930), 176–208; Lewis Hyde, *The Gift: Imagination and the Erotic Life of Property* (New York: Random House, 1983), 175.

10. Reynolds, *Walt Whitman,* 240.

11. For example, Psalms 103:15, 16: "As for man, his days are as grass: / As a flower of the field, so he flourisheth. / For the wind passeth over it, and he is gone; / And the place thereof shall be known no more"; see also Psalms 90:5, 6.

12. Andrew Michael Ramsay, *The Philosophical Principles of Natural and Revealed Religion* (Glasgow, 1748), 11–12, quoted in Jonathan Edwards, *Images or Shadows of Divine Things,* ed. Perry Miller (New Haven: Yale UP, 1948), 58.

13. Ivan Marki, *The Trial of the Poet: An Interpretation of the First Edition of Leaves of Grass* (New York: Columbia UP, 1976), 123–125.

14. Ann Douglas, *The Feminization of American Culture* (New York: Alfred A. Knopf, 1977), 223; Douglas, "Heaven Our Home," 49–60, 63.

15. Lamont, *Illusion of Immortality*, 132; Robert K. Martin, *The Continuing Presence of Walt Whitman: The Life after the Life* (Iowa City: U Iowa P, 1992), 31.

16. Jones, *Some Exponents of Mystical Religion*, 185.

17. *Notes & Fragments*, 38, cited in Marki, *Trial of the Poet*, 132.

18. Joseph Campbell, *The Flight of the Wild Gander: Explorations in Mythological Dimension* (New York: Viking, 1969), 166–168. James Nolan reads this passage in terms of shamanism in *Poet-Chief: The American Poetics of Walt Whitman and Pablo Neruda* (Albuquerque: U New Mexico P, 1994) 201.

19. Quoted in Marion Walker Alcaro, *Walt Whitman and Mrs. G.: A Biography of Anne Gilchrist* (Rutherford, N.J.: Farleigh Dickinson UP, 1991) 221.

20. Stephen J. Tapscott, "Leaves of Myself: Whitman's Egypt in "Song of Myself" in *On Whitman: The Best from American Literature*, ed. Edwin H. Cady and Louis J. Budd (Durham: Duke UP, 1987), 203–227.

21. Harold Aspiz, "Walt Whitman: The Spermatic Imagination," in *On Whitman*, 273–289.

22. In 1867, Whitman modified line 4 in section 23 of "Song of Myself" to emphasize the role of the self in his interpretation of cosmic time: "Here or henceforward it is all the same to me; I accept Time absolutely . . . That mystic wonder that completes all." The workings of time, he assumed, would eventually resolve the separation of the spiritual and material worlds.

23. Robert J. Scholnick, "'The Password Primeval': Whitman's Use of Science in 'Song of Myself,'" in *Studies in the American Renaissance: 1986*, ed. Joel Myerson (Charlottesville: UP of Virginia, 1986), 386, 392. The essay is a valuable discussion of Whitman and science.

24. Andrew W. Delp, "Andrew Jackson Davis and Spiritualism," and Robert C. Fuller, "Mesmerism and the Birth of Psychology," both in *Pseudo-Science and Society in Nineteenth-Century America*, ed. Arthur Wrobel (Lexington: UP of Kentucky, 1987), 7, 105, 212–213.

25. Edward Carpenter, *My Days and Dreams* (London: George Allen & Unwin, 1921), 205.

26. "Cosmic Emotion," *Nineteenth Century* 2 (October 1879), cited in Clara Barrus, *Whitman and Burroughs Comrades* (1931; reprint, Port Washington, N.Y.: Kennikat Press, 1959), 169.

27. The lexicographer is probably William Swinton, with whose language research Whitman may have collaborated; the chemist possibly the renowned Dr. William Draper, whose textbook on chemistry Whitman reviewed, the "grammarian of the old cartouches" the Egyptologist Dr. Henry Abbott; and "he who works with the scalpel" Dr. Edward H. Dixon, editor of *The Scalpel*, who was a popular lecturer on medical topics mentioned in Whitman's journalism. See *WWBB*, 58–61.

28. *NUPM*, 1:172–173; Frederick William Conner, *Cosmic Optimism: A Study in the Interpretation of Evolution by American Poets from Emerson to Robinson* (Gaines-

ville: U Florida P, 1949), 96–97, suggests that in this passage Whitman was trying to pour old wine into new bottles.

29. "Spirit that Form'd this Scene" (1881), *LG*, 486.

30. Phoebe Lloyd, "Posthumous Mourning Portraiture," in *A Time to Mourn: Expressions of Grief in Nineteenth-Century America,* ed. Martha V. Pike and Janice Gray Armstrong (Stony Brook, N.Y.: Museum of Stony Brook, 1980), 75.

31. Roger Asselineau, *Leaves of Grass: The Evolution of a Book* (Cambridge: Harvard UP, 1962) 13, 27, cited in Miller, *Walt Whitman's "Song of Myself,"* 100.

32. Lawrence Kramer, *Music and Poetry: The Nineteenth Century and After* (Berkeley: U California P, 1984), 141

33. *NUPM*, 1:126–127. On the Bettini connection, see Reynolds, *Walt Whitman,* 189. On Alboni, see *WWC,* 9:49–50. Alboni, a student of Rossini, in whose roles she excelled, sang in the United States in 1852. On Whitman's relation to the opera, also see Donald Barlow Stauffer, "Opera and Opera Singers," in *Walt Whitman: An Encyclopedia,* ed. J. R. LeMaster and Donald D. Kummings (New York: Garland, 1998), 484–486.

34. Rainer Marie Rilke, *Duino Elegies,* trans. David Young (New York: Norton, 1978), 19.

35. Quoted from *NUPM*, 1:151 in Byrne R. S. Fone, *Masculine Landscapes: Walt Whitman and the Homoerotic Text* (Carbondale: Southern Illinois UP, 1992), 102.

36. See, for example, the "wholesome relief, repose, content" in the closing lines of "Spontaneous Me" *LG1860,* 308–309.

37. Karl Kerényi, *Hermes Guide of Souls: The Mythologies of the Masculine Source of Life* (Zurich: Spring Publications, 1976), 71.

38. Donald Pease, *Visual Compacts: American Renaissance Writing in Cultural Context* (Madison: U Wisconsin P, 1987), 137.

39. Quoted in George B. Hutchinson, *The Ecstatic Whitman: Literary Shamanism and the Crisis of the Union* (Columbus: Ohio State UP, 1986), 36. See the discussion of the *zoe* in relation to "Children of Adam," in chapter 4, below.

40. See Frederick J. Hoffman, *The Mortal No: Death and the Modern Imagination* (Princeton: Princeton UP, 1964), 323, 334.

41. Marki, *Trial of the Poet,* 161.

42. See *LGVar,* 1:43, for variant readings of the line.

43. Hoffman, *Mortal No,* 349–350.

44. James Nolan calls it a "shamanistic migration" in *Poet-Chief,* 180.

45. *LG,* 65–66n; Reynolds, *Walt Whitman,* 328–329.

46. Such a reading would accord with the beliefs of Spiritualism, which had a widespread appeal during this period. In 1857 *The Practical Christian* (organ of the Hopedale Community, of which Whitman's close friend Abby Price had been a prominent member) listed sixty-seven periodicals or books devoted to Spiritualism. John Humphrey Noyes, founder of the Oneida Community, noted in 1868 that "the surge of Swedenborgianism which [the Fourierists] started, swept on among their constituents, and under the force of Spiritualism, is sweeping on to this day." Spiritualism was a sort of *omnium gatherum* of related causes and ideologies, "taking form from each of the ideologies that have emptied into it," including Swedenborgianism,

mysticism, Fourierism, various "socialisms," Unitarianism, and Shakerism. Spiritualism professed to embrace both science and spirit—the sort of duality that is evident in much of Whitman's own thinking. See Noyes, *History of American Socialisms* (1870; reprint, New York: Hillary House, 1961), 537, 565, 567, and passim. Spiritualism brought together sexual reformers, labor advocates, feminists, and others. See also Sherry Ceniza, *Walt Whitman and Nineteenth-Century Women Reformers* (Tuscaloosa: U Alabama P, 1998), 45–95.

The idea of a continuum in the material and spiritual worlds in *Leaves of Grass*, and particularly in "Song of Myself," was anticipated, after a fashion, by the spiritualist (and Whitman's sometime neighbor) Andrew Jackson Davis whose book, *The Principles of Nature, Her Divine Revelations, and Voice to Mankind* was an "encyclopedic work" that "included an account of the relations between the spirit and the material world, and a plan for the reorganization of society on socialist lines." See Geoffrey K. Nelson, *Spiritualism and Society* (New York: Schocken, 1969), 53.

47. Kuebrich, *Minor Prophecy*, 101–102.

48. Thomas L. Brasher, *Whitman as Editor of the Brooklyn Daily Eagle* (Detroit: Wayne State UP, 1970) 238–239, n.5; see also *Encyclopedia Americana* (1951 edition), 13:38–39, 14:449. An authoritative historic treatment is Clarence Wharton, *Remember Goliad* (Glorieta, N.M.: Rio Grande Press, 1968)—a volume based on original documents.

49. Brasher, *Whitman as Editor*, 88.

50. *Encyclopedia Americana* (1951), 11:10.

51. Wharton, *Remember Goliad*, 40. Whitman's depiction of the Goliad episode, based on newspaper reports, is contradicted by contemporary data showing that some Americans were spared and others were less than heroic.

52. In 1860, Whitman changed the timing of the body burning from "The second Sunday morning" to "The second First-day morning," apparently to confer a tone of Quaker holiness on the incident.

53. For Whitman's use of sources for this passage, see David Goodale, "Some of Walt Whitman's Borrowings," *American Literature* 10 (1938), 202–203.

54. "The Artilleryman's Vision" and its aborted manuscript draft represent Whitman's only other extended poetic descriptions of a battle and the attendant carnage.

55. On Whitman and painting, see Ruth L. Bohan, "'The Gathering of the Forces': Walt Whitman and the Arts in Brooklyn," *The Mickle-Street Review* 12 (1990), 10–30; M. Wynn Thomas, *The Lunar Light of Whitman's Poetry* (Cambridge: Harvard UP, 1987), 94–96 and passim.

56. Whitman reported on the 1849 epidemic in the *Brooklyn Freeman;* see Rubin, *Historic Whitman*, 29. Whitman's allusion in "To Think of Time" to "the infected in the immigrant hospital" refers to the Emigrant Refuge Hospital, where hundreds of cholera victims were treated. And in the 1880s he considered adding a passage on the cholera victims in *Specimen Days* if he were to revise the work; see Whitman, "Diary in Canada," *Daybooks and Notebooks*, 348. See also James J. Walsh, *History of Medicine in New York* (New York, 1919), 2:106–110, 173–174, 3:826; also *WWBB*, 56, 259 n. 64.

57. Ronald Wallace, *God Be with the Clown: Humor in American Poetry* (New York: Columbia UP, 1984), 74.

58. Marki, *Trial of the Poet,* 172.

59. Harold Aspiz, "Mark Twain and 'Doctor' Newton," *American Literature* 44 (1972), 130–136; on Whitman as healer, see chapter 5, passim.

60. *LG,* 153–154. On the efflux of sweat as an agency of spiritual expression, see John James Garth Wilkinson, *The Human Body in Its Connection with Man* (Philadelphia: Lippincott, Grambo, and Co., 1851), 266–267.

On Whitman and Wilkinson, see *NUPM,* 1:146. Wilkinson, a leading English Swedenborgian, argued that heart reaches out to heart by "magnetic fingers."

61. White, *Daybooks and Notebooks,* 764; Goodale, "Some of Walt Whitman's Borrowings," 208–210, shows that many details in this passage were taken from C. F. Volney's *The Ruins.*

62. Walt Whitman, *Walt Whitman's Workshop: A Collection of Unpublished Manuscripts,* ed. Clifton Joseph Furness (Cambridge: U Harvard P, 1928), 44.

63. The dictionary definition of "ambush" is to attack from a concealed position; Whitman's usage is quite unusual.

64. *LG1855,* 49; *LGVar,* 70 ("Song of Myself," section 43).

65. Kuebrich, *Minor Prophecy,* 21.

66. Quoted in Hick, *Death and Eternal Life,* 251.

67. "When I walked at night by the shore and looked up at the countless stars, I asked of my soul whether it would be filled and satisfied when it should become god enfolding all these, and open to the life and delight and knowledge of everything in them or of them; and the answer was plain to me as the breaking water on the sands at my feet: and the answer was, No, when I reach there, I shall want to go further still." *UPP,* 2:267, 64.

Historically, Moses is supposed to have died on Mount Nebo.

68. Joseph Brodsky, *On Grief and Reason: Essays* (New York: Farrar Straus Giroux, 1995), 96.

69. The radical Deist position is discussed in Reichert, *Partisans of Freedom,* 43. Many of these values were shared by liberal religionists and radical reformers.

70. Quoted ibid.

71. Stephen Pearl Andrews, *The Science of Society* (New York, 1851), quoted ibid., 83.

72. Bloom, "Death and the Native Strain," 87.

73. Edmond Holmes, *Whitman's Poetry: A Study and Selection* (1902; reprint, New York: Haskell House, 1973), 60.

74. See Joseph Beaver, *Walt Whitman—Poet of Science* (New York: King's Crown Press, 1974), 53.

75. "Walt Whitman and His Poems," *United States Review* 5 (September 1855), reprint, Maurice Hindus, ed., *Walt Whitman: The Critical Heritage* (New York: Barnes and Noble, 1972), 38.

76. Passages from Kant's *Critique of Practical Reason* (1788) are quoted in Lamont, *Illusion of Immortality,* 162–163.

77. "*Preface 1876*—Leaves of Grass and Two Rivulets," in *LG,* 753; Marki, *Trial of the Poet,* 169–170.

78. Ralph Waldo Emerson, "The Transcendentalist," in *Selections from Ralph*

*Waldo Emerson,* ed. Stephen E. Whicher (Boston: Houghton Mifflin, 1957), esp. 198–199.

79. Brinton's remarks appear in the *Walt Whitman Fellowship Papers* 3 (May 1897), 34 (verso of a numbered sheet).

80. Tapscott, "Leaves of Myself," 220.

81. Hyde, *The Gift,* 17–18.

82. Jacques Derrida, *The Work of Mourning* (Chicago: U Chicago P, 2001), 9.

# Chapter 2

1. Emerson, "Immortality," 832–833.

2. Pike and Armstrong, *A Time To Mourn,* 15; Philippe Ariès, "The Reversal of Death: Changes in Attitudes towards Death in Western Societies," trans. Valerie M. Stannard, in *Death in America,* ed. David E. Stannard (Philadelphia: U Pennsylvania P, 1975), 139. See also Louis O. Saum, "Death in the Popular Mind in Pre–Civil War America," ibid., 43–44.

On the use of camphor as a liniment, relaxant, a specific against opium, or as an incense to counteract sickroom odors, see John Heineman, *Heineman's Encyclopedia of Healing Herbs and Spices* (West Nyack, N.Y.: Heineman, 1996), 114–116.

3. Kübler-Ross, *Wheel of Life,* 172. Such reports, of course, tend to be based on personal testimony or on hearsay.

4. Quoted in Ann Braude, *Radical Spirits: Spiritualism and Women's Rights in Nineteenth-Century America* (Boston: Beacon, 1989), 55.

5. "I suppose it can be said of Bryant—he felt it [death] was a natural fact—as such to be noted as you pass" (*WWC,* 6:313); "I have often tried to think of myself as writing Leaves of Grass in Thanatopsis verse." Noting that Bryant was a classicist in method and approach, Whitman adds "Breaking loose is the thing I do: breaking loose, resenting the bonds, opening new ways . . . I expected hell: I got it" (*WWC,* 3:515). The comment on Bryant's modernism is from Whitman's "Street Yarns" in *Life Illustrated,* August 1856, reprinted in Emory Holloway and Ralph Adimari, eds. *New York Dissected* (New York: Rufus Rockwell Wilson, 1936), 172.

"He that was President" apparently refers to Zachary Taylor, who died in office in 1850. On Whitman's attitude toward Taylor, see Martin Klammer, *Whitman, Slavery, and the Emergence of Leaves of Grass* (University Park: Pennsylvania State UP, 1995).

6. When Whitman revised this passage in 1871, he added a rather Wordsworthian introduction that suggests a more tepid enthusiasm for the working classes:

A reminiscence of the vulgar fate,
A frequent sample of the life and death of workmen,
Each after his kind.

7. See Stanley French, "The Cemetery as Cultural Institution: Mount Auburn and the Rural Cemetery Movement," in *Death in America,* ed. David E. Stannard, 77. On undertaking establishments, see P. G. Buckley, "Mourning on Long Island," in *A Time to Mourn: Expressions of Grief in Nineteenth-Century America,* ed. Pike and

Armstrong (Stony Brook, N.Y.: Museum of Stony Brook, 1980) 107–124. In 1881, Whitman made a return visit to the family burial grounds on Long Island. *A Time to Mourn* includes a photograph of the Huntington Burial Hill Cemetery.

8. Madeleine B. Stern, *Heads and Headlines: The Phrenological Fowlers* (Norman: U Oklahoma P, 1971), 109–141. See also *WWBB*, 99–123. Many interesting parallels between Whitman's thinking and that of contemporary reformers (especially women) are illustrated in Ceniza, *Walt Whitman and Nineteenth-Century Women Reformers*.

9. When all of humanity is unmuzzled, it was argued, it will have outgrown its bestial traits. Johann Kaspar Lavater's *Essay on Physiognomy*, 1778, a crudely evolutionary and racialist work that diagnosed character in terms of facial features argued that some peoples (non-Nordics) and some individuals exhibited bestial features that mark their arrested state of development. The attribution of bestial features to non-European and non-Christian persons antedated Lavater by centuries. On earlier hostile analyses of peoples in terms of their physical characteristics, see David E. Stannard, *American Holocaust: Columbus and the Conquest of the New World* (New York: Oxford UP, 1992).

10. The concept that American democracy is best served by a cadre of exceptional heroes is clearly expressed in "Song of the Broad-Axe," "Pioneers! O Pioneers!" and *Democratic Vistas*.

11. Paul Tillich, "The Eternal Now," in *The Meaning of Death*, ed. Herman Feifel (New York: McGraw-Hill, 1959), 53.

12. Lucretius, *On the Nature of Things*, trans. Cyril Bailey, cited in Lamont, *Illusion of Immortality*, 26.

13. John Dryden, *Aureng-Zebe*, ed. Frederick M. Link (Lincoln: U Nebraska P, 1975), 75. Another passage (p. 79) reads: "Grim though it be, death pleases when it frees."

14. Quoted in Mariasusai Dhavamony, "Death and Immortality in Hinduism," in *Death and Immortality in the Religions of the World*, ed. Paul Badham and Linda Badham (New York: Paragon House, 1987), 99–100.

15. Samuel Clemens, "[Three Statements of the Eighties]," in *What Is Man?* ed. Paul Baender (Berkeley: U California P, 1973), 57.

16. James E. Miller Jr., *Walt Whitman* (New York: Twayne, 1962), 107.

17. Whitman, *Daybooks and Notebooks*, 770.

18. For an insight into this subject, see Hick, *Death and Eternal Life*, 143. In an "uncertain" conclusion, Hick suggests that "the spirits, particularly the controls, who seem to be communicating directly during the mediumistic trance, are some kind of secondary personality of the medium." He speculates that they may be "tapping some kind of telepathic impressions" from the living or the dead.

19. Kübler-Ross, *Wheel of Life*, 189–191. Gates, roads, bridges, she reports, commonly occur in such visions as they do in Whitman's imagery of the passage to, and beyond, death.

20. Barrus, *Whitman and Burroughs Comrades*, 225.

21. The episode of the foundered ship resembles Henry Thoreau's reportage of a similar tragedy in the first chapter of *Cape Cod*, 1865. The essay was first published in

*Putnam's Monthly Magazine* in June, 1855, a month before the appearance of *Leaves of Grass.*

22. *LG1855,* 75–76; *LGVar,* 243–244. Compare the "unseen something" to the sexually suggestive lines in "Song of Myself," section 24: "Something I cannot see puts upward libidinous prongs, / Seas of bright juice suffuse heaven."

23. "Faces" (untitled), *LG1855,* 82–85; St. Augustine, *Enchridion,* chapters 85–87, quoted in Lamont, *Illusion of Immortality,* 115.

According to the laws formulated in Orson S. Fowler's *Hereditary Descent,* a copy of which Whitman owned, the sins of the parents—disease, debility, sexual abuse, or promiscuity—are visited upon their children but can be gradually bred out by judicious choice of mates and by cultivating sound health and good morals. Whitman often implies that obeying the "laws" of physical nurture promotes the nurture of the soul.

24. Edwards, *Images and Shadows of Divine Things,* 94.

25. In 1952 the psychoanalyst Gustav Bychowski analyzed Whitman's frequent association of mother and death in the poems as "a fright of annihilation for which he was secretly longing" because it would serve to restore "the dual unity with his mother." The acceptance of death, Bychowski argued, was a way of promoting such unity, since "his ego [was] never completely freed from its prenatal fixation." "Walt Whitman: A Study in Sublimation," in *A Century of Whitman Criticism,* ed. Edwin Haviland Miller (Bloomington: U Indiana P, 1969), 205–206.

# Chapter 3

1. See Stern, *Heads and Headlines,* 116–119.

2. David Cavitch speculates that the poem may have been occasioned by the death of Whitman's father and the indifference of his mother and siblings to the event. "The Lament in 'Song of the Broad-Axe,'" in *Walt Whitman Here and Now,* ed. Joann Krieg (Westport, Conn.: Greenwood, 1985), 126. However, Whitman expresses his terror of death in several of the 1856 and 1860 poems. (Unless noted, the cited poems follow the usage of the 1856 edition.)

3. *The Westminster Study Edition of the Bible* (Philadelphia: Westminster Press, 1948), 308. The emphasis is added. Compare the words of Jesus before his death in John 12:24: "Verily, verily, I say unto you, Except a corn or wheat fall into the ground and die, it abideth alone; but if it die, it bringeth much fruit." See also John 35–38, wherein the sown grain can be harvested by true believers.

4. Savage, *Life beyond Death,* 79–80. Savage remarks that Paul was vague about resurrection, perhaps not believing in the upraising of the soul when the body died but in the upraising of the soul from Hades. Paul's world had a limited cosmology, but the ever-expanding universe in Whitman's day offered a limitless prospect for defining life and immortality.

5. Whitman enthusiastically reviewed Liebig's *Chemistry* in the *Brooklyn Daily Eagle* on June 28, 1847, and in 1857 quoted Dr. Edward H. Dixon's explanation of miasma in the *Brooklyn Daily Times.* But he expressed some skepticism about the phenomenon in the *Brooklyn Daily Times* in 1858. See *WWBB,* 63, 260, n.83; John T.

Matteson, "Liebig, Justus," in *Walt Whitman: An Encyclopedia,* ed. J. R. LeMaster and Donald D. Kummings (New York: Garland, 1998), 392.

6. Cited in Brodsky, *On Grief and Reason,* 46.

7. "Ashes of Soldiers" (1865), *LG,* 490–492; *Democratic Vistas,* in *PW1892,* 2:382.

8. Arthur Wrobel, ed., *Pseudo-Science and Society in Nineteenth-Century America* (Lexington: UP of Kentucky, 1987), 6, 229–230.

9. Stern, *Heads and Headlines,* 99–123; Harold Aspiz, *"Leaves of Grass,* 1856 Edition," in *Walt Whitman: An Encyclopedia,* ed. J. R. LeMaster and Donald D. Kummings (New York: Garland, 1998), 359–361.

10. Alfred Still, *Soul of Lodestone* (New York: Murray Hill Books, 1946), 200–222.

11. *LGVar,* 216–217.

12. *LGVar,* 248–249.

13. Holmes, *Whitman's Poetry,* 64

14. D. T. Suzuki, *Outlines of Mahayana Buddhism* (New York: Schocken, 1963), quoted in Reichenbach, "Buddhism, Karma, and Immortality," 149. Similar ideas can be found in "Compensation," "Fate," and other essays by Emerson.

15. *LGVar,* 241.

16. R. Laurence Moore, *In Search of White Crows: Spiritualism, Parapsychology and American Culture* (New York: Oxford UP, 1977), 54. See also, Douglas, "Heaven Our Home," 49–68.

17. George Bush, *Mesmer and Swedenborg* (New York, 1847), 47, 129, quoted in Fuller, "Mesmerism and the Birth of Psychology," 217.

18. For Whitman's borrowings throughout the poem, see Goodale, "Some of Walt Whitman's Borrowings," 203–213.

19. The "sabians" (more accurately Sabaeans) were ancient astrologers and star worshipers who possessed an elaborate priesthood. The name possibly refers to an ancient Arabic people dating back to 1000 B.C. and, less likely, to an early Christian sect that accepted John the Baptist rather than Jesus as the true Messiah (see *Encyclopedia Americana* [1951], 24:76–77).

Tacitus identified Mona with the island of Anglesey, located in the Irish Sea north of Wales; other ancient writers identified it with the Isle of Man.

20. On Whitman and the Thorvaldsen statuary, see Paul Benton, "Whitman, Christ, and the Crystal Palace Police: A Manuscript Source Restored," *WWQR* 17 (2000), 136–165.

21. See Cavitch, "Lament in 'Song of the Broad-Axe,'" 32–33; Rubin, *Historic Whitman,* 300.

22. James Bonwick, *Egyptian Belief and Modern Thought* (Indian Hills, Colo.: Falcon Wing Press, 1956), 105–106. The French archaeologist was Theodule Deveria; the churchman was Eusebius. Kneph has been associated with various deities and assigned various physical attributes and powers.

23. Kerényi, *Hermes Guide of Souls,* 74–75, 79, 80, 89, and passim. Goodale, "Some of Whitman's Borrowings," 202–213, documents the borrowings from Volney concerning the classic gods (and the Scandinavian "cairns"); Hermes's impressive plea is borrowed from that source almost verbatim.

24. "Starting from Paumanok," *LG,* 27; "By Blue Ontario's Shore," *LG,* 313.

25. Savage, *Life beyond Death*, 31.

26. Many scholars have lauded Whitman as one who afforded dark-skinned peoples equal respect with whites; he observed that his personal kindness to blacks was part of his nature. But some crudely racist comments that he made the closing days of his life, together with the admission that his expression of similar views in the past had upset some of his friends, confirm his lingering anti-black prejudice. See *WWC*, 8:439; *WWC*, 9:48–49. Like Carlyle and proslavery apologists—and many Free Soilers—Whitman was chiefly concerned with the deleterious effect the blacks might have upon the *white* population.

27. *LGVar*, 174; *LG1856*, 120. For the three-line verse quoted above, the 1860 edition reads:

> I do not refuse you my hand,
> I do not say one word against you.

See Eric Foner, *Politics and Ideology in the Age of the Civil War* (Oxford: Oxford UP, 1988), 77–93 (the quotation is from p. 90). On the prevailing racialist theories of the day, see also John S. Haller, *Outcasts from Evolution: Scientific Attitudes of Racial Inferiority 1859–1900* (Urbana: U Illinois P, 1971).

28. *LGVar*, 175.

29. *UPP*, 2:67; T. R. Rajahsekhariah, *The Roots of Whitman's Grass* (Rutherford, N.J.: Farleigh Dickinson UP, 1970), 401; Conner, *Cosmic Optimism*, 121.

30. Perry Miller's introduction to Jonathan Edwards's *Images or Shadows of Divine Things*, 23; Edwards's quotation appears on p. 130.

31. *LG*, 157; *LGVar*, 236.

32. James O. Wheatley, "Reincarnation—How It Stands, What It Entails: Reflections on Paul Edwards' *Reincarnation*," *The Journal of the American Society for Psychical Research* 91 (July 1997), 230–231.

33. Lamont, *Illusion of Immortality*, 164–166. Davis is quoted in Braude, *Radical Spirits*, 51.

34. On the possible postmortem retention of human faculties, see Arthur Flew, "The Logic of Mortality," in *Death and Immortality in the Religions of the World*, ed. Badham and Badham, 179–180.

35. Moore, *In Search of White Crows*, 53. Moore declares that spiritualists, rejecting Calvinist teachings, derived many of their ideas of Heaven and Hell from Swedenborg, although they generally rejected any belief in Hell (56–58).

36. John Hick, "The Survival of the Disembodied Mind," in *Death and Eternal Life*, 265–269. All of the material in this paragraph is quoted or derived from this source. In turn, Hick's comments rely heavily, he says, on a paper by H. H. Price called "Survival and the Idea of 'Another World.'"

37. Perhaps this is what Edward Carpenter had in mind when he called Whitman "a savage in the happy hunting ground, with all his faculties restored"; see Edward Carpenter, *Edward Carpenter—1844–1920—Democratic Author and Poet* (London: Friends of Dr. Williams's Library, 1970), 11 [pamphlet].

38. The phrase occurs in Nolan, *Poet-Chief,* 180.

39. Tenny Nathanson, *Whitman's Presence: Body, Voice, and Writing in Leaves of Grass* (New York: New York UP, 1992), 465–466.

40. Bucke, *Notes and Fragments,* 23, quoted in *Walt Whitman's Autograph Revision of the Analysis of Leaves of Grass,* ed. Quentin Anderson and Stephen Railton (New York: New York UP, 1974), 35.

41. Emerson, "Immortality," 827.

42. Lamont, *Illusion of Immortality,* 139.

43. For example, these lines in "Starting from Paumanok" (*LGVar,* 275):

One generation [of Americans] playing its part and passing on,
Another generation playing its part and passing on in its turn,
With faces turned sideward or backward towards me to listen,
With eyes retrospective towards me.

44. Stephen Railton, "As If I Were with You: The Performance of Whitman's Poetry," in *The Cambridge Companion to Walt Whitman,* ed. Ezra Greenspan (Cambridge: Cambridge UP, 1995), 20–21.

45. Stephen A. Black, *Whitman's Journey into Chaos: A Psychological Study of the Poetic Process* (Princeton: Princeton UP, 1975), 202–203.

46. *LGVar,* 225; *LG1856,* 221.

# Chapter 4

1. W. C. Harris, "Whitman's *Leaves of Grass* and the Writing of the New American Bible," *WWQR* 16 (1999), 180, 182.

2. *LGVar,* 290–292, 312–313. The "purged lumine" apparently are those enlightened seers whose thoughts are enlightened and intelligent, expressing luminous ideas; they are "purged" in the sense that they are free from sin, guilt, or corruption. For a summary of Whitman's relations to spiritualism, see *WWBB,* 64–166, 272 n.64.

3. "Leaves-Droppings," in *Leaves of Grass* (Brooklyn, 1856), 365–366; Walt Whitman, *Corr,* 1:43, 206–208; Loving, *Walt Whitman,* 353.

4. Nelson, *Spiritualism and Society,* 8.

5. Noyes, *History of American Socialisms,* 538–539, 565, 567, 617–618. In 1857 *The Practical Christian* counted sixty-seven books and periodicals devoted to spiritualism. See Gilbert Seldes, *The Stammering Century* (New York: Harper and Row, 1965), 336.

6. Anonymous self-review in *United States Review,* 1855; included in *Leaves of Grass Imprints* (1860), 7–13, reprinted in Hindus, *Walt Whitman,* 34–41 (the quotation appears on 39).

7. Richard Maurice Bucke, et al., eds. *The Complete Writings of Walt Whitman* (New York: G. P. Putnam's Sons, 1902) 9:150–151, quoted in Frederick William Connor, *Cosmic Optimism: A Study of the Interpretations of Evolution by American Poets from Emerson to Robinson* (Gainesville: U Florida P, 1949), 114.

8. *LG,* 15n.

9. *LG,* 182. Whitman revised the 1860 version of the poem extensively, eliminating the couplet about "the mad-sweet drops" of his genitalia (*LG1860,* 268).

10. The mockingbird's arias may owe something to Whitman's infatuation with the popular contralto Marietta Alboni. See Robert D. Faner, *Walt Whitman and Opera* (Carbondale: Southern Illinois UP, 1972), 67, 177.

11. Claire Rossini's intriguing reading of the poem suggests that the bird, and, by extension, the persona's alter ego, may have descended into the realm of death, as the persona does in "Song of Myself," section 49. See Rossini, "The Rebound Seed: Death in Whitman's Poetry" (Ph.D. diss. Columbia University, 1990), 81–91.

The poem's "arias" are not without musical echoes of Tennyson.

12. C. G. Macaulay, "Walt Whitman," *Nineteenth Century* [London] 12 (1882), 903–918, cited in Kenneth Price, ed., *Walt Whitman: The Contemporary Reviews* (New York: Cambridge UP, 1996), 265.

13. Colum, "The Poetry of Walt Whitman," 58.

14. "To a Locomotive in Winter," *LG,* 472.

15. Kuebrich, *Minor Prophecy,* 118.

16. *LGVar,* 350.

17. Rossini, "The Rebound Seed," 89–91.

18. Richard Chase, *Walt Whitman Reconsidered* (New York: William Sloane Associates, 1955), 123.

19. Kuebrich, *Minor Prophecy,* 113. Kuebrich's interpretation of the poem cites Whitman's 1872 preface; see *PW1892,* 459.

20. See Stephen E. Whicher, "Whitman's Awakening to Death," in *Walt Whitman: A Collection of Criticism,* ed. Arthur Golden (New York: McGraw Hill, 1974), 93; Ned J. Davison, "'The Raven' and 'Out of the Cradle Endlessly Rocking,'" *Poe Newsletter* 1 (April 1968), 5.

21. Black, *Whitman's Journey into Chaos,* 72.

22. When Whitman deleted these lines in 1867 he changed the poem's essential balance and, to a degree, blunted its meaning. See *LGVar,* 350 n.

23. Black, *Whitman's Journey into Chaos,* 56; Tenny Nathanson maintains that this is a critical poem announcing the poet's inability to translate himself into the ghost-Whitman, unable to attain a wished-for relation with his audience (*Whitman's Presence,* 465–466).

24. *LGVar,* 319. In accepting the poem, James Russell Lowell, editor of the *Atlantic Monthly,* required Whitman to delete two lines that graphically described a corpse; see Loving, *Walt Whitman,* 222.

25. Rossini, "The Rebound Seed," 100. Rossini provides a thoughtful discussion of the poem.

26. See "On the Beach at Night Alone" and "Eidòlons," *LG,* 5–8, 260–261.

27. Does Whitman's reference to the "oceans both" suggest that the poem was written at, or inspired by, Montauk Point, where the Atlantic Ocean and Long Island Sound can both be seen?

28. Black, *Whitman's Journey into Chaos,* 61.

29. *LG1860,* 199.

30. Staten, *Eros in Mourning,* 60; Kerényi is quoted in Hyde, *The Gift,* 32.

31. "Myself and Mine," originally "Leaves of Grass, 10," *LG1860,* 224–226 (not a "Children of Adam" poem). Whitman deleted two self-accusatory lines from the 1860 version of the poem: "Let others deny the evil their enemies charge against them—but how can I do the like? / Nothing ever has been, or ever can be, charged against me, half as bad as the evil I really am."

32. Ludowick Muggleton, *The Acts of the Witnesses of the Spirit* (London, 1699 [1694]), 21; see Genesis 14:17–20. In Melville's *Pierre* (1852) Pierre Glendinning's mother compares the youth's infatuated conduct to that of "milksops and Muggletonians."

33. The Doyle testimony is cited in Emory Holloway, "Whitman Pursued," in *On Whitman: The Best from American Literature,* ed. Edwin H. Cady and Lewis J. Budd (Durham: Duke UP, 1987), 105. Loving indicates (*Walt Whitman,* p. 381) that Whitman showed some interest in certain women. An amusing application of this antic (and sexist) theory of the semen appears in Laurence Sterne's account of his hero's birth in *The Life and Opinions of Tristram Shandy, Gent.* On Whitman's and the era's interest in "sound begetting," see *WWBB,* 199–200; also "Unfolding the Folds."

34. "With All Thy Gifts" (1872), *LG,* 401; Henry C. Wright, *Marriage and Parentage: Or, The Reproductive Element in Man* (1855; reprint, New York: Arno Press, 1974), 237–239, 246–251.

35. "Enfans d'Adam" no. 11, *LG1860,* 312–313; Bucke, *Complete Writings of Walt Whitman,* 10:40.

36. "One Hour to Madness and Joy" ("Enfans d'Adam 6"), *LG1860,* 307–309.

37. Gay Wilson Allen, *The New Walt Whitman Handbook* (New York: New York UP, 1975), 89; an enlightening discussion of "Live Oak, with Mosses" to "Calamus" is Hershel Parker, "The Real 'Live Oak with Moss': Straight Talk about Whitman's 'Gay Manifesto,'" *Nineteenth-Century Literature* 51 (September 1996), 147–160.

38. The relation between the persona's spermatic ("seminal") experience and his literary and mystical expression is discussed in Aspiz, "Walt Whitman: The Spermatic Imagination," 273–289.

39. Lamont, *Illusion of Immortality,* 116–117. Lamont cites Kant's *Critique of Practical Reason,* Book 2, ch. 2.

40. *LG1860,* 362–363.

41. This line does not appear in any published version of the poem, but only in a manuscript in the Barrett Collection; still, it helps to indicate Whitman's intent. The poem's earlier version announced that the poet was "thirty-eight years old," placing its composition in 1857. See *LG,* 136–137; *LGVar,* 407–408.

42. *LG,* 118–119; Kuebrich (*Minor Prophecy,* 148) construes the calamus, the hardiest of grasses, as a symbol of the victory of life over death.

43. Rossini, "The Rebound Seed," 62; see also Vivian Pollak, "Death as Repression, Repression as Death: A Reading of Whitman's 'Calamus' Poems," *The Mickle Street Review* 11 (1989), 64. Lewis Hyde says that this poem inspired D. H. Lawrence to call Whitman the great poet of death (*The Gift,* 182).

44. Lawrence, "Whitman," 13.

45. Tapscott, "Leaves of Myself," 221–222.

46. *NUPM*, 4:1366; Allen Ginsberg, "I Love Old Whitman So," in *Walt Whitman: The Measure of His Song*, ed. Jim Perlman, Ed Folsom, Dan Campion (Duluth: Holy Cow Press, 1998), 353.

47. Nathanson, *Whitman's Presence*, 315.

48. *NUPM*, 3:1137.

49. Kenneth M. Price and Cynthia G. Bernstein, "Whitman's Sign of Parting: 'So Long!' as 'l'envoi,'" *WWQR* 9 (1991), 65–76; Faner, *Walt Whitman and Opera*, 137–138.

50. *LG*, 504–505; *LGVar*, 451.

51. Quoted in *The Nation*, February 12, 1996, p. 33.

52. See *LG1860*, p. 56; Kerényi, *Hermes Guide of Souls*, 71. The butterfly in the well-known photograph of Whitman with a butterfly on his finger is, alas, only a paper butterfly.

53. Kübler-Ross, *Wheel of Life*, 284 (thus punctuated in the original text). A lovely example of butterfly-soul image occurs in *Platero and I: An Andalusian Elegy*, by the Nobelist Juan Ramón Jiménez (New York: New American Library, 1960). At the graveside of Platero, his beloved donkey and virtual soul mate, he wonders whether the buried animal can still see him. "As if to answer my question, a delicate white butterfly, which I had not seen before, flew insistently from iris to iris, like a soul."

54. "Starting from Paumanok," *LG*, 18.

55. Staten, *Eros in Mourning*, 15.

56. Attributed to Holmes by Osler, *Science and Immortality*, 3.

57. Stevenson quoted in Lamont, *Illusion of Immortality*, 265.

58. "I Heard You Solemn-Sweet Pipes of the Organ," *LG*, 110. Whitman placed this 1861 lyric in the "Children of Adam" cluster in 1871, thus giving it the cachet of a heterosexual poem.

59. See Nathan Ausubel, *The Book of Jewish Knowledge* (New York: Crown Publishers, 1964), 136–137. A *gilgul* in Hebrew lore is a disembodied soul that takes possession of a living person; a *dybbuk* is a *gilgul* with a malign purpose. Ausubel calls attention to similar beliefs among ancient Egyptians, Brahmins, Buddhists, Neo-Platonists, etc.

60. James M. Cox, "Whitman, Death, and Mark Twain" (paper delivered at the 11th Annual Conference of the American Literature Association, Long Beach, Calif., May 26, 2000).

61. *LGVar*, 138. I am indebted for this information to a brilliant article by W. C. Harris, "Whitman's *Leaves of Grass*," 166.

62. The concept of a spiritual spouse is discussed in Hutchinson, *Ecstatic Whitman*, 130–131.

63. "To Him That Was Crucified." *LG*, 384–385. Originally part of the 1860 "Messenger Leaves" cluster, it was later to be transferred to the "Autumn Rivulets" cluster. Christ is named seven times in *Leaves of Grass*.

64. Isaac Watt, hymn 19, book 1, quoted in Staten, *Eros in Mourning*, 60.

65. *WWC*, 8:23, 99. He esteemed Jesus's teaching as opposed to the false doctrines of contemporary preachers.

66. *LG*, 450–451.

67. *LGVar*, 452.

68. See Kuebrich, *Minor Prophecy.* 21.

69. Rajahsekhariah, 418; *Roots of Whitman's Grass,* quoting from James C. Thomson's translation of the *Bhagavadgita,* a copy of which was presented to Whitman (70).

70. Hick, *Death and Eternal Life,* 361. Hick is following Buddhist scripture, and defines the term "rebecoming" as "unprocreated." Hick also cites Saint Augustine's observation (251) that "the inherent gravitation of our being" is toward God.

# Chapter 5

1. Thomas Donaldson, *Walt Whitman, the Man* (New York, 1896), 205–206. On Whitman's hospital service, see *WWBB,* 77–105; Robert Leigh Davis, *Whitman and the Romance of Medicine* (Berkeley: U California P, 1997); Loving, *Walt Whitman,* 1–25, 251–295.

2. Charles I. Glicksberg, ed., *Walt Whitman and the Civil War: A Collection of Original Articles and Manuscripts* (1933; reprint, New York: A. S. Barnes, 1963), 121–126.

3. *Memoranda During the War [and] Death of Abraham Lincoln,* ed. Roy P. Basler (Bloomington: Indiana UP, 1962), 3–5; on the relation between the notebooks and the *Memoranda,* see introduction, 23 (separately paginated). Whitman was not unique in keeping informal pocket notebooks of his hospital experiences—the famed nurse Clara Barton kept similar ones; see Gary Laderman, *The Sacred Remains: American Attitudes toward Death, 1799–1883* (New Haven: Yale UP, 1996), 131.

4. F. DeWolfe Miller, ed., *Walt Whitman's Drum-Taps (1865) and Sequel to Drum-Taps (1865–6)* (Gainesville, Fla.: Scholars' Facsimiles & Reprints, 1959), xxvi; on Whitman's attempts to get his book published, see xxvi–xxxi.

5. *Sequel to Drum-Taps* also contained two poems reflecting a spirit of personal despair, possibly left over or reworked from the 1850s—"O Me, O Life" and "Ah Poverties, Wincings and Sulky Retreats"—each concluding on a note of half-hope. "Ah Poverties" is a compact masterpiece possibly related to "As I Ebb'd with the Ocean of Life."

6. See Julianne Ramsey, "A British View to the American War: Walt Whitman's 'Drum-Taps' Cluster and the Editorial Influence of William Michael Rossetti," *WWQR* 14 (1997), 166–175.

7. *LGVar,* 456n.; *LG,* 501. Originally included in "Shut Not Your Doors to Me Proud Libraries."

8. Miller, *Walt Whitman's Drum-Taps (1865) and Sequel to Drum-Taps,* xxvii–xxix.

9. An interesting discussion on this point is Barbara Ehrenreich, *Blood Rites: Origins and History of the Passions of War* (New York: Henry Holt, 1997), 162.

10. Manuscript fragment, quoted in Glicksberg, *Walt Whitman and the Civil War,* 17. Apparently parts of the original were missing or undecipherable.

11. Glicksberg, *Walt Whitman and the Civil War,* 29, 82–83; on the genesis of a couple of *Drum-Taps* poems, see 121–126.

12. Loving, *Walt Whitman,* 9. The rousing "recruitment" poem appeared in *Har-*

*per's Weekly* and the *New York Leader* on September 28, 1861; see Joann P. Krieg, *A Whitman Chronology* (Iowa City: U Iowa P, 1998), 46.

13. *LG,* 284–291.

14. Quoted in Ehrenreich, *Blood Rites,* 218, 222.

15. On the piano as Whitman's symbol for conventional, effeminate verse, see also "To a Certain Civilian" and "To a Locomotive in Winter," *LG,* 323, 471–472.

"Well-gristled" literally means well-endowed with cartilage, or soft tissue. Possibly Whitman meant strong-boned or perhaps even well-*grizzled,* like his graying self. Samuel Johnson's *Dictionary of the English Language* (London, 1818) cites "Grisled. See Grizzled."

16. Whitman, *Memoranda During the War,* 7.

17. On Whitman's attitude toward hanging, see Rubin, *Historic Whitman,* 117; *UPP,* 2:15–16; Loving, *Walt Whitman,* 496, no. 28. On Whitman's enthusiasm for the Mexican War, see Thomas L. Brashear, *Whitman as Editor of the Brooklyn Daily Eagle* (Detroit: Wayne U Press, 1970), 87–90.

18. Ellen Calder cited in Myerson, *Whitman in His Own Time,* 208 (the words attributed to Whitman are only an approximation, according to Mrs. Calder). The "secession slave-power" is mentioned in *Democratic Vistas,* in *PW1892,* 2:377.

19. *Corr,* 1:114–115 ( July 7, 1863).

20. A few weeks after he began visiting soldiers at the Washington hospitals, he noted that he had spent about two hours every day doing so: *NUPM,* 2:582. Considering the many overnight visits and vigils and many longer visits, the total hours may be reckoned in the thousands.

21. Whitman, *Memoranda During the War,* 57–58.

22. In covertly editing Dr. Richard Maurice Bucke's *Walt Whitman* (1883), Whitman changed John Burroughs's reference to his "maternal soul" to read "paternal soul"; see Harold Jaffe, "Bucke's *Walt Whitman:* A Collaboration," *Walt Whitman Review* 15 (1969), 192. Homosexuality had not been defined by midcentury, and the references to Whitman's supposedly "feminine" side, observed by both men and women contemporaries, deserve further study; see also page 000 and note 57, below.

23. Davis, Whitman and the Romance of Medicine, 14, 50–51.

24. Paul Zweig, *Walt Whitman: The Making of a Poet* (New York: Basic Books, 1984), 343.

25. Introduction to Whitman, *Memoranda During the War,* 17.

26. *WWC,* 2:52–53. On Whitman's photographic imagery, see also Ed Folsom, *Walt Whitman's Native Representations* (Cambridge: Cambridge UP, 1997), 126.

27. Introduction to Whitman, *Memoranda During the War,* 14–15.

28. Glicksberg, *Walt Whitman and the Civil War,* 121–123.

29. For a gallery of Whitman photographs, see *WWQR* 4 (1986–1987), 1–72.

30. Glicksberg, *Walt Whitman and the Civil War,* 82 n. The quotation, from *Notes & Fragments,* 96, appears in Howard J. Waskow, *Whitman's Exploration in Form* (Chicago: U Chicago P, 1966), 54. In 1859 Whitman credited Dante with "a great vigor, a lean muscular ruggedness, and the fascination there always is in a well-told tragedy, no matter how painful and repulsive," but free from the florid style of Shakespeare (*NUPM,* 5:163).

31. *LGVar,* 493–494; "staunch" was later correct to the more commonly used "stanch."

32. See, for example, M. Wynn Thomas, "Fratricide and Brotherly Love: Whitman and the Civil War," in *The Cambridge Companion to Walt Whitman,* ed. Ezra Greenspan (New York: Cambridge UP, 1995), 40.

Whitman's insistence on the calm and serene acceptance of death by his heroic soldier boys, if not mythic, is far from representative of all soldiers facing death. Christopher Knox, recalling his own fear and the fears of his fellow soldiers in the Spanish Civil War, cites two literary examples of the soldier's *timor mortis* when they were near death: "In Homer's *Iliad,* for example, the greatest of all war books. Hector 'went singing down to the House of Death / wailing his fate, leaving his manhood far behind, his young and supple strength.' And Virgil's Turnus goes the same road . . . 'his life with a groan fled angry to the shades below . . . angry because he was young'" (cited in a review of books on the Spanish Civil War by Christopher Hitchens, *Los Angeles Times Book Review,* July 15, 2001, 2–3).

33. Laderman, *Sacred Remains,* 37 and passim; Introduction to Whitman, *Memoranda During the War,* passim. On burial rites, see also Thomas Lynch, *The Undertaking* (New York: Norton, 1997), 5, 13.

34. Oliver Wendell Holmes, "My Hunt After 'The Captain,'" in *Pages from an Old Volume of Life* (Boston: Houghton Mifflin, 1890), 29.

35. "November Boughs," in *PW1892,* 614.

36. Thomas, "Fratricide and Brotherly Love," 36.

37. Richard A. Shryock, "A Medical Perspective on the Civil War," *American Quarterly* 14 (summer 1962), 161.

38. See John Carlos Rowe, *At Emerson's Tomb: The Politics of Classic American Literature* (New York: Columbia UP, 1997), 156.

39. Ariès, "The Reversal of Death," 148.

40. Lynch, *Undertaking,* 22.

41. *NUPM,* 2:514. On the poem's genesis, see Loving, *Walt Whitman,* 20–21; on military burial practice, see Laderman, *Sacred Remains,* 46.

42. On Whitman's relations with some wartime physician, see *WWBB,* 81–84.

43. "November Boughs" in *PW1892,* 618; *NUPM,* 2:508–509, quoted in Loving, *Walt Whitman,* 20–21; Jerome Loving, personal correspondence.

44. *Corr,* 1:127.

45. Mesmerists and "electrical healers" claimed that their words, their letters, and even their telegrams could heal at long distance. Thus there is an entire chapter, "Healing at a Distance," in *The Modern Bethesda, Or the Gift of Healing Restored* (New York, 1879), 139–154, a purported record of the cures effected by the self-pronounced "healer" J. R. Newton, many of them performed in the 1860s. Mark Twain credited Newton with having cured his wife-to-be of her chronic neurasthenia.

46. Davis, *Whitman and the Romance of Medicine,* 67–68.

47. *Corr,* 1:122, also 112, 153, 157, 231, 261; Introduction to Whitman, *Memoranda During the War,* 8–9, 38–39; *Specimen Days,* in *PW1892,* 1:308–309; Charles E. Feinberg, "Walt Whitman and His Doctors," *Archives of Internal Medicine* 114 (1964), 834. On Whitman's healing touch, see, for example, *November Boughs,* which possibly

ends with a quote of Whitman placing his hands on a certain Wallace, who then slept peaceably (*PW1892*, 265).

48. *Specimen Days*, in *PW1892*, 75; Walter Lowenfels, *Walt Whitman's Civil War* (New York: Knopf, 1978), 123.

49. *LG*, 308–309 n.

50. Shryock, "Medical Perspective on the Civil War," 161–175. Lamenting the lack of complete "mortuary statistics," Whitman asserts that more than thirty thousand Union soldiers died "largely of actual starvation" in Southern prisons. See "Last of the War Cases," in *PW1892*, 2:614–615.

51. "The Return of the Heroes," *LG*, 360; *WWC*, 3:293.

52. *NUPM*, 2:519; Shryock, "Medical Perspective on the Civil War," 165.

53. On Whitman and the junior physicians, see *WWBB*, 71–75.

54. *Corr*, 1:112, 114, 122.

55. Whitman, *Memoranda During the War*, 21 (text section).

56. *Corr*, 1:230–232. This letter of June 4, 1864, affectingly describes Whitman's awareness of his own impending emotional and physical crisis.

57. Whitman spoke these words to Charles Eldridge. See Barrus, *Whitman and Burroughs Comrades*, 13; on Farnham, see Harold Aspiz, "An Early Feminist Tribute to Whitman," *American Literature* 51 (1979), 405.

58. "Last of the War Cases," in *PW1892*, 620–621, a note inscribed May 23, 1864. For soldiers' often hostile attitudes toward dying, see note 32 above.

59. M. Wynn Thomas, "Whitman's Obligations of Memory," *WWQR* 28 (1982), 43.

60. Stanton Garner, *The Civil War World of Herman Melville* (Lawrence: (U Kansas P, 1993), 324, 361, 388. Melville's seventy-two poems are reflections on the war's battles its ironies. Apparently Whitman sensed a challenge (almost amounting to a resentment) in James Russell Lowell's pindaric "Ode Recited at the Commencement to the Living and Dead Soldiers of Harvard University." Lowell is disparagingly mentioned several times in *WWC*, vols. 8 and 9.

61. *LGVar*, 144–146. See "Resurgemus" ("Europe, the 72d and 73d Years of These States," *LG*, 266–268), which predicts that the spirits of the martyrs of the failed European revolutions of 1849 would return to inspire living young men with the spirit of freedom. See also the discussion of "Scented Herbage of My Breast" in chapter 4.

62. "Specimen Days," in *PW1892*, 1:102–104.

63. The inclusion of "Chanting the Square Deific" in *Sequel to Drum-Taps*—a poem that Whitman admitted he could not explain with "mathematical precision"—appears to be an anomaly, but it does reflect his attitude toward the just concluded war. Three sides of the poem's "square" are occupied by figures of the Christian Trinity, augmented by loosely related pagan figures. The fourth side is inhabited by the figure of Satan. The Jehovah figure's judgments are declared to be "inexorable without the least remorse," thus suggesting that the war and its carnage resulted from an unavoidable fate. The Satan figure embodies both the spirit of rebellion against tyranny and oppression and also the contradictory spirit of perversity and evil, thus representing the complex motivations that caused men to participate in the conflict. In sharp

contrast, the third "side" of the square is occupied by a Whitmanlike figure—a composite of Christ, Hermes, and Hercules—who brings "hope and all-enclosing charity," and who declares, "All the world I have given up for my brothers' and sisters' sake, for the soul's sake" and who proposes to speak "with fresh and sane words— mine only." The fourth side belongs to Santa Spirita, the universal "breather of life," who embodies Whitman's faith that everything—including ostensible evil—becomes integrated into the divine plan. The poet implores Santa Spirita to "breathe [her] breath through these songs." The poem anticipates Whitman's later "philosophical" poems.

See *LG,* 442–443; *LGVar,* 544n.; *WWC,* 1:156; George L. Sixbey, "Chanting the Square Deific: A Study in Whitman's Religion," *American Literature* 9 (1937), 171–195. On Cronos (one of the Jupiter grouping) as a symbol of tyranny, "human sacrifice, bloody suffering and even cannibalism, but still revered as a bringer of peace," see H. S. Veronel, "Greek Myth and Ritual: the Case of Kronos" in *Interpretations of Greek Mythology,* ed. Ian Bremmer (Totowa, N.J.: Barnes & Noble, 1986), 127–129. On Jehovah as a warrior God, see Ehrenreich, *Blood Rites,* 62.

64. John Bailey, *Walt Whitman* (New York: Macmillan, 1926), 175–176.

65. See Gay Wilson Allen, *The Solitary Singer: A Critical Biography of Walt Whitman* (New York: Macmillan, 1955), 383.

66. John Burroughs, *Notes on Walt Whitman, Poet and Person* (1867; reprint, New York: Haskell House, 1971), 101–102; italics are mine.

67. Edward Said, "Musical Retrospection," *The Nation,* October 16, 1992, 481. See also Faner, *Walt Whitman and Opera,* 154–159, and Robert Strassburg, "Whitman and Music," in *Walt Whitman: An Encyclopedia,* ed. J. R. LeMaster and Donald D. Kummings (New York: Garland Publishing Co., 1998), 437–439.

68. "Spirit That Form'd This Scene," (1881); *LG,* 486. Perhaps to tweak his critics, Whitman's verse included some half dozen examples of iambic hexameter.

69. Quoted from Bucke's *Walt Whitman* in Myerson, *Whitman in His Own Time.* On Whitman and the English classics, see Kenneth Price, *Whitman and Tradition: The Poet and His Century* (New Haven: Yale UP, 1990).

70. Richard P. Adams, "Whitman's 'Lilacs' and the Tradition of the Pastoral Elegy," *PMLA* 72 (1957), 479–487; Peter M. Sacks, *The English Elegy: Studies in the Genre from Spenser to Yeats* (Baltimore: Johns Hopkins UP, 1985), 316–317; Helen Vendler, *The Music of What Happens: Poems, Poets, Critics* (Cambridge: Harvard UP, 1988), 141–145.

71. Introduction to Whitman, *Memoranda During the War,* 5–6; *LG,* 339.

72. Ralph Waldo Emerson, "Abraham Lincoln," in *The Complete Writings of Ralph Waldo Emerson* (New York: William H. Wise and Co., 1929), 1217–1220.

Robert Milder, review of Stanton Garner, *The Civil War of Herman Melville* in *American Literature* 68 (1996), 239, and Hutchinson, *Ecstatic Whitman,* 156, respectively, refer to Lincoln as "the prairie Christ" and "the American Osiris," ideas that are latent in Whitman's treatment of the deceased President. Lincoln's death softened the opinions of some of the president's critics. Thus the first two volumes of Whitman's Washington friend Count Adam de Gurowski's wartime diaries are hostile to Lincoln's policies, but the third volume, published after Lincoln's death celebrates him as a hero-martyr. On Gurowski see LeRoy Fisher, *Lincoln's Gadfly: Adam Gurowski* (Norman: U Oklahoma P, 1964).

73. R. Gerald McMurtry, "The Lincoln Funeral Car," in *The Poet and the President: Whitman's Lincoln Poems*, ed. William Coyle (New York: Odyssey Press, 1962), 124–131.

74. See Laderman, *Sacred Remains*, 157–163, and the photographs following 116. Photographs and commercial reproductions of Lincoln's iconic corpse, which to the untrained eye seemed almost alive and beyond decay, were widely printed in the media.

75. Zweig, *Walt Whitman*, 129.

76. On the literature of consolation, see Douglas, "Heaven Our Home," 49–68.

77. On the concept that war is an instrument of progress as well as a national purgative, see Barbara Ehrenreich, *Blood Rites*, 222 and passim.

78. Emerson's statement quoted in Laderman, *Sacred Remains*, 128.

79. Hutchinson, *Ecstatic Whitman*, 153.

80. Derrida, *Work of Mourning*, 142–143; Staten, *Eros in Mourning*, xii, 11.

81. Sacks, *English Elegy*, 317.

82. Edwin Haviland Miller, ed., *Walt Whitman's Poetry: A Psychological Journey* (Boston: Houghton Mifflin, 1968), 189.

83. Miklos Udvarty, *The Audubon Society Field Guide to the Birds of North America: Western Region* (New York: Knopf, 1977), 743.

84. W. David Shaw, *Elegy and Paradox: Testing the Conventions* (Baltimore: Johns Hopkins UP, 1994), 165.

85. Lynch, *Undertaking*, 13, 21.

86. "Elegy for Jane, My Student Thrown from a Horse," 1953, in *The Collected Poems of Theodore Roethke* (New York: Doubleday, 1966), 102.

87. Loving, *Walt Whitman*, 285–286, notes Whitman's favorable observations of Lincoln and his fascination with his physiognomy, recorded in some of his newspaper pieces and other writings. But he also notes that Whitman (who creates a mythic bond with the President in "Lilacs," section 8) later in life exaggerated his intimacy with Lincoln, going so far as to repeat the tale in his Lincoln lectures that he was seated close to Lincoln in Ford's Theater when the president was fatally shot. See also *PW1892*, 59–61.

88. See Adams, "Whitman's 'Lilacs' and the Tradition of Pastoral Poetry," *PMLA* 72 (1957), 481.

89. Jeffrey Steele, "Poetic Grief Work in Whitman's 'Lilacs,'" *WWQR* 2 (winter 1984), 15.

90. Leo Marx, *The Machine in the Garden: Technology and the Pastoral Ideal in America* (New York: Oxford UP, 1967), 222.

91. Rosemary L. Gates, "Egyptian Myth and Whitman's 'Lilacs,'" *WWQR* 5 (summer 1987), 24; Edwards, *Images and Shadows of Divine Things*, 58. Gates remarks that "The sun does not represent Osiris per se, but rather the immortality of Osiris, who made immortality possible and who was symbolically cradled in the arms of the sun."

92. Quoted Gates, "Egyptian Myths," 31, no. 17.

93. Sigmund Freud, "Mourning and Melancholy," *The Standard Edition of the Psychological Works* (London: Hogarth, 1964), 14:255.

94. James E. Miller Jr., *A Critical Guide to "Leaves of Grass"* (Chicago: U Chicago Press, 1957), 117. Also see, Shaw, *Elegy and Paradox*, 147.

95. Vendler, *Music of What Happens*, 142–143.

96. See, especially, Lyman L. Leathers, "Music, Whitman's Influence On," in *Walt Whitman: An Encyclopedia*, ed. J. R. LeMaster and Donald D. Kummings (New York: Garland, 1998), 439–441.

97. Kuebrich, *Minor Prophecy*, 125. Helen Vendler, on the other hand, interprets section 15 as a song of "ultimate despair of human solutions to violence" (*Music of What Happens*, 143).

98. Stephen E. Whicher, "Whitman's Awakening to Death: Toward a Biographical Reading of 'Out of the Cradle Endlessly Rocking,'" *A Century of Whitman Criticism*, ed. In Edwin Haviland Miller, 290.

99. Cited in Laderman, *The Sacred Remains*, 161. The bishop was Matthew Simpson of Illinois.

# Chapter 6

1. Waggoner, *American Visionary Poetry*, 35, 42; Bucke's letter is quoted in *WWC*, 8:103.

2. Rufus M. Jones, "The Mystical Element in Walt Whitman" in *Some Exponents of Mystical Religion*, 174; M. Jimmie Killingsworth, "Whitman's Sexual Themes during a Decade of Revision: 1866–1876," *WWQR* 4 (summer 1988), 7–15.

3. *The Galaxy* published only two installments of the essay; the declaration, in the third section, that America needed poets of death was not published until 1871, when the author himself published *Democratic Vistas*.

4. Anonymous, "Poems by Walt Whitman," *Lloyds's Weekly London Newspaper*, April 19, 1868, reprinted in Price, *Walt Whitman*, 158; Anne Gilchrist, "A Woman's Estimate of Walt Whitman," *The Radical* (Boston, May 1870), reprinted in Hindus, *Walt Whitman*, 139; Edward Dowden, "The Poet of Democracy: Walt Whitman," *Westminster Review*, July 1871, reprinted in Price, *Walt Whitman*, 207.

5. "*Preface 1872—As a Strong Bird on Pinions Free*," *LG*, 744–745.

6. "Darest Thou Now O Soul" became the lead poem in the group "Whispers of Heavenly Death" in the final ("Deathbed") edition of *Leaves of Grass; LG*, 441–442.

7. *LG*, 454.

8. "These Carols," *LG*, 502.

9. *NUPM*, 2:522–523; Allen, *Solitary Singer*, 342–343. Allen says that several such drafts exist.

10. Friedrich Engels, "Natural Science and the Spirit World," in *The Dialectics of Nature*, 297–310. Among the distinguished scientists turned spiritualists whom Engels names are Darwin's rival in evolutionary theory Alfred Russell Wallace, the discoverer of thalium William Crookes, and the celebrated pathologist Rudolf Virchow.

11. William Rounseville Alger's *Doctrine of a Future Life,* cited in William Sloane Kennedy, "The Germ Idea of Whitman's 'Noiseless Patient Spider' Poem," *Conservator* 14 (January 1904), 173.

12. Savage, *Life beyond Death,* 164.

13. Lloyd, "Posthumous Mourning Portraiture," 75; for Whitman's remark, see *NUPM,* 3:1163.

14. Arthur Golden, "Passage to Less than India: Structure and Meaning in Whitman's 'Passage to India,'" *PMLA* 88 (1973), 1095–1103. Golden demonstrates that about one-third of the poem is constructed from earlier manuscript poems.

15. Golden, "Passage to Less than India," 1096–1097, quoting from manuscript. On the presumed relation between material and spiritual progress, see Lisa M. Steinman, *Made in America: Science, Technology, and American Modernist Poetry* (New Haven: Yale UP, 1987), 58. An article on cosmic emotion in the October 1877 issue of *Nineteenth Century* credits Whitman's work with being more consistent with the spirit of modern science than that of any contemporary poet, while agreeing with him that science alone provides little evidence for a future existence; cited in Barrus, *Whitman and Burroughs Comrades,* 160.

16. *"Preface 1876*—Leaves of Grass and Two Rivulets," *LG,* 747 n.

17. J. B. S. Haldane, "When I Am Dead," in *Possible Worlds and Other Papers* (New York: Harper and Brothers, 1928), 219–220. Haldane was a well known British biologist and Marxist.

18. John Williamson Nevin, *The Mystical Presence,* 1846, quoted in Laderman, *Sacred Remains,* 54.

19. Savage, *Life beyond Death,* 152.

20. Quoted in Rajasekhariah, *Roots of Whitman's Grass,* 206. Whitman may have had access to the translation of the *Vedas* by Sir William Jones (*Works,* [1799], 6:421–422). Thoreau utters a similar prayer in the verse, "Light-winged Smoke, Icarian Bird," in chapter 13 of *Walden.*

21. On Whitman's Eastern influence, see V. K. Chari, *Whitman in the Light of Vedantic Mysticism* (Lincoln: U Nebraska P, 1964).

22. *LG,* 206–210; Folsom, *Whitman's Native Representations,* 69, 76–77.

23. Some of Whitman's contemporaries protested against the 40 million board feet of lumber being cut from Northern California forests in the name of "progress" as a desecration of nature. Protestors included James Fenimore Cooper, Henry Thoreau, the painter Thomas Cole, and John Cole Morris, author of "Woodman, Spare That Tree." By way of contrast, Emerson's "Ode Inscribed to W. H. Channing" proclaims "'tis fit the forest fall, / The steep be graded"; see Thomas, *Lunar Light of Whitman's Poetry,* 138–140.

24. The germinal treatment of Whitman's relation to Native Americans is Ed Folsom's "Whitman and American Indians," in *Walt Whitman's Native Representations,* 55–98.

25. Geoffrey Sill, "Whitman on the 'Black Question': A New Manuscript," *WWQR* 8 (1990), 69. The brief manuscript deals only with African Americans, not with Native Americans.

26. Henry Seidel Canby calls the poem's music "Tennysonian," and compares it to "the last aria of the tenor in a tragic opera" (*Walt Whitman, an American: A Study in Biography* [Boston: Houghton Mifflin, 1943], 286–287).

27. *NUPM*, 4:1390–1391; Henry Thoreau, "The Shipwreck," published in *Putnam's Monthly* in June 1855 and collected posthumously in *Cape Cod*, 1865; see *Cape Cod*, reprint, ed. Dudley C. Lunt (New York: Norton, 1951), 13–15, 21–22. In 1856 Thoreau presented Whitman with a copy of *A Week on the Concord and Merrimac Rivers.* See also Fred Stovall, *The Foreground to Leaves of Grass* (Charlottesville: U Virginia P, 1974), 172.

28. *WWC*, 3:243–244.

29. Allen, *Solitary Singer*, 458–459; Stovall, *The Foreground of Leaves of Grass*, 262–263.

30. Saum, "Death in the Popular Mind of Pre–Civil War America," 43.

31. *The Life and Voyages of Christopher Columbus*, ed. John Harmon McElroy, in *The Complete Works of Washington Irving* (Boston: Twayne, 1981), 11:582 and passim.

32. *"Preface 1872—As a Strong Bird on Pinions Free," LG*, 741–742.

33. The image of a noble and pious Columbus, as conceived by Whitman's generation, contrasts sharply with his record of unspeakable depredation of the Caribbean peoples; see Stannard, *American Holocaust*, 66–67, 197–201, and passim.

34. *LG*, 449. Originally a "Calamus" poem, it was shifted in 1871 to the "Whispers of Heavenly Death" cluster.

35. For example, Allen, Solitary Singer, 460; Chari, Whitman in the Light of Vedantic Mysticism, 156–157.

36. Lee S. McCollester, "Universalism," *Encyclopedia Americana* (1951 ed.), 27:569. On Universalism and Spiritualism, see Braude, *Radical Spirits*, 34, 37, 46–47. A Universalist clergyman may have been exaggerating when he declared that half the Universalist ministers were Spiritualists in the 1870s (ibid., 47).

37. "Democratic Vistas," in PW1892, 2:424.

38. Russell E. Miller, *The Larger Hope: The First Century of the Universalist Church in America, 1770–1870* (Boston: Unitarian Universalist Assosciation, 1979), 27, 100, 570–571. Universalism has certain affinities to spiritualist doctrines.

39. "Roaming in Thought" (1881), *LG*, 274. The couplet is subtitled "After Reading Hegel" but is consistent with Universalist thought.

40. Holmes, *Walt Whitman's Poetry*, 65.

41. Gary Wihl, "The Manuscript of Whitman's 'Sunday evening Lectures'." *WWQR* 18 (2001), 111; the reference to Kennedy is from *LG*, 5 n. David S. Reynolds finds the influence of Balfour Stewart and P. G. Tait's *Unseen Universe*, which argues that everything on earth has a spiritual double (*Walt Whitman*, 514–515). On Whitman's "doubles" as a Swedenborgian principle, see Harris, "Whitman's *Leaves of Grass*," 177–190. Donald E. Pease finds that "There are no individuals in Whitman's world but only 'presences,' which he calls eidolons who call for further development to and for 'other presences'" (*Visual Compacts*, 154).

42. Edwards, *Images and Shadows of Divine Things*, 54. Sharon Cameron observes that in *Moby-Dick* and the tales of Hawthorne "what stands behind the body is an-

other different body" (*The Corporeal Self: Allegories of the Body in Hawthorne and Melville* [Baltimore: Johns Hopkins UP, 1981], 2).

43. *LG,* 744–748. Lynch, *Undertaking,* 18, attributes to the British prime minister William Gladstone the observation "that he could measure with mathematical precision a people's respect for the laws of the land by the way they cared for their dead."

44. "Last of Ebb, and Daylight Waning," *LG,* 515.

45. Gay Wilson Allen calls attention to the fact that some of these verses were leftover odds and ends from earlier periods (*New Walt Whitman Handbook,* 155–156).

46. None of the brief memorial poems that Whitman composed add to his luster. Among them, "Outlines for a Tomb" (1870) commemorates the death of the New England millionaire philanthropist George Peabody by poetically decking his tomb with the vision of a fraternal, sororal America, somewhat in the manner of the decking of Lincoln's tomb in "Lilacs." The chauvinistic "From Dark Dakota's Canyons" (1876) eulogizes the deaths of General Custer and his men at the Battle of Little Big Horn. Whereas the Indians are described in the poem as crafty, Custer "of the tawny flowing hair" and "erect head" is said to exemplify "the old, old legend of our race, / The loftiest life upheld by death"—the heroic spirit of the Civil War. For John Mulvany's large painting as a possible source of "From Dark Dakota's Canyons," see Folsom, *Walt Whitman's Native Representations,* 62–64. "The Dead Emperor" honors Prussia's Wilhelm I as "a good old man." "Interpolations" (*LG,* 545) appeared a couple of days after the death of General Sherman. And "Going Somewhere" (1887) is a restrained brief verse for his "science friend" Anne Gilchrist, who had moved to America for his sake and died in 1885.

47. *LG,* 574. "After the Supper and Talk" is the concluding poem in a cluster of poems called "Sands at Seventy" and appended as an "annex" to *Leaves of Grass.*

48. *LG,* 536.

49. *LG,* 561.

50. *LG,* 530–532.

51. Oliver Wendell Holmes, *Over the Teacups* (Boston: Houghton Mifflin, 1894), 39. For a similar thought, see Longfellow's sonnet "Nature."

52. *LG,* 532 n.

53. "You Lingering Sparse Leaves of Me," 532; *LG,* 513.

54. *WWC,* 1:464. Toward the end of his life, Whitman read several novels by Cooper, expressing a preference for Cooper's sea novels over the others: *WWC,* 9:125.

55. "My 71st Year," *LG,* 541; Susan Hunter Walker, "I Knew Walt Whitman," in *1980: Leaves of Grass at 125,* ed. William White (Detroit: Wayne State UP, 1980), 72; Loving, *Walt Whitman,* 474.

56. Folsom, *Walt Whitman's Native Representations,* 76–77.

57. *LG,* 551–553.

58. "Queries to My Seventieth Year"; "As I Sit Writing Here," *LG,* 509–510. These reports of Whitman's physical condition had a counterpart in the steady flow of postal cards to Dr. Bucke, reporting on his aches and pains, his fading energy, his paralysis and his digestion.

59. "L. of G.'s Purport," *LG,* 555–556.

60. "Old Age's Ship & Crafty Death's" and "Sail Out for Good Eidòlon Yacht," *LG*, 543, 539.

61. *LG*, 534. See Mrs. Herbert S. Harned Jr., "The Origin of 'The Dismantled Ship,'" *WWQR* 16 (1998), 37; a photograph of the etching appears on the back cover of this issue.

62. Daniel Longaker, "The Last Sickness and Death of Walt Whitman," in *In Re Walt Whitman*, ed. Richard Maurice Bucke, Horace Traubel, and Thomas Harned, 393–411, reprinted in Myerson, *Whitman in His Own Time*, 43.

63. Bucke's letters, quoted in Artem Lozynsky, ed., *Richard Maurice Bucke, Medical Mystic: Letters of Dr. Bucke to Walt Whitman and His Friends* (Detroit: Wayne State UP, 1977), 140, 172.

64. "Continuities," *LG*, 523–524.

65. Alma Calder Johnston, "Personal Memories of Walt Whitman," *Bookman*, 1917, quoted in Myerson, *Whitman in His Own Time*, 272.

66. "Whitman," *Fortnightly Review*, 1886, reprinted in Hindus, *Walt Whitman*, 206; *The Complete Letters of Oscar Wilde*, ed. Merle Holland and Rupert Hart-Davis (New York: Henry Holt, 2000), 144. On Whitman's status as a guru and seer among the Whitmanites, see Carmen Sarracino, "Redrawing Whitman's Circle," *WWQR* 14 (1996–1997), 113–127.

67. David D. Anderson, *Robert Ingersoll* (New York: Twayne, 1972), 122. For Whitman's exchanges with Ingersoll, see, for example, "Walt Whitman's Birthday: A Delightful Dinner in Honor of the Venerable Poet's 69th Birthday," *New York Times*, 1 June, 1890, 5:2; *WWC*, 5:47.

68. *WWC*, 8:369, 477; *WWC*, 9:24; *WWC*, 8:556–557. In a more accepting frame of mind, Whitman said that he found something uplifting both in Christianity and in Ingersoll: *WWC*, 8:30–31.

69. *WWC*, 9:576; Traubel notes that he transcribed these words hurriedly as the poet could barely manage to speak. The elderly Whitman had frequently praised Tennyson. Whittier, whose poetry he regarded highly, wrote many attractive poems on death.

70. "A Death-Bouquet" (January, 1890), *PW1892*, 671–673.

71. Lozynsky, *Richard Maurice Bucke*, 117, 167–178.

72. *WWC*, 8:142; *WWC*, 9:234, 433.

73. Myerson, *Whitman in His Own Time*, 101–102.

74. *WWC*, 9:277. Volumes 8 and 9 of *With Walt Whitman in Camden* may comprise the most complete record of the sickness and dying of any literary personality—several hundred detailed pages. It is remarkable that throughout his prolonged final illness Whitman exhibited a sweetness of demeanor, a powerful memory retention, and moments of startling lucidity. To the very last, he was concerned with his reputation, the regard of his contemporaries and acolytes, and the publishing progress of his books.

75. See Longaker, "Last Sickness and Death," 93. Dr. Longaker was Whitman's last attending physician. For a later analysis of Whitman's terminal condition, see Josiah C. Trent, "Walt Whitman: A Case History," *Surgery, Gynecology, Obstetrics* 87 (July 1948), 113–121. Dr. Trent speculated that Whitman's medical symptoms indic-

ated possible "eunuchoidism," attributable to an androgen deficiency. See also *WWBB*, 31–33.

76. Ernest Rhys, *Everyone Remembers* (New York: Cosmopolitan, 1932), quoted in Myerson, *Whitman in His Own Time*, 328; *New York Times*, January 26, 1890, 1:4.

77. On the periodical coverage of Whitman's death, see Allen, *Solitary Singer*, 541–542. On Whitman as a photographic subject, see Folsom, *Whitman's Native Representations*, 147 and passim; for an impressive photograph of the mourners gathered before Whitman's house on Mickle Street, see Loving, *Walt Whitman*, following 368.

78. On Whitman's tomb and his funeral, see *WWC*, 6:146–147, 210–212; Loving, *Walt Whitman*, 479–481. His friend and literary executor Thomas B. Harned paid $1,500 toward the cost of the tomb (see Reynolds, *Walt Whitman*, 572); Barrus, *Whitman and Burroughs Comrades*, 296, 341. William Roscoe Thayer, among others, objected to Whitman's pretence of poverty while setting aside money for his tomb; see Thayer's "Personal Recollections of Walt Whitman" (1919), reprinted in Myerson, *Whitman in His Own Time*, 304. On the destruction of Whitman's brain by the American Anthropometric Society, see Brian Burrell, "The Strange Fate of Whitman's Brain," *WWQR* 20 (2003), 103–133; Philip W. Leon, *Walt Whitman and Sir William Osler* (Toronto ECW Press, 1999), 194–205.

79. *WWC*, 8:483.

80. Longaker, "Last Sickness and Death," 103.

81. John L. Coulehan, review of Walt Whitman and Sir William Osler: A Poet and his Physician, by Philip W. Leon, *Academic Medicine* 71 (1996), 930.

82. Lozynsky, *Richard Maurice Bucke*, 185. Bucke repeated this sentiment in letters to various friends. On Burroughs's remarks, see Barrus, *Whitman and Burroughs Comrades*, 299. Burroughs was surely aware of Whitman's several comparisons of his persona to that of Christ in *Leaves of Grass*.

83. Bucke, *Cosmic Consciousness*, 257. "At the Graveside of Walt Whitman," *Conservator* (memorial issue, April 1892).

84. "At the Graveside of Walt Whitman," cited by Scott Giantvalley, *Walt Whitman, 1838–1939: A Reference Guide* (Boston: G. K. Hall, 1981), 114.

85. Traubel felt, or perhaps imagined, that in a final gesture Whitman had made him his heir-designate. In a rather awkward poem about the poet's last hours he wrote that as he sat bedside his "dead comrade":

I sat by your bedside, I held your hand;
Once you opened your eyes: O look of recognition! O look of bestowal!
Reaching through me, through others through me, through all at last,
    our brothers,
A hand to the future.

Quoted in Walker, "I Knew Walt Whitman," 73.

86. See, especially, Joann P. Krieg, "Without Walt Whitman in Camden," *WWQR* 14 (1997), 85–112. Three more examples follow: In 1892 Julian Hawthorne's American literature text characterized Whitman as "incontinently" showing off "like a bull in a china shop"; Max Nordau's widely circulated *Degeneration* called him "mystically

mad"; James Gibbons Huneker, the literary and musical critic, who had once viewed Whitman favorably, attacked him, in what has been called "the first *explicit* reference by an American literary critic" to Whitman's homosexuality. In an acerbic pun, Huneker labeled the "Calamus" poems "inflated humbuggery."

On Hawthorne see Miller, *Walt Whitman's "Song of Myself,"* 47. Nordau, whose book was translated into English in 1895, is cited in Hindus, *Walt Whitman*, 243–245. On Huneker, see Arnold T. Schwab, *James Gibbons Huneker: Critic of the Seven Arts* (Stanford: Stanford UP, 1963), 80–81, 319; Schwab, "James Gibbons Huneker," *Dictionary of American Literary Biography: American Critics and Scholars, 1800–1900*, ed. James W. Rathbun and Monica M. Green (Detroit: Gale, 1988), 7:96.

87. Francis Howard Williams, *Poet-Lore* 7 (summer 1997), cited in Giantvalley, *Walt Whitman*, 155–156.

88. LeRoy Ireland, *The Works of George Inness: An Illustrated Catalogue Raisonné* (Austin: U Texas P, 1965), 515, 540.

89. *Harper's New Monthly Magazine*, 84 (April 1892), 707–709; *LG*, 580–581. The original first stanza, which remained in manuscript during the poet's lifetime, is published in *LG*, 581, as "On the Same Picture." Inness's painting is located at Vassar College.

90. "Death of a Nature Lover," *EPF*, 30–32.

91. "Death's Valley" and "On the Same Picture," *LG*, 580–581.

# Bibliography

Adams, Richard P. "Whitman's 'Lilacs' and the Tradition of the Pastoral Elegy." *PMLA* 72 (1957): 479–487.

Alegría, Fernando. "Whitman in Spain and Latin America." In Allen and Folsom, 71–96.

Gay Wilson Allen. *The New Walt Whitman Handbook.* New York: New York UP, 1975.

———. Introduction to 1856 edition of *Leaves of Grass* (facsimile ed.). Norwood, Pa.: Norwood Editions, 1976.

———. *The Solitary Singer: A Critical Biography of Walt Whitman.* New York: Macmillan, 1955.

Allen, Gay Wilson and Ed Folsom, eds. *Walt Whitman and the World.* Iowa City: U Iowa P, 1995.

Amyot, Gerald F. "Contrasting Views of Death in the Poetry of Poe and Whitman." *Walt Whitman Review* 19 (1973): 103–111.

Anderson, David D. *Robert Ingersoll.* New York: Twayne, 1972.

Ariès, Philippe. "The Reversal of Death: Changes in Attitudes towards Death in Western Societies." Translated by Valerie M. Stannard. In David E. Stannard, *Death in America,* 134–158.

Aspiz, Harold. "An Early Feminist Tribute to Whitman." *American Literature* 51 (1979): 404–409.

———. "Mark Twain and 'Doctor' Newton." *American Literature* 44 (1977): 130–136.

———. *Walt Whitman and the Body Beautiful.* Urbana: U Illinois P, 1980.

———. "Walt Whitman: The Spermatic Imagination." In Cady and Budd, 273–289.

"At the Graveside of Walt Whitman. *Conservator.* Special issue, April 1892.

Ausubel, Nathan. *The Book of Jewish Knowledge.* New York: Crown, 1964.

Badham, Paul. "The Christian Hope Today." In Badham and Badham, 37–50.

Badham, Paul and Linda Badham, eds. *Death and Immortality in the Religions of the World.* New York: Paragon House, 1987.

Bailey, John. *Walt Whitman.* New York: Macmillan, 1926.

Barrus, Clara. *Whitman and Burroughs Comrades.* 1931. Reprint, Port Washington, N.Y.: Kennikat, 1959.

Beach, Christopher. *The Politics of Distinction: Whitman and the Discourses of Nineteenth-Century America.* Athens: U Georgia P, 1996.

——. "Walt Whitman, Literary Culture, and the Discourse of Distinction." *WWQR* 12 (1994): 73–85.

Beaver, Joseph. *Walt Whitman—Poet of Science.* 1951. Reprint, New York: Octagon Books, 1974.

Benton, Paul. "Whitman, Christ, and the Crystal Palace Police: A Manuscript Source Restored." *WWQR* 17 (2000): 146–165.

Benwick, James. *Egyptian Belief and Modern Thought.* Indian Hills, Colo.: Falcon's Wing, 1956.

Black, Stephen A. *Whitman's Journey into Chaos: A Psychological Study of the Poetic Process.* Princeton: Princeton UP, 1975.

Blatt, Martin Henry. *Free Love and Anarchism: The Biography of Ezra Heywood.* Urbana: U Illinois P, 1989.

Bloom, Harold. "Death and the Native Strain in American Poetry." In *Death and the American Experience,* edited by Airen Mack, 83–96. New York: Schocken Books, 1973.

Bohan, Ruth L. "'The Gathering of the Forces': Whitman and the Arts in Brooklyn." *Mickle-Street Review* 12 (1990): 10–30.

Brasher, Thomas L. *Whitman as Editor of the Brooklyn Daily Eagle.* Detroit: Wayne State UP, 1970.

Braude, Ann. *Radical Spirits: Spiritualism and Women's Rights in Nineteenth-Century America.* Boston: Beacon, 1989.

Briggs, Arthur E. *Walt Whitman: Thinker and Artist.* New York: Philosophical Library, 1952.

Brinton, Daniel. Eulogy. *The Walt Whitman Fellowship Papers.* May, 1892. n.p.

Bucke, Richard Maurice. *Cosmic Consciousness: A Study of the Evolution of the Human Mind.* 1907. Reprint, New York: E. P. Dutton, 1951.

Burrell, Bryan. "The Strange Fate of Whitman's Brain," *WWQR* 20 (2003), 103–133.

Burroughs, John. *The Heart of Burroughs's Journals.* Ed. Clara Barrus. 1928. Reprint, New York: Kennikat Press, 1967.

——. *Notes on Walt Whitman as Poet and Person.* 1867. Reprint, New York: Haskell House, 1971.

Bychowski, Gustav. "Walt Whitman: A Study in Sublimation." In Miller, *A Century of Whitman Criticism,* 203–215.

Cady, Edwin H., and Louis J. Budd, eds. *On Whitman: The Best from American Literature.* Durham: Duke UP, 1987

Cameron, Sharon. *The Corporeal Self: Allegories of the Body in Hawthorne and Melville.* Baltimore: Johns Hopkins UP, 1981.

Campbell, Joseph. *The Flight of the Wild Gander: Explorations of the Mythological Dimension.* New York: Viking, 1951.

Canby, Henry Seidel. *Walt Whitman, an American: A Study in Biography.* Boston: Houghton Mifflin, 1943.

Carpenter, Edward. *Edward Carpenter—1840–1920—Democratic Author and Poet.* London: Friends of Dr. Williams's Library, 1970. [pamphlet]

Cavitch, David. "The Lament in 'Song of the Broad-Axe.'" In *Walt Whitman Here and Now,* edited by Joann P. Krieg, 125–135. Westport, Conn.: Greenwood, 1985.

Ceniza, Sherry. *Walt Whitman and Nineteenth-Century Women Reformers.* Tuscaloosa: U Alabama P, 1998.

Chari, V. K. Whitman in the Light of Vedantic Mysticism. Lincoln: U Nebraska P, 1964.

Chase, Richard. *Walt Whitman Reconsidered.* New York: William Sloane Associates, 1955.

Claire, Sister Miriam. "The Sea and Death in *Leaves of Grass.*" *Walt Whitman Review* 10:1 (March 1964): 14–16.

Clemens, Samuel. *What Is Man? and Other Philosophical Writings,* edited by Paul Baender. Berkeley: U California P, 1973.

Cohn-Sherbok, Daniel "Death and Immortality in the Jewish Tradition." In Badham and Badham, 24–36.

Colum, Padraic. "The Poetry of Walt Whitman." In Allen and Folsom, 57–58.

Conner, Frederick William. *Cosmic Optimism: A Study in the Interpretation of Evolution by American Poets from Emerson to Robinson.* Gainesville: U Florida P, 1949.

Coulehan, John L. Rev. of Philip W. Leon. "Walt Whitman and Sir William Osler: A Poet and His Physician." *Academic Medicine* 71 (1996): 930–931.

Darwin, Charles. *Darwin: A Norton Critical Edition.* New York: Norton, 1975.

Davis, Robert Leigh. *Whitman and the Romance of Medicine.* Berkeley: U California P, 1997.

———. "Wound-Dresser and House Calls: Medical Representations in Whitman and Williams." *WWQR* 6 (1989): 133–139.

Davison, Ned J. "'The Raven' and 'Out of the Cradle Endlessly Rocking.'" *Poe Newsletter* 1 (1968): 5–6.

Delp, Robert W. "Andrew Jackson Davis and Spiritualism." In Wrobel, 100–121.

Derrida, Jacques. *The Work of Mourning.* Chicago: U Chicago P, 2001.

Dharanny, Mariasusai. "Death and Immortality in Hindusim." In Badham and Badham, 95–108.

Donaldson, Thomas. *Walt Whitman the Man.* New York: 1896.

Douglas, Ann. *The Feminization of American Culture.* New York: Knopf, 1977.

———. "Heaven Our Home: Consolation Literature in the Northern United States, 1830–1880." In David E. Stannard, ed., *Death in America,* 49–68.

Dryden, John. *Aureng-Zebe.* 1675. Edited by Frederick M. Link. Lincoln: U Nebraska P, 1975.

Edwards, Jonathan. *Images or Shadows of Divine Things.* Edited by Perry Miller. New Haven: Yale UP, 1948.

Ehrenreich, Barbara. *Blood Rites: Origins and History of the Passions of War.* New York: Henry Holt, 1997.

Ellis, Havelock. *The New Spirit.* 1890. Reprint, New York: Boni and Liveright, 1921[?].

Emerson, Ralph W. *The Complete Writings of Ralph Waldo Emerson.* New York: William H. Wise and Co., 1929.

Engels, Friedrich. *Dialectics of Nature.* New York: International, 1960.

Faner, Robert D. *Walt Whitman and Opera.* Carbondale: Southern Illinois UP, 1972.

Fisher, LeRoy. *Lincoln's Gadfly: Adam Gurowski.* Norman: U Oklahoma P, 1964.

Flew, Arthur. "The Logic of Mortality." In Badham and Badham, 171–187.

Folsom, Ed. *Walt Whitman's Native Representations.* New York: Cambridge UP, 1997.

Fone, Byrne R. S. *Masculine Landscapes: Walt Whitman and the Homoerotic Text.* Carbondale: Southern Illinois UP, 1992.

Foner, Eric. *Politics and Ideology in the Age of the Civil War.* Oxford: Oxford UP, 1980.

French, Stanley. "The Cemetery as Cultural Institution: Mount Vernon and the Rural Cemetery Movement." In David E. Stannard, *Death in America,* 69–91.

Freud, Sigmund. "Mourning and Melancholy." *The Standard Edition of the Psychological Works,* 14:243–258. London: Hogarth P, 1964.

———. "Our Attitude Towards Death." *The Standard Edition of the Psychological Works,* 14:289–296. London: Hogarth P, 1964.

Fuller, Robert C. "Mesmerism and the Birth of Psychology." In Wrobel, 205–222.

Garner, Stanton. *The Civil War World of Herman Melville.* Lawrence: U Kansas P, 1993.

Gates, Rosemary L. "Egyptian Mythology and Whitman's 'Lilacs.'" *WWQR* 5 (1987): 21–31.

Giantvalley, Scott. *Walt Whitman, 1838–1939: A Reference Guide.* Boston: G. K. Hall, 1981.

Glicksberg, Charles I., ed. *Walt Whitman and the Civil War: A Collection of Original Articles and Manuscripts.* 1933. Reprint, New York: A. S. Barnes, 1963.

Gohdes, Clarence. "Section 50 in Whitman's 'Song of Myself.'" *Modern Language Notes* 75 (1965): 653–656.

Golden, Arthur. "Passage to Less Than India: Structure and Meaning in Whitman's 'Passage to India.'" *PMLA* 88 (1973): 1095–1103.

Goodale, David. "Some of Walt Whitman's Borrowings." *American Literature* 10 (1938): 202–213.

Greenspan, Ezra, ed. *The Cambridge Companion to Walt Whitman.* New York: Cambridge UP, 1995.

Haldane, J. B. S. "When I Am Dead." In *Possible Worlds and Other Papers,* 214–221. New York: Harper and Brothers, 1928.

Harned, Thomas. "At the Graveside of Walt Whitman." *Conservator.* Special issue, April 1892.

Harris, W. C. "Whitman's *Leaves of Grass* and the Writing of the New American Bible." *WWQR* 16 (1999): 172–190.

Hick, John. *Death and Eternal Life.* New York: Harper and Row, 1976.

Hindus, Milton, ed. *Walt Whitman: The Critical Heritage.* New York: Barnes and Noble, 1972.

Hitchens, Christopher. Review of Spanish Civil War books. *Los Angeles Times Book Review,* July 15, 2001, 6–8.

Hoffman, Frederick J. *The Mortal No: Death and the Modern Imagination.* Princeton: Princeton UP, 1964.

Hollis, C. Carroll. *Language and Style in Leaves of Grass.* Baton Rouge: Louisiana State UP, 1983.

Holmes, Edmond. *Whitman's Poetry: A Study and a Selection.* 1902. Reprint, New York: Haskell House, 1973.

Holmes, Oliver Wendell. *Over the Teacups.* Boston: Houghton Mifflin, 1894.

———. *Pages from an Old Volume of Life.* Boston: Houghton Mifflin, 1890.

Hutchinson, George B. *The Ecstatic Whitman: Literary Shamanism and the Crisis of the Union.* Columbus: Ohio State UP, 1986.

Hyde, Lewis. *The Gift: Imagination and the Erotic Life of Property.* New York: Random House, 1983.

Ingersoll, Robert. "At the Graveside of Walt Whitman." *Conservator.* Special issue, April 1892.

Ireland, LeRoy. *The Works of George Inness: An Illustrated Catalogue Raisonée.* Austin: U Texas P, 1965.

Irving, Washington. *Life and Voyages of Christopher Columbus.* New York: Perkins Book Co., n.d.

Jaffe, Harold. "Bucke's *Walt Whitman:* A Collaboration." *Walt Whitman Review* 15 (1969): 190–194.

Jiménez, Juan Ramón. *Platero and I: An Andalusian Elegy.* New York: American Library, 1960.

Jones, Rufus M. *Some Exponents of Mystical Religion.* New York: Abingdon, 1930.

Kennedy, William Sloane. "The Germ Idea of Whitman's 'Noiseless Patient Spider' Poem." *Conservator* 14 (1904): 173.

Kepner, Diana. "From Spears to Leaves: Walt Whitman's Theory of Nature in 'Song of Myself.'" *American Literature* 51 (1974): 179–204.

Kerényi, Karl. *Hermes Guide of Souls: The Mythologies of the Masculine Source of Life.* Zurich: Spring Publications, 1976.

Killingsworth, M. Jimmie. *The Growth of Leaves of Grass: The Organic Tradition in Whitman Studies.* Columbia, S.C.: Camden House, 1993.

———. "Whitman's Sexual Themes during a Decade of Revision: 1866–1876." *WWQR* 4 (1988): 7–15.

Klammer, Martin. *Whitman, Slavery, and the Emergence of Leaves of Grass.* University Park: Pennsylvania State UP, 1995.

Kramer, Lawrence. *Music and Poetry: The Nineteenth Century and After.* Berkeley: U California P, 1984.

Krieg, Joann. *A Whitman Chronology.* Iowa City: U Iowa P, 1998.

———. "Without Walt Whitman in Camden." *WWQR* 14 (1996–1997): 85–112.

Kübler-Ross, Elisabeth. *The Wheel of Life: A Memoir of Living and Dying.* New York: Scribner, 1997.

Kuebrich, David. *Minor Prophecy: Walt Whitman's New American Religion.* Bloomington: Indiana UP, 1989.

Laderman, Gary. *The Sacred Remains: American Attitudes toward Death, 1799–1883.* New Haven: Yale UP, 1996.

Lamont, Corliss. *The Illusion of Immortality.* New York: Frederick Ungar, 1965.

Lawrence, D. H. "Whitman." In *Whitman: A Collection of Essays,* edited by Roy Harvey Pearce, 11–23. Englewood Cliffs, N.J.: Prentice Hall, 1962.

Leathers, Lyman L. "Music, Whitman's Influence On." In LeMaster and Kummings, 439–444.

LeMaster, J. R., and Donald D. Kummings, eds. *Walt Whitman: An Encyclopedia*, New York: Garland, 1998.

Leon, Philip. *Walt Whitman and Sir William Osler: A Poet and His Physician*. Toronto: ECW Press, 1996.

Lloyd, Phoebe. "Posthumous Mourning Portraiture." In Pike and Armstrong, 75–77.

Longfellow, Henry Wadsworth, trans. *The Inferno*, by Dante Alighieri. Garden City, N.Y.: Dolphin Books, n.d.

Loving, Jerome. *Walt Whitman: The Song of Himself*. Berkeley: U California P, 1999.

Lowenfels, Walter. *Walt Whitman's Civil War*. New York: Knopf, 1978.

Lozynsky, Artem, ed. *Richard Maurice Bucke, Medical Mystic: Letters of Dr. Bucke to Walt Whitman and His Friends*. Detroit: Wayne State UP, 1977.

Lynch, Thomas. *The Undertaking*. New York: Norton, 1997.

Marki, Ivan. *The Trial of the Poet: An Interpretation of the First Edition of Leaves of Grass*. New York: Columbia UP, 1976.

Marriage, Anthony X. "Whitman's 'This Compost,' Baudelaire's 'A Carrion': Out of Decay Comes an Awful Beauty." *Walt Whitman Review* 17 (1971): 143–149.

Martin, Robert K., ed. *The Continuing Presence of Walt Whitman: The Life after the Life*. Iowa City: U Iowa P, 1992.

Marx, Leo. *The Machine in the Garden: Technology and the Pastoral Ideal in America*. New York: Oxford UP, 1967.

Mattson, John. "Liebig, Justus." In LeMaster and Kummings, 392.

McCollester, Lee S. "Universalism." *Encyclopedia Americana*, 27:569. 1951 edition.

McMurtry, R. Gerald. "The Lincoln Funeral Car." In *The Poet and the President: Whitman's Lincoln Poems*, edited by William Coyle, 124–131. New York: Odyssey Press, 1962.

Milder, Robert. Review of *The Civil War of Herman Melville*, by Stanton Garner. *American Literature* 68 (1996), 239–240.

Miller, Edwin Haviland. *Walt Whitman's Poetry: A Psychological Journey*. Boston: Houghton Mifflin, 1968.

Miller, Edwin Haviland, ed. *A Century of Whitman Criticism*. Bloomington: U Indiana P, 1969.

———. *Walt Whitman's "Song of Myself": A Mosaic of Interpretations*. Iowa City: U Iowa P, 1989.

Miller, F. DeWolfe. Introduction. *Walt Whitman's Drum-Taps (1865) and Sequel to Drum-Taps*. Gainesville, Fla.: Scholars' Facsimiles and Reprints, 1959.

Miller, James E., Jr. *A Critical Guide to "Leaves of Grass."* Chicago: U Chicago P, 1957.

———. *Walt Whitman*. New York: Twayne, 1962.

Miller, Russell E. *The Larger Hope: The First Century of the Universalist Church in America, 1770–1870*. Boston: Unitarian Universalist Association, 1979.

Moore, R. Laurence. *In Search of White Crows: Spiritualism, Parapsychology, and American Culture*. New York: Oxford UP, 1977.

Muggleton, Ludowick. *The Acts of the Witnesses of the Spirit*. London, 1699 (1694).

Myerson, Joel, ed. *Whitman in His Own Time: A Biographical Chronicle of His Life Drawn from Recollections, Memoirs, and Interviews by Friends and Associates*. Detroit: Omnigraphics, 1991.

Nathanson, Tenney. *Whitman's Presence: Body, Voice, and Writing in Leaves of Grass.* New York: New York UP, 1992.

Nelson, Geoffrey K. *Spiritualism and Society.* New York: Schocken, 1969.

Newton, R. J. *The Modern Bethesda, Or the Gift of Healing Restored.* New York: 1879.

Nolan, James. *Poet-Chief: The American Poetics of Walt Whitman and Pablo Neruda.* Albuquerque: U New Mexico P, 1994.

Noyes, John Humphrey. *History of American Socialisms.* 1870. Reprint, New York: Hillary House, 1961.

Osler, William. *Science and Immortality.* 1904. Reprint, New York: Arno, 1977.

Parker, Hershel. "The Real 'Live Oak, with Moss': Straight Talk about Whitman's Gay Manifesto." *Nineteenth-Century Literature* 51 (1996): 145–160.

Pascal, Richard. "'What Is It Then between Us': 'Crossing Brooklyn Ferry' as Dramatic Meditation." In *Leaves of Grass at 125,* edited by William White, 59–70. Detroit: Wayne State UP, 1980.

Pease, Donald. *Visual Compacts: American Renaissance Writing in Cultural Context.* Madison: U Wisconsin P, 1987.

Pennypacker, William. "Genealogy." In LeMaster and Kummings, 807–812.

Perlman, Jim, Ed Folsom, and Dan Campion, eds. *Walt Whitman: The Measure of His Song.* Duluth: Holy Cow Press, 1998.

Pike, Martha V., and Janice Gray Armstrong, eds. *A Time to Mourn: Expressions of Grief in Nineteenth Century America.* Stony Brook, N.Y.: Museum of Stony Brook, 1980.

Pollak, Vivian R. "Death as Repression, Repression as Death: A Reading of Whitman's 'Calamus' Poems." *Mickle Street Review* 11 (1989), 56–70.

Price, Kenneth M., ed. *Walt Whitman: The Contemporary Reviews.* New York: Cambridge UP, 1996.

———. *Whitman and Tradition: The Poet and His Century.* Yale UP, 1990.

Price, Kenneth M., and Cynthia G. Bernstein. "Whitman's Sign of Parting: 'So Long!' as *l'envoi.*" *WWQR* 9 (1991): 67–76.

Railton, Stephen. "'As if I Were with You': The Performance of Whitman's Poetry." In Greenspan, 7–26.

Rajahsekhariah, T. R. *The Roots of Whitman's Grass.* Rutherford, N.J.: Farleigh Dickinson UP, 1970.

Ramsey, Julianne. "A British View to an American War: Whitman's 'Drum-Taps' Cluster and the Editorial Influence of William Michael Rossetti." *WWQR* 14 (1997): 166–175.

Reichenbach, Bruce R. "Buddhism, Karma, and Immortality." In Badham and Badham, 141–157.

Reichert, William O. *Partisans of Freedom: A Study of American Anarchism.* Bowling Green, Ohio: Bowling Green U Popular Press, 1976.

Reynolds, David S. *Walt Whitman: A Cultural Biography.* New York: Alfred A. Knopf, 1995.

Rilke, Rainer Marie. *Duino Elegies.* Translated by David Young. New York: Norton, 1973.

Rossini, Claire. "The Rebound Seed: Death in Whitman's Poetry." Ph.D. Diss., Columbia University, 1990.

Rowe, John Carlos. *At Emerson's Tomb: The Politics of Classic American Literature.* New York: Columbia UP, 1997.

Rubin, Joseph Jay. *The Historic Whitman.* University Park: Pennsylvania State UP, 1973.

Sacks, Peter M. *The English Elegy: Studies in the Genre from Spenser to Yeats.* Baltimore: Johns Hopkins UP, 1985.

Said, Edward W. "Musical Retrospective." *The Nation,* October 20, 1992, 481–483.

St. Armand, Burton Levi. *Emily Dickinson and Her Culture: The Soul's Society.* Cambridge: Cambridge UP, 1984.

Salska, Agnieszka. *Walt Whitman and Emily Dickinson: Poetry of the Central Consciousness.* Philadelphia: U Pennsylvania P, 1985.

Saracino, Carmine. "Redrawing Whitman's Circle." *WWQR* 14 (1996–1997), 113–127.

Saum, Lewis O. "Death in the Popular Mind of Pre–Civil War America." In David E. Stannard, *Death in America,* 30–48.

Savage, Minot Judson. *Life beyond Death.* 1899. Reprint, New York: G. P. Putnam's Sons, 1905.

Scholnick, Robert J. "'The Password Primeval': Whitman's Use of Science in 'Song of Myself.'" In *Studies in the American Renaissance,* edited by Joel Myerson, 385–425. Charlottesville: UP of Virginia, 1986.

———. "Science." In LeMaster and Kummings, 616–619.

Schwab, Arnold T. "James Gibbons Huneker." *Dictionary of American Literary Biography: American Critics and Scholars, 1800–1900,* edited by James W. Rathbun and Monica M. Green, 7:90–101. Detroit: Gale, 1988.

———. *James Gibbons Huneker: Critic of the Seven Arts.* Stanford: Stanford UP, 1963.

Seldes, Gilbert. *The Stammering Century.* New York: Harper and Row, 1965.

Selley, April. "Satisfied Shivering: Emily Dickinson's Deceased Speakers." *ESQ: A Journal of the American Renaissance* 37 (1991): 215–238.

Selsam, Howard. *What Is Philosophy? A Marxist Introduction.* New York: International Publishers, 1962.

Shaw, W. David. *Elegy and Paradox: Testing the Conventions.* Baltimore: Johns Hopkins UP, 1994.

Shryock, Richard A. "A Medical Perspective on the Civil War." *American Quarterly* 14 (1962): 161–175.

Sill, Geoffrey. "Whitman on 'The Black Question': A New Manuscript." *WWQR* 8 (1990): 69–75.

Smith, Barbara Herrnstein. *Poetic Closure: A Study in How Poems End.* Chicago: U Chicago P, 1968.

Stannard, David E., ed. *American Holocaust: Columbus and the Conquest of the New World.* New York: Oxford UP, 1992.

———. *Death in America.* Philadelphia: U Pennsylvania P, 1975.

Staten, Henry. *Eros in Mourning: Homer to Lacan.* Baltimore: Johns Hopkins UP, 1995.

Steele, Jeffrey. "Poetic Grief Work in Whitman's 'Lilacs.'" *WWQR* 2 (1984): 10–16.

Steinman, Lisa. *Made in America: Science, Technology, and American Modernist Poetry.* New Haven: Yale UP, 1987.

Stern, Madeleine B. *Heads and Headlines: The Phrenological Fowlers.* Norman: U Oklahoma P, 1971.

Stovall, Floyd. *The Foreground of Leaves of Grass.* Charlottesville: U Virginia P, 1974.

———. "Main Drifts in Whitman's Poetry." In Cady and Budd, 1–19.

Strassburg, Robert. "Whitman and Music." In LeMaster and Kummings, 437–439.

Symonds, John Addington. *Walt Whitman: A Study.* 1893. Reprint, New York: Benjamin Blom, 1967.

Tapscott, Stephen J. "Leaves of Myself: Whitman's Egypt in 'Song of Myself.'" In Cady and Budd, 203–227.

Taylor, Lawrence. "The Anthropological View of Mourning Ritual in the Nineteenth Century." In Pike and Armstrong, 39–48.

Tenner, Edward. *Why Things Bite Back: Technology and the Revenge of Unintended Circumstances.* New York: Knopf, 1997.

Thomas, M. Wynn. "Fratricide and Brotherly Love: Whitman and the Civil War." In Greenspan, 27–44.

———. *The Lunar Light of Whitman's Poetry.* Cambridge: Harvard UP, 1987.

———. "Whitman's Obligations of Memory." *WWQR* 28 (1982): 43–54.

Thoreau, Henry. *Cape Cod.* 1865. Reprint, edited by Dudley C. Lunt. New York: Norton, 1951.

Tillich, Paul. "The Eternal Now." In *The Meaning of Death,* edited by Herman Feifel, 30–38. New York: McGraw-Hill, 1938.

Traubel, Horace, comp., *The Book of Heavenly Death by Walt Whitman Compiled from Leaves of Grass.* Portland, Me.: Thomas B. Mosher, 1907.

Traubel, Horace, comp. *With Walt Whitman in Camden.* Volume 1. 1905. Reprint, New York: Rowman and Littlefield, 1961.

———. *With Walt Whitman in Camden.* Volume 2. 1908. Reprint, New York: Rowman and Littlefield, 1961.

———. *With Walt Whitman in Camden.* Volume 3. 1912. Reprint, New York: Rowman and Littlefield, 1961.

———. *With Walt Whitman in Camden.* Volume 4. Edited by Sculley Bradley. Carbondale: Southern Illinois UP, 1959.

———. *With Walt Whitman in Camden.* Volume 5. Edited by Gertrude Traubel. Carbondale: Southern Illinois UP, 1964.

———. *With Walt Whitman in Camden.* Volume 6. Edited by Gertrude Traubel and William White. Carbondale: Southern Illinois UP, 1982.

———. *With Walt Whitman in Camden.* Volume 7. Edited by Jeanne Chapman and Robert MacIsaac. Carbondale: Southern Illinois UP, 1992.

———. *With Walt Whitman in Camden.* Volume 8. Edited by Jeanne Chapman and Robert MacIsaac. Oregon House, Calif.: W. L. Bentlely, 1996).

———. *With Walt Whitman in Camden.* Volume 9. Edited by Jeanne Chapman and Robert MacIsaac. Oregon House, Calif.: W. L. Bentlely, 1996.

Trent, Joshua C. "Walt Whitman: A Case History." *Surgery, Gynecology, Obstetrics* 87 (July 1948): 113–121.

Udvarty, Miklos D. F. *The Audubon Guide to North American Birds: Western Region.* New York: Knopf, 1977.

Vendler, Helen. *The Music of What Happens: Poems, Poets, Critics.* Cambridge: Harvard UP, 1988.

Veronel, H. S. "Greek Myth and Ritual: The Case of Kronus." In *Interpretations of Greek Mythology,* edited by Jan Bremmer, 121–152. Totowa, N.J.: Barnes & Noble, 1986.

Waggoner, Hyatt H. *American Visionary Poetry.* Baton Rouge: Louisiana State UP, 1982.

Walker, Susan Hunter. "I Knew Walt Whitman." In *Leaves of Grass at 125,* edited by William White, 71–74. Detroit: Wayne State UP, 1980.

Wallace, Ronald. *God Be with the Clown: Humor in American Poetry.* New York: Columbia UP, 1984.

"Walt Whitman's Birthday: A Delightful Dinner in Honor of the Venerable Poet's 69th Birthday." *New York Times,* June 1, 1890, p. 5, col. 2.

"Walt Whitman's Cheerful Views on Death: The Aged Poet Thinks Philosophy Conduces to Long Life." *New York Times,* 26 January 1890, p. 1, col. 4.

Waskow, Howard J. *Whitman's Exploration in Form.* Chicago: U Chicago P, 1966.

Wharton, Clarence. *Remember Goliad.* Glorietta, N.M.: Rio Grande Press, 1968.

Wheatley, James O. "Reincarnation—How It Stands, What It Entails: Reflections on Paul Edwards' *Reincarnation.*" *Journal of the American Society for Psychical Research* 91 (1997): 227–240.

Whicher, Stephen E. "Whitman's Awakening to Death: Towards a Biographical Reading of 'Out of the Cradle Endlessly Rocking.'" In *Walt Whitman: A Collection of Criticism,* edited by Arthur Golden, 77–96. New York: McGraw-Hill, 1974.

*Whitman, Walt. *The Correspondence.* Edited by Edwin Haviland Miller. 6 volumes. New York: New York UP, 1961 et seq.

*———. *Daybooks and Notebooks.* Edited by William White. 3 volumes. New York: New York UP, 1978.

*———. *The Early Poems and the Fiction.* Edited by Thomas L. Brashear. 3 volumes. New York: New York UP, 1963.

———. *The Gathering of the Forces.* Edited by Cleveland Rodgers and John Black. New York: G. P. Putnam's Sons, 1920.

*———. *Leaves of Grass.* Comprehensive Readers Edition. Edited by Harold W. Blodgett and Sculley Bradley. New York: New York UP, 1965. Reprint, New York: Norton, 1975.

———. *Leaves of Grass.* Brooklyn, 1855. Reprint, edited by Richard Bridgman, San Francisco: Chandler, 1968.

———. *Leaves of Grass.* New York, 1856. Reprint, edited by Gay Wilson Allen, Norwood, Pa.: Norwood Editions, 1976.

———. *Leaves of Grass.* Boston: Thayer and Eldridge, 1860. Reprint, edited by Roy Harvey Pearce, Ithaca: Cornell UP, 1961.

*———. *Leaves of Grass: A Textual Variorum of the Printed Poems.* Edited by Sculley Bradley, et. al. 3 volumes. New York: New York UP, 1980.

*The starred Whitman volumes are part of New York University's uniform edition of *The Collected Writings of Walt Whitman.* General editors: Gay Wilson Allen and Sculley Bradley.

———. *Memoranda During the War [and] Death of Abraham Lincoln.* Edited by Roy P. Basler. Bloomington: U Indiana P, 1962.

———. *New York Dissected.* Edited by Emory Hollowy and Ralph Adimari. New York: Rufus Rockwell Wilson, 1936.

*———. *Notes and Unpublished Prose Manuscripts.* Edited by Edward F. Grier. 6 volumes. New York: New York UP, 1984.

———. *Passage to India.* Washington, 1870. Reprint, New York: Haskell House, 1969.

*———. *Prose Works 1892.* Edited by Lloyd Stovall. 2 volumes. New York: New York UP, 1964.

———. *Walt Whitman's* DRUM-TAPS *(1865) and Sequel to* DRUM-TAPS *(1865–66).* Reprint, edited by F. DeWolfe Miller, Gainesville, Fla.: Scholars' Facsimiles and Reprints, 1959.

———. *Walt Whitman's Workshop: A Collection of Unpublished Manuscripts.* Edited by Clifton Joseph Furness. Cambridge: Harvard UP, 1928.

Wihl, Gary. "The Manuscript of Whitman's 'Sunday Evening Lectures.'" *WWQR* 18 (2001), 107–133.

Wilde, Oscar. *The Complete Letters of Oscar Wilde.* Edited by Merle Holland and Rupert Hart-Davis. New York: Henry Holt, 2000.

Wilkinson, John James Garth. *The Human Body in Its Connection with Man.* Philadelphia: Lippincott, Grambo, and Co., 1851.

Wright, Henry C. *Marriage and Parentage: Or, The Reproductive Element in Man.* 1855. Reprint, New York: Arno Press, 1974.

Wrobel, Arthur, ed. *Pseudo-Science and Society in Nineteenth-Century America.*, Lexington: UP of Kentucky, 1987.

Zweig, Paul. *Walt Whitman: The Making of a Poet.* New York: Basic Books, 1984.

# Index

## Index of Names and Subjects

# Index of Poems and Essays